JEREMY DUQUESNAY ADAMS is Assistant Professor of History at Yale University, where he has served as Director of Graduate Studies for the Medieval Studies Program. His doctoral thesis, *Sense of Community in the Early Middle Ages: 'populus' and other socio-political terms in the works of Jerome, Augustine, and Isidore of Seville*, is now being considered by university presses. At present he holds a fellowship from the National Endowment for the Humanities for 1969–70 to work on a book on alien-exclusion policies in Visigothic Spain (fifth–eighth centuries A.D.).

PATTERNS OF MEDIEVAL SOCIETY

Patterns of
MEDIEVAL SOCIETY

Jeremy duQuesnay Adams

Prentice-Hall, Inc., *Englewood Cliffs, New Jersey*

Current printing (last number):
10 9 8 7 6 5 4 3 2 1

PRENTICE-HALL INTERNATIONAL, INC. (*London*)
PRENTICE-HALL OF AUSTRALIA, PTY. LTD. (*Sydney*)
PRENTICE-HALL OF CANADA, LTD. (*Toronto*)
PRENTICE-HALL OF INDIA PRIVATE LIMITED (*New Delhi*)
PRENTICE-HALL OF JAPAN, INC. (*Tokyo*)

CONTENTS

The Legal Order

Upward Mobility

The Cities of the Bourgeoisie

INTRODUCTION

The selections which appear in this volume of readings in the social history of medieval western Europe have been chosen with a two-fold purpose: to acquaint the general reader with the sort of evidence normally examined by professional historians and to explore questions which may not be too remote from the modern reader's current concerns. Although these two purposes may, superficially at least, strike some readers as being incompatible, I think that each can serve the other well if the individual student remains conscious both of the real distinction between them and of the pleasure he can get from exploring those areas in which they may be congruent.

In order to facilitate the twentieth-century student's approach to the authentically medieval problems examined in the following pages, I have adopted some analytical categories which have been made familiar by modern sociology. The use of terms such as "class," "outgroup," and the like need do no essential violence to standards of historical purity if it is remembered that these terms function simply as pedagogical aids rather than as final judgments. It should also be pointed out that medieval men who thought and wrote about such matters made constant use themselves of terms like "order," "estate," and "rank" which will strike the ordinarily sensitive modern reader as being very similar to the "classes" of which we tend to speak, at any rate in our less technical or doctrinaire moments.

There are those who may object to the use of the term "Christendom" to denote the broadest general category of medieval social association or identity, encompassing the four social classes (the clergy, the nobles, the peasants, and the bourgeoisie) with which we are concerned here. I feel strongly, however, that some such master group must be proposed if an exercise like this is to result in any valid comprehensive view of the relationship of these classes to each other as well as to the conception of the cosmos which existed in the minds of the men who made them up. I hope this hypothesis defends itself adequately in the course of Chapter I.

1

In addition to the studies of the four classes around which the subsequent chapters have been organized, there are other broad issues of social concern for which evidence may be gathered throughout the book. Some are indicated in the extensive footnotes which are intended to place the quoted texts in fairly deep historical perspective. Others will, I hope, suggest themselves to the reader as he peruses the book. One question, which may serve as a useful model for similar exploration of other such issues, is the position of women in medieval Europe. This topic is treated explicitly in I, 5, but the attitudes presented there can be filled in and qualified by information gathered from other selections. The scandalous bishop's wife and the rambunctious nuns of sixth-century Gaul in II, 3, and the strictures imposed on his young wife by a fourteenth-century Parisian bourgeois in V, 8, combine to document the sources and extent of male distrust which strongly marked the attitudes of the medieval clergy and bourgeoisie (although the emancipation of women in our own century has surely been a direct corollary of the latter class' ultimate ascendancy).

By way of contrast, a look at the tactics of the forceful and admired Countess Richeldis of feudal Hainaut (III, 2) and the economic and legal equality enjoyed by peasant women in the thirteenth-century Ile-de-France (IV, 8) may help to dispel some favorite modern misconceptions on the subject. References to marriage and other related forms of social linkage recur throughout these selections, as tends to be the case in records of the human scene of any age.

A special effort has been made throughout to include several kinds of source materials. Chronicles and biographies of the conventional sort constitute the nucleus of the collection, as is fitting for any work with a basically historical orientation. But legal documents, both in the raw authenticity of charters, contracts, court records, and the like (with extensive footnoting to banish some of their technical mystery) and in the more seductive and questionable form of the legal treatise (e.g., the complementary selections of III, 3, and IV, 6) are represented in no small number. Finally, I have defied the taboos of much of my own training and included a fair share of literary and even fictional material, in the abiding but rather beleaguered conviction that the writers of such material tell us a good deal about their basic social attitudes— sometimes a good deal more than they intended.

Although some apologies to the American reader may be in order for not including a map, care has been taken to document most of the selections with geographical data where it seemed appropriate to an understanding of the text in question. In any event, the interested reader should have no difficulty in locating these references with the aid of any current atlas. Although I have attempted to cover as much of the surface of Latin Christendom as is feasible in the space allotted, I have consciously concentrated evidence in those areas most usually studied in American curricula. France and Britain easily dominate the rest of Europe in this respect, but Germany, Italy, and Spain have by no means been ignored; in a few cases the selections go even further afield. In the documents relating to France, the area within 100 miles of Paris receives the most attention, appearing in several overlapping selections. In Britain, the north and the receding Celtic frontier of Norman England come in for somewhat more extensive treatment than is the rule in collections of this sort, while most of the readings from Germany concentrate on the Rhineland and Venice has a rather special place in the Italian documents (see V, 2—which isn't even Italian— and V, 9, as well as the final, and in some ways summary offering, V, 12). It should be noted here that translations not otherwise attributed are my own.

* * *

I am deeply grateful for the advice and expert assistance of Mrs. Caroline Walker Bynum of Harvard University; Professors Joel Kraemer, Stephan G. Kuttner, Robert S. Lopez, and Harry Miskimin of Yale; and Professor Edward M. Peters, now of the University of Pennsylvania. Indispensable to this book's preparation have been the kind services of Miss Mary I. Blake, Mrs. Donald H. Akenson, and Mrs. Marjorie Van Cleef; the contribution of my wife in all phases and aspects of this enterprise is as far beyond ordinary gratitude as it is beyond description.

CHRISTENDOM   I

In the fifth century A.D. most of the reflective inhabitants of western Europe thought of themselves as associated with the Roman Empire in some capacity, whether as magistrates, subjects, or conquering inheritors. They may have had other loyalties as well, perhaps to the Christian Church, the Visigothic nation, or their native city or province, but most such attachments either fitted within or overlapped significantly with a sense of belonging to the Roman world, which appeared to be a nearly universal entity embracing economic, cultural, and religious citizenship as well as political allegiance and a common law.

In the sixteenth century, western Europe was divided among a number of states, languages, trading areas, and Christian churches, but many of its inhabitants had come to think of themselves as belonging ultimately to something called Europe, an entity cultural as well as geographic, whose diverse members at least felt closer to one another in most everyday reflexes than they did to Muslims or Chinese or American Indians or even Russians.

What happened in between? It is conventional to say that the Middle Ages were a time of political and economic fragmentation in western Europe, and that the world of nearly everyone was bound by close horizons. Unfortunately, this judgment cannot be conveniently extended to the spheres of education, formal thought, or artistic style. In a few strata of society the Latin language was more generally current than any modern European tongue has been, and similar claims can be made for the widely influential canon law, academic degrees, and the code of aristocratic conduct. It has been said that for several centuries Europe was ruled by one kind of knight and one kind of monk. Furthermore, medieval Europeans of all classes were at least as enamored of travel as their modern descendants, and their endless pilgrimages, trading expeditions, and crusades knew other obstacles than the frozen national frontiers and intricate passport regulations of our day.

Many of the most successful foci of local or regional loyalty in the Middle Ages were men or institutions that appeared to embody a transcendent order. One cannot help thinking of all those political bishops whose license to rule territories or undertake public works depended on their being magistrates of the Universal Church, or those pragmatic kings who felt an urgent need to declare themselves either revivifications of the Roman Emperor or his equivalent in their own lands, as well as many humbler manifestations of the same tendency. In any case, it seems clear that local allegiances, however absorbing and intense, did not exhaust the medieval European capacity for communal solidarity. Few medieval men and women felt no pull of loyalty or fellowship from beyond their immediate communities.

The largest category of association which seems to have been effective for most classes was Christendom, a notion vague but splendid and capable of great emotional appeal. Theoretically it should have included all Christians, even those not strictly orthodox, but in practice it soon became restricted to those who led a Latin form of Christian life. It may be argued that western European civilization first came to an understanding of itself in the process of defining the content and limits of Christendom.

The Inner Order

1. ROGATION DAYS

As Christianity became the majority religion of the Roman Empire's western provinces, the Catholic bishops showed great ingenuity in devising public ceremonies to emphasize and symbolize the communal life of their congregations. With the collapse of the Empire's political order and the partition of its territory among a number of tenuous Germanic kingdoms, such liturgical ceremonies quickly became the chief civic acts in which the population of the surviving cities had any chance to participate. The public spirit of the Mediterranean type of city-state, which Roman rule had spread all over western Europe, had long found expression in venerable political rituals; originally sprung from pagan religious ceremonies, they gave way at the beginning of the Middle Ages to Christian rites.

Sometimes these new celebrations simply competed with ancient pagan rituals, gradually eclipsing or absorbing them. Such was the case with the Major Litanies, a chanting procession held at Rome on April 25, which happened to be both the feast of St. Mark the Evangelist and the date of the Robigalia—a procession to the walls of the city, culminating in the sacrifice of a dog's and a sheep's entrails to propitiate the god Robigus and thus prevent rust-blight (*robigo*), or mildew, from attacking the young wheat. In time the Major Litanies not only superseded the Robigalia but spread to every western diocese.

Second in popularity were the Minor Litanies, or Rogation Days, instituted in a more original fashion by Mamertus, Bishop of Vienne in southeastern Gaul from about 461 to 475. A specific earthquake and fire occasioned the first set of Rogation processions, but they suited the mood of an age familiar with general calamity and were widely imitated.

Selection (a) is from a sermon composed by Alcimus Ecdicius Avitus, Mamertus' successor as Bishop of Vienne from about 490 to 519. A cultivated Gallo-Roman aristocrat and a practitioner of the dying art of classical Latin rhetoric, Avitus shows considerable awareness of the psychological and political finesse needed to organize the diverse elements of a community for protracted penitential exercises.

Selection (b) consists of two letters from the pen of Sollius Apollinaris Sidonius, an elegant elder kinsman of Avitus. Born at Lyons (some 15 miles upriver from Vienne), he married the daughter of the Emperor Avitus in 452, became Prefect of the City (of Rome) in 468, and was elected Bishop of Clermont in 471 or 472. Clermont (about 75 miles west of Lyons) was the capital of a mountainous district now called Auvergne, once ruled by the Arverni, the last Gallic tribe to resist Julius Caesar; it was also the sentimental home of several of the greatest families of late Roman Gaul, including Sidonius' own. South of Auvergne lay the practically autonomous kingdom of the heretical Visigoths, who had settled there after sacking Rome herself in 410. When their new king, Euric, moved against Clermont in 474, Sidonius and his military brother-in-law Ecdicius organized the city's successful defense, and Sidonius found that the most effective means of bolstering morale was a spirited celebration of the Rogation Days, which he had just introduced for the purposes of a less militant piety. (About 60 years later another kind of disaster, the bubonic plague, inspired Sidonius' successor, Gall, to institute a new Rogations exercise—a 40-mile pilgrimage to the tomb of the wonder-working martyr Julian at Brioude.)

Selection (c) comes from the decrees of the First Council of Orleans, called by the Frankish king Clovis in 511, after he had united all Gaul under his rule and been baptized a Catholic.

Appreciating his orthodox protection, the assembled bishops of the Gallic Church reinstated old laws and looked around for new institutions that might be conducive to the endless goal of reform: one of the latter was Mamertus' invention of 50 years before. About 300 years later, Leo III, the Pope who crowned Charlemagne Emperor and was generally susceptible to Frankish influences, introduced the Rogations to Rome, and from there they spread to the entire Latin Church. Notice here the popular inducement of three consecutive holidays—making for quite a spring vacation, since the Sunday preceding and the Thursday following were already holidays—and the severity with which the bishops anticipate elite contempt.

Avitus: *Homily VI*

From Aviti Opera, *Homily VI, in Rudolf Peiper, ed.,* MGH, AA, *VI (Berlin: Weidmann, 1883), 108–11. Footnotes Supplied.*

The refreshing river of the Rogation Days observance is now flowing in a life-giving course not only through Gaul, but through almost the whole world, and an earth tainted by vices is being washed clean by the abundant flood of its annual satisfaction for sins. We have a very special cause for service to and joy in this institution, because it flowed forth from here for the welfare of all; it welled up first of all from our own spring. Surely the introduction of this entirely fresh institution may even now add luster to the condition of each one of us.

Moreover, when an ineffable necessity tamed the stiff hearts of the Viennans to this expression of humility, our church knew the cause of her own sickness, and thought that there was a great need to institute the present observance, not for herself foremost among all, but for herself alone of all; she was more concerned to get a remedy than a primacy.[1] Indeed, I know that many of us are calling to mind once again the causes of the terrors of that time. Frequent fires, constant earthquakes, dreadful sounds at night seemed to threaten some prodigious conflagration for the destruction of the whole world. Worst

---

[1] Because Vienne had been the capital of the civil "diocese" of the Seven Provinces of southern Gaul, its bishop (or archbishop) often claimed an ecclesiastical primacy over that area, and disputed Lyons' claim to primacy over all Gaul. Avitus himself was a kind of religious commissar for the kingdom of the Burgundians, whose king Sigismund he converted to Catholicism; later, closely allied to the pope, his influence became even wider.

of all was the sight of wild animals in the midst of thronged gatherings of men, God alone knew whether in an optical illusion or really present, brought forth as a portent.

Whichever may have been the case, whether the savage hearts of wild beasts had truly become so gentled, or whether phantoms of deluded vision had been produced so appallingly in the sight of terrified men, it was well understood to be a monstrous event. There was a wide range of opinion about all this among the common people, and theories differed from one order of society to the next. Some dissembled, attributing what they had experienced to chance, since they refused to recognize it as a cause for mourning. Others, in a healthier spirit, interpreted these new ill-omens according to their significance for the evils of their own condition. For who amid those close-packed fires did not think fearfully of the fiery rain that fell on Sodom? Who amid the trembling elements did not believe that the peaks were about to topple and the earth to split apart? What man who saw—or surely thought he saw—deer timid by nature penetrating the city from the narrow gates to the wide forum, did not shudder at the imminent sentence of the returning wilderness?

These occurrences stretched out amidst public fear and private rumor up to the night of the solemn vigil which yearly custom required with the celebration of the feast of the Lord's resurrection. And indeed all longed with one spirit for this night to bring help in their labors, an end to evils, and security for their fears. At last the venerable night itself was at hand, hopefully inaugurating a solemn votive service for public absolution. But just shortly thereafter, an exceptionally violent crash of thunder struck, with all the force of a lash cutting more deeply than before: it was as though one finally understood that nothing less drastic than chaos itself could follow. For the public court building, raised before the sight of all thanks to its position atop a steep slope at the highest point of the city, began to burn with terrible flames in the twilight.

The joy of the solemn rite was interrupted by the news of this disaster; the church was emptied of the fear-filled people. All were afraid lest a similar accident befall their houses or possessions through some spark from the blazing citadel. Nevertheless, the invincible bishop stayed in front of the festive altars, and adding fire to the heat of his faith with a flood of tears, he curbed the power permitted to the flames: the conflagration died down.

Putting away its desperation, the congregation returned to church, and as the glow of the flames was quenched, the beautiful light [of the Paschal candles] shone forth. And there was certainly no delay about taking the cure prescribed by repentance. For Mamertus the bishop, my predecessor and spiritual father since baptism, whom my father in the flesh[2] succeeded after some years, at a time acceptable in the sight of God, conceived the whole idea of the Rogations on that holy night of the Easter vigil of which we have been speaking. Then and there he silently arranged with God what the whole world proclaims with psalms and prayers today. When the Paschal solemnity had been brought to a close, a secret committee was summoned to consider, not *what* ought to be done, but when and how. Certain members of the senate of Vienne, whose court then bloomed with more men of distinguished rank than now, were of the opinion that invented rites could not hope to attract men who were scarcely moved by long-established and legitimate ones. But that pious and concerned shepherd, bountifully endowed with the salty wit of wisdom, used prayer to soften the hearts of the sheep he was about to tame, before he softened their hearing with oratory. Thus he opened up their dispositions, showed them the order to be followed, and explained its health-bestowing benefits. To a man like him, whose talents were religious as well as adroit, the fact that the mere proposal of the institution was winning adherents did not seem enough; he must attach to its very commencement some bond of a customary nature. And so, with God inspiring the hearts of the repentant, he was heard, acclaimed, and carried out on the shoulders of all. The present three-day period[3] was chosen as the time, so as to connect the holy celebration of the Ascension with the previous Sunday by a richly embroidered band of appropriate ceremonies.

As the bishop observed the enthusiasm which attended the beginning of these plans, he began to fear greatly lest a small turnout of the people deprive the observance of all prestige at its very inception. Consequently, he prescribed that the procession of the first day go as far as the basilica, which was then closer to the city walls. It took place with swift fervor amid a swelling crowd, and in a mood of high spiritual intensity, so that all the tears and efforts of the people made the procession seem short and strait.

Discerning from the results of lesser efforts the probable outcome of greater ones, the holy bishop instituted on the following day what we are about to undertake on the first day, that is, tomorrow, if God

---

[2] Hesychius, whom some have identified with Sidonius' brother-in-law Ecdicius.
[3] The Monday, Tuesday, and Wednesday before Ascension Thursday, which comes 40 days after Easter.

permits. In subsequent years several churches of Gaul began to follow
so commendable an example, but in such a way that it was not celebrated by all on the same days which were originally established
among us. Of course it would not matter a great deal which period
of three days were chosen, as long as the ritual of psalms and of public mourning were observed in annual ceremonies. Nevertheless, agreement among the priests increased along with love of the Rogations,
and a general concern has now assigned the same period, that is, the
present three days, to this observance.

But the point of all these introductory remarks is this: having heard
us recount these things, whether you were familiar with them or not,
be sure that all of you attend! The church which sent forth to others
the form of this institution, is many times over indebted to them for
the enthusiasm they have shown; and she who in a matter so necessary for all has been the mother of example, should be first also in the
exercise of her authentic repentance for sin.

Apollinaris Sidonius: *Letters*

From The Letters of Sidonius, *trans. O. M. Dalton (Oxford: Oxford University Press, 1915), II, 67–68, 95–97. Reprinted by permission of the Clarendon Press, Oxford. Footnotes supplied.*

To His Friend Aper (472–3). Are you taking your ease in your sunny
Baiae,[1] where the sulphurous water rushes from hollows of the porous
rock, and the baths are so beneficial to those who suffer either in the
lungs or liver? Or are you "camped among the mountain castles," [2]
looking for a place of refuge, and perhaps embarrassed by the number
of strongholds you find to choose from? Whatever the cause of your
delay, whether you are making holiday or going about your business,
I feel sure that the thought of the forthcoming Rogations will bring
you back to town. It was Mamertus our father in God and bishop who
first designed, arranged, and introduced the ceremonial of these prayers, setting a precedent we should all revere, and making an experi-
ment which has proved of the utmost value. We had public prayers of
a sort before, but (be it said without offence to the faithful) they were
lukewarm, irregular, perfunctory, and their fervour was destroyed

---

[1] One of several possible spas in central Gaul. Aper was an Arvernian aristocrat
whom Sidonius kept urging to spend more time in Clermont.

[2] An illusion to the *Aeneid*, V, 440. Many a large landowner was finding his
fortified country estate more secure than his town house.

by frequent interruption for refreshment; and as they were chiefly for rain or for fine weather, to say the least of it, the potter and the market-gardener could never decently attend together! But in the Rogations which our holy father has instituted and conferred upon us, we fast, we pray with tears, we chant the psalms. To such a feast, where penitential sighs are heard from all the congregation, where heads are humbly bowed, and forms fall prostrate, I invite you; and if I rightly gauge your spirit, you will only respond the quicker because you are called in place of banquets to a festival of tears. Farewell.

To the Lord Bishop Mamertus (474). Rumour has it that the Goths have occupied Roman soil; our unhappy Auvergne is always their gateway on every such incursion. It is our fate to furnish fuel to the fire of a peculiar hatred, for, by Christ's aid, we are the sole obstacle to the fulfilment of their ambition to extend their frontiers to the Rhône, and so hold all the country between that river, the Atlantic, and the Loire. Their menacing power has long pressed us hard; it has already swallowed up whole tracts of territory round us, and threatens to swallow more. We mean to resist with spirit, though we know our peril and the risks which we incur. But our trust is not in our poor walls impaired by fire, or in our rotting palisades, or in our ramparts worn by the breasts of the sentries, as they lean on them in continual watch. Our only present help we find in those Rogations which you introduced; and this is the reason why the people of Clermont refuse to recede, though terrors surge about them on every side. By inauguration and institution of these prayers we are already new initiates; and if so far we have effected less than you have, our hearts are affected equally with yours. For it is not unknown to us by what portents and alarms the city entrusted to you by God was laid desolate at the time when first you ordained this form of prayer. Now it was earthquake, shattering the outer palace walls with frequent shocks; now fire, piling mounds of glowing ash upon proud houses fallen in ruin; now, amazing spectacle! wild deer grown ominously tame, making their lairs in the very forum. You saw the city being emptied of its inhabitants, rich and poor taking to flight. But you resorted in our latter day to the example shown of old in Nineveh, that you at least might not discredit the divine warning by the spectacle of your despair. And, indeed, you of all men had been least justified in distrusting the providence of God, after the proof of it vouchsafed to your own virtues. Once, in a sudden conflagration, your faith burned stronger than the flames. In full sight of the trembling crowd, you stood forth all alone to stay them, and lo! the fire leapt back before you, a sinuous beaten fugitive. It was miracle, a formidable thing, unseen before and unexampled; the element which naturally shrinks from nothing, retired in awe at your approach. You therefore first enjoined a fast upon a few members of our sacred order, denouncing gross offences, announcing punishment, promising relief. You made it clear that if the penalty of sin was nigh, so also was the pardon; you proclaimed that by frequent prayer the menace of coming desolation might be removed. You taught that it was by water of tears rather than water of rivers that the obstinate and raging fire could best be extinguished, and by firm faith the threatening shock of earthquake stayed. The multitude of the lowly forthwith followed your counsel, and this influenced persons of higher rank, who had not scrupled to abandon the town, and now were not ashamed to return to it. By this devotion God was appeased, who sees into all hearts; your fervent prayers were counted to you for salvation; they became an ensample for your fellow citizens, and a defence about you all, for after those days there were neither portents to alarm, nor visitations to bring disaster.

We of Clermont know that all these ills befell your people of Vienne before the Rogations, and have not befallen them since; and therefore it is that we are eager to follow the lead of so holy a guide, beseeching your Beatitude from your own pious lips to give us the advocacy of those prayers now known to us by the examples which you have transmitted. . . .

Canons of the Council of Orleans

From MGH, Concilia, *I*, ed. Friedrich Maassen (Hanover: Hahn, 1893), 8. Footnotes supplied.

27. It has pleased the Council for Rogations, that is, public litanies, to be celebrated by all churches before the Ascension of the Lord, in such a manner that the three-day fast be completed on the feast day of the Lord's Ascension. During that three-day period let servants and serving-women[1] be released from all work, so that it may be more convenient for the whole people. On those three days let everyone practice abstinence and use Lenten foods.

28. If any clerics scorn to attend this holy work, let them be sub-

[1] The language of the original covers both "servants" and "slaves"—the latter a dwindling group which had had little or no share in the civic life of pagan antiquity.

ject to discipline according to the judgment of the bishop of the church.

2. CHURCH-BUILDING BROTHERHOODS

The "cities" which medieval Europe inherited from the Roman Empire shrank in size and urban character until they almost disappeared. Only the continuity of liturgical communities like those illustrated in the previous selections kept some conurbations alive, though they functioned more as the temple centers of a profoundly rural society than as nuclei of commerce, manufacture, or even of civil administration. From the tenth century onward, however, they underwent a great expansion and reanimation, thanks first to a real population explosion and then to a rebirth of distinctive institutions. Perhaps the most striking symbols of this revived sense of public identity and pride were the churches which rose in cathedral towns and elsewhere in the eleventh and twelfth centuries. Many an abbey lost its original solitude and became the occasion for a new town as steady streams of pilgrims produced the need for lodging and other services. Most of these expensive building projects were the creations of dynamic prelates or of lay magnates such as the Dukes of Normandy, but sometimes, to the clergy's delighted surprise, the initiative or an important phase of implementation came from below. Although such surges of spontaneous public edification were unpredictable, many of them were swiftly organized into fairly durable associations, clear signs of the corporate instinct of the times.

Selection (a) is from a letter written in 1145 by a Norman abbot to the dependent priory of Tutbury in England. Little is known of Haimo, the author, beside the fact that he succeeded Richard of Aquila as abbot of the monastery of St. Mary at St.-Pierre-sur-Dives in central Normandy sometime between 1140 and 1143, and died in that post in 1148. The abbey church had been started in 1040 through the munificence of a Countess Lesceline, but destructive wars between the sons of William the Conqueror and other interruptions had kept it from completion. Word of the new abbot's determination to remedy this neglect spread through the valley of the Dives, and the response was startling.

Selection (b) is a sober confirmation of Haimo's excited report from the pen of a sophisticated ecclesiastical statesman, Hugh de

Boves. Born near Laon of a lordly family, Hugh had been educated in that city under the renowned masters Anselm and Ralph, and entered the reforming order of Cluny around 1112. He was made prior of Cluniac houses at Limoges (in central France) and Lewes (in southern England), and about 1125 became abbot of Henry I's rich new foundation at Reading on the Thames. In 1129 he was elected archbishop by the cathedral chapter of Rouen, the civil and ecclesiastical capital of Normandy, and won royal approval for that unexpected honor the following year. The next 35 years of his life were spent largely in diplomatic missions, advancing the construction of his cathedral church, founding an abbey at Aumale, enforcing discipline throughout his archdiocese, and quietly but resolutely asserting the prerogatives of his office against subordinate bishops, abbots, kings, and a host of lesser lay lords. He died in 1164, having also composed half a dozen works in various genres on a wide range of topics, a side of his accomplishments which the brusqueness of this letter to an episcopal colleague may not lead one to suspect.

Letter of Haimo

Letter of Haimo *and* Letter of Hugh *from* Annales Ordinis Sancti Benedicti, ed. J. Mabillon and E. Martène (Lucca: L. Venturini, 1745), VI, 361–63. Footnotes supplied.

God has instituted a new kind of piety according to which He may be sought; new, I repeat, and unheard of in any other age. For who ever saw, who in all the generations gone by ever heard that rulers, princes mighty in the world, swollen with honors and wealth, men and women of noble birth, lowered their haughty and tumid necks to take the traces of carts, and weighted down with wine, wheat, oil, lime, stones, logs, and other things necessary either for provisioning or for the construction of the church, dragged them to the asylum of Christ[1] in the manner of dumb animals? But what seems more marvelous is this: in the act of dragging these things, when sometimes a thousand or more men and women are hitched to the carts (so massive is the pile of materials, the building equipment, and the whole burden of the project), so great a silence descends that no voice or murmuring can be heard; and if one did not use his eyes, he would judge that no man of all that multitude were present. Whenever a halt is called along

[1] One of several favorite monastic epithets for a monastery, stressing its separation from the ordinary course of worldly society.

the road, nothing can be heard besides the confession of sins and suppliant and pure prayer to God in order to obtain pardon for offense. And there while the priests preach peace, enmities fall asleep, disagreements are driven away, debts are lightened, and unity of spirit is restored. And if anyone so persists in evil that he refuses to forgive someone who has sinned against him, or to obey the priests when he receives a pious admonition, his offering is immediately thrown out of the cart like something unclean, and he is expelled from the fellowship of the sacred people with much shame and ignominy. . . .

There, thanks to the prayers of the faithful, you would see certain sick men, feeble from various illnesses, rise with renewed health from the carts on which they had been placed; you would see dumb men open their mouths to the praise of God, and those vexed by demons receive a healthier state of mind. You would see the priests of Christ presiding over the individual carts, exhorting all to penance, to confession, to lamentation, to resolutions of a better life, and you would see those exhorted stretched out the full length of their bodies on the ground, and kissing the earth over and over. You would see old men along with youths and children of trifling age crying out to the Mother of God, and directing to her in particular, with professions of repentance and praise, sobs and sighs from the intimacy of their innermost hearts. . . . But let me return to the very beginnings [of this event]. When the faithful people put itself back on the road to the blare of trumpets and the raising of the banners that led them on, the whole business was carried out with such ease that no obstacle (marvelous to relate!), neither steep hills nor the depth of intervening bodies of water, delayed their progress. Just as the ancient Hebrew people of whom we read entered the Jordan in crowded array, so these, when they came unexpectedly upon a river which had to be crossed, entered it under the Lord's guidance without hesitation; indeed, when they crossed a stretch of the sea at the place called Sainte-Marie-du-Port,[2] its surf fell still at their arrival, as is reliably asserted by many who made the crossing. . . . And when at last they had reached the church, the wagons were placed in a circle around it like a spiritual encampment, and all that night the whole army kept watch with hymns and canticles. Then candles and lamps were lighted here and there among the carts; then the sick and enfeebled were gathered together; then relics of saints were brought forward to give

[2] Perhaps 25 miles away, a considerable distance in view of the loads and the probable state of the roads.

them aid: then the priests and clerics undertook to organize a procession, which the people joined as one with the utmost devotion and concern, imploring the clemency of the Lord and of His Blessed Mother for the recovery of the sick. . . .

This rite of divine institution first arose at the Church of Chartres, and then was ratified in ours with innumerable prodigies; thereafter it flourished far and wide through almost the whole of Normandy, and has settled down particularly in those places dedicated to the Mother of Mercy.

Letter of Hugh

Hugh, priest of Rouen, sends to the reverend Father Thierry, bishop of Amiens, the wish that he may always prosper in Christ. "Great are the works of the Lord, and subtle in all his judgments." At Chartres they have begun with great humility to draw wagons and building materials to the work of constructing the church, and their humility is sparkling with miracles. The report of this celebrated development has spread all around, and finally aroused our Normandy. Our own people, consequently, after getting our blessing, traveled thither in fulfillment of pilgrimage vows. Then they began in a similar fashion to approach their mother church in our diocese, throughout the district under our episcopal control, on the condition that no one should join their company unless he had previously gone to confession and received absolution, and unless any of them who had been enemies put away their anger and ill will and joined together in harmony and firm peace. After these preliminaries, one of their number is chosen as the leader, at whose command they put their shoulders to drawing the wagons in humility and silence, and they bring forward their offering with a good deal of both tears and discipline. The three things which we have mentioned, to wit, confession, penance, and the harmony deriving from a renunciation of ill will and the humble agreement to proceed obediently, are the conditions which we require of them when they come to us, and if they promise those three we receive them lovingly, absolve them, and bless them. When, given form in this manner, they proceed on their route, and especially when they arrive in the churches, miracles happen thick and fast, especially among those associates whom they had brought along with them in ill health, and bring back home well. . . . And we permit our own people to travel thus outside our diocese, although we keep them from going to visit those under excommunication or interdict. All these things have taken place in the year 1145 after the Incarnation of the Word. Farewell.

3. PEACE ASSOCIATIONS WITHIN THE CHRISTIAN COMMUNITY

Men have always banded together for defense if public authority proves incapable of protecting their persons or those activities which they consider necessary. In the late tenth century local self-policing arrangements sprang up in many areas of western Europe. Some of them, like the London guilds organized in 940, resembled the vigilante committees of the nineteenth-century American frontier; and like them, they disturbed civil and ecclesiastical authorities almost as much as the brigandage they set out to attack. More distinctive and more influential were sworn associations which strove, usually under the patronage of the bishop, to involve the entire local population in a regular program for suppressing violence. The earliest recorded attempt of this sort occurred in 989 at the Council of Charroux in west-central France, one of the most anarchic regions of Europe. Bishop Guy of Le Puy in Auvergne organized the first successful militia of this type in 990, and the example began to spread. Peace brotherhoods flourished in central and southern France for nearly two centuries, gradually becoming more democratic and more radical until established authority (already more effective than in the past) could tolerate them no longer; but the counts and bishops who quashed the last brotherhoods were happy to perpetuate the regular system of war taxes they had established. In northern France the direction of such movements was taken firmly in hand by lay lords such as the Count of Flanders (1030) and the Duke of Normandy (1047); a French pope (Urban II) and Norman invaders introduced the movement to southern Italy at the end of the eleventh century; and in 1077 Emperor Henry IV sanctioned and sponsored similar efforts within his realms. In time, the promulgation of new peace regulations became a favorite occasion for general legislation on the part of German rulers, and similar legislative practices arose in northeastern Spain. Documents describing the emergence of self-governing communes in towns all over Europe are full of terms and techniques developed by the peace associations.

Two kinds of programs were typical of this movement: the "Peace of God," which forbade violence against certain classes of persons or things, and the "Truce of God," which forbade violence against anyone at certain times. This decree combines both programs, and seems to envision universal jurisdiction. Notice the rigor of the penalties: in the casual anarchy of the earlier Middle Ages, public authorities preferred to control violence by regularizing vengeance (whether of the "state" or of offended families "at feud") and by making money compensation possible, even for murder. Now, with an irony typical of reform, higher standards of public order and higher respect for human life brought with them a tendency toward judicial severity which would grow harsher in centuries to come. Notice also that for this emperor, despite his endless troubles with popes and bishops and despite the universal claims of his own imperial office, society in general is still "the holy Church," and the ultimate sanctions are still sacramental.

Decree of the Emperor Henry IV

From Select Historical Documents of the Middle Ages, *trans. and ed. Ernest F. Henderson (London and New York: George Bell & Sons, 1896), pp. 208–11. Footnotes supplied.*

Whereas in our times the holy church has been afflicted beyond measure by tribulations through having to join in suffering so many oppressions and dangers, we have so striven to aid it, with God's help, that the peace which we could not make lasting by reason of our sins, we should to some extent make binding by at least exempting certain days. In the year of the Lord's incarnation, 1085, in the 8th indiction, it was decreed by God's mediation, the clergy and people unanimously agreeing: that from the first day of the Advent of our Lord until the end of the day of the Epiphany,[1] and from the beginning of Septuagesima until the 8th day after Pentecost,[2] and throughout that whole day, and on every Thursday, Friday, Saturday, and Sunday, until sunrise on Monday, and on the day of the fast of the four seasons, and on the eve and the day itself of each of the apostles—moreover on every day canonically set apart, or in future to be set apart, for fasting or for celebrating,—this decree of peace shall be observed. The purpose of it is that those who travel and those who remain at home may enjoy the greatest possible security, so that no one shall commit murder or arson, robbery or assault, no man shall injure another with a whip or

[1] About six weeks, ending January 6.
[2] A period of 17 consecutive weeks, including Lent, Easter, the Rogation Days, etc.

a sword or any kind of weapon, and that no one, no matter on account of what wrong he shall be at feud, shall, from the Advent of our Lord to the 8th day after Epiphany, and from Septuagesima until the 8th day after Pentecost, presume to bear as weapons a shield, sword, or lance—or, in fact, the burden of any armour. Likewise on the other days—namely, on Sundays, Thursdays, Fridays, Saturdays, and on the eve and day of each of the apostles, and on every day canonically fixed, or to be fixed, for fasting or celebrating,—it is unlawful, except for those going a long distance, to carry arms; and even then under the condition that they injure no one in any way. If, during the space for which the peace has been declared, it shall be necessary for any one to go to another place where that peace is not observed, he may bear arms; provided, nevertheless, that he harm no one unless he is attacked and has to defend himself. Moreover, when he returns, he shall lay aside his weapons again. If it shall happen that a castle is being besieged, the besiegers shall cease from the attack during the days included in the peace, unless they are attacked by the besieged, and are obliged to beat them back.

And lest this statute of peace be violated with impunity by any person, the following sentence was decreed by all present: If a freeman or a noble shall have violated it—that is, if he shall have committed murder, or shall have transgressed it in any other way,—he shall, without any payments or any friends being allowed to intervene, be expelled from within his boundaries, and his heirs may take his whole estate; and if he hold a fief, the lord to whom it belongs shall take it. But if, after his expulsion, his heirs shall be found to have given him any aid or support, and shall be convicted of it, the estate shall be taken from them and shall fall to the portion of the king. But if he wish to clear himself of the charges against him, he shall swear with 12 who are equally noble and free. If a slave kill a man he shall be beheaded; if he wound him he shall have his right hand cut off; if he have transgressed in any other way—by striking with his fist, or a stone, or a whip, or any thing else—he shall be flogged and shorn. But if the accused (slave) wish to prove his innocence, he shall purge himself by the ordeal of cold water: in such wise, however, that he himself, and no one in his place, be sent to the water. But if, fearing the sentence that has been passed against him, he shall have fled,— he shall be forever under the bann. And wherever he is heard to be, letters shall be sent there announcing that he is under the bann, and that no one may hold intercourse with him. The hands may not be cut off of boys who have not yet completed their 12th year; if boys, then, shall transgress this peace, they shall be punished with whipping only. It is not an infringement of the peace if any one order a delinquent slave, or a scholar, or any one who is subject to him in any way, to be beaten with rods or with whips. It is an exception also to this statute of peace, if the emperor shall publicly order an expedition to be made to seek the enemies of the realm, or shall be pleased to hold a council to judge the enemies of justice. The peace is not violated if, while it continues, the duke, or other counts, or bailiffs, or their substitutes hold courts, and lawfully exercise judgment over thieves and robbers, and other harmful persons. This imperial peace has been decreed chiefly for the security of all those who are at feud; but not to the end that, after the peace is over, they may dare to rob and plunder throughout the villages and homes. For the law and judgment that was in force against them before this peace was decreed shall be most diligently observed, so that they be restrained from iniquity;—for robbers and plunderers are excepted from this divine peace, and, in fact, from every peace. If any one strive to oppose this pious decree, so that he will neither promise the peace to God nor observe it, no priest shall presume to sing a mass for him or to give heed to his salvation; if he be ill, no Christian shall presume to visit him, and, unless he come to his senses, he shall do without the Eucharist even at the end. If any one, either at the present time or among our posterity forever, shall presume to violate it, he is banned by us irrevocably. We decree that it rests not more in the power of the counts or centenars,[3] or any official, than in that of the whole people in common, to inflict the above mentioned punishments on the violators of the holy peace. And let them most diligently be on their guard lest, in punishing, they show friendship or hatred, or do anything contrary to justice; let them not conceal the crimes of any one, but rather make them public. No one shall accept money for the redemption of those who shall have been found transgressing. Merchants on the road where they do business, rustics while labouring at rustic work—at ploughing, digging, reaping, and other similar occupations,—shall have peace every day. Women, moreover, and all those ordained to sacred orders, shall enjoy continual peace. In the churches, moreover, and in the cemeteries of the churches, let honour and reverence be paid to God; so that if a robber or thief flee thither he shall not at all be seized, but shall be besieged there until, induced by hunger, he shall be compelled to surrender. If any one

---

[3] Centenars (or *hundredmen*) were representatives of the count who presided throughout the year over courts handling minor or ordinary cases in a subdivision of the county.

shall presume to furnish the culprit with means of defence, arms, victuals, or opportunity for flight, he shall be punished with the same penalty as the guilty man. We forbid under our bann, moreover, that any one in sacred orders, convicted of transgressing this peace, be punished with the punishments of laymen—he shall, instead, be handed over to the bishop. Where laymen are decapitated, clerks shall be degraded; where laymen are multilated, clerks shall be suspended from their positions; and, by the consent of the laity, they shall be afflicted with frequent fasts and flagellations until they shall have atoned. Amen.

4. RANKS AND DIVIDED FUNCTIONS WITHIN THE HOUSE OF GOD

What attitudes were dominant concerning the proper division of labor or functions within the Christian community? For most of the Middle Ages such attitudes were rudimentary, schematic, and utterly traditional. Even though many new and complex social forms emerged after the twelfth century, medieval speculation on such subjects remained to the end strangely oblivious to novel realities. The following selection is part of a semi-satirical didactic poem and hence may seem an unlikely source of sociologically respectable evidence. But it expresses a perfectly commonplace set of ideas despite its pretentious phrasing, and in "The Bishop's" impatience with "The King's" sympathy for the dreary lot of the lower classes, it reveals a new current of social concern as well as its conservative author's contempt for such notions. Adalbero (950?–1030) was the scion of a family proud of its descent from the stock of Charlemagne and sure of its innate right to direct both Church and State. His father was Count of Bastogne; the ranks of his uncles and great-uncles included a Count of Luxemburg and a Duke of Upper Lorraine; Adalbero himself was probably named for a great-uncle who was Bishop of Metz and an uncle who became Archbishop of Reims. Educated at both Metz and Reims, he was chancellor of the French King Lothair before becoming Bishop of Laon in 977. Having switched his allegiance from his own turbulent family to the upstart Capetian dynasty because of a personal feud with the Carolingian claimant to the crown of France, but perfectly willing to change sides whenever so moved, he was treated gingerly by the patient Capetian king Robert the Pious (996–1031). Adalbero wrote this poem about 1015, in irritation at Robert's patronage of low-born clerics, the reform movement of the monastery of Cluny, and other novelties. This passage begins just after his assertion that Robert, in order to do an acceptable job as king, must have an appropriate understanding of the "heavenly Jerusalem," which the Fathers and liturgy of the Church described in eloquent mystical language. We must not demand too much originality or semantic consistency from this arrogant and conventional prelate in his attempt to bring that transcendental symbol down to earth. Educated men of policy in his generation had many things to worry about besides precision in the use of terms like *Church, House of God, the Faith, law,* etc. His general sentiments would probably have won the general assent of most respectable men for two centuries (at least) on either side of his own lifetime.

Adalbero of Laon: *Panegyric to King Robert the Pious of France*

From *Adalbero of Laon,* Carmen ad Rotbertum regem Francorum, *ed. H. Valesius (Paris: J. duPuis, 1663), pp. 247–49. Footnotes supplied.*

There are two orders in the heavenly City, and it is on this pattern that earthly society is said to be modeled. Through Moses and the Law which He gave to the former Chosen People, the Lord established a rule of order for the ministers of His Church (which then was called the Synagogue, a name that reveals its function[1]). . . .

If the condition of the Church here below is to enjoy a tranquil peace, its constitution must be in accord with two laws, that is, those formed by divine and by human authority.

The divine law sets up no division among her ministers; it makes them all of equal condition, however disparately nature or rank may bring them forth: the son of an artisan is not inferior to the heir of a king. This pious law segregates the Church's ministers from every sordid earthly function. They do not plow open the earth, they do not tread behind the oxen. They are scarcely involved in the culture of vines or trees, or even of gardens. They are not hangmen, keepers of taverns, swineherds, trackers of goats, or shepherds; they sift no wheat through a sieve, no greasy warming pan is their fire. They tie no pigs to the backs of oxen for market. They are not laundrymen, they scorn to boil cloth for the fuller. But to cleanse their minds and their bodies, that is their duty; arrayed in good morals themselves, they guard the morals of others. The eternal law of God commands

[1] *I.e.,* "a gathering together," the sort of causal etymology that delighted ordinarily reflective men in the Middle Ages.

them to be clean in this manner, and judges that they should be free of servile obligations. The Lord has chosen them as His servants[2] alone; He judges them Himself and His voice from Heaven demands that they be chaste and sober. His decree has subjected to them all classes of men—and when it says *all*, no prince is excepted. He orders these ministers to teach men how to preserve the true Faith, and to plunge those they have taught in the holy baptismal font. He has established them as doctors of souls, to apply the cautery of their preaching to any putrefying wound of the spirit. He has commanded the priest alone to enact in fitting rites the sacrament of His body and blood. They shall ascend the first seats in the kingdom of heaven, but here they should also keep watch, avoid much eating or feasting, and always pray on account of the ruined state of the people and of their own selves. And so they are of equal condition: the single House[3] of God is ruled by a single law.

Now the substance of the Faith is an undifferentiated whole, but it exists in three distinct states. Human law applies to the two other orders, those of the noble and serf, who are subject to disparate laws.

Of the nobles, two hold first rank. One holds royal power, the other issues commands: under their rule the Commonwealth appears secure. There are other nobles, whom no authority restricts so long as they avoid those crimes for which the royal scepter has sanctions. These men are warriors, guardians of the Churches, defenders of the greater and the lesser folk among the common people: they are to protect both themselves and all other men in comparable fashion.

The second order is composed of those of servile condition.

The King. That afflicted class possesses nothing beyond its labor. Who could keep track, even with the counters on an abacus, of the worries, the rounds, the immense travail of the serfs?

The Bishop. The serfs provide all other men with treasure, garments, and food. Without serfs no free man is capable of living. When there is work to be done, or the cost of something is needed, kings and bishops appear to be serfs of the serf. The lord is fed by the serf, who hopes to be fed by him.

The King. There is no end to the tears and the groans of the serfs!

The Bishop. Now therefore the house of God, which is believed in and trusted as one, is threefold in order. Some pray, some fight, and others work. These three must function together, and cannot en-

---

[2] The original term can also mean "slave" or "serf."
[3] The original term can mean both "house" and "household."

dure separation: the duty of one engages the others, and each gives support to all. And so this triple connection is simple and one: it was thus that law prevailed, and the world was at rest in peace. But now the laws have decayed, and all peace has vanished. The customs of men are corrupted, and order is changed. You, O king, hold by right the scale of the balance: it is up to you to protect the world. Hold back with the reins of law those men inclined to do harm!

5. WOMAN'S PLACE

This set of selections aims to suggest the official—that is, male and clerical—view of the role of women in a properly ordered society. The first three passages come from a history of the progressive Christianization of England composed by Bede, an exceptionally learned and gentle Northumbrian monk. He completed this work in 731, but took great care to base his narrative on verbal witness and on documents from earlier centuries. In Book I, Chapter 27, he reproduces letters sent by Pope Gregory the Great (590–604) to Augustine of Canterbury, the missionary legate he had sent to convert the pagan Angles and Saxons. Augustine, who had been a monk in Gregory's own Roman monastery before becoming the first Archbishop of Canterbury, had asked for advice on several points of discipline. It is important for the modern reader to realize that Gregory was relatively liberal in this expression of his views; everyone for centuries past had been convinced both that woman was designed for subordination to man and that the specifically different things about her sex were peculiar reminders of all that was defiling in human nature. Passages (b) and (c) show what surprising scope individual women blessed with eminent rank and evident virtue could nevertheless enjoy, providing they conformed heroically to masculine ideals.

The last passage shows what happened to women who behaved in a less conventional fashion, particularly in the increasingly intolerant atmosphere of the later Middle Ages. The author, Johann Nider, was an average intellectual of the period which rediscovered witchcraft. He seems to have been a man of naturally benign disposition, but his distinguished career as a student at the universities of Vienna and Cologne and as a professor at the former, had taught him the error of certain laxities. A Dominican renowned for his achievements as an inquisitor, he went as a delegate to the Council of Basle in 1431, the year in which Joan of Arc was burned at Rouen after being convicted of various things by an ecclesiastical court largely influenced by Dominican inquisitors. In the same year he began the didactic work from which this selection is taken, completing it before he died in 1438.

Nider was just one of many intelligent Christians who undertook, from the fifteenth to the eighteenth century, a sustained attack upon the primitive folk religion of western Europe. The missionaries of earlier centuries had adapted many of the features of that cult; one durable example of this assimilative practice is their conversion of the old winter festival and its preceding vigil to All Hallows' Eve and the Feast of All Saints (October 31 and November 1). By the later Middle Ages, however, leaders of both Church and State were determined to extirpate any independent survivals of that native form of paganism. The old religion seems to have offered its adherents a sense of intense and special solidarity, approved outlets for vengeance, and a feeling of control over the potency and general health of animals and men. Originally the cult had been directed by priests (wizards) as well as priestesses (witches), and had worshiped male manifestations of divinity (whom Christian theologians and judges identified with the Devil). The male clergy of medieval Christendom seem to have been more upset by its female practitioners, with their claims to foreknowledge and exotic sexual mastery, than by any other aspect of the ancient "witchcraft."

Bede: *Ecclesiastical History*

From *Bede's* History of the English Church and People, *trans. Leo Sherley-Price (Baltimore: Penguin Books, Inc., 1955), pp. 76–81, 233–34, 240–43, Reprinted by permission of the publisher.*

Book I, Chapter 27. Augustine's eighth question: May an expectant mother be baptized? How soon after childbirth may she enter church? And how soon after birth may a child be baptized if in danger of death? How soon after childbirth may a husband have relations with his wife? And may a woman properly enter church at certain periods? And may she receive Communion at these times? And may a man enter church after relations with his wife before he has washed? Or receive the sacred mystery of Communion? These uncouth English people require guidance on all these matters.

Pope Gregory's reply: I have no doubt, my brother, that questions such as these have arisen, and I think I have already answered you:

but doubtless you desire my support for your statements and rulings. Why should not an expectant mother be baptized?—it is no offence in the sight of Almighty God to bear children. For when our first parents sinned in the Garden, they justly forfeited God's gift of immortality. But although God deprived man of immortality for his sin, he did not destroy the human race on that account, but of his merciful goodness left man his ability to continue the race. . . .

As you are aware, the Old Testament lays down the interval that must elapse after childbirth before a woman may enter church; that is, for a male child thirty-three days and for a female, sixty-six. But this is to be understood as an allegory, for were a woman to enter church and return thanks in the very hour of her delivery, she would do nothing wrong. The fault lies in the bodily desires, not in the pain of childbirth; the desire is in the bodily union, the pain is in the birth, so that Eve, the mother of us all, was told: *"In sorrow shalt thou bring forth children."* If, then, we forbid a woman who is delivered of a child to enter church, we make this penalty into a sin. . . .

Until a child is weaned, a man should not approach his wife. For a bad custom has arisen among married people that women disdain to suckle their own children, and hand them over to other women to nurse. This custom seems to have arisen solely through incontinency, for when women are unwilling to be continent, they refuse to suckle their children. So those who observe this bad custom of giving their children to others to nurse must not approach their husbands until the time of their purification has elapsed. For even apart from childbirth, women are forbidden to do so during their monthly courses, and the Old Law prescribed death for any man who approached a woman during this time. But a woman should not be forbidden to enter church during these times, for the workings of nature cannot be considered culpable, and it is not just that she should be refused admittance, since her condition is beyond her control. We know that the woman who suffered an issue of blood, humbly approaching behind our Lord, touched the hem of his robe, and was at once healed of her sickness. If, therefore, this woman was right to touch our Lord's robe, why may not one who suffers nature's courses be permitted to enter the church of God? . . .

A woman, therefore, should not be forbidden to receive the mystery of Communion at these times. If any out of a deep sense of reverence do not presume to do so, this is commendable; but if they do so, they do nothing wrong. Sincere people often acknowledge their faults even when there is no actual fault, because a blameless action may often spring from a fault. For instance, eating is no fault, but being hungry originates in Adam's sin; similarly, the monthly courses of woman are no fault, because nature causes them. . . . For while the Old Testament makes outward observances important, the New Testament does not regard these things so highly as the inward disposition, which is the sole true criterion. For instance, the Law forbade the eating of many things as unclean, but in the Gospel our Lord says: *"That which enters the mouth does not defile a man, but that which issues from his mouth."* He also said: *"Out of the mouth proceed evil thoughts."* Here Almighty God clearly shows us that evil actions spring from evil thoughts. Similarly, Saint Paul says: *"To the pure all things are pure, but to those who are corrupt and unbelieving, nothing is pure."* And later, he indicates the cause of this corruption, adding: *"For even their mind and conscience are corrupt."* If, therefore, no food is unclean to one of a pure mind, how can a woman who endures the laws of nature with a pure mind be considered impure?

It is not fitting that a man who has approached his wife should enter church before he has washed, nor is he to enter at once, though washed. The ancient Law prescribed that a man in such cases should wash, and forbade him to enter a holy place before sunset. But this may be understood spiritually, for when a man's mind is attracted to those pleasures by lawless desire, he should not regard himself as fitted to join in Christian worship until these heated desires cool in the mind, and he has ceased to labour under wrongful passions. And although various nations have differing views on this matter and observe different customs, it was always the ancient Roman usage for such a man to seek purification, and out of reverence to refrain awhile from entering a holy place. In making this observation, we do not condemn marriage itself, but since lawful intercourse must be accompanied by bodily pleasure, it is fitting to refrain from entering a holy place, since desire itself is not blameless. For even David, who said: *"Behold, I was conceived in iniquity, and in sin my mother brought me forth,"* was not himself born of any illicit union, but in lawful wedlock. . . . Lawful intercourse should be for the procreation of offspring, and not for mere pleasure; to obtain children, and not to satisfy lust. But if any man is not moved by a desire for pleasure, but only by a desire for children, he is to be left to his own judgement either as to entering church, or to receiving the Communion of the Body and Blood of our Lord; for we have no right to debar one who does not yield to the fires of temptation. But when lust takes the place of desire for children, the pair have cause for regret; and although the holy teachings give them permission, yet this carries a warning with it. For when the Apostle Paul said: *"Whoever cannot contain, let him marry,"* he at once added, *"This I say by way of permission, not as a command."* This concession makes it lawful, yet not good; so when he spoke of permission, he indicated that it was not good.

It should be carefully considered that when God was about to speak to the people on Mount Sinai, he first ordered them to abstain from women. And if such a degree of bodily purity was required in those who were to hear the word of God when he spoke to men through a subject creature, how much the more should women preserve themselves in purity of body when about to receive the Body of Almighty God himself, lest they be overwhelmed by the very greatness of this ineffable mystery?

Book IV, Chapter 19. King Egfrid married Etheldreda, a daughter of Anna, King of the East Angles, of whom I have often spoken; he was a very devout man, noble in mind and deed. Before her marriage to Egfrid, Etheldreda had been married to Tonbert, a prince of the South Gyrwas, but he died shortly after the wedding and she was given to King Egfrid. Although she lived with him for twelve years, she preserved the glory of perpetual virginity, which fact is absolutely vouched for by Bishop Wilfrid of blessed memory, of whom I made enquiry when some people doubted it. He said that Egfrid promised to give estates and much money to anyone who could persuade the queen to consummate the marriage, knowing that she loved no man so well as himself. But there is no doubt that the same thing could happen in our own day, when reliable histories record it as having happened on several occasions in the past through the grace of the same Lord who has promised to remain with us until the end of the world. For the miraculous preservation of her body from corruption in the tomb is evidence that she had remained untainted by bodily intercourse.

For a long time Etheldreda begged the king to allow her to retire from worldly affairs and serve Christ the only true King in a convent. And having at length obtained his reluctant consent, she entered the convent of the Abbess Ebba, King Egfrid's aunt, at Coludi,[1] where she received the veil and clothing of a nun from the hands of Bishop Wilfrid. A year later she was herself made Abbess of Elge,[2] where she built a convent and became the virgin mother of many virgins vowed to God, displaying the pattern of a heavenly life in word and deed. It

---

[1] Coldingham.
[2] Ely.

is said that from the time of her entry into the convent, she never wore linen but only woolen garments, and that she washed in hot water only before the greater festivals such as Easter, Pentecost, and the Epiphany, and then only after she and her assistants had helped the other servants of Christ to wash. She seldom had more than one meal a day except at the greater festivals or under urgent necessity, and she always remained at prayer in the church from the hour of Matins until dawn unless prevented by serious illness. Some say that she possessed the spirit of prophecy, and that in the presence of all the community, she not only foretold the plague that was to cause her death, but also the number who would die of it in the convent. She was taken to Christ in the presence of her nuns seven years after her appointment as abbess, and in accordance with her instructions, she was buried among them in the wooden coffin in which she died.

Etheldreda was succeeded in the office of abbess by her sister Sexburga, who had been wife of King Earconbert of Kent. . . .

Book V, Chapter 23. In the following year, that is the year of our Lord 680, Hilda, abbess of the monastery of Whitby, a most religious servant of Christ, passed away to receive the reward of eternal life on the seventeenth of November at the age of sixty-six, after a life full of heavenly deeds. Her life fell into two equal parts, for she spent thirty-three years most nobly in secular occupations, and dedicated the remainder of her life even more nobly to our Lord in the monastic life. She was nobly born, the daughter of Hereric, nephew to King Edwin, with whom she received the Faith and sacraments of Christ through the preaching of Paulinus of blessed memory, first bishop of the Northumbrians, and she preserved this Faith inviolate until she was found worthy to see him in heaven.

When she decided to abandon the secular life and serve God alone, she returned to the province of the East Angles, whose king was her kinsman; for having renounced her home and all that she possessed, she wished if possible to travel on from there into Gaul, and to live an exile for our Lord's sake in the monastery of Cale.[1] In this manner she hoped the more easily to attain her eternal heavenly home, for her sister Hereswith, wife of Aldwulf, King of the East Angles, was living there as a professed nun and awaiting her eternal crown. Inspired by her example, Hilda remained in the province a full year, intending to join her overseas; but when Bishop Aidan was recalled home, he

---

[1] Chelles, near Paris.

granted her one hide of land on the north bank of the River Wear, where she observed the monastic rule with a handful of companions.

After this, Hilda was made abbess of the monastery of Heruteu,[2] founded not long previously by Heiu, a devout servant of Christ who is said to have been the first woman in the province of Northumbria to take vows and be clothed as a nun, which she did with the blessing of Bishop Aidan. But soon after establishing the monastery she left for the town of Calcaria, which the English call Calcacestir,[3] and settled there. Then Christ's servant Hilda was appointed to rule this monastery, and quickly set herself to establish a regular observance as she had been instructed by learned men; for Bishop Aidan and other devout men, who knew her and admired her innate wisdom and love of God, often used to visit and advise her.

When she had ruled this monastery for some years, constantly occupied in establishing the regular life, she further undertook to found or organize a monastery at a place known as Streaneshalch, and carried out this appointed task with great energy. She established the same regular life as in her former monastery, and taught the observance of justice, devotion, purity, and other virtues, but especially in peace and charity. After the example of the primitive Church, no one there was rich or poor, for everything was held in common, and none possessed any personal property. So great was her prudence that not only ordinary folk, but kings and princes used to come and ask her advice in their difficulties. Those under her direction were required to make a thorough study of the Scriptures and occupy themselves in good works, in order that many might be found fitted for Holy Orders and the service of God's altar.

Subsequently, five bishops were chosen from this monastery—Bosa, Hedda, Oftfor, John, and Wilfrid—all of them men of outstanding merit and holiness. . . .

. . . Her life was the fulfilment of a dream which her mother Breghusyth had when Hilda was an infant, during the time that her husband Hereric was living in banishment under the protection of the British king Cerdic, where he was poisoned. In this dream she fancied that he was suddenly taken away, and although she searched everywhere, she could find no trace of him. When all her efforts had failed, she discovered a most valuable jewel under her garments, and as she looked closely, it emitted such a brilliant light that all Britain was

---

[2] Hartlepool.
[3] Possibly Tadcaster.

lit by its splendour. This dream was fulfilled in her daughter, whose life afforded a shining example not only to herself, but to all who wished to live a good life.

Johann Nider: *Formicarius*

From Life in the Middle Ages, *ed. and trans.* G. G. Coulton *(Cambridge: Cambridge University Press, 1930), I, 81–84. Reprinted by permission of the publisher.*

Pupil. In your opinion, have some good men been deceived by sorceresses or witches in our own day?

Master. In what here follows, I suspend my judgment; but I will tell you what is repeated by public rumour and report. We have in our days the distinguished professor of divinity, brother Heinrich Kaltyseren, Inquisitor of Heretical Pravity. Last year, while he was exercising his inquisitorial office in the city of Cologne, as he himself told me, he found in the neighbourhood a certain maiden who always went about in man's dress, bore arms and dissolute garments like one of the nobles' retainers; she danced in dances with men, and was so given to feasting and drink that she seemed altogether to overpass the bounds of her sex, which she did not conceal. And because at that time, (as, alas! even to-day) the see of Trèves was sorely troubled by two rivals contending for the bishopric, she boasted that she could and would set one party upon the throne, even as Maid Joan, of whom I shall presently speak, had done shortly before with Charles king of France, by confirming him in his kingdom. Indeed, this woman claimed to be that same Joan, raised up by God. One day therefore, when she had come into Cologne with the young count of Württemberg, who protected and favoured her, and there, in the sight of the nobles, had performed wonders which seemed due to magic art, she was at last diligently scrutinized and publicly cited by the aforesaid inquisitor, in order that she might be examined. For she was said to have cut a napkin in pieces, and suddenly to have restored it whole in sight of the people; to have thrown a glass against the wall and broken it, and to have repaired it in a moment, and to have shown many such idle devices. But the wretched woman would not obey the commands of the Church; the count protected her from arrest and brought her secretly out of Cologne; thus she did indeed escape from the inquisitor's hands but not from the sentence of excommunication. Thus bound under curse, she quitted Germany for France, where she married a certain knight, to protect herself against ecclesiastical interdict and the sword. Then a certain priest, or rather pimp, seduced this witch with talk of love; so that she stole away with him at length and went to Metz, where she lived as his concubine and showed all men openly by what spirit she was led.

Moreover, there was lately in France, within the last ten years, a maid of whom I have already spoken, named Joan, distinguished, as was thought, both for her prophetic spirit and for the power of her miracles. For she always wore man's dress, nor could all the persuasions of any doctors [of divinity] bend her to put these aside and content herself with woman's garments, especially considering that she openly professed herself a woman and a maid. "In these masculine garments," she said, "in token of future victory, I have been sent by God to preach both by word and by dress, to help Charles, the true king of France, and to set him firm upon his throne from whence the king of England and the duke of Burgundy are striving to chase him"; for, at that time, those two were allied together, and oppressed France most grievously with battle and slaughter. Joan, therefore, rode constantly like a knight with her lord, predicted many successes to come, was present at some victories in the field, and did other like wonders, whereat not only France marvelled, but every realm in Christendom. At last this Joan came to such a pitch of presumption that, before France had been yet recovered, she already sent threatening letters to the Bohemians, among whom there were then a multitude of heretics. Thenceforward layfolk and ecclesiastics, Regulars and Cloisterers began to doubt of the spirit whereby she was ruled, whether it were devilish or divine. Then certain men of great learning wrote treatises concerning her, wherein they expressed not only diverse but also adverse opinions as to the Maid. But, after that she had given great help to king Charles, and had confirmed him for some years upon his throne, then at last, by God's will, as it is believed, she was taken in arms by the English and cast into prison. A great multitude were then summoned, of masters both in Canon and in Civil Law, and she was examined for many days. And, as I have heard from Master Nicolas Amici, Licentiate of Theology, who was ambassador for the University of Paris, she at length confessed that she had a familiar angel of God, which, by many conjectures, and proofs, and by the opinion of the most learned men, was judged to be an evil spirit; so that this spirit rendered her a sorceress; wherefore they permitted her to be burned at the stake by the common hangman; and the king of England gave a like account of this story, at great length, in a letter to our emperor Sigismund. At this same time two women arose near Paris, preaching publicly that they had been sent by God to help Maid Joan; and, as I heard from the very lips of the aforesaid Master Nicolas, they were forthwith arrested as witches or sorceresses by the Inquisitor for France, and examined by many Doctors of Theology, and found at length to have been deceived by the ravings of the evil spirit. When therefore one of these women saw that she had been misled by an angel of Satan, she relinquished that which she had begun, by the advice of her masters, and, as was her duty, abjured her error forthwith. But the other abode in her obstinacy and was burned.

Pupil. I cannot sufficiently marvel how the frail sex can dare to rush into such presumptuous things.

Master. These things are marvellous to simple folk like thee; but they are not rare in the eyes of wise men. For there are three things in nature, which, if they transgress the limits of their own condition, whether by diminution or by excess, attain to the highest pinnacle whether of goodness or of evil. These are, the tongue, the ecclesiastic, and the woman; all these are commonly best of all, so long as they are guided by a good spirit, but worst of all if guided by an evil spirit.

Defining the Boundaries

6. THE EXTENT OF THE "ROMAN WORLD"

Most of the continental European territory of Latin Christianity was politically united under the rule of the heroic Frankish king Charlemagne (768–814), whose coronation as Emperor in Rome on Christmas Day, 800, was supposed to restore the Roman Empire in the west. Although the title and some of the dream would endure for a thousand years, the reality of this artificial and backward-looking enterprise collapsed quickly because of shortages of wealth and manpower within, and relentless assault from without by Saracens, Vikings, and Magyars in the ninth and tenth centuries. Western Europe proved its resilience in the latter tenth and eleventh centuries by absorbing its Viking and Magyar invaders, reviving the Empire on a more practical scale, and inaugurating a rapid expansion of population which continued until the middle of the fourteenth century. Economic and cultural revivals followed swiftly; with them came a new set of questions about the internal coherence and external limits of Latin Christendom, whose concerned members clearly felt themselves somehow unified despite a high degree of political fragmentation.

The following selection attempts to suggest what semi-educated public opinion may have considered the territorial limits of that unity in the mid-eleventh century. Ralph Glaber was born about 985 in Burgundy, roughly at the geographical center of Latin Christendom. Sent to a monastery by his family at the age of twelve, he led a restless and truculent life, belonging to seven or eight French monastic communities before his death around 1050. His only long journey was a trip to Italy in 1028, but he listened avidly to the tales of the pilgrims, merchants, and military adventurers who suddenly seemed to be everywhere on the move, and for whom monasteries were normal dispensers of hospitality. Under the firm hand of the great Abbot Odilo of Cluny (994–1049) he settled down to write, undertaking the first general history of contemporary events in more than two centuries. Books III and IV were probably finished at the monastery of St. Germain at Auxerre between 1037 and 1044. Thanks to his paranoid personality and defective education, his work is both bad history and an excellent sample of a wide range of popular feeling. Like most men, Ralph equated the importance of events with his knowledge of and interest in them; it is fortunate for our purposes that he was almost obsessed with threats to the inner security of his world and fascinated with what he took to be its alien margins, whether receding or expanding.

Ralph Glaber: *History of His Times*

From *Radulfus Glaber*, Quinque Historiarum Libri, *III and IV, in Migne*, PL, *CXLII, cols. 645–46, 651, 657–58, 680, 682, 683. Footnotes supplied.*

III, 1. At that time, the nation of the Hungarians, which dwells along the Danube, was converted along with its king to the faith of Christ. To their king, called Stephen at his baptism, and an exemplary Christian, the emperor Henry gave his sister in marriage.[1] From that time on, almost all the pilgrims from Italy and the Gauls who desired to go to the Lord's sepulcher at Jerusalem, began to abandon the traditional route by sea, and to make their way through the territory of that country. And Stephen made that road very safe for all; he received as brothers whomever he saw, and bestowed magnificent gifts on them. Encouraged by the graciousness of this behavior, an innumerable multitude both of nobles and of the common people made the journey to Jerusalem.

At that time also the Emperor Basil [2] of the Holy Empire of Constantinople commanded a certain satrap of his, the one designated

[1] (St.) Stephen I (997–1038); (St.) Henry II (1002–24); Gisela of Bavaria. Granted an "Apostolic Crown" by Pope Silvester II and Emperor Otto III (983–1002), Stephen organized his kingdom along Frankish and Roman lines.

[2] Basil II (963–1025), under whom the Empire reached a zenith of military power, conquered Bulgaria, and expanded in Italy and Syria (his co-Emperor John I nearly took Jerusalem in 976).

Catapont (because he held authority along the coasts), to go exact tribute from the cities across the sea which belonged to the Roman Empire. He obeyed with a will, and sent a Greek fleet to carry away the property of the Italians. This operation was stretched out over a period of two years, and no small part of the province of Benevento was subjugated by the Greeks. But it happened also at that time, that a certain extremely audacious Norman by the name of Rodolphus displeased his count Richard, and fearing his wrath, journeyed with all the possessions he could collect to Rome, to plead his case before Benedict, the Supreme Pontiff.[3] The Pope, discovering that he was a splendid warrior indeed, began to unfold his grievance at the Greek invasion of the Roman Empire, and to express his great regret that there was scarcely anyone among his men who could repel those men of foreign birth.

III, 4. About three years after the year 1000, it happened throughout almost the whole world, although especially in Italy and in the Gauls, that the basilicas of the churches[4] were built anew, although most of them were in such decent condition that they scarcely needed renovation. Nevertheless each Christian nation entered into a rivalry with the next one to have a more attractive church. It was as though the whole world, with one accord, had cast off its old age and was dressing itself everywhere with a white robe of churches. The faithful then altered thoroughly not only almost all the cathedrals, but also several monasteries of diverse saints, and even the lesser churches of the villages.

III, 6. When the whole world had, as we have said, arrayed itself in a white robe of renewed churches, a little thereafter, about the year 1008 of the Lord's incarnation, there were revealed, thanks to diverse accounts and indications, many relics of the saints, which had lain hidden for a long time thereto. The saints themselves came at God's command to reclaim the honor of a resurrection on earth, and appeared to many of the faithful, to whose minds they brought a great deal of solace. It is known that this sort of revelation began first in Sens, a city in Gaul, in the church of Saint Stephen the martyr. Archbishop Leuteric, who presided over that see, made some discoveries of sacred antiquities which are wonderful to relate. Indeed, among many other objects which had lain hidden there, there was said to be a part of the rod

---

[3] Pope Benedict VIII (1012–24), in whose reign Norman knights flocked to Italy. Richard II (the Good), 996–1026, ruled Normandy with an iron hand. He also pushed the conversion of Norway, standing sponsor in Rouen for the baptism of its future king, (St.) Olaf (1016–28).

[4] Presumably the cathedral churches of the various dioceses.

of Moses. At the news of this discovery the faithful gathered, not only from the provinces of Gaul but also from almost the whole of Italy and from regions overseas, and at the same time not a few ailing people returned home cured through the intervention of the saints.

III, 7. Also at that time, that is, in the ninth year after the aforesaid millennium, the church at Jerusalem which contained the sepulcher of Our Lord and Savior, was leveled to its foundations by order of the prince of Babylon.[5] The occasion for this destruction is now known to have arisen as I shall relate. Since a vast multitude was traveling to Jerusalem from all over the world to visit that famous memorial of the Lord, the Devil became envious, and began to spread the poison of his iniquity towards the worshipers of the true Faith through his favorite nation, the Jews. There was at Orleans, a royal city of Gaul, no small number of this race, who were found to be more ambitious, envious, and audacious than the rest of their nation. Having laid the plans for their criminal project, they corrupted with money a certain vagabond in pilgrim's garments named Robert, who was actually a fugitive serf of the convent of St. Mary at Moutiers. Taking him into their scheme they sent him in secret to the prince of Babylon with a letter in Hebrew characters, which they had enclosed in a stick with small iron pins, lest it fall out in some accident.

He set out, and brought to the prince that letter full of treachery and wickedness, to the effect that unless he swiftly destroyed that venerable temple of the Christians, he would soon see himself deprived of every dignity as his kingdom was occupied by them. When the prince heard this, he was straightaway swept into a rage, and sent to Jerusalem some of his men to destroy the aforesaid temple. They went and did as they had been ordered. They even tried to shatter the hollow interior of the sepulcher with iron hammers, but their strength was inadequate. At the same time in Ramleh they also destroyed the church of the blessed martyr George, whose might had once greatly cowed the Saracen nation: he is said often to have inflicted blindness on those of them who wished to enter his church for pillage.

And when, as we have related, the temple had been torn down, it became utterly clear after a little while that the wickedness of the Jews had perpetrated this crime. And when this was divulged throughout the world, it was decided by the common consent of all Christians that all

[5] Al-Hakim, Fatimid calif of Cairo (996–1020), who declared himself a manifestation of God and insisted on the public humiliation of *dhimmis* (see I, 10). He had a Christian minister sign the decree authorizing the unprecedentedly inflammatory act of the church's demolition.

Jews should be thoroughly expelled from their lands or cities. And so held in universal contempt, they were expelled from the cities; some were killed by the sword, others drowned in the rivers, and others done away with in several kinds of death. Not a few killed themselves in a scattered slaughter, so that when this just vengeance had been exacted, very few of them could be found in the Roman world. And then it was decreed by the bishops that no Christian might associate himself with them in any business whatever. But if some of them wished to be converted to the grace of baptism and to disavow all Jewish customs and behavior, it was decreed that they alone might be accepted. But most of those who did so were driven more by love of this present life and by fear of death than out of any desire for the joys of eternal life. For whichever ones of them requested that this be done, soon thereafter returned insolently to their former way of life.

IV, 6. About the same time[6] the perfidious hatred of the Saracens in North Africa for the Christian people revived; they persecuted whomever they could find on land or sea, skinning some alive and cutting others to pieces. Much slaughter occurred for a long time on either side, and many blows were struck by each party, until finally it was decided that both parties would come together to stage a pitched battle. They, presumptuously reposing confidence in the rabid ferocity of their immense multitude, expected that they would be victorious. But our side, despite the fact that they were few in number, invoked the aid of almighty God through the intervention of his mother Mary and of Peter, the holy prince of the apostles, and of all the saints, faithfully hoping to obtain victory from them. They counted especially on the vow which they made as they marched to battle: they had sworn that, if the powerful hand of the Lord would deliver that most perfidious nation over to them, they would send to Peter the prince of the Apostles, to his abbey of Cluny, all the gold, silver, and other spoils that would fall to them. For as we have remarked earlier, the many religious men of that nation who have taken up the habit of the holy rule in that monastery, have inspired their whole nation with a love for that holy place.[7]

IV, 8. Now Germany, which stretches from the River Rhine all the way to the northern shore of the world, is inhabited by a great number of very ferocious and indiscriminate nations. . . . In Farther Rhaetia

[6] About 1033.
[7] Latin Christianity seems to have died out in North Africa about two centuries later. Peter the Venerable, abbot of Cluny 1122–56, had translations made of the Koran and other Muslim books, as part of an effort to prepare missionaries.

dwells the barbarous nation of the Letts, fiercer than any other nation in every cruelty, whose name derives from *lutum* [mud]:[8] for all their habitat lies along the Northern Sea, [*i.e.*, the Baltic] among filthy swamps. . . . In the year 1000 after the Lord's Passion they advanced from their hiding places, laying waste with surpassing cruelty the neighboring provinces of the Saxons and also those of other barbarians; they razed to the ground the possessions of Christian people and slaughtered men and women in massacres. The Emperor Conrad [9] went against them with a very great army, and several times he felled many of their number, but not without casualties among his own men. For that reason the clergy and people of the whole Church of his kingdom performed penances and besought God to grant a judgment of vengeance against the madness of the barbarians, so that the Christians might achieve a victory to the honor of His name. Conrad subsequently fell upon them and wiped out a large part of them. The others, taking refuge in flight, escaped in great terror to the inaccessible regions of their swamps. This victory revived the Emperor's confidence; he collected his army again and marched into Italy, advancing as far as the city of Rome, where he stayed for a year putting down all the rebels who attempted to rise against him.

7. THE CALL TO CRUSADE

At the end of the eleventh century, western Europe took the offensive against Islam in an extraordinary mass movement, the First Crusade. Starting with a papal call to arms late in 1095, the movement quickly gained a following which amazed contemporaries for its fervor, size, and variety. Half a dozen ill-disciplined armies passed through Constantinople, whose Emperor had appealed to the West for mercenary troops, but not for this new horde of barbarians. After suffering colossal losses and some bitter disillusionments, the remnants of the host broke through the walls of their goal, the earthly Jerusalem, on July 15, 1099, and consummated their victory by an unparalleled massacre of its Muslim and Jewish inhabitants. Subsequent crusades were directed against pagans, heretics, and Greek Christians as well as Muslims before the movement faded away in the fifteenth century, although Columbus headed west in 1492 with red crosses

---

[8] Fantastic geographical and etymological identification; an attempt to be learned.
[9] Conrad II (1024–39). See I, 8.

on his sails and, in a certain sense, the West has never lost the habit of going on crusade.

The First Crusade at least was an armed pilgrimage as much as a military expedition in the usual sense of the term. Its object was the liberation of the historical homeland of Christianity as much as colonization or conquest—several Latin states were established in the Levant as a result of the First Crusade, but most of the host's survivors returned to Europe. It was also a manifestation of the popular consciousness and common enthusiasm of Latin Christendom; the astonishing fact of its success testifies to the vigor of those forces.

Pope Urban II (1088–99) called the Crusade into being in the last week of November, 1095. Born to a very noble family in Champagne about 1042, he had been archdeacon of Reims, a prior at Cluny, cardinal-bishop of Ostia, and papal legate in Germany before becoming Pope. An astute judge of human motivation and a realistic diplomat, he reconciled many of the rulers alienated from the Papacy by his predecessors' reforms and moved to improve relations with the Greek Church and Eastern Empire. At the same time, he was a firm supporter of Norman rule in Sicily, the Christian reconquest in Spain, and the Truce of God wherever practical. Robert the Monk (1055?–1122?) wrote this account of Urban's speech around 1120. He had attended the Council of Clermont as abbot of the monastery of St. Remi in his native Reims and then gone with the army to Jerusalem. By 1120 he had retired to a priory of St. Remi's in the wooded Ardennes district and made a point of recording his vivid memories in "rustic and plebeian" Latin.

Robert the Monk: *The Jerusalemite History*

From O. J. Thatcher and E. H. McNeal, A Source Book for Mediaeval History *(New York: Charles Scribner's Sons, 1905), pp. 518–21.*

In 1095 a great council was held in Auvergne, in the city of Clermont. Pope Urban II, accompanied by cardinals and bishops, presided over it. It was made famous by the presence of many bishops and princes from France and Germany. After the council had attended to ecclesiastical matters, the pope went out into a public square, because no house was able to hold the people, and addressed them in a very persuasive speech, as follows: "O race of the Franks, O people who live beyond the mountains [that is, reckoned from Rome], O people loved and chosen of God, as is clear from your many deeds, distinguished over all other nations by the situation of your land, your catholic faith, and your regard for the holy church, we have a special message and exhortation for you. For we wish you to know what a grave matter has brought us to your country. The sad news has come from Jerusalem and Constantinople that the people of Persia, an accursed and foreign race, enemies of God, 'a generation that set not their heart aright, and whose spirit was not steadfast with God' [Ps. 78:8], have invaded the lands of those Christians and devastated them with the sword, rapine, and fire. Some of the Christians they have carried away as slaves, others they have put to death. The churches they have either destroyed or turned into mosques. They desecrate and overthrow the altars. They circumcise the Christians and pour the blood from the circumcision on the altars or in the baptismal fonts. Some they kill in a horrible way by cutting open the abdomen, taking out a part of the entrails and tying them to a stake; they then beat them and compel them to walk until all their entrails are drawn out and they fall to the ground. Some they use as targets for their arrows. They compel some to stretch out their necks and then they try to see whether they can cut off their heads with one stroke of the sword. It is better to say nothing of their horrible treatment of the women. They have taken from the Greek empire a tract of land so large that it takes more than two months to walk through it. Whose duty is it to avenge this and recover that land, if not yours? For to you more than to other nations the Lord has given the military spirit, courage, agile bodies, and the bravery to strike down those who resist you. Let your minds be stirred to bravery by the deeds of your forefathers, and by the efficiency and greatness of Charles the Great, and of Louis his son, and of the other kings who have destroyed Turkish kingdoms, and established Christianity in their lands. You should be moved especially by the holy grave of our Lord and Saviour which is now held by unclean peoples, and by the holy places which are treated with dishonor and irreverently befouled with their uncleanness.

"O bravest of knights, descendants of unconquered ancestors, do not be weaker than they, but remember their courage. If you are kept back by your love for your children, relatives, and wives, remember what the Lord says in the Gospel: 'He that loveth father or mother more than me is not worthy of me' [Matt. 10:37]; 'and everyone that hath forsaken houses, or brothers, or sisters, or father, or mother, or wife, or children, or lands for my name's sake, shall receive a hundredfold and shall inherit everlasting life' [Matt. 19:29]. Let no possessions keep you back, no solicitude for your property. Your land is shut in on all sides by the sea and mountains, and is too thickly populated. There is not much wealth here, and the soil scarcely yields enough to support you. On this account you kill and devour each other, and carry on war and mutually destroy each other. Let your hatred and quarrels cease, your civil wars come to an end, and all your dissensions stop. Set out on the road to the holy sepulchre, take the land from that wicked people, and make it your own. That land which, as the Scripture says, is flowing with milk and honey, God gave to the children of Israel. Jerusalem is the best of all lands, more fruitful than all others, as it were a second Paradise of delights. This land our Saviour made illustrious by his birth, beautiful with his life, and sacred with his suffering; he redeemed it with his death and glorified it with his tomb. This royal city is now held captive by her enemies, and made pagan by those who know not God. She asks and longs to be liberated and does not cease to beg you to come to her aid. She asks aid especially from you because, as I have said, God has given more of the military spirit to you than to other nations. Set out on this journey and you will obtain the remission of your sins and be sure of the incorruptible glory of the kingdom of heaven."

When Pope Urban had said this and much more of the same sort, all who were present were moved to cry out with one accord, "It is the will of God, it is the will of God." When the pope heard this he raised his eyes to heaven and gave thanks to God, and, commanding silence with a gesture of his hand, he said: "My dear brethren, today there is fulfilled in you that which the Lord says in the Gospel, 'Where two or three are gathered together in my name, there am I in the midst' [Matt. 18:20]. For unless the Lord God had been in your minds you would not all have said the same thing. For although you spoke with many voices, nevertheless it was one and the same thing that made you speak. So I say unto you, God, who put those words into your hearts, has caused you to utter them. Therefore let these words be your battle cry, because God caused you to speak them. Whenever you meet the enemy in battle, you shall all cry out, 'It is the will of God, it is the will of God.' And we do not command the old or weak to go, or those who cannot bear arms. No women shall go without their husbands, or brothers, or proper companions, for such would be a hindrance rather than a help, a burden rather than an advantage. Let the rich aid the poor and equip them for fighting and take them with them. Clergymen shall not go without the consent of their bishop, for otherwise the journey would be of no value to them. Nor will this pilgrimage be of any benefit to a layman if he goes without the blessing of his priest. Whoever therefore shall determine to make this journey and shall make a vow to God and shall offer himself as a living sacrifice, holy, acceptable to God [Rom. 12:1], shall wear a cross on his brow or on his breast. And when he returns after having fulfilled his vow he shall wear the cross on his back. In this way he will obey the command of the Lord, 'Whosoever doth not bear his cross and come after me is not worthy of me' " [Luke 14:27]. When these things had been done, while all prostrated themselves on the earth and beat their breasts, one of the cardinals, named Gregory, made confession for them, and they were given absolution for all their sins. After the absolution, they received the benediction and the permission to go home.

8. WHAT ABOUT THE GREEKS?

The people of Latin Christendom were united with the subjects of the Byzantine Empire by a common faith, but separated by differences of liturgy, culture, and political habits. The early Middle Ages were full of misunderstandings between the sophisticated Byzantines and the semi-barbarous inhabitants of the Romano-Germanic West, but as the Latins began to approach the Greeks in wealth and cultivation and to surpass them in commercial inventiveness and military vigor, the lack of comprehension became acute. In the late eleventh and twelfth centuries, the religion which earlier had seemed the chief link between the two cultures turned into an occasion for constant wrangling, and after the conquest of Constantinople in 1204 by the Franco-Venetian Fourth Crusade, it became the primary focus for mutual resentment. If the Greeks could be insufferably arrogant, the Latins could be absurdly paranoid. It was almost as though Latin Christendom felt a need to define its emerging identity by nervous comparison with that richer, subtler, and more venerable realm of Christendom—a process bound to be invidious in at least one direction.

Perhaps the Crusades contributed more than anything else to this alienation. Westerners felt that the Byzantines ought to be grateful and cooperative, while most Byzantines saw them as uninvited tamperings with the delicate balance of power in their own part of the world, or even as excuses for Latin adventurers to scout the scene of future depredations. Both sets of convictions reached a climax of self-justification during the Fourth Crusade, but that eruption had been prepared by at least a century of intensified suspicion. The slow boil on the Latin side is well represented by the following selection from the official French account of the crusade undertaken by King Louis VII (1137–80) and the German Emperor Conrad III (1138–52) from 1147 to 1149. Despite the personal participation of these two powerful monarchs and the passionate ideological inspiration of St. Bernard of Clairvaux, prime spokesman of the Catholic conscience, the crusade accomplished practically nothing while suffering massive casualties. Blame had to be fixed, and the intricacies of Byzantine diplomacy provided Latins once again with an ideal (and probably rather valid) excuse. But the hostility went deeper than that.

Odo had been sent along as Louis' chaplain by Suger, abbot of his monastery of St. Denis (whom Odo would succeed as abbot from 1152 to 1162) and powerful adviser of both Louis and his father. Sharing none of his abbot's skepticism about the crusade, Odo published his bitter but well-informed account after his return to France. This passage begins after Odo's account of a clash between advance elements of the French army and barbarian cavalry in the Byzantine service; the Emperor Manuel I (1143–80) disclaimed responsibility for the incident and arranged for the French to make camp and buy provisions without harassment—but under close supervision.

Odo of Deuil: *The Journey of Louis VII to the East*

From Odo of Deuil, The Journey of Louis VII to the East, *trans. and ed. Virginia G. Berry (New York: Columbia University Press, 1948), III, 55, 57, 59. Reprinted by permission of Columbia University Press. The footnotes originally accompanying this selection have been deleted with the permission of the publisher.*

This outcome would have satisfied the messengers if they had not judged one crime in the light of another; for they learned that the emperor had an agreement with the Turks and that the very man who had written to our king that he was going to accompany him in fighting the infidels and had won a recent and renowned victory over them had actually confirmed a twelve-year armistice with them. Also, his treachery was increased and made manifest by the fact that only a great number could get through his realm in safety; for the bishop of Langres and the count of Warenne and certain others, who had sent a few men ahead to Constantinople to provide arms and food for the journey, had suffered a considerable loss of possessions and were mourning their wounded and dead. And this did not happen just once; for from the time when we entered his territory we endured the robberies which his people perpetrated on us because our strength did not equal theirs. Perhaps this condition would have been bearable, and it could have been said that we deserved the evils which we suffered on account of the evils which we had committed, if blasphemy had not been added. For instance, if our priests celebrated mass on Greek altars, the Greeks afterwards purified them with propitiatory offerings and ablutions, as if they had been defiled. All the wealthy people have their own chapels, so adorned with paintings, marble, and lamps that each magnate might justly say, "O Lord, I have cherished the beauty of Thy house," if the light of the true faith shone therein. But, O dreadful thing! we heard of an ill usage of theirs which should be expiated by death; namely, that every time they celebrate the marriage of one of our men, if he has been baptized in the Roman way, they rebaptize him before they make the pact.[1] We know other heresies of theirs, both concerning their treatment of the Eucharist and concerning the procession of the Holy Ghost,[2] but none of these matters would mar our page if not pertinent to our subject. Actually, it was for these reasons that the Greeks had incurred the hatred of our men, for their error had become known even among the lay people. Because of this they were judged not to be Christians, and the Franks considered killing them a matter of no importance and hence could with the more difficulty be restrained from pillage and plundering.

But let us return to the king, who, although he received new messengers from the emperor nearly every day, nevertheless complained about the delay of his own ambassadors, because he did not know what had happened to them. The Greeks always reported good news, but they never showed any proof of it, and they were the less believed because on every occasion all used the same prefatory flattery. The king accepted, but considered of slight value, their *polychroniae* (for that is the name of the gestures of honor which they exhibit, not only toward kings, but even toward certain of their nobles, lowering the head and body humbly or kneeling on the ground or even prostrating them-

[1] Which implied that the Latins were less validly Christian than many heretics were considered to be.

[2] The laity of the Greek rite received the wine as well as the bread of the Eucharist. Greek theologians taught that the Holy Ghost proceeded from the Father rather than from the Father *and* the Son.

selves). Occasionally the empress[3] wrote to the queen.[4] And then the Greeks degenerated entirely into women; putting aside all manly vigor, both of words and of spirit, they lightly swore whatever they thought would please us, but they neither kept faith with us nor maintained respect for themselves. In general they really have the opinion that anything which is done for the holy empire cannot be considered perjury. Let no one think that I am taking vengeance on a race of men hateful to me and that because of my hatred I am inventing a Greek whom I have not seen. Whoever has known the Greeks will, if asked, say that when they are afraid they become despicable in their excessive debasement and when they have the upper hand they are arrogant in their severe violence to those subjected to them. However, they toiled most zealously in advising the king to turn his route from Adrianople to St. George of Sestos and there to cross the sea the more swiftly and advantageously. But the king did not wish to undertake something which he had never heard that the Franks had done.[5] Thus, by the same paths, but not with the same omens, he followed the Germans who had preceded us, and when a day's journey from Constantinople met his own messengers, who told him the stories concerning the emperor which we have already related in part. There were those who then advised the king to retreat and to seize the exceedingly rich land with its castles and cities and meanwhile to write to King Roger, who was then vigorously attacking the emperor,[6] and, aided by his fleet, to attack Constantinople itself. But, alas for us, nay, for all St. Peter's subjects, their words did not prevail! Therefore, we proceeded, and when we approached the city, lo, all its nobles and wealthy men, clerics as well as lay people, trooped out to meet the king and received him with due honor, humbly asking him to appear before the emperor and to fulfil the emperor's desire to see and talk with him. Now the king, taking pity on the emperor's fear and obeying his request, entered with a few of his men and received an imperial welcome in the portico of the palace. The two sovereigns were almost identical in age and

[3] Bertha of Sulzbach, sister-in-law of Conrad III, who had married Manuel in 1146 after changing her uncouth Frankish name to Irene.

[4] Eleanor of Aquitaine, already very discontented with her pious husband; she found Constantinople and all the East an exhilarating experience.

[5] Louis and his commanders were determined to follow the exact route not only of the First Crusade but also of the mythical expedition of Charlemagne, two accounts of which were composed at St. Denis.

[6] Roger II, Norman king of Sicily (1130–54), whose family had been plotting against the Byzantine Empire for two generations. His raid of 1147 managed to capture Corinth and Thebes before retreating.

stature, unlike only in dress and manners. After they had exchanged embraces and kisses, they went inside, where, when two chairs had been arranged, they both sat down.[7] Surrounded by a circle of their men, they conversed with the help of an interpreter.

9. THE HEATHEN OF THE NORTHEAST

For a thousand years between the crumbling of the Roman Empire in the west and the official conversion of Lithuania in 1386, Latin Christendom had to deal with significant groups of pagans to the north and east. The drive to convert these barbarous neighbors to the true religion and to the culture for which it served as vehicle was undertaken with sporadic but continuous zeal. A peculiar note of secular militancy was added during the twenty-five bloody years of Charlemagne's successful struggle against the Saxons (778–804) in northern Germany. By 1000 the major Slavic peoples had accepted Christianity in either the Latin or the Greek form, and in the following century and a half most of the Scandinavians embraced the Latin version. The lesser Slavic tribes along the Baltic coast proved surprisingly resistant, whether from a sluggish contentment with their backward culture or a high-spirited resentment of the ethnic insolence and territorial ambitions of Christian princes, both ecclesiastical and lay. The region between the rivers Elbe and Oder was eventually Christianized in the latter twelfth century more by conquest and the introduction of colonies of German peasants than by an enduring conversion of the natives; in the early thirteenth century the crusading order of the Teutonic Knights was established by papal and imperial charter to carry the good work and the frontier further.

This selection is from a twelfth-century Saxon priest's account of two of the numerous Slavic uprisings which in the tenth and eleventh centuries nearly stopped the eastward advance of the German Empire's missionary archdioceses of Magdeburg and Hamburg-Bremen. Helmold (1120?–72?) was probably born in Westphalia, perhaps of peasant parents. As a young man he joined the vigorous reforming order of Prémontré, whose founder, St. Norbert, had become archbishop of Magdeburg in 1126. Helmold was appointed pastor of the church at Bosau in the diocese of Oldenburg, which had been founded as a dependency

---

[7] A tender point of protocol. The parallel Byzantine account by Cinnamus has Louis sitting on a stool at a lower level than the enthroned Manuel. Manuel actually tended to be enthusiastic about Western culture.

of Hamburg-Bremen by Emperor Otto I in 968, but wiped out in the rising of 983–96, revived under the patronage of the Slavic prince Gottschalk, destroyed once more at his death in 1066, and effectively reorganized only in 1149, at the conclusion of military campaigns which had been planned in conjunction with the crusade of Conrad III and Louis VII to the Holy Land. For his information about Gottschalk, the exceptionally broad-minded Helmold relied on lively oral traditions, both Slavic and German, as well as on earlier historians.

Helmold: *Chronicle of the Slavs*

From Helmold, Chronicle of the Slavs, *trans. F. J. Tschan (New York: Columbia University Press, 1935), pp. 90–96. Reprinted by permission of Columbia University Press. The footnotes originally accompanying this selection have been deleted by permission of the publisher.*

19. The Persecution of Gottschalk. In those days there was a firm peace in Slavia because Conrad [1] who succeeded the pious Henry in the Empire wore down the Winithi in successive wars. Nevertheless, the Christian religion and the service of the house of God made little headway, since it was hindered by the avarice of the duke and of the Saxons, who in their rapacity let nothing remain either for the churches or for the priests. The chiefs of the Slavs were Anadrag and Gneus, and a third Udo, a bad Christian. On this account and also because of his cruelty he was suddenly stabbed by a Saxon deserter. His son named Gottschalk was being instructed in the learned disciplines at Lüneburg. When he heard of his father's death he rejected the faith along with his studies and, crossing the river,[2] came to the tribe of the Winithi. Having brought together a multitude of robbers, he smote, out of vengeance for his father, the whole land of the Nordalbingians. Such slaughter did he perpetrate on the Christian people that his cruelty exceeded all measure. Nothing in the land of the Holzatians and of the Sturmarians and of those who are called Ditmarshians[3] escaped his hands, except those well-known fortified places, Itzehoe and Bökelnburg. Thither certain armed men had betaken themselves with their women and children and the goods that had escaped pillage.

[1] Conrad II, 1024–39. *Cf.* I, 6.
[2] The Elbe. Lüneburg, where Gottschalk was studying at St. Michael's monastery, is 10 miles west of it (about 30 miles south of Hamburg).
[3] Three subdivisions of the Nordalbingian Saxons, whose expanding territories lay east of the Elbe, right against Slavic lands.

One day, however, as the said chieftain coursed like a robber through field and thicket and saw what had at one time been a country teeming with men and churches reduced to a waste solitude, he shuddered at the work of his own savagery and "it grieved him at his heart." [4] He deliberated how at length to stay his hands from their nefarious undertakings. He therefore presently withdrew from his associates and, going out as if into ambush, unexpectedly came upon a Saxon who was a Christian. And when the latter fled from the armed man as he approached from a distance, Gottschalk raised his voice and exhorted him to stop, swore even that he would do him no harm. When the timid man took courage and paused, Gottschalk began to inquire of him who he was and what news he had. "I am," said he, "a poor man born in Holzatia. Daily we get sinister reports that that prince of the Slavs, Gottschalk, is bringing many evils upon our people and country and that he longs to slake his cruel thirst with our blood. It were time, indeed, that God, the Vindicator, should avenge our injuries."

Gottschalk answered him:

> You seriously arraign that man, the prince of the Slavs. Yet he has, in very truth, brought many afflictions upon your land and people. A splendid avenger of his father's murder is he. But I am the man about whom we are now speaking and I have come to talk with you. I am sorry that I have done God and the worshipers of Christ so much wrong and I earnestly desire to return to the favor of those on whom I am beginning to realize I have unjustly inflicted such enormities. Heed, then, my words and go back to your people. Tell them to send trustworthy men to a designated place that they may secretly treat with me about an alliance and a covenant of peace. This done, I shall deliver into their hands that whole band of robbers with whom I am engaged more from necessity than from choice.

And with these words he set for him the place and the time.

When the man came to the stronghold in which the Saxon survivors were staying in great trepidation, he made known to the elders the saying that was hid and urged them by all means to send men to the place fixed for the conference. But they, thinking it a trick rife with guile, did not heed him.

And so some days later that prince was captured by the duke[5] and was thrown into chains, as if he had been a robber chieftain. The duke, however, reckoned that a man so brave and warlike would be useful to

---

[4] Like God grieving that He had made man, in Genesis 6:6.

[5] Bernhard II of Saxony (1011–59), whose exactions had been resented by clergy of independent mind and by both Christian and pagan Slavs.

him. He entered into an alliance with Gottschalk and permitted him to depart honorably laden with gifts. On being dismissed, the prince went to the king of the Danes, Cnut, and remained with him many days and years, winning for himself glory by his valor in various warlike deeds in Normandy and in England. Wherefore, also, was he honored with the hand of the king's daughter.[6]

20. The Faith of Gottschalk. After the death of King Cnut, Gottschalk went back to the land of his fathers. Finding that his heritage had been seized by certain usurpers, he determined to fight and, since victory was his, he got back his possessions in their entirety with the principate. He at once directed his mind to winning glory and honor for himself before the Lord and strove to rouse the Slavic peoples, who still lived forgetful of the Christian religion which they had held of old, that they might receive the grace of faith and take thought for the well being of the Church. And the work of God so prospered in his hands that a countless multitude of pagans thronged to receive the grace of baptism. Throughout the whole country of the Wagiri and even in that of the Polabi and Abodrites the churches which had been demolished of old were rebuilt. The call went out into all the lands for priests and ministers of the Word, who were to instruct the untutored pagans in the teachings of the faith. The faithful, therefore, rejoiced over the increase of the new plantation and it came to pass that his territories abounded in churches, and the churches in priests. Now the Kicini and the Circipani and all the tribes who lived along the Peene River also received the grace of faith. This is that Peene River at the mouth of which is located the city of Demmin.[7] Thither the limits of the diocese of Oldenburg at one time extended.

All the Slavic peoples who pertained to the cure of Oldenburg devoutly kept the Christian faith all the time that Gottschalk lived. This very devout man is said to have been inflamed with such zeal for the divine religion that he himself often made discourse in church in exhortation of the people, because he wished to make clearer in the Slavic language matters which were abstrusely preached by the bishops and the priests. Surely in all Slavia there has never arisen anyone mightier or anyone so fervent in the Christian religion. If a longer life had been granted him, he would have disposed all the pagans to embrace Chris-

[6] Sigrid, daughter not of Cnut (1028–35) but of his successor Sweyn Estridsson (1047–74). Apparently Gottschalk's travels lasted from 1029 to 1043.

[7] Ninety miles east-southeast of Oldenburg, 120 miles east-northeast of Hamburg (and about 90 miles due north of Berlin, which does not appear in the records until 1230).

tianity, since he converted nearly a third of those who had under his grandfather, Mistivoi,[8] relapsed into paganism. Then were also founded in several cities communities of holy men who lived according to canonical rule; also communities of monks and of nuns, as those who saw the several houses in Lübeck, Oldenburg, Ratzeburg, Lenzen, and in other cities bear witness. In Mecklenburg, which is the foremost city of the Abodrites, there are said in fact to have been three communities of those who served God.

21. The War of the Tholenzi. In those days[9] a great uproar occurred in the eastern country of the Slavs who fell upon each other in civil war. There are of those called Lutici, or Wilzi, four peoples, of whom we know the Kicini and Circipani lived beyond the Peene, the Redarii and Tholenzi on this side of the Peene. Among these peoples there arose mighty contention over leadership and power. The Redarii and Tholenzi desired to rule because of the high antiquity of their stronghold and the great reputation of the fane in which there is exhibited an image of Redigast. They claimed for themselves special preferment in respect of nobility because, on account of the oracle and the annual offerings of sacrifices, they were frequently visited by all the Slavic people. The Circipani and Kicini on their part refused to do them service; indeed, they were determined to defend their freedom by arms. As the dissension gradually waxed, a war at length broke out in which the Redarii and the Tholenzi were vanquished in very fiercely fought battles. The war was renewed a second time and a third time, and again the same ones were overcome by the selfsame victors. Many thousands of men were killed on both sides. The Circipani and Kicini on whom necessity had imposed the war were the victors. The Redarii and Tholenzi who were fighting for glory, stung to the quick by the shame of their defeat, summoned to their aid the most powerful king of the Danes and Bernhard, the duke of the Saxons, as well as Gottschalk, the prince of the Abodrites; each and every one of these with their armies. For six weeks they maintained this great multitude from their own resources. The war against the Circipani and Kicini then grew fiercer and, overwhelmed by so great a multitude, they did not have the strength to resist. Thus there was cut down a very great number of them and very many were led into captivity. At last they bought peace for fifteen thousand marks, and the princes divided the money among themselves. Of Christianity there was no mention, and they did not

[8] Mistivoi had led the uprising of 983 and even succeeded in burning Hamburg.
[9] About 1057.

give glory to God who had awarded them the victory in battle. From this fact may be discerned the insatiable greed of the Saxons who, though they surpass in arms and in the art of war the other peoples who are contiguous to the barbarians, are ever more intent upon increasing the tribute than upon winning souls for the Lord. Through the perseverance of the priests Christianity would long ago have grown in the esteem of Slavia if the avarice of the Saxons had not stood in the way. Therefore, let commendation and unbounded praise be heaped upon the most worthy Gottschalk, who, sprung from the barbarian peoples, restored to his race the gift of faith, the grace of belief through the abounding fervor of his love; let the Saxon chiefs be censured, who, sprung from Christian forefathers and reared in the bosom of Holy Mother Church, are found ever sterile and empty in the work of God.

22. The Rebellion of the Slavs. In the course of the years in which by the mercy of God and the virtue of that most religious man, Gottschalk, the state of the Church and the priestly service flourished becomingly in Slavia, the church of Oldenburg on the death of Abelinus was divided into three bishoprics. This division, indeed, was by no means effected by an imperial order but was clearly ordained as an invention of the great Adalbert, archbishop of Hamburg. For he was an ambitious man and very influential in the realm, since he had the most powerful Caesar Henry, the son of Conrad, as well as Pope Leo,[10] well disposed and agreeable to his wishes in all matters. He exercised the authority of an archbishop and functioned as papal legate in all the northern kingdoms, to wit, Denmark, Sweden, and Norway. Not content with these distinctions, he desired to attain to patriarchal dignity and, consequently, he wished to erect twelve bishoprics within the limits of his diocese in keeping with this rank. Of this design it is more than idle to speak for the reason that it appeared to judicious men as something absurd and witless. There gathered at his court, too, many priests and religious, and also many bishops who had been driven from their sees, and they partook of his table. Wishing to unburden himself of these men, he sent them out among the heathen, giving definite sees to some, indefinite sees to others. Thus, he put Ezzo in the place of Abelinus in Oldenburg, appointed to Ratzeburg a certain Aristo who had come from Jerusalem, and assigned John to Mecklenburg. This John, who had out of his love for roving come from Ireland

---

[10] Henry III (1039–56) and his cousin, the vigorous reforming Pope Leo IX (1049–54). Adalbert was archbishop 1043–72.

to Saxony, was kindly received by the archbishop (as were all) and was not long after sent into Slavia to Gottschalk. In the days he was with Gottschalk he is said to have baptized many thousands of pagans.[11]

10. THE SARACEN FRONTIER

In the early eighth century Muslim armies conquered Spain and penetrated Gaul almost as far as Tours, thus bringing Latin Christendom face-to-face with Islam. It was to be a long and tense confrontation with a dynamic civilization also organized around the conscious nucleus of a religion also derived from the Hebrew revelation, but militarily more effective than the civilization of western Europe and culturally far superior. In the eleventh century Europeans began to develop economic and military techniques that tipped the balance against Islam in the western Mediterranean; the Spanish *reconquista* was completed by the fall of Granada in 1492 to Ferdinand of Aragon and Isabella of León and Castile. However, in the eastern Mediterranean the eleventh century saw the beginnings of Turkish power, which absorbed the impact of the Crusades, finally overwhelmed the Byzantine Empire in 1453, and in the 1520's destroyed the Latin kingdom of Hungary and laid siege to Vienna.

Ethnically and socially less homogeneous than Latin Christendom, Islam contained within its boundaries several subjugated religious minorities, among whom various types of Christians were the most numerous. Muslim law granted them the special status of *Ahl-al-Dhimmah*, or People of the Covenant, who were disarmed and taxed in return for protection of their persons and property and permission to abide by the religious and civil laws of their community. They were naturally not allowed to convert Muslims or engage in public discussions of religion, and were not supposed to have any part in the making of political decisions; even self-defense against attack from individual Muslims was curtailed. Occasionally rulers would crack down on the *dhimmis,* requiring them to wear distinctive dress, forbidding them to ride horses, build taller houses than Muslim neighbors, raise their voices or ring bells during the liturgy, give testimony in Muslim courts, etc., and making *dhimmi*-murder by a Muslim punishable merely by a fine. The earlier centuries of Islam saw a great deal of tolerance, however; in Syria and Spain, areas with large and well-entrenched Christian majorities at first, many Christians and Jews rose to positions of public eminence. The structure of group

[11] Adalbert also sent him on a mission to Iceland.

status was especially complex in Spain. On top was an Arab elite, followed by a larger group of Berber origin which enjoyed the same legal standing but lower social prestige; next came the Muwallads, the "new Muslims," who paid a land tax originally levied on their *dhimmi* ancestors, and were the most mobile and restless element in society. Among the *dhimmis,* who paid a head as well as a land tax, the Jews were somewhat more favored than the threateningly numerous Christians; the latter were in turn divided between the Mozarabs, who had adopted Arabic language and culture, and the more backward elements who valued their links with the past and with Latin Christians beyond the frontier. There was also a considerable number of slaves of non-Muslim origin, from whose ranks came powerful ministers and officers as well as the most degraded instruments of public convenience. Christian *dhimmis* who wished to preserve their religious (and hence, legal) identity in this society faced four alternatives: subsiding into the isolation of a cultural ghetto; assimilation in the ambiguously promising manner of the Mozarabs; flight to an area under Christian rule; or working for Christian reconquest of the homeland.

The following two selections offer illustrations of the last three alternatives. Louis the Pious' charter is a statement of the Frankish Empire's refugee settlement policy, offering either assimilation to nascent Frankish feudalism or preservation of Spanish identity. A letter which he wrote in 828 to the Christians of Mérida, urging them to create an anti-tax rebellion deep in the southwest of the peninsula, suggests the long-range goal of this policy. The second selection is from a provincial history by Lisan-al-Din ibn-al-Khatib (1313–74), one of the two greatest historians of western Islam (his friend Ibn-Khaldun being the other). Born in Granada of an Arab family which had come from Syria during the Conquest, he directed the world-renowned schools of Granada under the Sultans Yusuf ibn-al-Hajjuj (1333–54) and Muhammad V (1354–59, 1362–91), who gave him the lofty title of "He of the Two Vizirates" (*i.e.,* minister of the sword and of the pen). Author of sixty works, historical, geographical, philosophical, medical, poetic, and epistolary, he is a late representative of the cultivated semi-tolerance which typified Muslim Spain before the hardening of positions which set in at the end of the eleventh century. By the ninth century Granada had become one of the most heavily Mozarabic regions of Spain, and in the mid-eleventh century its Berber rulers had even appointed two Jews in succession to the post of vizir, or chief minister. But the coming of the Almoravids, a puritanical North African sect which held sway briefly from

Ghana to Toledo, put an end to that. It is an appropriate co-incidence that the Almoravid emir Yusuf ibn-Tashfin decreed the destruction of Granada's most illustrious church in the same year which witnessed the bloody capture of Jerusalem by the Crusaders and the death in Valencia of Rodrigo Díaz de Vivar, who had won his epithet, the Cid, while fighting against Aragon in the service of a Muwallad dynasty and before that had been the champion of Castilian kings who sought to rule the "Three Religions" of Spain even more tolerantly than had the most liberal Muslim califs.

Charter of Louis the Pious for Spanish Refugees, 815

From Histoire générale de Languedoc, *2nd ed.* (*Toulouse, 1875*), *II, cols. 97–100. Footnotes supplied.*

In the name of the Lord God and our Saviour Jesus Christ. Louis, Emperor and Augustus by the ordination of divine providence, to all those faithful to the holy Church of God and to ourself, both present and to come, residing in the regions of Aquitaine, Septimania, Provence, and Spain.

We do not think that notice has eluded any of you of the way in which certain men, on account of the iniquitous oppression and most cruel yoke placed on their necks by the Saracens, that race most hostile to Christianity, have fled to us from various regions of Spain, abandoning their own homes and the possessions which belonged to them by hereditary right. They have come together to make settlements in Septimania and in that portion of Spain which has been reduced to a wilderness by our frontier commanders, and withdrawing themselves from the power of the Saracens, they have on their own initiative and of their own free will subjected themselves to our dominion. Therefore we wish every man of you to be notified of what regulations we have decreed that those same men, whom we have taken under our protection and defense, shall in full liberty observe:

I. Let them proceed to the gathering of the host with their count just as other free men do, and in our March[1] let them not fail to make those scouting and patrolling expeditions called *wactae* in current

[1] The Spanish March (or frontier command district), established by Charlemagne some years after his disastrous expedition across the Pyrenees in 778 (Roland and the rear guard were ambushed by Christian Basques on the way back). In 801 the Franks took Barcelona, about 100 miles south of the Pyrenees; in 809 Louis himself led an expedition 100 miles further, to Tortosa at the mouth of the river Ebro.

speech, following the reasonable orders and admonitions of the same count. Let them make all preparations to receive those of our *missi*[2] or our sons whom we shall send to those regions as the occasion demands, or any envoys who shall be sent to us from various parts of Spain; let them provide horses for their transport. But no other charge may be levied upon them by the count or by his dependents or servants.

II. Let them not in any sense refuse to attend the court[3] of their count for major cases, such as homicides, kidnappings, arsons, depredations, loss of limbs, thefts, robberies, usurpations of others' property, and whenever they will have been charged by a neighbor[4] with either a criminal or a civil offense, and ordered to come to a judicial reckoning. But they shall not be prohibited from settling other minor cases among themselves according to their customs, as they have hitherto been capable of doing.

III. And if any one of them shall attract other men, whatever their place of origin, to settle with him in his portion of that region which he has occupied for settlement, and which is called an *adprisio*,[5] he may employ their labor without any reservation or impediment, and it shall be lawful for him to compel them to abide by such justice as they can establish among themselves. But other justice, that is, criminal actions, shall be reserved to the jurisdiction of the count.

IV. And if any of those men who were attracted and given a place to settle in their portions, shall leave the place, that place shall not be withdrawn from the lordship of the man who held it before.

V. If they, on account of sympathetic treatment on the part of their count, offer him some gift from their property as a token of their appreciation and respect, that shall not be counted as some form of tribute or fee, nor shall the count or his successors presume to consider it a custom. Nor shall he force them to provide quarters or give posthorses or render himself or his men any fee or tribute or service other than that which has been defined above. On the contrary, let these Spaniards who at the present time reside in the aforesaid places, as well as those who shall trickle hither to our obedience and Faith[6] in

[2] High-ranking agents sent on special tours of inspection and correction by Charlemagne and his successors.

[3] A court observing Frankish, Roman, or other local legal customs, and so perhaps not familiar with the Romano-Visigothic law of Spain—although Visigothic codes of the fifth century had had considerable influence on the customary law of the areas in question.

[4] *I.e.*, not under Visigothic law.

[5] The technical term for such frontier-filling settlements.

[6] The original *fidem* seems to cover both feudal and theological fidelity.

flight from the power of the unjust, and who, settling down in abandoned and uncultivated places with our permission or that of our count, shall erect buildings and cultivate fields,—let them reside in liberty under our defense and protection in the aforesaid manner, and with enthusiastic fidelity render to us what we have established above, both in the company of their count and in that of his envoys as the time demands.

VI. Let those same Spaniards understand, however, that they have our permission to become vassals of our counts in the accustomed manner. And if any of them shall obtain a fief from the man to whom he has commended himself, let him realize that he shall owe his lord such service from it as our own men are accustomed to owe their lords from a like fief.

VII. In consequence whereof, we have ordered that they be given this authoritative document of ours, in which we command and decree that this constitution of our liberality and mercy toward them be observed inviolably and perpetually in the same tenor by all those faithful to the Holy Church of God and to ourself. It is our wish that there be three copies of this constitution in each *civitas*[7] where the aforesaid Spaniards are known to reside: one for the bishop of that *civitas,* a second for the count, and a third for the Spaniards sojourning in that place. We have ordered that an official transcript be placed in the archives of the Palace, so that if ever (as often happens)[8] they shall clamor for redress or the count or someone else shall have a complaint against them, a definition of the issues can be obtained from inspecting it.

And so that this constitution may be more truly believed and more diligently observed through all future time by those faithful to the Holy Church of God and to ourself, we have signed it with our own hand and ordered that it be sealed with our own ring.

> *(The seal of the lord Louis, most serene Emperor. Durandus the deacon, acting for Helisachar, authenticated it.)*

> *(Granted on the first of January, in the first year of the reign of the lord Louis, most pious Emperor, in the 8th indiction. Done at Aachen in the royal Palace felicitously in the name of God. Amen.)*

[7] Either a county-sized unit of civil and ecclesiastical administration or its "urban" center.

[8] In 812 Charlemagne had delivered a judgment favorable to the Spaniards in such a case; in 844 Louis' son Charles the Bald would confirm and extend all these privileges.

Ibn Al-Khatib: *Book of the Deeds of Distinguished Men*

From La España musulmana, *ed. Claudio Sánchez-Albornoz (Buenos Aires: El Ateneo, 1946), II, 182–86. Translated by permission of the publisher. Footnotes supplied.*

When the Muslims established themselves in this noble province and the emir Abu'l-Hattar had assigned dwellings to the Arab tribes from Syria, giving them a third of the agricultural produce of the protected ones,[1] those tribes settled themselves firmly there among the Christians who cultivated the fields and lived in villages under chiefs of their own religion. These chiefs were men of experience and intelligence, manageable men, who knew how much each of their coreligionists had to pay for the head tax.[2] The last one, whose name was Ibn-al-Qallas, was quite renowned, and enjoyed a considerable reputation among the rulers of the province.

These Christians had a famous church, at two bowshots from the city, opposite the Elvira gate. It had been built by a great lord of their religion, whom a certain prince had put at the head of a numerous army of Rumis.[3] It was unique in the beauty of its construction and in its ornaments; nevertheless, the emir Yusuf ibn-Tashfin,[4] yielding to the ardent desire of the *faqihs*,[5] who had already delivered a judgment to that effect, ordered its destruction. Ibn al-Saraifi has written about it as follows:

> The men of Granada were to destroy it on Monday, the last day of Jumada II of the year 492 [May 23, 1099]. It was completely demolished, and each one of them took something from the spoil and from the objects consecrated for the liturgy. Even in our days the place where this temple was is known, and its walls, which partly survive, give evidence that it was very solidly built. Part of the space which it occupied is at present the well-known cemetery of Salh-ibn-Malik.

[1] *I.e.*, the *dhimmis.*
[2] The head tax, or *jizyah*, in Spain usually ranged from 12 to 48 *dirhams* a year. (A *dirham* was a coin of silver or silver-alloy weighing on the average three grams.)
[3] *I.e.*, "Romans"—the term applied by the Muslims to most free Christian peoples. The church dated from the Visigothic period (late fifth to early eighth century).
[4] Second ruler of the Almoravids (1061–1106), founder of Marrakesh. Entered Spain to assist local emirs against Alfonso VI of Castile in 1086, returned to conquer in 1090. In their zeal to reform the laxity of the native emirs, he and his son Ali (1106–43) were very concerned to curb the privileges of *dhimmis*, both Christian and Jewish.
[5] Teachers of Islamic law and theology.

Under the regime of the Almoravids, when the arms of the king Ibn-Rademiro, the enemy of God, were still victorious—the Eternal One, as is well known, annihilated his power at the battle of Fraga[6]—the protected Christians of this province conceived a hope of satisfying their resentment and making themselves lords of the country. They addressed themselves to Ibn-Rademiro, sent him letter after letter and envoy after envoy, begging him to make ready and to arouse himself and come to Granada. Then, seeing that he had his doubts, they presented him with a list which contained the names of 12,000 of their best fighting men, and in which no old man and no youth had been included. They told him, furthermore, that in addition to the persons enumerated therein and whom they knew because they lived in their vicinity, there were many others who could not be registered because they lived at a great distance, but who would present themselves as soon as the king would make himself seen.

In this way they inspired him with the desire to attempt the enterprise, and tried besides to arouse his covetousness by describing the excellent things that are found in Granada and that make it the fairest country in the world. They spoke of their great plain and of its produce, its wheat, barley, flax, its abundance of silk, vineyards, olive groves, and every kind of fruit, of its streams and rivers, the strong situation of their capital city, the gentle manners of their villagers, the courtesy of their city-dwellers, and the beauty of their meadows and hills. They added that once this blessed province was conquered, it would serve as a base for the conquest of others, and that, as one can read in its histories, Granada has been described by kings as the best part of Spain. In brief, they aimed so well at the mark that they struck it dead center. The king assembled his best troops and took the field, accompanied by four thousand Aragonese knights and their men-at-arms, who had sworn on the Gospels never to abandon one another.

The king left Saragossa[7] at the beginning of Sha'aban of the year 519 [early September, 1125], keeping secret the object of his undertaking. He passed near Valencia, where there was an Almoravid garrison under the command of the sheikh Abu Muhammad ibn-Badr ibn-Warka. While he was attacking that city, a great number of the protected Christians united themselves to him, to swell the ranks of his army, serve as guides, and show him what he should do in order to cause

---

[6] Alfonso the Battler, king of Aragon 1104–34; son of Sancho Ramirez (1063–94), grandson of Ramiro I (1035–63). His major inroads into Almoravid territory were decisively reversed at Fraga in 1134.

[7] About 325 miles north of Granada as the crow flies, and much farther by the route actually taken.

the greatest damage possible to the Muslims and succeed in his enterprise. Immediately thereafter he arrived at Alcira, which he attacked for several consecutive days; but he lost many men and gained no advantage from the attack. From there he went towards Denia, where he fought on the night of the Breaking of the Fast [October 31], and traveled all over the East Coast in daily stages, sacking the regions which lay along his line of march. . . . [The next two months were spent in half a dozen unsuccessful sieges.]

The author of the book entitled *Al-Anwar al-Jalia* writes in these terms:

Meanwhile, the plot of the protected Christians of Granada was discovered, and it was verified that the king had been summoned by them. The governor of Spain, Abu'l-Tahic Tamin ibn-Yusuf, whose residence was in Granada, wished to take them prisoners then and there, but he had to forego that intention. The Christians took advantage of the situation to assemble in the king's camp, following a number of different routes. In the meantime, Muslim troops came from all directions to place themselves at the orders of the governor, and his brother, the Commander of the Faithful, sent him a great army from Africa. In this way the Muslim hosts came to form a circle, so to speak, around Granada.

Having left Gaudix, Ibn-Rademiro camped at the *pueblo* of Diezma. On the day of the Feast of the Sacrifice [January 7, 1126] the men of Granada recited the prayer called the Prayer of Dread, and on the following day, almost at noon, they discerned the tents of the Rumis at Al-Nibar, to the east of the city. For a while there was fighting about six miles from Granada; the rabble had already fled from the marketplace and the other inhabitants of the same type were crowded together in the streets.

When he arrived in the outskirts of Granada, Ibn-Rademiro counted 50,000 men[8] under his banners. . . . He spent more than ten days at the village of Al-Nibar. But since it rained a great deal and froze frequently, he could not send troops around the countryside, and so it was the protected Christians who supplied his provisions.

Seeing that he would not succeed in taking the city, he raised camp on the twenty-sixth of Dzu'l-Hicha of 519 [January 23], after having reprimanded those who had summoned him and above all, their chief Ibn-al-Qallas; but they excused themselves, saying that he himself was responsible for the small success of the expedition, since his slowness and his frequent delays had given time for the Muslim forces to gather. They added that they had sacrificed all for him, since they could not hope for pardon from the Muslims. . . . [It took Alfonso nearly another year to

[8] Like all medieval statistics, this figure should be taken with a grain of salt.

get the remnants of his army, slowed down by Granadan refugees, back
to Aragon.]

When the Muslims took stock of what had taken place, and especially
of the treason of their neighbors, the protected ones, they became as
disturbed as they were irritated. At the same time that they were taking all sorts of precautions, the cadi[9] Abu'l-Walid ibn-Ruzd thought
he would perform a meritorious service. Taking it upon himself to go
to Africa, he went to Marrakesh, and there exposed the state of affairs
in Spain to the emir Ali ibn-Yusuf ibn-Tashfin. He recounted the tribulations which the Muslims of that country had had to undergo because
of the crime of the protected Christians who had called in the Rumis.
He added that such Christians had in that way broken their ancient
compact with the Muslims, and had lost the right to be protected. Then
he voiced a solemn opinion according to which the guilty ones, in the
case of those for whom a rather mild penalty was sought, should be
exiled from their country. His advice was adopted and appeared to
that effect in an edict of the emir.

In the month of Ramadan of that year [September-October, 1126],
many Christians were therefore transported to Africa. Some, expelled
in all directions, perished on the road, and others scattered throughout
the country. Nevertheless, many Christians remained in Granada, and
thanks to the protection accorded them by certain princes, managed
to become powerful and rich; but in the year 557 [1162] occurred a
battle in which nearly all were exterminated. Today a small group survives, accustomed after long years to contempt and humiliation. May it
please God to grant His servants triumph in the end.

11. THE JEWISH PROBLEM

Most societies reserve a place for strangers, especially if they
perform a valued function. They will usually be free from
molestation and may even become objects of marked favor, as
long as two conditions are met: they must not threaten the
security of a decisive sector of the host society, and the specifically
different things about them must not be too disturbing to that
society's sense of its own identity. The relationship of Jewish
communities to Latin Christendom was complicated and subject to extreme fluctuation. Sometimes groups of Jews were treated

---

[9] A judge with ultimate authority over all legal matters in a given area.

with appreciation as well as a high degree of tolerance, sometimes they were slaughtered or expelled. In general, their position worsened as medieval European society became more complex, dynamic, and self-conscious. They would undoubtedly have received less attention of either sort if they had dealt less skilfully in money and medicine, or if their religious heritage had not been so intimately connected with that of the Christians among whom they lived.

The following selections give some sense of the variety of treatment received by European Jews in the decisive twelfth century. The first two documents represent the classic theory, according to which the Jews were to enjoy the privileges and disabilities of religiously distinct body, their status guaranteed by the highest secular and sacred authority. The Emperor Frederick Barbarossa (1154–98) was a vigorous wielder of the law, whose formulae he treated with the utmost seriousness in his efforts to bind his vassals and subjects more tightly to his rule and to dispute the claims of popes, mere kings, and other rivals. Bishop Rudeger (1073–90) was a magnate of more modest scope, but his Rhineland see was a proud one. The bishops of Speyer were its secular rulers from 969 to 1111; Rudeger's predecessors had secured the assistance of two emperors in the erection of a huge cathedral which is still the largest Romanesque church in Germany, and now contains the tombs of eight emperors and many empresses. He clearly felt that a Jewish suburb would enhance the prestige as well as the prosperity of his city.

The bishops and cathedral chapter of Béziers in the south of France felt very differently about their city's Jews. So attached were they to the traditional ritual insult that it took their lord eight years to get a new bishop to ratify his profitable concession. The incident is best appreciated against the turbulent political background of that Mediterranean-coast city. The previous bishop had been so hostile to Raymond that he made an alliance with the Count of Toulouse against him; a few years after Bishop William's ratification, Raymond was murdered at the altar of the church of Mary Magdalen by a group of vengeful bourgeois. His son was reinstated some years later by the King of Aragon, after promising a general amnesty for which he promptly substituted a general massacre. The city was probably full of Albigensian heretics during these goings-on, which help to illustrate the ambiguities of local practice with which the Jews of Europe had to contend. Selection (e) shows lower-class resentment triggering a multilevel outburst against the Jews of London right in the middle of the ceremonies surrounding Richard the Lion-Heart's coronation in 1189. Such moments of public solemnity were becoming increasingly dangerous for those who could not participate in the central ritual. Sporadic outbreaks of violence occurred throughout England for another year, and in exactly a century the realm would be emptied of these once-favored aliens. Roger of Hoveden (died 1201?) was a Yorkshireman, a clerk in the entourage of Richard's father Henry II since 1174. At the time of Richard's coronation he was probably serving as an itinerant royal justice in the North, but his contacts were good and his details are usually reliable. He may have begun his composition of the *Annals* that same year.

The final selection shows that a desire to include the Jews through conversion could have harsher consequences than the urge to exclude or to segregate them in ghettos. The opening years of the First and Second Crusades—1096 and 1146—produced thousands of Jewish martyrs in France and Germany. Leading preachers of the Crusade, like St. Bernard, uttered eloquent condemnation of such behavior, but a great many of the "average Crusaders" followed their own impulses instead. This strange tale of ferocity and concern (the usual blend of fanaticism) comes from the autobiography of Guibert de Nogent (1053–1121?), a rambling memoir that gives expression to most of the enthusiasms current in his time and part of the world. Born in Picardy to a family of the middle nobility, he entered monastic life at twelve, and became abbot of Nogent-sous-Coucy (near Laon) in 1104. He had almost certainly heard Urban II's speech at Clermont in 1095 (see I, 7). Author of a history of the Crusade entitled *The Deeds of God through the Franks*, he also wrote a number of scriptural and devotional treatises, and began his autobiography in 1114.

Charter of Frederick I to the Jews of Worms

Charter of Frederick I to the Jews of Worms *and* Charter of Bishop Rudeger to the Jews of Speyer *from O. J. Thatcher and E. H. McNeal,* Source Book for Mediaeval History *(New York: Charles Scribner's Sons, 1905), pp. 574–78.*

In the name of the holy and undivided Trinity. Frederick, by the grace of God emperor of the Romans, Augustus. Be it known to all bishops, abbots, dukes, counts, and all others subject to our laws, that we have confirmed by our royal authority, expressed in the present law, the statutes in favor of the Jews of Worms and their fellow-religionists which were granted to them by our predecessor emperor Henry, in the time of Solomon, rabbi of the Jews.

1. In order that they may always look to us for justice, we command by our royal authority that no bishop or his official, and no count, *Schultheiss*, or other official except those whom they choose from among their own number, shall exercise any authority over them. The only official who may exercise such authority is the man whom the emperor puts over them in accordance with their choice, because they are entirely under the control of our treasury.

2. No one shall take from them any property which they hold by hereditary right, such as building sites, gardens, vineyards, fields, slaves, or any other movable or immovable property. No one shall interfere with their right to erect buildings against the walls of the city, on the inside or outside. If anyone molests them contrary to our edict he shall forfeit our grace and shall restore twofold whatever he took from them.

3. They shall have free right to change money with all men anywhere in the city except at the mint or where the officials of the mint have established places for changing money.

4. They shall travel in peace and security throughout the whole kingdom for the purpose of buying and selling and carrying on trade and business. No one shall exact any toll from them or require them to pay any other public or private tax.

5. Guests may not quarter themselves on the Jews against their will. No one shall seize one of their horses for the journey of the king or the bishop, or for the royal expedition.

6. If any stolen property is found in the possession of a Jew, and he says that he bought it, he shall say under oath according to Jewish law how much he paid for it, and he shall restore it to its owner on receipt of that amount.

7. No one shall baptize the children of Jews against their will. If anyone captures or seizes a Jew and baptizes him by force, he shall pay twelve pounds of gold to the royal treasury. If a Jew expresses a wish to be baptized, he shall be made to wait three days, in order to discover whether he abandons his own law because of his belief in Christianity, or because of illegal pressure; and if he thus relinquishes his law, he shall also relinquish his right to inheritance.

8. No one shall entice away from them any of their pagan slaves under pretext of baptizing them into the Christian faith. If anyone does this, he shall pay the ban, that is, three pounds of gold, and shall re-

store the slave to his owner; the slave shall obey all the commands of his owner, except those that are contrary to his Christian faith.

9. Jews may have Christian maid-servants and nurses, and may employ Christian men to work for them, except on feast days and Sundays; no bishop or other clergyman shall forbid this.

10. No Jew may own a Christian slave.

11. If a Jew brings suit against a Christian or a Christian against a Jew, each party shall follow the process of his own law as far as possible. The Jew has the same right as the Christian to prove his case and to release his sureties by his oath and the oath of another person of either law [*i.e.*, Christian or Jew].

12. No one may force a Jew to undergo the ordeal of hot iron, hot water, or cold water, or have him beaten with rods or thrown into prison, but he shall be tried according to his own law after forty days. In a case between a Christian and a Jew, the defendant cannot be convicted except by the testimony of both Christians and Jews. If a Jew appeals to the royal court in any case, he must be given time to present his case there. If anyone molests a Jew contrary to this edict, he shall pay the imperial ban of three pounds to the emperor.

13. If anyone takes part in a plan or plot to kill a Jew, both the slayer and his accomplice shall pay twelve pounds of gold to the royal treasury. If he wounds him without killing him, he shall pay one pound. If it is a serf who has wounded or slain the Jew, the lord of the serf shall either pay the fine or surrender the serf to punishment. If the serf is too poor to pay the fine, he shall suffer the penalty which was visited upon the serf who in the time of our predecessor, emperor Henry, slew the Jew named Vivus; namely, his eyes shall be torn out and his right hand cut off.

14. If the Jews have any suit or any matter to be settled among themselves, it shall be tried by their peers and by no others. If any Jew refuses to tell the truth in any case which arises among the Jews, he shall be forced to confess the truth by his own rabbi. But if a Jew has been accused of a serious crime, he shall be allowed to appeal to the emperor, if he wishes to.

15. Besides their wine, they shall have the right to sell spices and medicines to the Christians. As we have commanded, no one may force them to furnish horses for the expedition of the emperor, or to pay any other public or private tax.

Charter of Bishop Rudeger, to the Jews of Speyer

1. In the name of the holy and undivided Trinity. I, Rudeger, by cognomen Huozman, humble bishop of Speyer, when I wished to make a city of my village of Speyer, thought that it would greatly add to its honor if I should establish some Jews in it. I have therefore collected some Jews and located them in a place apart from the dwellings and association of the other inhabitants of the city; and that they may be protected from the attacks and violence of the mob, I have surrounded their quarter with a wall. The land for their dwellings I had acquired in a legal way; for the hill [on which they are to live] I secured partly by purchase and partly by trade, and the valley [which I have given them] I received as a gift from the heirs who possessed it. I have given them this hill and valley on condition that they pay every year three and one-half pounds of money coined in the mint of Speyer, for the use of the brothers [monks of some monastery which is not named here].

2. I have given them the free right of changing gold and silver coins and of buying and selling everything they wish within their own walls and outside the gate clear up to the boat-landing [on the Rhine] and also on the wharf itself. And they have the same right throughout the whole city.

3. Besides, I have given them a piece of the land of the church as a burial-ground. This land they shall hold forever.

4. I have also granted that, if a Jew comes to them from some other place and is their guest for a time, he shall pay no tolls [to the city].

5. The chief priest of their synagogue shall have the same position and authority among them as the mayor of the city has among the citizens. He shall judge all the cases which arise among them or against them. If he is not able to decide any case it shall be taken before the bishop or his chamberlain.

6. They are bound to watch, guard, and defend only their own walls, in which work their servants may assist them.

7. They may hire Christian nurses and Christian servants.

8. The meats which their law forbids them to eat they may sell to Christians, and the Christians may buy them.

9. To add to my kindness to them I grant them the most favorable laws and conditions that the Jews have in any city of the German kingdom. . . .

Geoffrey of Vigeois: *Chronicle*

From Life in the Middle Ages, *ed. and trans.* G. G. Coulton *(Cambridge: Cambridge University Press, 1930), II, 23. Reprinted by permission of the publisher.*

Raymund Trenchaval, viscount of Béziers, returned from Jerusalem in the year of Grace 1152, whereupon he received money to release the Jews from the affliction which they suffered from the Christians in the week of our Lord's Passion. I will narrate the matter at length to such as may be ignorant of it. Many Jews have dwelt in the town of Béziers from time immemorial; on Palm Sunday the bishop, having preached a mystic sermon to the people, was wont to exhort them in many words to the following effect: "Lo! ye see before you the descendants of those who condemned the Messiah, and who still deny that Mary was the Mother of God. Lo! here is the time wherein our heart echoes more often to the injury done to Christ. Lo! these are the days wherein ye have leave from the prince to avenge this so great iniquity. Now therefore, taught by the custom of your ancestors and fortified with our benediction after that of the Lord, cast ye stones against the Jews while there is yet time, and, in so far as in you lieth, atone manfully for the evil done to our Lord." When, therefore, the bishop had blessed them and (as in former days) the prince had given them the customary leave, then they would batter the Jews' houses with showers of stones, and very many were oftentimes wounded on either side. This fight was commonly continued from Palm Sunday until Easter Eve, and ended about the fourth hour; yet none were permitted to use other arms but stones alone. All this, as we have said, was forgiven to the faithless Jews by this Raymund.

Exemption Granted by Bishop William III to the Jews of Béziers

From Cartulaire de Béziers, *ed. J. Rouquette (Paris-Montpellier: Picard-Valat, 1918), pp. 266–68. Footnotes supplied.*

In the name of the Lord. In the year 1160 of His Nativity, in the reign of King Louis,[1] on the sixth day before the Nones of May:

---

[1] Louis VII of France (1137–80), who was generally sympathetic to his Jewish subjects, unlike his son, Philip II (1180–1223). William III was bishop 1160–67.

let it be known to all who hear this, that I, William, Bishop of Béziers, by the authority of our clergy and the consent of the whole [cathedral] chapter, do remit to you, Trencavel, and to all your successors and to all you [Jews] present and to come, residing in the city of Béziers, on my behalf and that of all my successors, the customary attack and insult and warfare of stoning which (whether rightly or wrongly) the Christians have been accustomed to wage against [the Jews] of this city by day or night from the first hour of the Saturday before Palm Sunday until the last hour of Easter Tuesday.[2]

And if by chance it should happen that anyone of my clergy or of their households shall on those forbidden days or nights throw a stone against the Jews or against the walls of their houses, from which that warfare may have occasion to arise, entry to the churches shall be forbidden him by my authority and that of my successors and clergy, and we shall place him under sentence of excommunication.

And if any of the laity of this city shall act contrary to the aforesaid prohibition, neither I nor any of my successors or clergy shall support him in this or provide him defense.

And on account of this remission and quittance, you have given me, William the bishop, 600 *solidi* of Melgueil[3] for the use of the church of St. Nazaire;[4] I have received all this money from you [Jews], and no debt remains to me on your part.

And for the aforesaid remission and quittance, you the aforesaid and your successors shall forever contribute, each year on Palm Sunday, four pounds of Melgueil to the church of St. Nazaire for its adornment, in such a way that neither the bishop nor any of the clergy shall be able to commute those four pounds to other uses.

And the Jews do this of their own will and by the authority of the Lord Trencavel.

The signatures of Hugh de Corneillan the archdeacon, William of Béziers the precentor, Macfred the archdeacon, Raymond of Montpaon the chamberlain, Bernard of Narbonne,[5] Deodatus of Antignac, Guillem, William de Margone, master Stephen and Raymond the cantor,

---

[2] Seventeen days in all.

[3] Equal to 12 marks of silver in 1158, a great deal of money. The coinage of Melgueil was struck by counts of Melgueil (60 miles northeast of Béziers, on a lagoon of the Mediterranean) and by bishops of Montpellier and Maguelonne in the eleventh and twelfth centuries.

[4] The cathedral, built from the twelfth to the fourteenth centuries.

[5] Treasurer of the cathedral. His native city, the archiepiscopal see, is about 20 miles southwest of Béziers.

and William Pelapullus; all of whom have approved this document. The witnesses of this transaction, in whose presence it was enacted at Béziers within the city walls on the first floor of the bishop's old residence, are William Arnaud, Berengar of Béziers, William Sigarius, Peter Sigarius, Arnaud of Maureillan, Gaucerand the vicar, Pons de Bessan, Alcher de Corneillan and Peter Raimund de Cellavinaria.[6]

Written by Bernard the hebdomadary of St. Aphrodisius[7] at the request of Lord William the bishop and all the aforesaid canons and witnesses, and at the dictation of master Marchesius and Bernard Sicfredus.

[6] Most of the gentlemen listed as members of the chapter and as witnesses seem to be from the immediate region. All the identifiable place-names refer to small communities within a 20-mile radius of Béziers, with the exception of Montpaon, which is about 50 miles northwest of Béziers, just beyond the watershed of the Orb, Béziers' river.

[7] A parish church named for the first Bishop of Béziers, martyred either in the first century or about 250. The title *hebdomadary* was usually applied to that member of a monastery or church chapter who had been selected to sing the key liturgical selections of a given week. Sometimes, one man might become, paradoxically enough, a permanent hebdomadary; in other atypical situations, the title was applied to the official in charge of the wine cellar, food supply, or some other important resource of the community.

Roger of Hoveden: *Annals*

From *Roger of Hoveden*, Annals, *trans. H. T. Riley (London: H. G. Bohn, 1853), II, 119–20. Footnote supplied.*

The mass having been concluded, and all things solemnly performed, the two bishops before-named, one on the right hand the other on the left,[1] led him [Richard] back from the church to his chamber, crowned,

[1] The Bishops of Durham (225 miles north of London) and Bath (90 miles west of London), who represent admirably the background of worldly clerical interests against which this dramatic outburst of persecution was enacted.

Hugh de Puiset (1125–95), who walked on Richard's right, was a great-grandson of William the Conqueror, and hence Richard's second cousin once removed. When Hugh was made Bishop of Durham in 1154, he became thereby secular Earl-palatine (see III, 8) of Durham in Northumberland. A few days after the coronation, Hugh bought from Richard the whole earldom of Northumberland, which was co-extensive with his diocese. Hugh paid 2000 marks for that large frontier territory, and another 1000 marks for the post of justiciar; he got the money from the funds which he had been collecting since 1188 for the Third Crusade. Hugh resented Richard's appointment of Bishop William Longchamp as Chief Justiciar; when Longchamp went to York to punish those who had persecuted the Jews there, Hugh tried to block the

and carrying a sceptre in his right hand and the rod of royalty in his left, the procession going in the same order as before. Then the procession returned to the choir, and our lord the king put off his royal crown and robes of royalty, and put on a crown and robes that were lighter; and, thus crowned, went to dine; on which the archbishops and bishops took their seats with him at the table, each according to his rank and dignity. The earls and barons also served in the king's palace, according to their several dignities; while the citizens of London served in the cellars, and the citizens of Winchester in the kitchen.

While the king was seated at table, the chief men of the Jews came to offer presents to him, but as they had been forbidden the day before to come to the king's court on the day of the coronation, the common people, with scornful eye and insatiable heart, rushed upon the Jews and stripped them, and then scourging them, cast them forth out of the king's hall. Among these was Benedict, a Jew of York, who, after having been so maltreated and wounded by the Christians that his life was despaired of, was baptized by William, prior of the church of Saint Mary at York, in the church of the Innocents, and was named William, and thus escaped the peril of death and the hands of the persecutors.

The citizens of London, on hearing of this, attacked the Jews in the city and burned their houses; but by the kindness of their Christian friends, some few made their escape. On the day after the coronation, the king sent his servants, and caused those offenders to be arrested who had set fire to the city; not for the sake of the Jews, but on account of the houses and property of the Christians which

---

sentence. His resistance was further motivated by the fact that the penalty fell heavily on the Percy family, with whom Hugh was connected (he had at least two illegitimate sons by a lady of that house).

Hugh was also a patron of learning and good works. He commissioned the monk Reginald of Durham to write a life of the saintly Godric of Finchale (see V, 3), which Reginald dedicated to him despite Godric's prediction that Hugh's worldliness would cost him seven years of blindness.

Reginald Fitzjoceline (1140–91), who walked on Richard's left, was one of Longchamp's chief supporters. He was the illegitimate son of Jocelin de Bohun, a great Norman noble who became Bishop of Salisbury. After being educated in Italy, Reginald joined a high-spirited group of courtiers around Thomas à Becket. In 1174 he was made Bishop of Bath and Wells, thanks to his skillful handling of the negotiations between King Henry II and Pope Alexander III after Becket's murder. Four years later he served on a commission trying cases of heresy at Toulouse and Albi in southern France. After the coronation he may have tried to buy the Chancellorship of England from Richard for £4000. In 1191 he was elected Archbishop of Canterbury, but died before being consecrated.

they had burnt and plundered, and he ordered some of them to be hanged.

On the same day, the king ordered the before-named William, who from a Jew had become a Christian, to be presented to him, on which he said to him, "What person are you?" to which he made answer, "I am Benedict of York, one of your Jews." On this the king turned to the archbishop of Canterbury, and the others who had told him that the said Benedict had become a Christian, and said to them, "Did you not tell me that he is a Christian?" to which they made answer, "Yes, my lord." Whereupon he said to them, "What are we to do with him?" to which the archbishop of Canterbury, less circumspectly than he might, in the spirit of his anger, made answer, "If he does not choose to be a Christian, let him be a man of the Devil"; whereas he ought to have made answer, "We demand that he shall be brought to a Christian trial, as he has become a Christian, and now contradicts that fact." But, inasmuch as there was no person to offer any opposition thereto, the before-named William relapsed into the Jewish errors, and after a short time died at Northampton; on which he was refused both the usual sepulture of the Jews, as also that of the Christians, both because he had been a Christian, and because he had, "like a dog, returned to his vomit." [2]

On the second day after his coronation, Richard, king of England, received the oaths of homage and fealty from the bishops, abbots, earls, and barons of England.

[2] *Prov.* 26:11; *II Pet.* 2:22.

Guibert de Nogent: *On His Own Life*

From The Autobiography of Guibert, Abbot of Nogent-sous-Coucy, *trans. C. C. Swinton Bland (New York: E. P. Dutton & Co., 1929), pp. 121–23. Reprinted by permission of Routledge & Kegan Paul Ltd. Footnotes supplied.*

In the monastery[1] there was a monk who was a Jew by birth. When the beginning of the pilgrimage to Jerusalem began to be bruited throughout the Latin world, he was thus rescued from his superstition.

[1] Of St. Germer-de-Fly, in the *pays* of Bray, on the border between Normandy and the county of Clermont (see III, 3), and about 80 miles west of Nogent-sous-Coucy. This richly endowed royal monastery was founded in the seventh century and restored (after Viking destruction) in the eleventh. Guibert received the monastic habit and most of his education there.

On a certain day when the people of Rouen who had joined in that expedition under the badge of the cross, began to complain to one another, "We, after traversing great distances towards the East, desire to attack the enemies of God there. But this is wasted labour, since before our eyes there are Jews, of all races the worst foes of God." Saying this and seizing their weapons, they herded them into a certain church, driving them in either by force or guile, and without discrimination of sex or age put them to the sword, but allowed those who accepted Christianity to escape slaughter. During this massacre a certain nobleman, seeing a little boy, rescued him and took him to his mother.

She was a lady of high worth, formerly the wife of the Count of Eu. Eu is the castle on which looks the abbey of St. Michel by the sea called Treport.[2] This excellent woman, therefore, receiving the child in a kindly way, asked him if he would like to come under Christian law. And when he did not refuse, thinking that otherwise he would certainly be put to death like his people, they hastily made the necessary preparations for baptism and came to the font. After the holy words had been said and he had received the sacrament, when they came to the part where a candle is lighted and the melted wax is dropped on the water, a drop of it was seen to fall separately all by itself, taking the shape of a tiny cross on the water so exactly in its minute substance that no human hand could have so fashioned it with so little. This the Countess told me herself, being a friend exceptionally well-known to me, always calling me son, and the priest too, both solemnly protesting by God that the tale was true. I should have treated the incident less seriously had I not seen without any doubt the remarkable progress of the boy. Now the name of the countess was Helisandis. Her son who rescued him and stood godfather to him, was named William;[3] therefore he gave his name to the boy who had thus come to him.

When he was a little older, he was transferred from the Hebrew language in which he had been first taught, to Latin with which he soon became familiar. And being afraid he might be recovered by his family (for they had long tried without success) and returned to

[2] The castle was begun by Rollo, first Duke of Normandy (911–33). The county was set up in 996 for Duke Richard I's illegitimate son Geoffrey. The abbey, named for the militant Archangel dear to the Normans, was founded in 1059.

[3] William II of Eu, who is said to have been punished by castration for the crime of rape, also in 1096. His brother Hugh was Bishop of Lisieux, and an uncle was William Busac, Count of Soissons.

his earlier condition, he entered the monastery of Fly. Being now given over to the monastic life, such love did he shew for Christianity, with such keenness of mind did he drink in all divine knowledge, with such calm did he endure all that was put upon him by way of discipline, that the victory over his wicked nature and his former turbulent spirit drew from all the greatest respect. Now he had chosen as his secret guardian, whilst a boy, a teacher of grammar, who being a very religious man, and considering that a knowledge of our law was necessary to the youth, took pains in teaching him which were well rewarded. For his naturally acute intellect was so sharpened daily that among the distinguished circle of men there, there was not one who was thought to shew greater distinction of understanding. Able as he was in thought, and therefore no envier or backbiter, his manners were always cheerful and of special purity. To increase the strength of his unbroken faith, I sent to him a little treatise, which about four years before I had written against the Count of Soissons, a Judaizer and a heretic,[4] with which, I hear, he was so delighted that he matched my work with a compilation on Reasons for the Faith. Therefore the cross at his baptism seems to have been formed not by chance, but by Providence, as a sign of the acceptance of our faith by a man of Jewish race, which was most unusual at that time.

12. HERETICS: SECESSION

In a way the most upsetting kind of religious non-conformity was heresy. The pagan Franks of the fifth century certainly had an easier time getting along with the Catholic populations of the Roman West than did Arian Christian peoples like the Visigoths or Lombards. All the Germanic invaders were converted to Catholic orthodoxy by the end of the seventh century, and from then until the Crusades began, Latin Christendom knew heresy only in minor and rather esoteric appearances. The twelfth century changed the situation for good. Most of the outbursts of internal heresy which marked that ebullient century arose from conflicts over discipline and the proper style of Christian life rather than from dogmatic controversy, and so they agitated society in general as well as elite circles used to theological speculation and disagreement. Attempts to restore religious conform-

---

[4] John, Count of Soissons and brother of its bishop, a strange and rather violent man, scion of a scandalous family, who seems to have enjoyed shocking public opinion with his libertine and skeptical opinions. The treatise was on the Incarnation; Guibert dedicated it to the archdeacon of Soissons cathedral.

ity became ever more intense, organized, and repressive. One result was the Inquisition, a papal court whose exclusive competence was heresy; it reinforced powerfully any current tendency to suspect the presence of subversive elements which, unless converted or eradicated, could shake society to its foundations. Perhaps even more divisive was the capacity of heresy (or the fear of it) to act as a catalyst for social and political ferment of entirely non-religious origin. It was largely through this function that the issue of heresy finally dissolved the fading unity of Latin Christendom during the Reformations of the sixteenth century.

Of the major groups of twelfth-century heretics, the Cathars were the most extreme and the Waldensians the most successful. The Cathars, or Albigensians, were adherents of a dogmatic and ethical system combining Christian teachings with elements of Zoroastrianism, Manichaeism, and other exotic traditions from the East. Between 1209 and 1245 several waves of Crusades were directed against the Cathars and those who supported or would tolerate them in the south of France, which had become the center of their activity. As might have been expected, issues of orthodoxy and of regional autonomy became hopelessly entangled. After the fourteenth century the Cathars disappear from historical record.

Less alien to the West were the Waldensians, who began as a radical evangelical protest against worldliness. Many strains of social and doctrinal dissatisfaction were combined in their tradition, which survives today in northern Italy. Waldes and his followers received cautious approval from Pope Alexander III at the Third Lateran Council in 1179, but were condemned by Pope Lucius III at the Council of Verona in 1184 (among their less theological errors was such deviant behavior as the absolute rejection of capital punishment and the wearing of a distinctive type of sandal).

Bernard Gui (1261?–1331) encountered one of the more conservative segments of the Waldensian movement after a century of crystallization. A native of central France, Gui entered the Dominican Order (founded for the express purpose of combating heresy) in 1280. For the next quarter-century he studied and taught logic and theology at several Dominican schools in southern France. After being prior of four Dominican houses in that still restive area, he was made Inquisitor of Toulouse in 1307, an office of prestige and real authority, which he exercised with comparative moderation for the next seventeen years. Selection (a) comes from the manual which he wrote for the use of others charged with that responsibility. Historical narrative was his chief avocation: in the midst of a busy and scrupulous career he found time to compose a universal history, studies on the history of his Order, and biographies of saints, kings of France, etc.

Caesarius of Heisterbach (1180?–1250?) became prior of the Cistercian house of that name, close to his native Cologne, in 1220. Enjoying considerable repute in the Rhineland as a theologian, canonist, and preacher, he composed the *Dialogue of Miracles* around 1235. The incidents presented in selection (b) are examples of his skill in sensing the mood of a crowd rather than of his delight in the preternatural—although it was the combination of those qualities that made his book a favorite for three centuries. Raynald of Dassel was Archbishop of Cologne from 1159 to 1167. Son of a Saxon count, former student at Paris, and Chancellor of the Empire for Frederick Barbarossa, he had scant patience with partisans of error, whether they were supporters of his enemy Pope Alexander III or Cathar heretics. Note that the solutions offered the beautiful heretic by the suddenly compassionate crowd were social arrangements; can we assume that her rejection of them was a choice any more doctrinal or individual in nature? Bertram, sixtieth bishop of Metz (1180–1212), was a contentious man, determined to remain secular lord of his city despite the rising political ambitions of the bourgeoisie. His debate with Waldensian missionaries around 1199 went so badly that he had to appeal to Pope Innocent III for help, which came in the form of three learned preachers who staged a public burning of six copies of the vernacular Bible then in circulation. Bertram's heterodox counterpart was *Barbe* ("uncle" in Provençal) Crespin, who found the political situation in Metz no small help to his mission.

Bernard Gui: *The Inquisitor's Manual*

From The Portable Medieval Reader, *ed. James Bruce Ross and Mary Martin McLaughlin (New York: The Viking Press, Inc., 1949), pp. 202–4, 207–9, 211–12. Copyright 1949 by The Viking Press, Inc. Reprinted by permission of The Viking Press, Inc. Footnotes supplied.*

Concerning the Waldensian Sect and First of All Concerning Their Origins and Beginnings. The sect and heresy of the Waldensians began in about the year 1170 A.D. Its founder was a certain citizen of Lyons, named Waldes or Waldo, from whom his followers were named. He was a rich man, who, after having given up all his wealth, determined to observe poverty and evangelical perfection, in imitation of the apostles. He caused to be translated into the French tongue, for his use, the Gospels, and some other books of the Bible, and also some authoritative sayings of Saints Augustine, Jerome, Ambrose, and Gregory, arranged under titles, which he and his followers called "sentences." They read these very often, and hardly understood them, since they were quite unlettered, but infatuated with their own interpretation, they usurped the office of the apostles, and presumed to preach the Gospel in the streets and public places. And the said Waldes or Waldo converted many people, both men and women, to a like presumption, and sent them out to preach as his disciples.

Since these people were ignorant and illiterate, they, both men and women, ran about through the towns, and entered the houses. Preaching in public places and also in the churches, they, especially the men, spread many errors around about them.

They were summoned, however, by the archbishop of Lyons, the Lord Jean aux Belles-Mains,[1] and were forbidden such great presumption, but they wished by no means to obey him, and cloaked their madness by saying that it was necessary to obey God rather than man. They said that God had commanded the apostles to preach the Gospel to all men, applying to themselves what was said to the apostles whose imitators and successors they boldly declared themselves to be, by a false profession of poverty and the feigned image of sanctity. They scorned the prelates and the clergy, because they abounded in riches and lived in pleasantness.

So then, by this arrogant usurpation of the office of preaching, they became masters of error. Admonished to cease, they disobeyed and were declared contumacious, and then were excommunicated and expelled from that city and their country. Finally in a certain council which was held at Rome before the Lateran council,[2] since they were obstinate, they were judged schismatic, and then condemned as heretics. Thus, multiplied upon the earth, they dispersed themselves through that province, and through the neighbouring regions, and into Lombardy. Separated and cut off from the Church, mingling with other heretics and imbibing their errors, they mixed the errors and heresies of earlier heretics with their own inventions. . . .

Concerning the Manner of Life of the Waldensians. Something

---

[1] Archbishop 1182–93. His attitude was very different from that of his predecessor.

[2] The Fourth Lateran Council, 1215. Nevertheless, Pope Innocent III (1198–1216) made many efforts to reconcile the Waldensians, and took several splinter groups of that movement under his personal protection.

should be said concerning the practices and way of life of the Waldensian heretics, in order that they may be known and recognized.

In the first place, then, it should be known that the Waldensians have and establish for themselves one superior whom they call their "majoral" and whom all must obey, just as all Catholics obey the lord pope.

Also, the Waldensians eat and drink at common meals. Also those who can and will, fast on Mondays and Wednesdays; those who fast, however, eat meat. Also, they fast on Fridays, and during Lent, and then they abstain from meat in order not to give scandal to others, since they say that to eat meat on any day whatsoever is not a sin, because Christ did not prohibit the eating of meat, nor order anyone to abstain from it.

Also, after they have been received into this society, which they call a "fraternity," and have promised obedience to their superior, and that they will observe evangelical poverty, from that time they should observe chastity and should not own property, but should sell all that they possess and give the price to the common fund, and live on alms which are given to them by their "believers" and those who sympathize with them. And the superior distributes these among them, and gives to each one according to his needs.

Also, the Waldensians recommend continence to their believers. They concede, however, that burning passion ought to be satisfied, in whatever shameful way, interpreting the words of the Apostle [Paul]: "It is better to marry than to burn," to mean that it is better to appease desire by any shameful act than to be tempted inwardly in the heart. This doctrine they keep very secret, however, in order not to seem vile to their "believers."

Also, they have collections made by their "believers" and friends, and what is given and received they take to their superior.

Also, each year they hold or celebrate one or two general chapters in some important town, as secretly as possible, assembling, as if they were merchants, in a house hired long before by one or more of the "believers." And in those chapters the superior of all orders and disposes matters concerning the priests and deacons and concerning those sent to different parts and regions to their "believers" and friends to hear confessions and to collect alms. He also receives the account of receipts and expenses.

Also, they do not work with their hands after they have been made "perfect," nor do they do any work for profit, except perchance in case it is necessary to dissimulate, so that they may not be recognized and apprehended.

Also, they commonly call themselves brothers, and they say that they are the poor of Christ or the poor of Lyons.

Also, they hypocritically insinuate themselves into the society of the religious and of the clergy, so that they may conceal themselves, and they bestow gifts or presents upon them and pay them reverence and services so that they may obtain a freer opportunity for themselves and theirs to hide, to live, and to injure souls.

Also, they frequent the churches and sermons, and in all externals conduct themselves with religion and compunction, and strive to use unctuous and discreet language. . . .

On the Method of Teaching of the Waldensians. One can distinguish two categories in this sect; there are the "perfect," and these are properly called Waldensians. These, previously instructed, are received into their order according to a special rite, so that they may know how to teach others. These "perfect" claim that they possess nothing of their own, neither houses nor possessions nor furnishings. Moreover, if they had had wives before, they give them up when they are received. They say that they are the successors of the apostles, and are the masters and confessors of the others. They travel through the country, visiting and confirming their disciples in error. Their disciples and "believers" supply them with necessities. Wherever the "perfect" go, the "believers" spread the news of their arrival, and many come to the house, where they are admitted to see and hear them. All sorts of good things to eat and drink are brought to them, and their preaching is heard in assemblies which gather chiefly at night, when others are sleeping or resting.

The "perfect," moreover, do not immediately in the beginning reveal the secrets of their error. First they say what the disciples of Christ should be like, according to the words of the Gospel and of the apostles. Only those, they say, should be the successors of the apostles who imitate and hold to the example of their life. On this basis, they argue and conclude that the pope, the bishops and prelates, and clergy, who possess the riches of this world and do not imitate the sanctity of the apostles, are not true pastors and guides of the Church of God, but ravening and devouring wolves, to whom Christ did not deign to entrust His spouse the Church, and so they should not be obeyed. They also say that an impure person cannot purify another, nor can one who is bound loose another, nor can an accused person influence a judge, already angered against him, in favour of another accused person. One who is on the road to perdition cannot lead another to heaven. In this way, they slander the clergy and the prelates, in order to render them odious, so that they will not be believed or obeyed.

The Waldensians, then, commonly say and teach to their "believers" certain things which seem good and moral, concerning the virtues which should be practised, the good works which should be done, and the vices to be avoided and fled from. Thus they are more readily listened to in other matters, and they ensnare their hearers. For they say that one should not lie, since everyone who lies slays his soul, according to the Scripture; also that one should not do to another, what he would not want done to him. One should obey the commandments of God. One should not swear in any case because God has forbidden all taking of oaths, saying in the Gospel: "Swear not at all; neither by heaven; for it is God's throne: Nor by the earth for it is the footstool of His feet, nor by any other creature, because a man cannot make one hair white or black, but let your speaking be yea, yea, and nay, nay; for whatever is more than these comes of evil." These words make a great impression on their "believers" and they receive no further interpretation of them. . . .

Caesarius of Heisterbach: *The Dialogue of Miracles, Book V*

From Caesarius of Heisterbach, The Dialogue of Miracles, *trans. H. von E. Scott and C. C. Swinton Bland (London: George Routledge & Sons, Ltd., 1929), I, 341–43. Reprinted by permission of Routledge & Kegan Paul Ltd.*

Chapter 19. About the same time several heretics were arrested at Cologne under archbishop Raynald, and after being examined and convicted by learned men, were condemned by the secular tribunal. Sentence was passed, and they were about to be led out to the stake, when one of them, by name Arnold, whom the rest acknowledged as their leader, begged, as was said by those present, that he might be given some bread and a bowl of water. Some thought that this request should be granted, but others who were wiser dissuaded them, saying that with these some diabolical charm might be wrought which would be a stumbling-block and perhaps ruin for the weak.

Novice. I cannot think what he can have wished to do with bread and water.

Monk. From the words of another heretic, who was arrested and burnt three years ago by the king of Spain, I think that he wished to use them for a sacrilegious communion, which would be a viaticum for his disciples to eternal damnation. For a Spanish abbot of our Order, who had been one of the bishops and prelates of the church who had condemned the errors of this heretic, told us, when passing our way, that part of his teaching was, that any rustic could make the Body of Christ at his own table out of the bread that he was eating; this accursed heretic was a blacksmith.

Novice. How then did it fare with the heretics of Cologne?

Monk. They were taken outside the town, and were together put into the fire near the Jewish cemetery. After the flames had taken strong hold of them, in the sight and hearing of a great crowd, Arnold placed his hand on the heads of his dying disciples, and exhorted them: "Stand fast in your faith, for this day you shall be with Laurence," and yet they were very far from the faith of Laurence. There was a maiden among them, beautiful though a heretic, and she was drawn from the fire by the compassion of some who promised that they would provide her with a husband, or if it seemed better, would place her in a nunnery. She consented to this in words, but when the heretics were now dead, she said to those who had charge of her: "Tell me, where does that seducer lie?" and when they pointed out to her where Master Arnold lay, she slipped from their hands, veiled her face with her robe, and threw herself upon the body of the dead man, and with him went down to burn for ever in hell.

Chapter 20. A few years ago, under the learned bishop Bertram, the Waldensian heresy sprang up in the city of Metz in the following way. On a certain feast the bishop was preaching to the people in the cathedral, when he saw two of the devil's servants standing in the crowd and cried: "I see the devil's messengers among you. See, there are the men," pointing to them with his finger, "who in my presence were condemned at Montpellier and cast out of the city for their heresies." They replied boldly to the bishop, and they had in their company a scholar, who barked at him like a dog attacking him with every kind of insult. When they left the church, they gathered a crowd round them, and preached their errors to them. Some of the clerks present said to them: "Sirs, does not the Apostle say, *How shall they preach, except they be sent* (Rom. x. 15)? We should like to know who sent you hither to preach," and they replied: "The Holy Spirit." Now the bishop was unable to use force against them, owing to certain powerful citizens, who befriended them in hatred of the bishop, because he had expelled from the church a certain dead usurer, their relative. In truth they had been sent out by the spirit of error, and by their preaching the Waldensian heresy was planted in that city, and to this day is not wholly extinguished.

Novice. Alas! that there should be to-day so many heresies in the church.
Monk. They are the fruit of the fury and malice of the devil.

The Universal Catastrophe

13. THE BLACK DEATH, 1347–50

Natural forces dealt the social order of medieval Latin Christendom a blow from which it never recovered. Free from demographic disasters since the middle of the eighth century, Europe was ravaged from one end to the other by bubonic and related forms of plague in the years 1347–50. The plague subsequently settled in Europe (among the fleas of its rats, to be exact), recurring sporadically and locally in epidemic form until 1720. A period of climatic irregularity seems to have occurred simultaneously, bringing with it agricultural disaster and resultant widespread and recurrent famine. The combination was too much for a civilization whose ambitious superstructure rested on an economy that had not developed far enough beyond the subsistence level. Although the greatest loss was in morale, the loss of manpower is easier to document. Florence, probably a city of 100,000 before the plague, had half that number of inhabitants after it, and did not regain its earlier population density until the second half of the eighteenth century. Rouen extended the circuit of its walls three times between 1150 and 1350, but did not again fill all the area within the widest circuit until the middle of the eighteenth century. According to the best estimates, the kingdom of England contained 3,700,000 people before the Black Death, and only 2,200,000 thirty years afterwards; at the beginning of the reign of Queen Elizabeth I, the English population was still 500,000 short of the pre-plague total.

Henry Knighton was a canon of St. Mary's Abbey in Leicester. His modest contribution to posterity is a chronicle of English history from the middle of the tenth century to 1366 (presumably the date of his death). The fourth and final book, covering the years since 1337, is probably original work, and certainly shows a good eye for local detail as well as a sense of the "whole world's" helplessness before overwhelming calamity.

Henry Knighton: *Compilation of Events in England, Book IV*

From The Portable Medieval Reader, *ed. James Bruce Ross and Mary Martin McLaughlin (New York: The Viking Press, Inc., 1949), pp. 216–20, 221–22. Copyright 1949 by The Viking Press, Inc. Reprinted by permission of The Viking Press, Inc. Footnotes supplied.*

In this year [1348] and in the following one there was a general mortality of men throughout the whole world. It first began in India, then in Tharsis [Taurus?], then it came to the Saracens, and finally to the Christians and Jews, so that in the space of one year, from Easter to Easter, as the rumour spread in the Roman curia, there had died, as if by sudden death, in those remote regions eight thousand legions, besides the Christians. The king of Tharsis, seeing such a sudden and unheard-of slaughter of his people, began a journey to Avignon with a great multitude of his nobles, to propose to the pope that he would become a Christian and be baptized by him, thinking that he might thus mitigate the vengeance of God upon his people because of their wicked unbelief. Then, when he had journeyed for twenty days, he heard that the pestilence had struck among the Christians, just as among other peoples. So turning in his tracks, he travelled no farther but hastened to return home. The Christians, pursuing these people from behind, slew about seven thousand of them.

There died in Avignon in one day one thousand three hundred and twelve persons, according to a count made for the pope, and, another day, four hundred persons and more. Three hundred and fifty-eight of the Friars Preachers[1] in the region of Provence died during Lent. At Montpellier, there remained out of a hundred and forty friars only seven. There were left at Magdalena only seven friars out of a hundred and sixty, and yet enough. At Marseilles, of a hundred and fifty Friars Minor,[2] there remained only one who could tell the others; that was well, indeed. Of the Carmelites, more than a hundred and sixty-six had died at Avignon before the citizens found out what had happened. For they believed that one had killed another. There was not one of the English Hermits left in Avignon. . . .

At this same time the pestilence became prevalent in England, beginning in the autumn in certain places. It spread throughout the

[1] Dominicans.
[2] Franciscans.

land, ending in the same season of the following year. At the same time many cities in Corinth and Achaia were overturned, and the earth swallowed them. Castles and fortresses were broken, laid low, and swallowed up. Mountains in Cyprus were levelled into one, so that the flow of the rivers was impeded, and many cities were submerged and villages destroyed. Similarly, when a certain friar was preaching at Naples, the whole city was destroyed by an earthquake. Suddenly, the earth was opened up, as if a stone had been thrown into water, and everyone died along with the preaching friar, except for one friar who, fleeing, escaped into a garden outside the city. All of these things were done by an earthquake. . . .

Then that most grievous pestilence penetrated the coastal regions [of England] by way of Southampton, and came to Bristol, and people died as if the whole strength of the city were seized by sudden death. For there were few who lay in their beds more than three days or two and a half days; then that savage death snatched them about the second day. In Leicester, in the little parish of St. Leonard, more than three hundred and eighty died; in the parish of the Holy Cross, more than four hundred, and in the parish of St. Margaret in Leicester, more than seven hundred. And so in each parish, they died in great numbers. Then the bishop of Lincoln sent through the whole diocese, and gave the general power to each and every priest, both regular and secular, to hear confessions and to absolve, by the full and entire power of the bishop, except only in the case of debt. And they might absolve in that case if satisfaction could be made by the person while he lived, or from his property after his death. Likewise, the pope granted full remission of all sins, to be absolved completely, to anyone who was in danger of death, and he granted this power to last until the following Easter. And everyone was allowed to choose his confessor as he pleased.

During this same year, there was a great mortality of sheep everywhere in the kingdom; in one place and in one pasture, more than five thousand sheep died and became so putrefied that neither beast nor bird wanted to touch them. And the price of everything was cheap, because of the fear of death; there were very few who took any care for their wealth, or for anything else. For a man could buy a horse for half a mark, which before was worth forty shillings, a large fat ox for four shillings, a cow for twelve pence, a heifer for sixpence, a large fat sheep for four pence, a sheep for threepence, a lamb for two pence, a fat pig for five pence, a stone of wool for nine pence. And the sheep and cattle wandered about through the fields and among the crops, and there was no one to go after them or to collect them. They perished in countless numbers everywhere, in secluded ditches and hedges, for lack of watching, since there was such a lack of serfs and servants, that no one knew what he should do. For there is no memory of a mortality so severe and so savage from the time of Vortigern, king of the Britons, in whose time, as Bede[3] says, the living did not suffice to bury the dead. In the following autumn, one could not hire a reaper at a lower wage than eight pence with food, or a mower at less than twelve pence with food. Because of this, much grain rotted in the fields for lack of harvesting, but in the year of the plague, as was said above, among other things there was so great an abundance of all kinds of grain that no one seemed to have concerned himself about it.

The Scots, hearing of the cruel pestilence in England, suspected that this had come upon the English by the avenging hand of God, and when they wished to swear an oath, they swore this one, as the vulgar rumour reached the ears of the English, "be the foul deth of Engelond." And so the Scots, believing that the horrible vengeance of God had fallen on the English, came together in the forest of Selkirk to plan an invasion of the whole kingdom of England. But savage mortality supervened, and the sudden and frightful cruelty of death struck the Scots. In a short time, about five thousand died; the rest, indeed, both sick and well, prepared to return home, but the English, pursuing them, caught up with them, and slew a great many of them.

Master Thomas Bradwardine was consecrated archbishop of Canterbury by the pope, and when he returned to England, came to London. In less than two days he was dead. He was famous above all other clerks in Christendom, in theology especially, but also in other liberal studies. At this same time there was so great a lack of priests everywhere that many widowed churches had no divine services, no masses, matins, vespers, sacraments, and sacramentals. One could hardly hire a chaplain to minister to any church for less than ten pounds or ten marks, and whereas, before the pestilence, when there were plenty of priests, one could hire a chaplain for five or four marks or for two marks, with board, there was scarcely anyone at this time who wanted to accept a position for twenty pounds or twenty marks. But within a short time a very great multitude whose wives had died of the plague rushed into holy orders. Of these many were

[3] For Bede, see I, 5. Vortigern ruled sometime in the latter part of the fifth century.

illiterate and, it seemed, simply laymen who knew nothing except how to read to some extent. The hides of cattle went up from a low price to twelve pence, and for shoes the price went to ten, twelve, fourteen pence; for a pair of leggings, to three and four shillings.

Meanwhile, the king[4] ordered that in every county of the kingdom, reapers and other labourers should not receive more than they were accustomed to receive, under the penalty provided in the statute, and he renewed the statute from this time. The labourers, however, were so arrogant and hostile that they did not heed the king's command, but if anyone wished to hire them, he had to pay them what they wanted, and either lose his fruits and crops or satisfy the arrogant and greedy desire of the labourers as they wished. . . .

After the aforesaid pestilence, many buildings, both large and small, in all cities, towns, and villages had collapsed, and had completely fallen to the ground in the absence of inhabitants. Likewise, many small villages and hamlets were completely deserted; there was not one house left in them, but all those who had lived in them were dead. It is likely that many such hamlets will never again be inhabited. In the following summer [1350], there was so great a lack of servants to do anything that, as one believed, there had hardly been so great a dearth in past times. For all the beasts and cattle that a man possessed wandered about without a shepherd, and everything a man had was without a caretaker. And so all necessities became so dear that anything that in the past had been worth a penny was now worth four or five pence. Moreover, both the magnates of the kingdom and the other lesser lords who had tenants, remitted something from the rents, lest the tenants should leave, because of the lack of servants and the dearth of things. Some remitted half the rent, some more and others less, some remitted it for two years, some for three, and others for one year, according as they were able to come to an agreement with their tenants. Similarly, those who received day-work from their tenants throughout the year, as is usual from serfs, had to release them and to remit such services. They either had to excuse them entirely or had to fix them in a laxer manner at a small rent, lest very great and irreparable damage be done to the buildings, and the land everywhere remain completely uncultivated. And all foodstuffs and all necessities became exceedingly dear. . . .

[4] Edward III (1327–77). See III, 8.

THE CLERGY   II

The clergy got its name from the Greek word *kleros*, meaning "lot" or "portion": it was that group within the community whose lot was the Lord's, whose members were to live from the proceeds of or the property attached to the altars which they served. This notion derives from the provision made for the priesthood of ancient Israel and has parallels in many societies. One of the distinctive characteristics of the medieval Latin clergy was the great influence exercised upon it by monasticism, a tradition of organized asceticism which was originally a quite separate institution. From the fifth century onwards, most pious Europeans considered the monastery the ideal model of Christian community. One reform after another tried to plan the life of the whole Church according to the monastic pattern; at the very least, there was a strong tendency to feel that a man trained in the monastery would make a better bishop than one whose whole experience had been "in the world." The paradoxical result was that monastic communities, designed to help their members withdraw from the world as completely as possible, were drawn into a close relationship with the rest of Christian society.

Development of Distinctive Behavior

1. THE MONASTIC RULE

Several varieties of monasticism flourished in western Europe in the early centuries, but by 800 most of the others had given way to the Benedictine type. The *Rule of St. Benedict*, composed in central Italy around 535, prescribes an independent, self-sufficient, remote community—a sort of male microcosm—dedicated to a regular program of prayer, manual work, and study (or at least reading). The *Rule*'s author had a profound distrust of property and of social or ecclesiastical distinctions: he envisaged a membership predominantly of laymen, whose only ranks, would correspond exactly to function. By 800, most Benedictine monks were priests and their monasteries were well endowed and deeply involved with secular politics, but the pristine ideal was still there for all who could read to reflect upon.

St. Benedict's Rule for Monasteries

From St. Benedict's Rule for Monasteries, *trans. Leonard J. Doyle (College-ville, Minn.: The Liturgical Press, 1948), pp. 79–84. Copyrighted by The Order of St. Benedict, Inc., Collegeville, Minnesota. Reprinted by permission of the publisher.*

Chapter 58. When anyone is newly come for the reformation of his life, let him not be granted an easy entrance; but, as the Apostle says, "Test the spirits to see whether they are from God." If the new-comer, therefore, perseveres in his knocking, and if it is seen after four or five days that he bears patiently the harsh treatment offered him and the difficulty of admission, and that he persists in his petition, then let entrance be granted him, and let him stay in the guest house for a few days.

After that let him live in the novitiate, where the novices study, eat and sleep. A senior shall be assigned to them who is skilled in winning souls, to watch over them with the utmost care. Let him examine whether the novice is truly seeking God, and whether he is zealous for the Work of God, for obedience and for humiliations. Let the novice be told all the hard and rugged ways by which the journey to God is made.

If he promises stability and perseverance, then at the end of two months let this Rule be read through to him, and let him be addressed thus: "Here is the law under which you wish to fight. If you can observe it, enter; if you cannot, you are free to depart." If he still stands firm, let him be taken to the above-mentioned novitiate and again tested in all patience. And after the lapse of six months let the Rule be read to him, that he may know on what he is entering. And if he still remains firm, after four months let the same Rule be read to him again.

Then, having deliberated with himself, if he promises to keep it in its entirety and to observe everything that is commanded him, let him be received into the community. But let him understand that, accord-ing to the law of the Rule, from that day forward he may not leave the monastery nor withdraw his neck from under the yoke of the

Rule which he was free to refuse or to accept during that prolonged deliberation.

He who is to be received shall make a promise before all in the oratory of his stability and of the reformation of his life and of obedience. This promise he shall make before God and His Saints, so that if he should ever act otherwise, he may know that he will be condemned by Him whom he mocks. Of this promise of his let him draw up a petition in the name of the Saints whose relics are there and of the Abbot who is present. Let him write this petition with his own hand; or if he is illiterate, let another write it at his request, and let the novice put his mark to it. Then let him place it with his own hand upon the altar; and when he has placed it there, let the novice at once intone this verse: "Receive me, O Lord, according to Your word, and I shall live: and let me not be confounded in my hope." Let the whole community answer this verse three times and add the "Glory be to the Father." Then let the novice brother prostrate himself at each one's feet, that they may pray for him. And from that day forward let him be counted as one of the community.

If he has any property, let him either give it beforehand to the poor or by solemn donation bestow it on the monastery, reserving nothing at all for himself, as indeed he knows that from that day forward he will no longer have power even over his own body. At once, therefore, in the oratory, let him be divested of his own clothes which he is wearing and dressed in the clothes of the monastery. But let the clothes of which he was divested be put aside in the wardrobe and kept there. Then if he should ever listen to the persuasions of the devil and decide to leave the monastery (which God forbid), he may be divested of the monastic clothes and cast out. His petition, however, which the Abbot has taken from the altar, shall not be returned to him, but shall be kept in the monastery.

Chapter 59. If anyone of the nobility offers his son to God in the monastery and the boy is very young, let his parents draw up the petition which we mentioned above; and at the oblation let them wrap the petition and the boy's hand in the altar cloth and so offer him.

As regards their property, they shall promise in the same petition under oath that they will never of themselves, or through an intermediary, or in any way whatever, give him anything or provide him with the opportunity of owning anything. Or else, if they are unwilling to do this, and if they want to offer something as an alms to the monastery for their advantage, let them make a donation of the property they wish to give to the monastery, reserving the income to themselves if they wish. And in this way let everything be barred, so that the boy may have no expectations whereby (which God forbid) he might be deceived and ruined, as we have learned by experience.

Let those who are less well-to-do make a similar offering. But those who have nothing at all shall simply draw up the petition and offer their son before witnesses at the oblation.

Chapter 60. If anyone of the priestly order should ask to be received into the monastery, permission shall not be granted him too readily. But if he is quite persistent in his resquest, let him know that he will have to observe the whole discipline of the Rule and that nothing will be relaxed in his favor, that it may be as it is written: "Friend, for what have you come?"

It shall be granted him, however, to stand next after the Abbot and to give blessings and to celebrate Mass, but only by order of the Abbot. Without such order let him not presume to do anything, knowing that he is subject to the discipline of the Rule; but rather let him give an example of humility to all.

If there happens to be question of an appointment or of some business in the monastery, let him expect the rank due him according to the date of his entrance into the monastery, and not the place granted him out of reverence for the priesthood.

If any clerics, moved by the same desire, should wish to join the monastery, let them be placed in a middle rank. But they too are to be admitted only if they promise observance of the Rule and their own stability.

Chapter 61. If a pilgrim monk coming from a distant region wants to live as a guest of the monastery, let him be received for as long a time as he desires, provided he is content with the customs of the place as he finds them and does not disturb the monastery by superfluous demands, but is simply content with what he finds. If, however, he censures or points out anything reasonably and with the humility of charity, let the Abbot consider prudently whether perhaps it was for that very purpose that the Lord sent him.

If afterwards he should want to bind himself to stability, his wish should not be denied him, especially since there has been opportunity during his stay as a guest to discover his character.

*   *   *

But if as a guest he was found exacting or prone to vice, not only should he be denied membership in the community, but he should even be politely requested to leave, lest others be corrupted by his evil life.

If, however, he has not proved to be the kind who deserves to be put out, he should not only on his own application be received as a member of the community, but he should even be persuaded to stay, that the others may be instructed by his example, and because in every place it is the same Lord who is served, the same King for whom the battle is fought.

Moreover, if the Abbot perceives that he is a worthy man, he may put him in a somewhat higher rank. And not only with regard to a monk but also with regard to those in priestly or clerical orders previously mentioned, the Abbot may establish them in a higher rank than would be theirs by date of entrance if he perceives that their life is deserving.

Let the Abbot take care, however, never to receive a monk from another known monastery as a member of his community without the consent of his Abbot or a letter of recommendation; for it is written, "Do not to another what you would not want done to yourself."

2. RECRUITMENT OF PRELATES

Despite the egalitarian message potentially present in Christianity, the leadership of the medieval Church tended to be recruited from the upper classes of lay society. More than mere rank was usually required, however. Aredius, now known as St. Yrieix, was the founder and first abbot of a type of urban monastic community widespread in the west before the Benedictine ascendancy. Tours was the seat of the proudest archdiocese of western Gaul. Its prestige derived both from the city's secular importance and from the spiritual legacy of St. Martin, its third bishop (372–97), who had been an exceptionally successful converter of rustic pagans in his life, and a mighty worker of miracles both before and after his death. Georgius Florentius, called Gregory after he entered the clergy, was the nineteenth bishop of Tours (573–94). His family, which considered Auvergne its home, belonged to the top level of Gallo-Roman aristocracy. The extent of its identification with the top of the ecclesiastical hierarchy may be deduced from Gregory's boast that thirteen of his predecessors at Tours were his relatives, and from his kinship to bishops Gregory and Tetricus of Langres (his great-grandfather and father), Nicetius of Lyons (his great-uncle), and Gall of Clermont (his uncle). Ill-educated but intensely concerned to preserve the record of his times, both good and bad, Gregory permits the readers of his historical and biographical works to sense, with unusual immediacy, the disorder, the vigor, and the ambitions of his age.

Gregory of Tours: *History of the Franks, Book X,* The Bishops of Tours, 460–473

From *Gregory of Tours,* History of the Franks, *trans. O. M. Dalton (Oxford: Oxford University Press, 1927), II, 465–68, 471, 473–75. Reprinted by permission of the Clarendon Press, Oxford. Footnotes supplied.*

29. I must now speak of the miracles and death of the abbot Aredius, who in this year[1] quitted this earth and at the summons of the Lord passed to heaven. He was a native of Limoges and of free birth, being sprung from parents in no mean station. He was sent in his youth to King Theudebert, and became one of the noble youths attached to the royal household. At that time Bishop Nicetius was at Trèves, a man of eminent holiness who enjoyed great fame among the people alike for the admirable eloquence of his preaching, and for his good works and his miracles. Noticing the boy in the palace, and discovering in his face I know not what quality that seemed divine, he bade him follow him. So Aredius left the royal palace and followed after him. And going into the bishop's cell, they talked together of the things relating to God; the youth then besought the holy bishop to correct, to teach, to influence him, and to instruct him in the knowledge of the Holy Scriptures. Thereafter he dwelled with the bishop, consumed with ardent zeal for this study, and had received the tonsure. One day, while the clergy were chanting psalms in the church, a dove descended from the ceiling, and lightly fluttering round him, perched upon his head, for a sign, as I hold, that already he was filled with the grace of the Holy Spirit. He sought to drive the bird away, not without confusion, but after circling round a little while, it settled once more upon his head, or on his shoulder; and not only in the church, but even when he went into the bishop's cell, it kept him company continually. This happened for several days, to the wonder of the bishop. Afterwards this man of God, filled, as I have said, with the Divine Spirit, returned to his own country, his father and brother being dead, to console his mother Pelagia,[2] who had none of her kindred to look to but this son alone. His time was

[1] *I.e.,* 591.
[2] Died 572. Her husband's name was Jocundus.

now all devoted to fastings and prayers, and he besought her to be responsible for all of the care of his house, whether in respect of the discipline of the servants, of the cultivation of the fields, or the tilling of the vineyards,[3] that there might be no interruption of his prayers. He claimed but one thing for himself, the privilege of superintending the erection of churches. What need to say more? He built churches of God in honour of the saints, sought and obtained their relics, made tonsured monks from those of his own household, and founded a monastery in which not only the Rule of Cassian was observed, but also the Rules of Basil[4] and other abbots who instituted the monastic life. His holy mother provided for every monk his food and raiment. But this heavy toil was not enough to hinder her from singing the praises of God; even when she was engaged on any work, she was ever constant in offering prayer to the Lord, as it were a fragrance of incense finding favour in His sight. In the meantime the sick began streaming from all sides to the holy Aredius, and he restored them to health by laying on of hands with the sign of the Cross. Were I to attempt to make several mention of them, I should never be able to go through their number or record their names; this one thing I know, that whoever went to him sick returned from him whole. I will only set forth some few facts concerning his greater miracles.

He was once making a journey with his mother on his way to the church of the blessed Julian the martyr.[5] They came with evening to a certain place which was very dry and sterile for want of running water. His mother then said to him: "My son, we have no water; how therefore can we abide here this night?" But he prostrated himself in prayer, and for a long while poured forth supplication to the Lord; then, rising up, he fixed a stick which he carried in the ground, and after making it revolve two or three times, he drew it out with great content; and soon so great a flow of water followed that they not only first drank of it themselves, but afterwards were able to water their beasts. A very short time ago he was on a journey, when a rain-cloud rapidly came up. As soon as he saw it he bowed his head a little over the horse which he rode, and stretched forth his hand towards the Lord. And when his prayer was over, lo! the cloud was divided into two parts, and all round them rain came down in torrents; but upon

---

[3] Aredius' will, which survives today, disposes of considerable wealth.

[4] John Cassian (early fifth century), a monk in the south of France; St. Basil (330?–79), author of the chief Greek monastic rule. Both are cited as sources of the Benedictine Rule.

[5] See I, 1.

themselves there fell hardly a drop. A citizen of Tours, Wistrimund, surnamed Tatto, suffered from violent toothache, which caused a swelling of the jaws. He complained of it to the holy man, who laid his hand upon the place, whereupon forthwith the pain was driven away and never afterwards revived to cause further trouble. It was the patient himself who told me the story. As for the miracles which the Lord wrought by his hands through the power of the blessed martyr Julian, and the blessed confessor Martin, I have recorded most of them in my books of Miracles, as he himself hath related them.

After these and many other miracles performed by Christ's aid, he came to Tours when the feast of the blessed Martin was over, and after a short sojourn told us that he should not be kept much longer in this world, and that his dissolution was surely near. He bade me farewell and departed, giving thanks to God that it had been granted him to kiss the tomb of the holy bishop before he passed away. Upon his return to his cell, he made his will, set all his affairs in order, and made the holy Martin and the holy Hilary his heirs; he then began to ail and was attacked by dysentery. On the sixth day of his sickness, a woman, often vexed by an unclean spirit, from which the holy man had not been able to deliver her, bound her hands behind her back, and began crying aloud, and saying: "Run, O citizens! leap for joy, O people! go forth to meet the martyrs and confessors who are now come together for the passing of the blessed Aredius. Lo, here is Julian come from Brioude, Privatus from Mende; here are Martin from Tours, and Martial from Aredius's own city. Here, too, are Saturninus from Toulouse, Denis from Paris, and many another now in heaven to whom ye pray as confessors and martyrs of God." When she thus cried aloud at nightfall, her master put her in bonds; but it was impossible to hold her; she burst the bonds and rushed to the monastery, uttering these same cries. Soon afterwards the holy man gave up the ghost, not without true testimony that he had been taken up of angels. During his funeral, when the grave closed upon him, he delivered the woman from the evil of the infesting demon, together with another woman vexed by a yet more evil spirit. And I believe it to have been by God's will that he should not heal these women in his lifetime, in order that his obsequies might be glorified by this miracle. And after they had been celebrated, a certain dumb woman with a wide gaping mouth came to his tomb and kissed it; after which she received the gift of speech.

*   *   *

31. The sixth bishop consecrated was Perpetuus,[6] likewise said to be descended from a senatorial family, and to have been a relative of his predecessor. He was very rich, and owned property in many cities. He pulled down the earlier basilica which Bishop Brice had erected over the holy Martin, and built another of greater size and wondrous workmanship, to the apse of which he translated the blessed remains of the venerable saint. It was he who instituted the fasts and vigils to be observed during the course of the year; of these we to-day preserve a written list, the order being as follows: . . .

Perpetuus built the church of Saint Peter, in which he placed the ceiling of the earlier church of the holy Martin, which is still preserved in our own day; he also erected the church of Saint Laurence at Montlouis. He built churches in the villages of Esvres, Mougon, Barrou, Balesmes, and Vernou. When he made his will he bequeathed all his possessions in divers cities to these churches, assigning no small part of his property to Tours. He occupied the see for thirty years, and was buried in the church of the holy Martin.

The seventh bishop consecrated was Volusianus,[7] of a senatorial family, a holy man, of great wealth, and related to his predecessor Bishop Perpetuus. In his time Clovis was already reigning over some of the cities of Gaul. On account of this the bishop was held in suspicion by the Goths, who feared that he wished to subject them to Frankish rule; they therefore condemned him to banishment in Toulouse, where he died. In his time were built the village of Manthelan and the church of Saint John at Marmoutier. He occupied the see seven years and two months.

The eighth bishop consecrated was Verus. He also was held in suspicion by the Goths for his zeal in the aforesaid cause, and sent into exile, in which he ended his days. His property he bequeathed to the churches and to persons of good desert. He held the see eleven years and eight days.

The ninth was Licinius, a citizen of Angers, who, for the love of God, went into the East, and visited the Holy Places. Returning thence he founded a monastery upon a property of his own within the territory of Angers. Afterwards he fulfilled the duties of abbot in the monastery in which the holy abbot Venantius was buried, and finally was elected bishop. In his time King Clovis returned as victor to Tours after defeating the Goths. He occupied the see twelve years, two months,

---

[6] Died 490. Perpetuus was a friend of Apollinaris Sidonius (see I, 1), and a relative of Gregory.

[7] Bishop 491–98.

and twenty-five days, and was buried in the church of the holy Martin.

In the tenth place Theodore and Proculus were appointed to the see by command of the blessed queen Clotild,[8] whom they had followed from Burgundy. There they were already bishops, but had been expelled from their cities by their enemies. They were both very old men, and together they governed the church of Tours for two years, and were buried in the church of the holy Martin.

The eleventh bishop was Dinifius, who also came from Burgundy. He reached the episcopate through the choice of the aforesaid queen, who endowed him with certain property from the royal domain, granting him the power to dispose of it as he would. And he took the better way, leaving the most part to his church; some portion also he gave to the deserving. He held the see ten months, and was buried in the church of the holy Martin.

The twelfth was Ommatius,[9] of senatorial family, a citizen of Clermont, who was exceeding rich in lands. Having made his will, he distributed his wealth among the churches of the towns in which his possessions lay. He erected within the walls of Tours, and adjoining them, a church consecrated to the relics of the holy Gervasius and Protasius. He began to build the church of Saint Mary within the city walls, which he left unfinished. Having occupied the see four years and five months, he died, and was buried in the church of the holy Martin.

The thirteenth, Leo, was abbot of the church of the holy Martin before he was consecrated bishop. He was a worker in wood, of which he made turrets covered with gold; some of these are still preserved among us. He was also accomplished in other kinds of work. He held the see for six months, and was buried in the church of the holy Martin.

The fourteenth bishop to be consecrated was Francilio, a member of a senatorial family, and citizen of Poiters, who had a wife named Clara, but no sons. Both he and his wife were very rich in lands, which for the most part they presented to the church of the holy Martin, though some they left to their kinsfolk. Francilio had occupied the see two years and six months when he died,[10] and was buried in the basilica of the holy Martin.

---

[8] A Burgundian princess, queen of Clovis (481–511). A Catholic, she and Bishop Remigius of Reims worked on the pagan Clovis until he agreed to be baptized a Catholic.

[9] King Chlodomer (511–24) "commanded" his consecration.

[10] Gregory reports elsewhere the suspicion that he was poisoned.

The fifteenth was Injuriosus,[11] a citizen of Tours, a man of low degree, yet of free birth. It was in his time that Queen Clotild passed away. He completed the church of Saint Mary within the walls of Tours; the church of the holy Germanus was also erected in his time. The villages of Neuilly and Luzillé were now founded. By his institution tierce and sext were said in the cathedral church, a usage which is continued in the name of God to this day. He was bishop sixteen years, eleven months, and twenty-six days, and was interred in the church of the holy Martin.

The sixteenth, Baudin, was referendary of King Lothar before being consecrated as bishop.[12] He had sons, and was much given to charity. He distributed among the poor the money which his predecessor left a sum amounting to more than twenty thousand pieces of gold. In his time was built the second village of Neuilly. He instituted the common table for canons. He held the see five years and ten months, and when he died was buried in the church of the holy Martin.

The seventeenth, Gunthar, was abbot of the monastery of the holy Venantius before he was consecrated. During his tenure of office he was a man of great discretion, and was often sent on embassies between the kings of the Franks. But after his consecration he became addicted to wine, until he seemed almost half-witted. This weakness so affected his understanding that he could not recognize guests whom he well knew, and often assailed them with taunts and abuse. He held the see two years, ten months, and twenty-two days. When he died he was buried in the church of the holy Martin. The see then remained vacant for the space of a year.

The eighteenth bishop to be consecrated was the priest Eufronius,[13] belonging to one of the families which I have above called senatorial, a man eminent in holiness, and a cleric from his early years. In his time the city of Tours with all its churches was burned in a great conflagration; two of the churches he himself afterwards restored, leaving the third and most ancient deserted. And afterwards the church of the holy Martin was itself burned by Wiliachar when he took refuge there after the revolt of Chramn;[14] at a later time this bishop, with

[11] Bishop 529–46. He resisted a royal demand that all churches pay one-third of their revenue as taxes.

[12] The referendary administered royal properties and revenues.

[13] He was chosen by a vote of the diocese called a *consensus;* although King Lothar preferred another priest, he agreed to Eufronius' election after a while.

[14] Chramn was a son of Lothar; Wiliachar, a rich priest of Tours, was his father-in-law.

aid from King Lothar, roofed it with tin. In his time the church of the holy Vincentius was built. Churches were erected in the villages of Thuré, Céré, and Orbigny.

3. SCANDALS AFFECTING CLERICAL ORDER

Needless to say, the daily life of religious communities was often not as orderly as might have been desired. Anarchic periods like the sixth century were particularly prone to such disedifying scandal, but no medieval century was free of it. The two examples which follow suggest some of the reasons why later leaders of ecclesiastical reform legislated as rigorously as they did, a code intended to segregate the cleric from his fellow Christians in certain visible and tangible ways. Urbicus ruled the church of Clermont as its second bishop before 350. Most prelates of the early Church came to the episcopal dignity after mature experience with other responsibilities, including marriage and fatherhood. Gregory is quite aware that the wife's argument had a great deal of validity. St. Radegund was a Thuringian princess, whose agreement to leave her husband for the religious life in 555 was quite similar to that of Urbicus and his wife. Her husband, the Frankish king Lothar I (511–61), did not reclaim his rights, however; on the contrary, he helped her build a sizeable convent at Poitiers, to which she attracted as many as 200 noblewomen by the time of her death in 587. The atmosphere of privileged autonomy prevailing at Radegund's convent thanks to her former status was healthy as long as the queen herself was on the scene, but after her death it proved too heady for the proud spirits she had collected there.

Gregory of Tours: *History of the Franks, Book I*

From Gregory of Tours, History of the Franks, *trans. O. M. Dalton (Oxford: Oxford University Press, 1927), II, 25–26. Reprinted by permission of the Clarendon Press, Oxford. Footnotes supplied.*

34. At Clermont, Stremonius, bishop and preacher, was succeeded by Bishop Urbicus, a convert of senatorial family, who was married. According to the custom of the Church, his wife lived religiously apart, not cohabiting with the bishop, and both devoted themselves to prayer,

charity, and good works. This being their way of life, the envious malice of the Enemy, ever jealous of holiness, was aroused against the woman, whom he inflamed to desire of her husband, making of her a new Eve. For she was kindled by concupiscence, and, covered with the darkness of sin, made her way through the shadows of night to the church house. Finding all shut fast, she began beating upon the doors of the house, and crying out with some such words as these: "How long wilt thou sleep, O bishop? how long wilt thou refuse to open these closed doors? Wherefore spurnest thou thy spouse? Wherefore dost thou harden thine ears to the precepts of Paul, who hath thus written: 'Return one to the other, lest the Devil tempt you?' [1] Lo! now I do return to thee, and to no strange vessel but to that which is mine own." As she continued a long time crying these words or the like, the scruples of the bishop at last grew faint; he caused her to be admitted to his chamber, and having lain with her, bade her depart. Afterwards he came to himself all too late, and to do penance for his misdeed withdrew to a monastery of his diocese; there having atoned for his offence with groans and tears, he returned to his own city. Having finished the course of his life, he departed from this world. Of his wife's conception was born a daughter, who passed her life in religion. The bishop was buried near the public way in a crypt at Chantoin with his wife and daughter. Legonus was made bishop in his place.

[1] I Cor. 7:5.

Gregory of Tours: *History of the Franks, Book IX*

From Gregory of Tours, History of the Franks, *trans. O. M. Dalton (Oxford: Oxford University Press, 1927), II, 409–10, 412–17, 421–22. Reprinted by permission of the Clarendon Press, Oxford. Footnotes supplied.*

---

39. In the monastery of Poitiers arose a great scandal. The Devil seduced the heart of Clotild, who boasted herself the daughter of King Charibert.[1] Relying upon her kinship with the royal house, she bound the nuns by oath to join in bringing charges against the abbess Leubovera, who should then be expelled from the monastery, while she herself should be chosen superior in her place. She now left the convent

[1] Son of Lothar; king 561–67. Clotild's mother was not of particularly illustrious rank, however.

with forty or more nuns, including her cousin Basina, daughter of Chilperic,[2] saying: "I am going to my royal kinsfolk, to make known to them the insults put upon us, how we are humiliated in this place as though we were not kings' daughters but the offsprings of low serving-women." Rash and unhappy woman, not remembering how conspicuous for humility was the blessed Radegund, foundress of that monastery. From which house she now went forth, and came to Tours; and giving me greeting, said: "I beseech thee, holy bishop, deign to take under thy protection and to maintain these virgins, reduced to great humiliation by the abbess of Poitiers, while I myself go to our royal kinsmen to make plain to them all that we suffer, and then come again." I made them answer: "If the abbess is in fault, or hath in anything transgressed any of the canons, let me go to my brother, Bishop Maroveus,[3] and together let us convict her of offence; then, when the matter is arranged, go ye back into the monastery, lest that be wantonly dispersed which the holy Radegund with perpetual fasts and prayers and with constant charity brought together." But she made reply: "Not so, but we will seek the kings." Then I said: "Wherefore do ye resist the voice of reason? For what cause do ye refuse to hear this my episcopal admonition? I fear me the assembled bishops of the churches may remove you from communion." For so it is set down in a letter written to the holy Radegund in the early days of her community by those who were before us, a copy of which I deem it fitting to insert in this place.

Copy of the Letter

To the most blessed lady and daughter of the Church in Christ, Radegund, the bishops Eufronius, Praetextatus, Germanus, Felix, Domitianus, Victorius and Domnolus.[4]

. . . We therefore before all things ordain that if a virgin cometh, as we have already said, from the places committed by God's providence to our episcopal control, who shall deserve to become a member of thy monastery in Poitiers, following the institution of Caesarius, bishop of Arles, of blessed memory,[5] it shall never be permitted to her to leave it,

---

[2] Son of Lothar; king 561–97. Basina's mother was his first wife Audovera, whom he sent to a convent when he tired of her. Chilperic later tried to take Basina out of the Poitiers convent for a convenient marriage to a Spanish prince, but she refused and Radegund protected her.

[3] Of Poitiers; died 590.

[4] Bishops of Tours, Rouen, Paris, Nantes, Angers, Rennes, and Le Mans.

[5] Caesarius of Arles, 471–542. While a monk at Lérins on the Mediterranean coast of Gaul, he made various reforms in the observance of John Cassian's Rule.

seeing that, as ordered by the Rule, she hath entered of her own desire; lest that which shineth forth honourable in the eyes of all be turned to dishonour by the base misdeed of one. If, therefore, which may God forfend, any nun, inflamed by some allurement of a distracted mind, shall wilfully cast down into the defilement of such great reproach her discipline, her glory, and her crown, so that by the guile of the enemy, like Eve forthdriven from Paradise, she consent to forsake the bars of the cloister, say rather of the kingdom of heaven, to be dragged and trampled in the vile mud of the streets, let her be sundered from our fellowship, let her be stricken with the dire wound of excommunication. So that if, Christ being thus forsaken, she shall desire, through the Devil's wiles, to espouse a man, not only shall she who hath eloped be held adulterous and base, but also he who shall wed her; he shall be rather a profaner of things sacred than a spouse. And any who, to bring this crime about, hath administered to her that which was poison rather than counsel, we will that he be smitten with a retribution like to hers, through the divine judgement, until, separated from her companion, with a penitence fitting her detestable offence, she deserve once more to be received and taken back to fellowship in the place from which she fled. We add hereto that the bishops who hereafter shall succeed us shall hold themselves bound to pass like condemnation upon such guilt. And if, which we are fain not to believe, the bishops shall desire to relax aught of that which our deliberation containeth, let them know that one day it shall be for them to defend their act against us before the Eternal Judge; for it is the general law of our salvation, that man keep inviolate his every promise made to Christ. That this our decision and decree may have due authority, we have thought fit to confirm it by signing it with our own hands, that, under the guardianship of Christ, it may be observed for evermore.

After the reading of this letter Clotild said: "Nothing whatever shall hinder us from presenting ourselves before the kings, whom we know to be our kinsmen." They had come from Poitiers on foot without a single horse to help them, so that they were exhausted and worn out: no one had provided them with any food on the way. They reached our city on the first day of March; great rains were falling, and the endless downpour had made quagmires of the roads.[6]

40. They also spoke in disparagement of their bishop, saying that it was through his deceit that they had been driven to forsake the

---

As archbishop of Arles (503–42) he was a vigorous preacher and reformer of the whole Gallic Church. For his sister Caesaria and her followers he wrote a monastic Rule based on those of Lérins and of St. Augustine: it stressed poverty, permanence, and autonomy from the bishop.

[6] Tours is about 65 miles north of Poitiers, across a low, well-watered plain.

monastery. But it will be well to set forth somewhat more fully the causes of this scandal.

In the time of King Lothar, when the blessed Radegund founded the monastery, she and her community were always submissive and obedient to the earlier bishops. In the time of Sigibert,[7] when Maroveus had obtained the see, the blessed Radegund, moved by her faith and devotion, sent clerics into the East to procure wood of the True Cross, and relics of the holy apostles and the other martyrs; they took with them letters from King Sigibert. They set forth, and duly returned with the relics. Upon the delivery of these, the queen requested the bishop himself to deposit them in the convent with chanting of psalms and all honour. But he disregarded her proposal, mounting his horse, and going off to a country estate. The queen then sent a fresh message to King Sigibert, begging him to command one of the bishops to place the relics in the convent with all the honour due to them, and in compliance with her vow. The king then enjoined the blessed Eufronius, bishop of Tours, to perform this task; who, coming with his clergy to Poitiers, in the absence of the bishop of that city, brought the holy relics to the monastery with much chanting of psalms, with pomp of gleaming tapers and incense. After this event Radegund on many occasions sought the good grace of the bishop of Poitiers; but she failed, and was forced to go to Arles with the abbess whom she had appointed.[8] There they received the Rule of the holy Caesarius and the blessed Caesaria, and on their return put themselves under the protection of the king, because they could find no care for their security in the man who should have been their pastor. The time for the passing of the blessed Radegund came when this cause of offence was still spreading from day to day. After her death the abbess once more begged her own bishop to take the monastery under his care. At first he was inclined to refuse, but afterwards, on the advice of those about him, he promised to become the father of the nuns, as it was meet that he should, and whenever need was, to take up their defence. He therefore went to King Childebert[9] and obtained a diploma granting him the regular control of this convent, such as he had over the rest of his diocese. But I believe that there remained in his heart some resentment which contributed, as the nuns declared, to cause the trouble in the monastery.

[7] Son of Lothar; king 561–75.
[8] Agnes. This occurred about 570.
[9] Son of Sigibert; king 575–95.

Since they now proposed, as I have written, to obtain audience of the king, we gave them this advice: "What ye propose is against reason; it is impossible for you so to order matters as to escape reproach. But if, as I say, ye ignore reason and will not hearken to wholesome counsel, at least get this into your minds, that it is best to let this wintry season pass which hath fallen upon us in the spring-time; then, with the coming of softer airs, ye shall be better able to travel whithersoever your purpose may lead you." They saw the sense of this advice, and when the summer came on, Clotild quitted Tours, commending the other nuns to the care of her cousin, and proceeded to King Guntram.[10] Having been received by him and honoured with gifts, she returned to Tours, leaving Constantina, daughter of Burgolen,[11] in the monastery of Autun. She now awaited the bishops whom the king had commanded to visit the city and investigate the matters in dispute between the nuns and the abbess. But before she had returned from this mission many of the nuns had been enticed by evil men, and entered the bonds of wedlock. The nuns kept awaiting the arrival of the bishops; but seeing that none came, they retraced their steps to Poitiers, and put themselves in safety in the church of the holy Hilary.[12] There they prepared themselves for resistance, gathering about them a gang of thieves, slayers of men, adulterers, and criminals of all kinds, for they said: "We are of blood royal, and we will not pass the threshold of our monastery unless the abbess be expelled."

At the time there was in the nunnery an anchoress who a few years earlier had dropped from the walls and taken refuge in the church of the holy Hilary, pouring forth many charges against the abbess, all of which we discovered to be false. But later she had herself drawn up by ropes into the monastery at the very spot from which she had got down, and asked permission to shut herself up in a secret cell, saying: "Greatly have I sinned against the Lord and against my lady Radegund" (for the queen was alive at that time), "and therefore am I fain to withdraw from all intercourse with the community, and to do penance for my sins. For I know that the Lord is merciful and forgiveth those who make confession of their sins." She then entered the cell. But when this disturbance arose, and Clotild had returned from King Guntram, she broke down her cell door in the night, and escaping

---

[10] Son of Lothar; king 561–93.

[11] A very rich magnate.

[12] St. Hilary, great fourth-century Bishop of Poitiers, enjoyed in that diocese the status that St. Martin had in Tours. The churches containing their tombs were places of sanctified refuge.

from the monastery, made her way to Clotild, venting accusations against the abbess, as she had done before.

41. Meanwhile Gundegisil, bishop of Bordeaux, associating with himself Nicasius of Angoulême, Safarius of Périgueux, and Maroveus of Poitiers, came to the church of the blessed Hilary, in his quality of metropolitan, to censure these nuns, hoping to get them back into their monastery. But they resisted with stubbornness, and when the bishops, in accordance with the letter above cited, pronounced sentence of excommunication, the gang of ruffians which I have mentioned rose up against them and handled them so roughly within the very walls of the church, that the bishops fell to the ground and could hardly rise, while the deacons and other clerics came forth covered with blood, and with their heads broken. So huge a terror seized them, as one may believe, by the Devil's prompting, that when they issued from the sacred place, they did not even take leave of each other, but went off home, every man by the first way open to him. Desiderius, deacon of Syagrius, bishop of Autun, was present at this disaster; without even searching for a ford, he plunged into the Clain at the first spot where he reached the bank, and swam his horse across to low ground on the farther shore.

Clotild now chose bailiffs, seized the lands of the monastery, and with stripes and blows compelled all the men whom she could force away from that house to enter her service; she further threatened, if she succeeded in entering the building, to throw the abbess down from the walls. When news of these disorders was brought to King Childebert, he sent authority to Count Macco,[13] commanding him to do his utmost to repress them. Gundegisil, after he had, in concert with the other bishops, excommunicated these nuns and so left them, wrote a letter in his own name and that of his brethren present with him to the bishops then assembled with King Guntram, receiving from them the following reply:

Copy of the Letter

To their ever dear lords Gundegisil, Nicasius, and Safarius, most worthy occupants of their apostolic seats, the bishops Aetherius, Syagrius, Aunacharius, Hesychius, Agricola, Urbicus, Felix, Veranus, Felix, and Bertram,[14] these. When the messenger delivered your letter, our happiness

[13] Count of Poitiers.
[14] Bishops of Lyons, Autun, Auxerre, Grenoble, Nevers, Riez, Belley, Cavaillon, Châlons-sur-Marne, and Le Mans.

in rejoicing at your safety was balanced by our affliction in bewailing beyond measure the outrage which ye report yourselves to have suffered, for not only have the prescriptions of the Church been transgressed, but all reverence for religion hath been forgotten. Ye have made known to us that the nuns who, hearkening to the voice of the Evil One, went forth from the monastery of Radegund of blessed memory refused either to hear your admonition, or to return within the walls of the convent which they had deserted; moreover, that they did outrage to the church of our lord Hilary, by the blows inflicted on you and upon your people. Ye have told us that for these offences it seemed good to you to suspend them from the privilege of communion, and ye have chosen to consult our mediocrity upon this matter. Therefore, inasmuch as we know that ye have well studied the canons, and that the Rule in its full content ordereth any who are caught in such excesses to be coerced not by excommunication alone, but also by a sufficent penance; and further, inasmuch as we hold you in veneration and feel for you the warmest brotherly love, we hereby declare, being of one mind and accord, that we consent unto your judgements and share your opinions. We leave the matter so, until we sit with you at the council to be held on the first day of November, and deliberate together how we may bridle the temerity of such offenders, to the end that none hereafter falling into such temptation may be led by vainglory to perpetrate the like deeds.

*   *   *

43. Thereafter Bishop Maroveus, having heard that these nuns were uttering reproaches against him, sent Porcarius, abbot of the church of the blessed Hilary, to Bishop Gundegisel and the other bishops of his province, to ask that they would grant him leave, after giving the communion to the nuns, to come before them and be heard; his request was, however, absolutely refused. King Childebert, who was vexed without ceasing from both sides, alike by the monastery and by the nuns who had abandoned it, dispatched the priest Theuthar to put an end to the recriminations which they kept up between them. Theuthar summoned Clotild and her companions before him. But they said: "We shall not come, because we are suspended from communion; if we are once more received into the Church, we will forthwith present ourselves before thee." At this reply, he returned to the bishops, and spoke with them upon this matter. But as he could obtain no result on the subject of their communion, he went back to Poitiers. The nuns were now separated; some returned to their relatives, others to their own houses, others to monasteries to which they had previously belonged, for together they could not bear the severity of winter, firewood being scarce. A few remained with Clotild and Basina. But even among these there were great discords, for each one of them wanted to set herself above the rest.

4. STANDARDS OF CONDUCT FOR PARISH PRIESTS

The Benedictine monastery of Prüm, 35 miles north of Trier in a valley of the rough Eifel mountains, was founded in 721 by Bertrada of Mürlenbach. Taken under royal protection by Charlemagne's father, it grew swiftly in wealth and importance. By the end of the ninth century it boasted an immunity (a territory subject to its own judicial control), a mint, market rights, fortifications (strong enough to resist two Viking attacks in 882 and 892), and more than 1500 agricultural estates. It remained a bastion of ecclesiastical privilege until Napoleon dissolved it in 1802. It is a little ironic that Prüm owes its widest influence to the work of Regino (840?–915), its abbot 892–99, who was deposed in order to make way for the brother of some powerful local lords. Ratbod, Archbishop of Trier (883–915), invited Regino to become abbot of the monastery of St. Martin in the cathedral city. From that post he collaborated actively with Ratbod's attempts at reform. The most enduring results of this joint effort were the *Two Books on Ecclesiastical Discipline,* completed in 906 and dedicated to the Archbishop of Mainz, the Primate of Germany. Book I deals with the clergy, Book II with the laity; each contains an anthology of decrees and instructions carefully selected from a variety of sources, along with a set of specific questions to be put to those under examination. Regino's manual was an immediate success in the Rhineland; when adopted in the following century by the famous lawyer-bishop Burchard of Worms (see IV, 5), it spread to the whole Latin Church. The questions presented here reveal, among other things, a conviction that the rank and file of the secular clergy should resemble their "brethren" in the monasteries more than their neighbors in the village and the field, the objects and associates of their daily work.

Regino of Prüm: *On Ecclesiastical Discipline*

From Regino of Prüm, De ecclesiasticis disciplinis, *I, in* PL, *XXXII, cols. 187–91. Footnotes supplied.*

Here begins the list of matters concerning which the bishop or his agents in each district should make inquiry throughout the settlements, countryside, and parishes of his diocese.

1. First of all, they must inquire in which saint's honor the church was consecrated, or by whom it was consecrated. After that they should examine the church building all around, to see if it is well roofed and vaulted and to make sure that no doves or other birds make their nests there—this last because of the uncleanliness of their droppings and the noisy disturbance of which they are capable.

* * *

3. [They must inquire] if hay, grain, or anything of that sort is kept in the church.

4. Then they should go up to the altar, and consider what sort of equipment it has; how much is new, how much old, and how cleanly it is maintained.

* * *

10. [They must inquire] if it has a complete Missal, book of Lessons, and book of Antiphons. For without these mass cannot be perfectly celebrated.

11. They should also see how many other books are there, and whether they are well bound; how many and what sort of priestly vestments are there, and if they are clean and kept in a clean place.

12. They must inquire about the lighting of the church, and how many dependents owe it dues in war.

13. They must check to see if the church possesses a *mansus*[1] and a cemetery close by, and a yard which connects the church and the priest's house, and four servants.

14. How many free *mansi* it has, and how many tilled by serfs or *hospites*,[2] from which the tithe may be collected.

15. They should also consider whether the entry to the church is strong enough and closed frequently enough to escape pollution from any unclean deed.

Questions About the Life and Associations of the Priest

16. They must inquire if the priest dwells in a room near the church, or in the vicinity of residences of a doubtful character.

17. If he is ill-famed with any woman, or if he has brought any strange woman into his house.

18. If he visits the sick, if he reconciles them, if he anoints them with oil as the Apostle commands, if he gives them communion with

---

[1,2] For an explanation of these terms see IV, 4.

his own hand and not through some layman. If he hands communion over to a layman or a woman to bring it to the sick—which is infamous.

19. If he exacts any fee for baptizing children or reconciling the sick or burying the dead.

20. This above all must be discovered: whether through the priest's negligence any child in the parish has died without baptism.

21. If he celebrates mass from house to house outside the church.

22. If he is given to drink or litigation.

23. If he bears arms in uprisings.

24. If he is given to games with dogs or birds.

25. If he drinks in taverns.

26. If he has with him a cleric to read the Epistle or Lesson and to deliver the responses at mass, and to sing psalms with him.

27. If he arises every night to recite Matins and Lauds.[3]

* * *

30. If he presumes—which God forbid!—to celebrate mass after having eaten and drunk.

* * *

32. If he proclaims the word of the Lord to the people.

33. If he celebrates mass at the prescribed time, that is, around the third hour of the day, and afterwards fasts until midday so that, if need be, he can sing mass for strangers and those on a journey.

34. If he takes care of the poor and pilgrims and orphans, and invites them to his table insofar as he is able.

35. If every Sunday before mass he puts blessed water into a clean and conveniently placed vessel, from which the people entering the church and standing in church can be sprinkled.

36. If he has presumed to give a chalice or paten or priestly vestment or book to a tavern-keeper or trader as a pledge (or collateral).

37. If he has accepted any gift or temporal advantage—rather spiritual damage—from any public sinner or incestuous person, so that he will conceal it from the bishop or his ministers.

38. If as a favor or from friendship or kinship, he has admitted to reconciliation[4] anyone who has done inadequate penance, or if he has given supporting evidence for such a reconciliation.

---

[3] Portions of the monastic Office, composed of hymns, lessons, and Biblical passages, which were sung or recited between midnight and dawn.

[4] *I.e.*, with the sacraments. This applied mainly to persons under the ban of excommunication.

39. If, when called on the third, seventh, or thirtieth day after some-one's death, or on the anniversary thereof, he has presumed to get drunk or utter prayers in Saints' names, or drink to the soul in ques-tion and influence others to drink, or glut himself at others' insistence, and engage in applause and disorderly laughter and disgraceful games and indecent songs.[5]

40. If, having no inheritance when he was admitted to ecclesiastical rank, he later bought possessions, in whose name they are.

41. If he collects usury, or has become a collection agent for his lord.

42. If he celebrates mass but does not receive communion.

43. If he permits women to approach the altar and touch the chalice of the Lord, which is not lawful.

44. If he was ordained through bribery, or bought the church in which he celebrates mass.

45. If he had another church before, and left it for another on ac-count of gain.

46. If he holds several churches without the help of other priests.

47. If he celebrates mass in another parish against the will or without the invitation of his fellow priest.

48. If he collects tithes belonging to another.

49. If he invites penitents to eat meat and drink wine, unless he does it as an act of charity.

50. If he acts as a notary or as his lord's agent.

*　　*　　*

54. [Inquire] about observance of the Greater Litany.

55. And of the Rogation Days.[6]

56. If he announces the Lenten fasting requirements in their en-tirety to the people.

57. If on Ash Wednesday he invites the people committed to his care to come to confession, and assigns a penance suitable to each kind of sin, not according to the promptings of his heart, but as is prescribed in the Penitential book.

58. If he admonishes all the faithful to come to the communion of the Lord's body and blood three times a year, that is, at Christmas, Easter, and Pentecost.

---

[5] Church authorities waged an endless campaign against the survival of various pagan rites connected with the burial of the dead. Anyone familiar with old-fashioned "Irish wakes"—actually widespread in European peasant culture—knows how incomplete their victory was.

[6] See I, 1.

59. If he also admonishes them at which times married men should abstain from their own wives.

60. Make sure that no cleric gets married.

* * *

63. Inquire if the priest puts off clerical dress to wear lay attire.

* * *

66. If he presumes to celebrate mass without an alb[7] or with the same alb which he uses in his daily activity.

* * *

69. If he teaches the people to observe Sundays and other feast days by abstaining from servile work from sunset to sunset.

70. If he admonishes the people that there is to be no singing at the church door, and no dancing of women,[8] but that they should enter the church and hear the word of God in silence.

71. If, by calling on Almighty God to witness, he forbids the diabolical songs which the lower elements of the common folk are accustomed to sing at night over the dead, and the loud laughter which they affect then.

* * *

74. After all these matters have undergone diligent investigation, the priest himself should be interrogated by the bishop or his vicar.

75. Whether he was born of free parents, or of serfs.

76. Whether he was born or ordained from the same parish or from another.

77. If from the same parish, he must be asked by which bishop he was ordained, and to which post he was assigned.

78. If he is of servile origin, he must show his charter of enfranchisement.

79. If he is from another parish, he must show his letters of introduction.

* * *

81. If he has with him a written explanation of the Creed according to the tradition of the orthodox Fathers, and fully understands it, and

---

[7] A long white robe over which the other vestments were worn: the basic priestly ritual garment.

[8] Like ¶71, another issue in the long attack on pagan ritual habits.

from it can instruct the people committed to him through earnest preaching.

82. If he understands adequately the prayers of the mass, the preface to the Canon and the Canon itself, and is capable of reciting them distinctly and from memory.

83. If he can read the Epistle and the Gospel well, and can explain at least their literal meaning.

*   *   *

94. If he has the forty homilies of Gregory[9] and studiously reads and understands them. Or if he cannot possess them, does he have at least the aforesaid Doctor's sermon on the seventy disciples sent by the Lord to preach, and does he recognize that he has been promoted to the ministry of the Church according to the model of those seventy disciples?

5. APPLYING THE STANDARDS

Eudes de Rigaud (1215?–75) was a model bishop of the High Middle Ages. Born near Paris, he entered the Franciscan Order in 1236, studied at the University of Paris, and became a professor of theology there in 1245. Three years later he was elected Archbishop of Rouen, to which office he was consecrated by no less a figure than the great canon lawyer, Pope Innocent IV. For the next 21 years Eudes sent his agents on rounds of inspection through his progressive Norman diocese: the following selection comes from one of the registers in which the results of those inquests were recorded. Discipline and harmony within the Christian community were perhaps Eudes' chief lifelong concerns. While at Paris, he collaborated on a commentary on the much-disputed Franciscan Rule which was to become a classic norm for its interpretation (it was later called the *Exposition of the Four Masters*); as Archbishop of Rouen he worked closely with St. Louis (King of France 1226–70) on a famously forthright treaty with England; at the Council of Lyons in 1274, he assisted all the efforts of Pope Gregory X and St. Bonaventure (Minister General of the Franciscans before becoming bishop and cardinal in 1273) to effect a reunion of the Greek and Latin Churches. The reports included in this selection should be taken as indications

[9] St. Gregory the Great (pope 590–604), the most authoritative writer on pastoral theology. See I, 5(a).

of the problems facing the application of Regino of Prüm's standards, rather than of normal clerical behavior; as always, good news was no news to the archbishop's inspectors. On the other hand, the growing difference between rural and urban vices is suggestive.

Register of the Visitations of Eudes de Rigaud

From Life in the Middle Ages, ed. and trans. G. G. Coulton (Cambridge: Cambridge University Press, 1930), I, 80–83, 95–96. Reprinted by permission of the publisher. Footnotes supplied.

March 19, 1248. We visited the Chapter of Rouen,[1] and found that they talk in choir contrary to rule. The clergy wander about the church, and talk in the church with women, during the celebration of divine service. The statute regarding the entrance [of lay folk] into the choir is not kept. The psalms are run through too rapidly, without due pauses. The statute concerning going out at the Office of the Dead is not kept. In begging leave to go forth, they give no reason for so going. Moreover, the clergy leave the choir without reason, before the end of the service already begun; and, to be brief, many other of the statutes written on the board in the vestry are not kept. The chapter revenues are mismanaged.

With regard to the clergy themselves, we found that Master Michael de Bercy is ill-famed of incontinence; *item,* Sir Benedict, of incontinence; *item,* Master William de Salemonville of incontinence, theft, and manslaughter; *item,* master John de St-Lô, of incontinence. *Item,* master Alan, of tavern-haunting, drunkenness, and dicing. *Item,* Peter de Auleige, of trading. Master John Bordez is ill-famed of trading; and it is said that he giveth out his money to merchants, to share in their gain. Of our own free will we have denounced these persons aforesaid to the Archdeacons of Greater and Lesser Calais; and the Chapter is bound to correct these offences through the aforesaid archdeacons, or through other officials, before the Assumption of the Blessed Virgin [Aug. 15]; otherwise (we said), we ourselves would forthwith set our hands on the business, as we have notified to them by letter; and it is for them to let us know how the corrections have been made.

* * *

[1] The clergy, usually of high social rank and advanced education, attached to the cathedral church.

January 19, 1249. *Deanery of Foucarmont.*[2] We found the priest of Neuilly ill-famed of trading, and ill-treating his father who is the patron of his benefice; and he fought bodily with drawn sword against a certain knight, with hue and cry and the help of his kinsfolk and friends. *Item,* the priest of Bazinval haunteth taverns. *Item,* the priest of Vieux-Rouen goeth about with a sword at his side and in unhonest garb. *Item,* the priest of Bouafles weareth no cassock and selleth his corn at a dearer price on account of a certain day. *Item,* the priest of Hamies is a leper, as it is thought. *Item,* the priest of Ecouis is a dicer and a player of quoits; he refused to take the pledged faith of espousal from a man, because he had not restored a legacy of his father; he haunteth taverns. *Item,* the priest of Petra hath celebrated mass, though suspended from his functions. *Item,* the priest of St Remy is ill-famed of drunkenness, weareth no cassock, playeth at dice, haunteth the tavern and is there oftentimes beaten. *Item,* the priest of Gilemerville dwelleth not in his parish, as he should, nor weareth the cassock, and sometimes he loseth his garments in taverns. *Item,* Robert, priest of Campneuseville, hath no cassock. *Item,* the priest of St Martin du Bois is litigious and a wanderer (*vagabundus*). *Item,* the priest of Pierrepont is drunken, and playeth at dice and quoits. *Item,* Master Walter, priest of Grandcourt, is ill-famed of overmuch drinking. *Item,* from Robert, priest of St Mary's church at Mortemer, (whom we found grievously ill-famed of misbehaviour, litigiousness, and tavern-haunting,) we have the letters here below.[3] *Item,* the priest of Realcamp, corrected by the Archdeacon, had promised that in case of relapse he would hold his benefice as resigned *ipso facto,* and hath since relapsed, even as he sometimes also loseth his garments in taverns. We have denounced the aforesaid priest as *ipso facto* deprived of the aforesaid church. *Item,* we found that the priest of Mesnil-David, oftentimes corrected by the Archdeacon, hath relapsed, and it is said that he hath celebrated in spite of suspension, wherefore we have bidden him purge himself in form of law from these accusations, or we would proceed to an inquisition against him. To which he answered that he would take counsel hereupon: we therefore have assigned him a day to answer these things.

January 20, 1249. *Deanery of Neufchâtel.*[4] Adam, priest of Neuilly, hath been corrected for drunkenness by the Archdeacon. *Item,* the

---

[2] Foucarmont is on the river Bresle, near the borders of Picardy, about 40 miles northeast of Rouen.

[3] *I.e.,* a written promise to resign one's benefice in case of relapse. Some of these priests were also charged with offenses against chastity.

[4] Ten miles closer to Rouen than Foucarmont; the chief crossroads in the sparsely settled *pays* of Bray.

priest of Sommery resideth not in his parish as he should, and rideth abroad like a vagabond. *Item,* Thomas, priest of Mesnil-Mauger, is said to buy and sell horses and to trade in other ways. *Item,* the priest of Fosse cometh not to [ruridecanal] chapters, nor to the synod. . . . *Item,* the priest of Malacopula frequenteth assizes and lay courts. *Item,* the priest of Lucy exacteth from each woman 13 pence; even though the child die before the churching, he will not church the mother until she pay 13 pence. *Item,* the priest of Haucourt buyeth and holdeth land on farm from the abbess of Buieval. The priest of Nogent hath no cassock. The priest of Louvechamp keepeth hunting hounds. *Item,* the priests of Salicosa Mara and Beaubec have no cassocks.

January 22, 1249. *Deanery of Eu.*[5] We found the priest of Panliu ill-famed of drunkenness; he selleth his wine and maketh his parishioners drunken. The priest of Auberville resideth not in his parish as he should. The Dean is ill-famed of exacting money, and it is said that he had forty shillings from the priest of Essigny for dealing gently with him in his incontinence. The prior of Criel is ill-famed of trading: he selleth rams. The priest of St Aignan is unhonestly dressed; *item,* the priest of Berneval is a trader in cider, corn, and salt. *Item,* the priest of Bouville selleth wine, as it is said.

Relations with the Rest of Society

6. THE CLERGY AND THE CRUSADE

This account of Pope Urban's launching of the First Crusade should be compared with that given in I, 7. This version reports a preliminary address to the assembled clergy as well as the great public speech that ended the council; it concentrates more on Urban's concern with the internal tranquillity of Europe, and presents the call to Crusade as a consistent extension of other clerical duties. The notion that the clergy had some sort of universal responsibility for the whole range of activity undertaken by Christendom (indeed, by the whole world) was dear to the hearts of the reformed Papacy. Fulcher was born in Chartres in 1059, attended the Council of Clermont, and went on the Crusade. He traveled first with Duke Robert of Normandy, then with Count Stephen of Blois, and finally with Baldwin, brother of Duke God-

---

[5] About 25 miles northeast of Neufchâtel, on the Channel coast. See I, 11(f).

frey of Lorraine, who became Count of Edessa (in Armenia) and then King of Jerusalem; Fulcher was his chaplain after the siege of Antioch. Some time before his death in Jerusalem in 1127, Fulcher composed his history of the origins and progress of this great "shaking-up" of "the whole Western People."

Speech of Pope Urban

From O. J. Thatcher and E. H. McNeal, A Source Book for Mediaeval History *(New York: Charles Scribner's Sons, 1905), pp. 514–17. Footnote supplied.*

"Most beloved brethren: Urged by necessity, I, Urban, by the permission of God chief bishop and prelate over the whole world, have come into these parts as an ambassador with a divine admonition to you, the servants of God. I hoped to find you as faithful and as zealous in the service of God as I had supposed you to be. But if there is in you any deformity or crookedness contrary to God's law, with divine help I will do my best to remove it. For God has put you as stewards over his family to minister to it. Happy indeed will you be if he finds you faithful in your stewardship. You are called shepherds; see that you do not act as hirelings. But be true shepherds, with your crooks always in your hands. Do not go to sleep, but guard on all sides the flock committed to you. For if through your carelessness or negligence a wolf carries away one of your sheep, you will surely lose the reward laid up for you with God. And after you have been bitterly scourged with remorse for your faults, you will be fiercely overwhelmed in hell, the abode of death. For according to the gospel you are the salt of the earth [Matt. 5:13]. But if you fall short in your duty, how, it may be asked, can it be salted? O how great the need of salting! It is indeed necessary for you to correct with the salt of wisdom this foolish people which is so devoted to the pleasures of this world, lest the Lord, when He may wish to speak to them, find them putrefied by their sins, unsalted and stinking. For if He shall find worms, that is, sins, in them, because you have been negligent in your duty, He will command them as worthless to be thrown into the abyss of unclean things. And because you cannot restore to Him His great loss, He will surely condemn you and drive you from His loving presence. But the man who applies this salt should be prudent, provident, modest, learned, peaceable, watchful, pious, just, equitable, and pure. For how can the ignorant teach others? How can the licentious make others modest? And how can the impure make others pure? If anyone hates peace, how can he make others peaceable? Or if anyone has soiled his hands with baseness, how can he cleanse the impurities of another? We read also that if the blind lead the blind, both will fall into the ditch [Matt. 15:14]. But first correct yourselves, in order that, free from blame, you may be able to correct those who are subject to you. If you wish to be the friends of God, gladly do the things which you know will please Him. You must especially let all matters that pertain to the church be controlled by the law of the church. And be careful that simony does not take root among you, lest both those who buy and those who sell [church offices] be beaten with the scourges of the Lord through narrow streets and driven into the place of destruction and confusion. Keep the church and the clergy in all its grades entirely free from the secular power. See that the tithes that belong to God are faithfully paid from all the produce of the land; let them not be sold or withheld. If anyone seizes a bishop let him be treated as an outlaw. If anyone seizes or robs monks, or clergymen, or nuns, or their servants, or pilgrims, or merchants, let him be anathema. Let robbers and incendiaries and all their accomplices be expelled from the church and anathematized. If a man who does not give a part of his goods as alms is punished with the damnation of hell, how should he be punished who robs another of his goods? For thus it happened to the rich man in the gospel [Luke 16:19]; for he was not punished because he had stolen the goods of another, but because he had not used well the things which were his.

"You have seen for a long time the great disorder in the world caused by these crimes. It is so bad in some of your provinces, I am told, and you are so weak in the administration of justice, that one can hardly go along the road by day or night without being attacked by robbers; and whether at home or abroad, one is in danger of being despoiled either by force or fraud. Therefore it is necessary to reenact the truce,[1] as it is commonly called, which was proclaimed a long time ago by our holy fathers. I exhort and demand that you, each, try hard to have the truce kept in your diocese. And if anyone shall be led by his cupidity or arrogance to break this truce, by the authority of God and with the sanction of this council he shall be anathematized."

After these and various other matters had been attended to, all who were present, clergy and people, gave thanks to God and agreed to the pope's proposition. They all faithfully promised to keep the decrees.

[1] The Truce of God. See I, 3.

Then the pope said that in another part of the world Christianity was suffering from a state of affairs that was worse than the one just mentioned. He continued:

"Although, O sons of God, you have promised more firmly than ever to keep the peace among yourselves and to preserve the rights of the church, there remains still an important work for you to do. Freshly quickened by the divine correction, you must apply the strength of your righteousness to another matter which concerns you as well as God. For your brethren who live in the east are in urgent need of your help, and you must hasten to give them the aid which has often been promised them. For, as the most of you have heard, the Turks and Arabs have attacked them and have conquered the territory of Romania [the Greek empire] as far west as the shore of the Mediterranean and the Hellespont, which is called the Arm of St. George. They have occupied more and more of the lands of those Christians, and have overcome them in seven battles. They have killed and captured many, and have destroyed the churches and devastated the empire. If you permit them to continue thus for awhile with impunity, the faithful of God will be much more widely attacked by them. On this account I, or rather the Lord, beseech you as Christ's heralds to publish this everywhere and to persuade all people of whatever rank, foot-soldiers and knights, poor and rich, to carry aid promptly to those Christians and to destroy that vile race from the lands of our friends. I say this to those who are present, it is meant also for those who are absent. Moreover, Christ commands it.

"All who die by the way, whether by land or by sea, or in battle against the pagans, shall have immediate remission of sins. This I grant them through the power of God with which I am invested. O what a disgrace if such a despised and base race, which worships demons, should conquer a people which has the faith of omnipotent God and is made glorious with the name of Christ! With what reproaches will the Lord overwhelm us if you do not aid those who, with us, profess the Christian religion! Let those who have been accustomed unjustly to wage private warfare against the faithful now go against the infidels and end with victory this war which should have been begun long ago. Let those who, for a long time, have been robbers, now become knights. Let those who have been fighting against their brothers and relatives now fight in a proper way against the barbarians. Let those who have been serving as mercenaries for small pay now obtain the eternal reward. Let those who have been wearing themselves out in both body and soul now work for a double honor. Behold! on this side will be the sorrowful and poor, on that, the rich; on this side, the enemies of the Lord, on that, his friends. Let those who go not put off the journey, but rent their lands and collect money for their expenses; and as soon as winter is over and spring comes, let them eagerly set out on the way with God as their guide."

7. CLERICAL SCHOOLING

During the greater part of the Middle Ages, the clergy possessed a near-monopoly of literacy, or at least of formal education. The most important official and learned language was Latin, mastery of which could not be gained without rigorous and sustained schooling. A fairly wide range of careers, with excellent prospects for advancement, awaited the successful graduate. Not the least of his assets was the set of friendships he had made in the course of those formative and impressionable years, one of the chief reasons why the alumnus of a good medieval school kept something of the cleric about him even if he was (and remained) a layman. The following selection conveys some of the atmosphere of those training centers of the administrative and intellectual elite. Note what it implies about the relative importance of prior social rank and subsequent academic achievement. It also expresses informally some current attitudes about the proper hierarchy of ranks and functions within the clergy.

Philip of Harvengt was born early in the twelfth century near Mons, the capital of Hainaut (now in southern Belgium), apparently of modest parentage. He received a good classical education at the cathedral school of Cambrai, some 50 miles to the southwest, and a short while after completing those studies entered the abbey of Bonne-Espérance (a few miles south of Mons), then recently founded by the reforming Order of Prémontré. His rise within the monastery was rapid until he tangled with Bernard of Clairvaux over the case of a monk who wanted to leave the Premonstratensians for a Cistercian house. Bernard had, as usual, the best of the exchange, and Philip was demoted and rusticated for a few years by his own Order. His recovery was swift, however. In 1158, seven years after his return from exile, he was elected abbot, in which office he served until his death (1183). Possessing an excellent command of Biblical, Classical, and Patristic literature, he especially admired St. Augustine, whose teachings he followed in his philosophical works and of whom he wrote a biography. He also composed several influential works on the training of monks and of clerics in general; many of his ideas were circulated in his correspondence, which won him the respect of his style-conscious contemporaries.

Philip of Harvengt: *Letter Thirteen*

From *Philip of Harvengt*, Epistolae, *in* PL, *CCIII, cols. 98–103. Footnotes supplied.*

When you and I were boys in boarding school for learning's sake, and were ruled by the teacher's rod lest untimely liberty do our restless spirits harm, a welcome comradeship brought us together into a sort of youthful compatibility, and bound our differing dispositions as though into one bundle. And although boys easily change their minds in their natural levity, now admiring, now full of aversion for one another, that sort of instability did not affect us; our scarcely formed friendship remained firm and lasting. When time moved on, boyhood faded away, and the advance of adolescence made us taller and perhaps more discerning, no comparable transformation altered the character of our mutual friendship, but rather a stronger impulse brought us to more generous affection. As my mind grew more acute with every passing day, I sought your approval ever more diligently, and the more solid and certain I perceived it to be, the more enthusiastic was my love for so fast a friend. Furthermore, you evidently possessed that calm integrity of character which merits the admiration of the genuinely wise—a quality rarely found in other boys who are aware that they come of distinguished blood. An adolescent of noble stock is usually so haughty that he feels distaste for the company of those he sees as his inferiors; he judges it beneath himself to seek a relationship of familiar give-and-take with lesser types, who ought more appropriately (in his judgment) to cultivate him. But you, endowed with brilliant lineage and yielding nothing to the reclining Maecenas,[1] treated your humbler classmates as well as your social equals with open-hearted amiability: a boy of naturally winning disposition, you showed yourself friendly to all. Before all others you joined yourself to me as though we were one in mind and spirit. Your affection treated me as an equal; in fact, you showed a certain awe of me as your senior, and although only in the number of your years could you have been considered a little less than I, you had no hesitation in deferring to me as though I

[1] The princely and opulent adviser of Augustus, patron of many poets, including Vergil and Horace.

surpassed you in other things as well. Towards me your generosity showed itself in particularly gracious gestures, striving to enter into no few conversations, and neither my uselessness to you nor the inequality of my estate kept back your friendliness; on the contrary, your goodness of heart inspired you disinterestedly to seek my friendship. . . .

In just such a way does Tullius Cicero[2] assert that true friendship first arises, and once having arisen, finds fitting nourishment: he will be found truly a friend who rejoices in his friend's virtue, and seeks no private advantage from their association. And since I was fully aware that our friendship conformed exactly to his description, I thought that we could rightly be counted among those peers of friendship about whom we were then together reading in the literature of the ancient pagans. Indeed it seemed to me a great and commendable thing that our affection deserved (as I thought) to be put on a par with that of rare and famous comrades like Theseus and Pirithous, Pylades and Orestes, Tydeus and Polynices, Patroclus and Achilles, Laelius and Scipio. . . .

I reached the end of adolescence before you, and following the ordinary sequence of events, crossed the contiguous frontiers of youth; . . . I led and you followed along the accustomed path. But my youth was like a vulnerable visitor to the interior of an unfamiliar house, and yours, all the more tender, still stood in the vestibule, when the grace of God struck me an unexpected blow, and dashed from my hands a delusive hope for secular advancement which I had cherished eagerly: perhaps it was because I had lived the longer, and along the way had compiled a longer record of offense.

And so I bade farewell to the world, discarding what I had solicited in my seduction. I held in great contempt what a little earlier I had yearned for; fleeing to the monastery I shut myself off from my former habitat and closed myself into cloistered lodging. When I began there to implore God's pardon for the past, and declined any further to incur present evil for the sake of future possibility, I felt that my position and recent experience would serve me well in attaining those salutary ends, and I rejoiced to no small extent in my new-found haven. . . .

Meanwhile, you continued to dwell with me in this residence of my heart. There you never eluded my company or conversation, and although no one ever beheld your presence, you became in all things more properly my own, because you had become in all things an interior companion. And my spirit conferred on me this benefit:[3] the one

---

[2] *I.e.*, in his dialogue *On Friendship*, a favorite text of the better twelfth-century schools.

[3] The original *beneficium* can also mean a fief or an ecclesiastical appointment.

whom my affections preferred before all others, although remote and unaware, my spirit brought before me constantly; indeed, his absence it entirely effaced. . . .

For several years I was engaged without interruption in this sort of intercourse, hoping and praying constantly for your salvation, when— behold!—that divine purpose with which no genuinely wise man presumes to quarrel, the loftiness of which "neither the wise man, nor the scribe, nor the investigator of this world" [4] may grasp, decided to elevate you, for whom I hoped an exile of the greatest worldly prosperity, to far greater honors in the ecclesiastical order. I grieved, I must confess; I groaned and wept, not disputing the subtlety of God's intent or envying your good fortune, but afraid lest so exalted a dignity do harm to your soul, as is usually the case, and make you look with aversion on the hard path of sanctity and of true religion. For although "all power is from God," [5] not an inconsiderable number of men, allured by the enticements of power, refuse to bend their backs to the burdensome demands of holiness: the higher the rank they attain in the Church, the farther they leave sanctity behind. And therefore anxious, therefore concerned, I was unable to rejoice in your honors, which one aspiring to spiritual perfection must recoil from as being the sort of thing which consumes one in external business and all too often involves one, intentionally or not, in the vices which keep such business company. . . .

And yet I, sitting in solitary silence in an impoverished corner, distinguished less by integrity of character than by the exterior apparel of holiness, look at myself and observe that, while I have taken on a little of the new man, a great deal of the old man yet persists. At least I will confess that my affection for you holds me still, and that I cannot but be deeply moved by it: indeed, when the interior taste experiences something old, it finds it all the sweeter, as can be attested from a certain wise man's words in sacred Scripture: "A new friend is like new wine which you drink with pleasure only when it has aged." [6] Although new wine does not really deserve to be utterly rejected, an old one is far more worthy of approval, because while the former can be drunk, it bites with the sharpness of novelty and sets the palate on edge, whereas the latter soothes and sweetens, having lost its tartar thanks to its maturity. A certain pagan author[7] puts it beautifully: "Those in a

---

[4] I Cor. 1:20.
[5] Rom. 13:1.
[6] Eccles. 9:10.
[7] Philip modestly feigns not to know that Horace is the author.

hurry may drink recent vintages; let my jug pour a venerable wine." . . .

I frequently felt a desire to reestablish more familiar contact with you, and confide in external words what I had been turning over in my mind. But whence comes access to the presence of such grandeur, especially for one restrained by the barriers of poverty? How indeed does one who is confined in a humble house of correction[8] gain access to a man surrounded in his palace by a multitude in attendance? How could such a one get through many gates and past so many gatekeepers, and penetrate to the lordly throne; rather, how could he expect to find you there with time to enter into any communication with him? How could you bear very long with his talk, from which you would think nothing weighty, nothing appropriate was likely to issue—particularly since, in the opinion of many, nothing is more intolerable than a poor man chattering uselessly with a rich one? Even if you possessed such extraordinary humility as to listen graciously to the speaker, and his speech possessed such utility that it deserved a comparable hearing, it would be no easy thing to resist the press of greater personages, or to postpone without loss the discussion of important cases. Even such humility could not permit one of your exalted dignity to keep himself very long available to me; whether you wished it so or not, your responsibilities would force you to turn back to more normal business. [So he decided to commit his thoughts to writing.]

Let the man who thinks in a prudent fashion know himself, what and for what he has been made. He should also recognize in what rank or order he has been established, and what mode of life has been prescribed for that order by the law of obedience [to God]. For we have all been made men, and so made to serve Him by whom we have been made, that what is subject to us may obey Him, too. This office has been imposed upon our reason, which must itself serve the sovereignty of God with diligent concern. Wherefore the prophet Micah says: "I shall show you, O man, what is good, and what the Lord demands of you. It is to do justice and to love mercy, and to walk humbly with your God." [9] But beside this law, which has been generally revealed to all men, and for disobedience to which effective damnation has been adjudged to some, another special law has been disclosed, according to which gradations of rank in the spiritual order are attributed. For when every assemblage of the faithful is divided into the

[8] A favorite metaphor of monastic writers for their monasteries.
[9] Mic. 6:8.

clergy and the laity, a lesser role is assigned to the laity, and a certain wider scope assigned the clergy. Neither of the two has any other basic duty than the service of God, but the clergy is commanded to perform its service with greater diligence. Within the clergy, the priests have precedence over those in lesser orders, because their hands are anointed with the sacred fluid of the Chrism so that they can consecrate the holy body and blood of Christ and lawfully dispense the other sacraments of salvation. Among the priests, those enjoy further distinction of rank who have taken up the pastoral staff. They are called abbots or bishops according to what they owe those subject to them: the former owe their cloistered sons the administration of discipline founded on a rule, the latter owe doctrinal instruction and the example of a good life both to those who dwell in cloisters and to everyone else. This is a lofty honor, but to it is joined a grave responsibility: its splendor will do no small damage to the man who bears it if he does not strive to be of loving profit to those over whom God's plan has given him an honorable preeminence. That is the purpose for which God has elevated some men in the Church, and subordinated others to them: that those who are more worthy may faithfully take care of the lesser ones, while the latter strive to obey the former with appropriate humility. Let those in authority exercise the ministry of spiritual instruction toward their subordinates, who in turn should show a filial obedience toward their superiors, and so may the force of unifying love, so much more efficacious than fleshly propagation, make them all like true fathers and sons.

8. THE FAIRS OF ST. DENIS

Far more complete than its control of learning was the clergy's monopoly of spiritual sanctions. The varieties of psychological resource available to the clergy covered a wide range of human appeal, extending all the way from refined ideological or legal persuasion to the manipulation of a rather crude type of magical awe. Such otherworldly leverage could win tangible secular privileges for ecclesiastical bodies capable of exercising them. Outstanding examples of this tendency in the economic sphere were the fairs sponsored several times a year by the abbey of St. Denis, either on its own home grounds or on the outskirts of Paris. Selection (a) is from a biography of the powerful and pious Frankish king Dagobert (623–39), probably written by Archbishop Hincmar of Reims (died 882), who was a monk of St. Denis before becoming Primate of the Franks. Note the discrepancies between the privileges claimed in that ninth-century history and those recognized in selection (b), an authentic decree of a rather ineffectual descendant of Dagobert.

Few European monasteries enjoyed greater fame or wealth than St. Denis. Its corporate origins may be due to St. Genevieve, the fifth-century aristocrat whose prayers were given credit for deflecting the Huns from Paris, and who seems to have built a church above the tomb of St. Denis and endowed a community of priests to tend it. By Dagobert's time the community had an abbot; in 656 it adopted the Benedictine Rule, which it followed with uneven rigor until its dissolution in 1792. Dagobert showered gifts upon the abbey and was buried there, beginning a tradition which was to last for nearly twelve centuries. King Louis VI (1106–37) adopted the abbey's red and gold banner—the Oriflamme—as the official banner of the French monarchy, an entirely fitting attribution in medieval eyes, since the kings of France had come to consider themselves the special vassals of St. Denis, and his abbey one of their most precious dependencies.

Gesta Dagoberti

Gesta Dagoberti *and* Judgment Rendered by Childebert III in Favor of the Monks of St. Denis *from* Histoire des institutions et des faits sociaux, *ed. J. Imbert, G. Sautel, and M. Boulet-Sautel (Paris: Presses universitaires, 1956), I, 358, 360–61. Footnotes supplied.*

About the same time King Dagobert returned to Paris. Out of love for the martyr Denis and his companions,[1] and on account of the miracles which the Lord, ever more greatly exalting their virtues,[2] worked daily at their sepulchers so worthy of veneration, the king handed over to their basilica certain pieces of land inside and outside the city of Paris, on either side of the city gate next to the prison of Glaucinus[3]—of which his merchant Solomon was then in charge—along with all the tolls levied there, to the extent that they were recognized

[1] Sts. Denis, Rusticus, and Eleutherius, martyred probably during the reign of the Emperor Decius (249–51), although another medieval tradition assigned their mission and martyrdom to the late first century. In either case, Denis was the first Bishop of Paris, Rusticus his priest, and Eleutherius another companion in orders. Tradition stated that after decapitation at Paris, their bodies drifted 15 miles down the Seine until they washed ashore at the site of the later abbey.

[2] The original word carries the second meaning of *powers*.

[3] On the north bank of the Ile de la Cité, near the present Quai aux Fleurs.

as due to the royal treasury. And he confirmed this grant in perpetuity through the authority of a decree signed with his own name and sealed with his ring.

At the same time he granted to the aforesaid holy place and to the monks who there served God and the holy martyrs, an annual fair which is held after the feast day of the same most excellent martyrs,[4] near the aforesaid monastery. He took care subsequently to implement this decree in such a way that the monks were granted the perpetual enjoyment, full and entire, without any exception or diminution, of every toll, any other revenue that might accrue to the royal fisc, and any fine that might be rightfully imposed by any judicial authority in the city itself and any of the other places within the *pays*[5] of Paris therein enumerated, during the whole period from the aforesaid feast day until the fair was finished. He made this concession for an eternal recompense, and in order that the aforesaid servants of God might take greater and more concerned pleasure in imploring divine clemency for him forever afterwards.

[4] *I.e.*, after October 4.

[5] In the original, *pagus,* which usually meant the rural area surrounding a *civitas,* formerly a center of Roman municipal government. *Civitas* and *pagus* together constituted a county. Boundaries dividing these units of administration tended to be quite vague in the seventh and eighth centuries.

Judgment Rendered by Childebert III in Favor of the Monks of St. Denis

Childebert, King of the Franks, to his *viri illustres.*[1] Before our presence and that of our magnates at Montmacq in our palace, came agents of the venerable Dalfinus, abbot of the basilica of our special patron St. Denis, where that worthy lord resides in the body.

Lodging a complaint against the agents of the *vir illuster* Grimoald, mayor of our palace, they declared that for a long time now Clovis, our departed grandfather, and thereafter Childeric our uncle, and then our lord and father Thierry, and again our cousin Clothair, have awarded [to the abbot] the entire toll paid by Saxon merchants or those of any other nation coming to the fair held near the basilica of St. Denis on the holy feast day of the Lord Denis; the grant provided that no toll be levied on behalf of the fisc, either now or in the future, upon men engaged in trade, whether at the fair itself or within the

[1] A title, of late Roman imperial origin, applied rather haphazardly to some of the highest officials and dignitaries of the Frankish court.

pays of Paris or in the city itself, but rather that the toll be conceded and awarded in entirety to the aforesaid basilica of St. Denis. As evidence whereof they presented the decrees of the aforesaid princes. When those decrees had been read through and examined, it was found that such concessions had indeed been made in their entirety to the aforesaid house of God.

Thereupon they declared that the agents of the aforesaid Grimoald, mayor of our palace and also count of the aforesaid *pays* of Paris, had taken half of the toll away from them and had snatched it from the revenues of the aforesaid basilica.

In reply the agents of the aforesaid Grimoald, mayor of our palace, submitted that for a long time it had been customary for the house of St. Denis to receive half, and for the other half to go to the count on behalf of our fisc.

The agents of St. Denis answered with the charge that the deceased Guerin, in his capacity as count of Paris, had introduced this custom by force and had on several occasions taken away half of the aforesaid toll; but the aforesaid agents had had recourse to the palace and had always had the former decrees renewed their entirety.

A second inquiry, made through several persons and through a reexamination of the aforesaid decrees, indicated that the aforesaid princes had conceded the toll in its entirety and had confirmed it at the beginning and subsequently. Therefore, with the assent of the aforesaid Grimoald on behalf of our fisc, his agents were to invest . . . the abbot's agents with the toll in its entirety: which they did.

However, this controversy has been notoriously subject to litigation, definition, comment, and judgment, as the *vir illuster* Sigofred, count of our palace, has borne witness; therefore we command that for all time henceforth the aforesaid monastery of St. Denis, where that worthy lord rests in the body, and Abbot Dalfinus and his successors, possess in its entirety, restored and secured after inspection of preceding decrees, the toll levied on the aforesaid feast day of St. Denis, whether upon the lands of the aforesaid basilica or in the same capacity at Paris. And since in former times, on account of disasters, the aforesaid fair was moved from the precincts of St. Denis and came to be held near the city of Paris between the basilicas of St. Martin and St. Lawrence,[2] in consequence whereof they[3] obtained princely decrees providing that the basilica of St. Denis would receive the tolls in their entirety whether

[2] A marketplace by a stream which crossed the road to St. Denis about one and a quarter miles north of the Seine, near the present Porte St. Denis.

[3] Presumably the abbots of St. Denis or their agents.

they settled down on the aforesaid feast day to transact their commerce and business in the aforesaid place or anywhere else; in like manner, if it should happen that the fair should be moved elsewhere because of disaster or some other inconvenience, the aforesaid tolls should remain for all time conceded and awarded in their entirety to the aforesaid house of God, to assure the illumination of the aforesaid St. Denis and out of reverence for the aforesaid holy place. And so be it in regard to all the controversy arisen between the interests of our fisc and the agents of St. Denis.

> *Actulius has taken cognizance of the act . . .*
> *Done at Montmacq in all felicity, in the*
> *month of December, on the thirteenth day,*
> *in the sixteenth year of our reign.*

9. AN EPISCOPAL PRINCIPALITY

The following selections show an ecclesiastical monopoly of political power, practically indistinguishable from the regime of lay princes. The cathedral church of St. Davids, around which grew the town of that name, long claimed to be the autonomous capital of the British (as opposed to the English) Church. One tradition claimed St. Patrick as its founder; it seems certain that St. David, the shadowy but historical patron saint of Wales, founded a monastery on the site of the later cathedral around 530. That monastery developed into a diocesan church with jurisdiction over the Kingdom of Dyfed (modern Pembrokeshire, along with parts of Carmarthen and Cardiganshire). It also exercised metropolitan authority over the other dioceses of Wales, asserting its independence of the Archdiocese of Canterbury until 1115, when St. Anselm of Canterbury persuaded King Henry I (1100–1135) to impose Bernard, a Norman monk, as bishop. St. Davids did not finally give up its fight for free elections and archdiocesan status until the death of Bishop Thomas Bek in 1293; after that it settled down to being a venerable and popular shrine and the seat of a small but honorable civil principality.

Selection (a) is a confirmation of the secular privileges accumulated by the diocese. Several of the Norman kings had made a point of cultivating the good will of St. Davids. William the Conqueror (1066–87) had gone on pilgrimage there; the pious Henry III (1216–72) had extended its secular powers, as though compensating for its failure to regain ecclesiastical autonomy; Richard II (1377–99) honored Bishop Adam Houghton (1361–

89) with several weighty responsibilities. Adam Houghton was a native of Whitchurch, near the cathedral of St. Davids, although his family name is Saxon or Norman rather than Welsh. He got a doctorate in civil law from Oxford about 1340. Ordained shortly thereafter to the priesthood, he was a canon of St. Davids, Hereford, and Chichester before Pope Innocent VI appointed him bishop of his home diocese. His active career in the royal service was stepped up rather than interrupted by his episcopal consecration: twice a negotiator of peace treaties with France, he was the last Chancellor of Edward III and the first of Richard II, who later sent him to arrange his marriage with Anne of Bohemia. Houghton attended many sessions of Parliament, and employed his legal talents in numerous trials and arbitrations. Despite all this secular business, Houghton was an attentive bishop. He undertook a major revision and expansion of the diocesan statutes, endowed the cathedral choir school, and founded the handsome College of St. Mary and another cathedral-connected school. Selection (b) is simply one example of the kinds of rights he inherited from his predecessors over the rural communities within this lordship on the southwest corner of Wales. It is an entry in a comprehensive register of the rents, services, and court customs due or subject to the bishop, compiled in 1326 under the direction of the diocesan chancellor. The exact location of Tydwaldy is difficult, perhaps impossible, to establish today. The enumeration of its dues indicates clearly enough that it was one of innumerable "manors" in which native Welsh tribal patterns were being blended with customs of Norman and English origin under the impact of English settlement and the assiduous pressure of lawyers.

Charter Roll of the Seventh Year of the Reign of King Richard II

From The Black Book of St. Davids, *ed. and trans. J. W. Willis-Bund (London: The Honorable Society of the Cymmrodorion, 1902), pp. 5–7, 55–57.*

Richard, by the grace of God King of England and France and Lord of Ireland, to the Archbishops, Bishops, Abbots, Priors, Dukes, Earls, Barons, Justices, Sheriffs, Reeves, Ministers, and all his Bailiffs and lieges greeting. The Venerable Father Adam, Bishop of St. David's, has besought us, that as he holds his Bishoprick and every parcel of the same freely from us as of our Crown, and as he and his predecessors Bishops of that See, have been accustomed to exercise royal jurisdiction in all their Lordships within the aforesaid Bishoprick, both in the hearing of all manner of pleas, whether personal or royal, and in enforcing the rights of the Crown, at their own prosecution, and that of others, with all manner of profits arising therefrom, according to the custom of those parts in all former times have been used and enjoyed, and so that neither without that we nor our progenitors, nor any other Lord Marcher or their Officers, have been accustomed or ought to intrude, by reason of any Lordship in Wales within the said Lordships of the said Bishop. And that the Lord Henry of glorious memory, son of King John, formerly King of England, our ancestor, by his charter granted and confirmed for himself and his heirs to Adam,[1] Bishop of the aforesaid church, that he and his successors in the said church should be for ever free from all pleas, suits, and actions, unless before himself, his heirs or his justices specially assigned for the purpose, and that the Bishop should hold his free Court for his men so that they should not be bound to answer in respect of any suit elsewhere than in the Court of their Lords, the Bishops of St. David's, save only before the King his heirs, or officers assigned for the purpose by special warrant of himself or his heirs, saving in all things the Royal dignity. Now we graciously desiring for the greater security and quiet of the said Bishop and his successors lest they may hereafter in any manner be impeached, molested, or taxed in any way, have for the honour of God and the Holy Church, as well at the special instance and request of the Venerable Father the Archbishop of Canterbury, our cousin, and all the clergy of his province, and on the request of the said Bishop, our great affection both to the Church of St. David and to the said Bishop also favourably inclining us thereto, have by our special grace granted and by this charter have confirmed for us and our heirs, that the aforesaid Bishop and his successors shall for ever possess, enjoy, and use all and singular the aforesaid liberties and all other liberties soever as fully and freely as the same are held and enjoyed by any Lords Marchers in their Lordships and Marches of Wales, and that all tenants of the said Bishop and his successors, whether residing in their Lordships within the Bishoprick or not, shall not be compelled, held, or bound to answer elsewhere than in the Courts of the said Bishop and his successors. And that the said Bishop and his successors

---

[1] An error for Anselm le Gras, bishop 1231–47.

shall be for ever released from all plaints, actions, suits, and demands brought or to be brought against them elsewhere, unless before us our heirs or our council, saving always our royal rights. Wherefore we will and firmly command for us and our heirs that the said Bishop and his successors have all and singular the liberties aforesaid and all manner of other liberties and enjoy and use them for ever, as fully and freely as any of the Lords Marchers have and use in their lordships and Marchers of Wales, and that all the tenants of the said Bishop and of his successors, or the residents in their lordships of the Bishoprick aforesaid shall be by no means bound to answer nor shall be compelled to answer elsewhere than in the Courts of the said Bishop and his successors. And that the said Bishop and his successors be for ever quieted from all pleas, actions, suits and demands brought or to be brought against them except before us our heirs or our council as aforesaid. These being witnesses, the Venerable Fathers William,[2] Archbishop of Canterbury, Primate of all England, R. London,[3] W. Winchester, Bishop,[4] John King of Castile and Leon, Duke of Lancaster, Edmund Earl of Cambridge, Thomas Earl of Buckingham, our dearest uncles: Richard Earl of Arundell, Hugo Earl of Stafford, Henry de Percy Earl of Northumberland, Michael de la Poole our Chancellor, Hugo de Segrave our Treasurer, John de Montacute, steward of our Household, and others. Given under our hand at our Manor of Shene the 21st day of December, the seventh year of our reign by letter of signet of the King himself.

[2] William Courtenay, 1381–96.
[3] Robert Braybrooke, 1382–1404.
[4] William of Wykeham, 1367–1404.

*　　*　　*

Tydwaldy. *Nannt'uan.* Item, they say that William Waur̃, Llewellyn ap Jevan, and their co-owners hold there one carucate[1] of land, and pay yearly at Michaelmas[2] 2s.

Services. And all the aforesaid at Tydwaldy give for heriot[3] the best beast or 5s. at the Lord's option, if they reside on the Lord's land, and if they are not resident they only give 5s. And they give for "leyrwyt"

[1] Nannt'uan, like Trefispoys at the end of this entry, seems to have been a small, hamlet-sized settlement farmed by a joint family group of Celtic type. A "carucate" amounted in this region to a little over 80 acres. It was divided into "bovates" of 7 acres or more (this terminology arose originally in the Danelaw).
[2] September 29.
[3] A payment due to the lord upon the death of a tenant; sort of an inheritance tax.

2s. if a maid, if not 12d.[4] And every third year they give collection of sheep, namely for each carucate of land 1, and the yearly value is 2s. And they do suit at the mill and are bound to carry the mill materials for wheels, spindles and sluices, with boards, and make sluices for the three mills above mentioned at their own cost. And the yearly value of that service for all Tydwaldy is 12d. And they do suit for the hundred court from fortnight to fortnight. And their common fine is 7s.

And they attend before the Steward whenever necessary and on being summoned. And they ought to do full service for each kind of corn, whether for the Lord or for the Court, growing in the Lord's manors of Pebidiauk as well as Burtoñ, Lawadeyñ, Trefdyñ, and Landogy, and if they do cartage to the manor where the Lord is residing, they have as food only one loaf of black bread, and they ought to reconvey the corn carried by them to Borton, and carry corn and straw[5] of each kind to and from Lantefey to Borton, and to all the manors of the Lord in Pebidiauk as often as neccessary. And each load will consist of 3 bushels of wheat, barley, and beans, and three of them will carry 20 bushels of oats. And they are bound to carry meat, fish, and the cooking utensils after the Lord's return, and if on a journey to the aforesaid manors they must carry as often as required all necessaries, the Lord finding food as aforesaid.[6] And they are bound to carry rabbits, geese, and fowls to the manors of Lantefey, Lawadeyñ, Landogy, and the other manors of the Lord in Pebidiauk, the Lord finding food as above. And each carriage of rabbits is worth 12d. and of fowls 6d. And they ought to receive the price of the carriage of rabbits at the house of the Reeve of St. David's. And as to wreck of the sea they do as the other men of the country.[7] And they pay toll for all beasts and sheep bought and sold. And they guard the Lord's market with the other men of the hundred. And they do services in war time with the others of the hundred. And when the Lord requires carriage he can insist on 24 services but on no more. And for each carriage the tenant works in the Lord's hay for three days. And the total yearly value is 6s. And they

---

[4] "Leyrwyt" was the fine due for having sexual intercourse with an unmarried tenant woman. As with the other payments, the amount of this fine is typical for the area.

[5] Or perhaps malt.

[6] The lord's feeding the tenant for such services is a Welsh survival, suggesting the relationship of a tribal chief rather than a feudal lord.

[7] They were bound to gather at the site of the wreck at the sound of a horn, and to guard the wrecked goods, which a recent royal decision had awarded to the local lord (*i.e.,* the bishop).

say that all at Tydwaldy from time immemorial were accustomed to pay flour and cheese for rent. But in the time of Bishop Gervase[8] that rent was commuted into money for the convenience of the church. And they also ought to carry the geese to Borton.

Trefispoys. Item, they say that Kedimor ap Coldu Retherch̃ ap Cadvan, and their co-owners hold there 2 bovates[9] of land at 2s. 6d. yearly at Michaelmas. And do all services as the men of Tidwaldy above mentioned. And they pay one fowl.

10. THE MENDICANT FRIARS IN TOWN

Nuclei of clerical life were constantly called upon to purify and refashion their links with lay society. One of the most imaginative responses to this demand was the emergence in the early thirteenth century of the Dominican and Franciscan Orders, designed by their founders as means to a dynamic reevangelization of the world. Rather than being attached to monasteries that were at least supposed to fortify one's permanent withdrawal from the world, the members of these new "mendicant" orders were to preach the Word through the highways and hedgerows, depending on spontaneous charity rather than endowments for food, lodging, and other inevitable resources. This primitive ideal was undone within one generation by a strange alliance of forces: the hierarchy's fear that the disciples of St. Dominic and St. Francis might prove an even greater threat to established orthodoxy than the Waldensians of the previous generation (see I, 12); and the friars' own spectacular success, which brought down upon them an avalanche of land, money, buildings, teaching and administrative functions, and adherents of every sort. By the end of the century the two orders were mighty corporations with complicated constitutions, great wealth, and hundreds of schools and convents in numerous provinces stretching from Morocco to the Mongol Empire. Latin Christendom witnessed once again the material transformation of an intense impulse to transcend the spirit of worldly society.

The Franciscan attempt to redeem Europe through the cultivation of Poverty and the rediscovery of the unadorned Life of the Gospels was socially more radical than the heresy-fighting Dominican program. Paradoxically enough, it seems to have had a special appeal for the rapidly expanding and suddenly self-conscious

[8] The period 1215–29.
[9] See note 1. There follows an enumeration of ten roughly similar settlements, and then a total: 6 carucates and 2 bovates of land, 6¼ sheep, 35 fowls worth 2s. 11d., and 62s. 3d. in money.

towns of the thirteenth century. Francis himself (1182–1226) was the son of a prosperous cloth merchant in the small but lively central Italian city of Assisi. He had his share of gallant enterprises, both romantic and military, before his conversion in 1205 or 1206. Within a decade after that experience he established regular modes of life (though not exactly *Rules* in the full conventional sense) for three groups of followers: the men (later called the First Order) who left all worldly ties in order to imitate Christ's original disciples; the smaller number of women (the Second Order) who pursued a similar ideal within settled convents rather than in groups always on the move; and the innumerable men and women of the Third Order who vowed to lead as rigorously ascetic a life as was consistent with the maintenance of secular vocations. Uncomfortable with any further systematization of his message, Francis spent the last seven years of his life in such bursts of personal inspiration as preaching to the astonished Sultan of Egypt, inventing Christmas cribs, and receiving the Stigmata. It was up to his followers and to a series of impressed but worried popes to search for organizational media that could communicate his simple and joyous ascetic vision to people he had never met, and at the same time defend its integrity against the swift ravages of spiritual or institutional entropy.

Bernard of Quintavalle, a "noble" of Assisi, was one of Francis' first two disciples. After Francis' death Bernard became one of the leaders of the Order's Moderate majority, which protested vigorously against the church-building projects of the Relaxed faction and the rigorist eccentricities of the Zealot faction. The following account of Bernard's mission to the city which was the seat of Europe's greatest school of law, comes from a late fourteenth-century translation of a Zealot (or "Spiritual") version of the Order's origins, composed in Italy about 1320. Its admiration for Bernard and lack of concern about the contradictions implicit in his success, represent an authentic memory of the Order's first encounters with the sophistication and opulence of large-scale urban life.

The Little Flowers of St. Francis

From The Little Flowers of Saint Francis, *trans. Leo Sherley-Price (London: Penguin Books Ltd., 1953), pp. 36–38. Reprinted by permission of the publisher. Footnote supplied.*

Chapter 4. Since Saint Francis and his companions were called and chosen by God to bear the cross of Christ within their hearts, to display it in their actions, and to preach it with their tongues, they appeared—and indeed were—men crucified, both in their clothing, the austerity of their lives, and their doings, for they desired to bear shame and insult for the love of Christ rather than receive worldly honour, respect, or praise from men. Indeed, they took delight in insults and were embarrassed by respect; they went about the world as strangers and pilgrims, carrying with them nothing but Christ Crucified. And because they were true branches of the True Vine, which is Christ, they bore rich and plentiful fruit in the souls they won to God.

In the early days of the Order Saint Francis sent Brother Bernard to Bologna to bear fruit for God there, according to the grace that God had given him. And having signed himself with the sign of the cross, Brother Bernard set out under holy obedience and arrived in Bologna.

When the children saw him in a ragged, shabby habit, they jeered at him and abused him, thinking him a madman;[1] but Brother Bernard bore all this patiently and gladly for the love of Christ. And in order to receive even worse treatment, he sat down openly in the market-place of the city. As he sat there a crowd of children and men gathered round him: one tugged at his cowl from behind, and another from in front; one threw dust at him, and another stones; one pushed him in this direction, and another in that. But Brother Bernard remained patient and unruffled, neither complaining nor moving away. And for several days he returned to the same place to endure similar treatment.

Since patience is evidence of perfection and proof of virtue, a wise doctor of laws, seeing Brother Bernard's great constancy and virtue, and considering how he remained undaunted by any ill-treatment and mockery during all these days, said to himself: "It is impossible that this is not a holy man." And coming up to him, he asked: "Who are you, and why have you come here?"

In reply Brother Bernard put his hand into his breast, and drawing out the Rule of Saint Francis, gave it him to read. When he had read it and recognized its sublime counsel of perfection, he turned to his friends with the greatest wonder and admiration, saying: "This is assuredly the highest form of the Religious Life of which I have ever heard. This man and his companions are the holiest men in the world,

---

[1] A favorite motif for Franciscans concerned to disavow traditional forms of respectability. Jacopone da Todi (1236–1306), one of the greatest Franciscan poets, wrote a poem entitled "How it is the highest wisdom to be reputed a madman for the love of Christ," containing such lines as "No philosophy so great has yet been seen at Paris," and "Go no more to Bologna, to get another mastery" (meaning both mastery of doctrine and, on a cruder but more immediate level, master's degree).

and whoever abuses him is the greatest of sinners, for he is the true friend of God and deserves the highest honour."

And he said to Brother Bernard: "If you need a place where you can serve God in a fitting manner, I will gladly provide it for the salvation of my soul."

Brother Bernard answered: "Sir, I believe that our Lord Jesus Christ has inspired you to make this offer, and I gladly accept it for the honour of Christ."

So the judge led Brother Bernard to his house with great joy and affection, and gave him the promised house, which he prepared and furnished at his own expense. And thenceforward he acted like a father to him, and was the foremost protector of Brother Bernard and his companions.

Because of the holiness of his life, Brother Bernard began to be greatly revered by all the people, so that any who could see or touch him counted himself blessed. But, as a disciple of Christ and of the humble Saint Francis, Bernard feared lest the respect of this world might impede the peace and salvation of his soul. So he left the town and returned to Saint Francis, saying: "Father, the friary has been established in Bologna. So send friars to occupy and maintain it, for I can do no good there; indeed, I fear to lose more than I could gain because of the excessive respect paid to me."

When Saint Francis had received a full account of all that God had done through Brother Bernard, he gave thanks to Him who had begun to increase the poor little disciples of the Cross in this manner. And he sent some of his companions to Bologna and into Lombardy, where they established many friaries in various places.

THE NOBLES   III

A Class of Fighters

Most aspects of European life in the Middle Ages were dominated by an aristocracy of some sort. The clergy was a vocational elite, formed by a fairly standard education and a ritual admission to membership. Conscious choice on the part of several individuals played a decisive role in that selective process. Less mobile and less precisely defined were the merchant patriciates of the towns or the prosperous peasant yeomanry. Least mobile of all was the medieval aristocracy *par excellence,* the feudal nobility, which from the twelfth century onwards enjoyed in most parts of Europe a separate status defined by law or theory and based on the fact (or legal fiction) of birth. This class derived its wealth from landholding, its power from the monopoly of certain military and political functions, and its sense of social distinction from special codes of behavior and a body of literature shaped for its particular environment and shaping it in turn. The upper ranks of the clergy were largely recruited from this class, and the commercial patriciate and rural yeomanry considered marriage with or admission to the nobility the summit of their own classes' social ambitions.

Scholarly opinion is still divided over the question of how much dynastic continuity there was within the noble class. Were the families endowed with noble status and privileges in the twelfth century the descendants of the legally defined aristocracies of the late Roman Empire and the invading Germanic nations, or were they sprung from families (or dynamic individuals) that had first seized power in the troubled and dark times following the collapse of the Carolingian Empire? We know that Roman law recognized and enforced the distinct and hereditary status of several social classes, of which the highest was the "senatorial order" (see I, 1(b) and II, 2), and that most Germanic societies recognized at least one hereditary class with special privileges above those of the ordinary freeman. On the other hand, it is equally clear that the Franks, whose laws and social habits exercised a great influence on the rest of Latin Europe, were an exception to the latter rule. Furthermore, the definition of noble status which prevailed on the continent in the twelfth century bears all the earmarks of a recent development, or at least of a recent crystallization of previous developments. Unfortunately, documentary evidence for the decisive period between the late ninth and the mid-eleventh centuries is none too plentiful, and what there is is often ambiguous. In any case, whatever the genetic composition or rate of turnover among its personnel, the noble class of the High Middle Ages was characterized by a social ethic remarkably like that of the pre-Carolingian aristocracies.

1. HEROIC LEADERSHIP

The most fundamental talent needed by a medieval nobleman was the ability to fight and to inspire other fighting men to follow him. An effective leader had to be generous with rewards and praise if he expected his men to be generous with their lives and safety. The reciprocal fidelity essential to the maintenance of such a relationship depended also on a lively consciousness of the honor of everyone involved. To be a really outstanding lord, one needed a certain eloquence along with a gift for the right gesture. With these qualities and a little luck, a man could get as much wealth as he needed; without them, a rich man would find his wealth little security indeed. On the other hand, it should be obvious that the lordly role was not an easy one to play without some material resources and some prior conditioning.

The following selection is the greater part of an Anglo-Saxon poem composed a few years after the heroic death of Birhtnoth, a great lord of Essex, in 991. Under the brilliant, patient leadership of Alfred the Great (king of Wessex from 871 to 899, and in his last years master of all England), the English had absorbed, survived, and defeated the most massive and sustained assault that the Vikings had flung against any part of Christendom. Under Alfred's successors the English kingdom achieved unity and an unprecedented degree of stability and coherence. Thanks largely to their patronage, Latin and vernacular literature, for which English culture had been particularly famous before the Vikings, flourished once again. The traditional values of the most purely Germanic society in Christian Europe appeared, at least, to have been firmly restored.

In the reign of Alfred's incompetent descendant Ethelred the Unready (978–1016) England was harassed once more by Vikings

—this time small bands of professional raiders seeking profit rather than large armies bent on conquest and settlement as well. Ethelred vacillated between paying them off and bursts of ill-considered vengeance, and the maintenance of security swiftly became a strictly local problem. The poet presents Birhtnoth as a model of the best traditional virtues: loyalty to his king, whose thane (personal vassal) as well as subject he was; far-seeing concern for the self-respect as well as the safety of the common people over whom he had been appointed *ealdorman* (roughly the equivalent of a Frankish count); and inspired leadership of his band of chosen retainers. Morally incapable of paying protection to the Vikings who had sailed up one of the tidal rivers of his coastal territory and not content with making them sail frustrated away, free to strike somewhere else, Birhtnoth forced a decisive engagement; by sending the horses away, he had removed from his own war band and from the local militia of common freemen the most convenient means of escape. His defeat in such a noble effort enriched Birhtnoth, his faithful companions, and all their kinsmen with enduring fame; the victorious Vikings had to be content with many casualties and not much booty. Although the poet prefers richly allusive turns of phrase to precise terminology, his subject matter still gives us a chance to see how wide a range of social status was represented in the actual war band of a well-known local magnate, the extent to which the thanes of every rank shared a common sense of function, and other items of suggestive social evidence.

The Battle of Maldon

The Battle of Maldon, *trans. E. Talbot Donaldson in* The Norton Anthology of English Literature, *Volume I, Revised, M. H. Abrams, General Editor (New York: W. W. Norton & Company, Inc., 1968), pp. 94–99. Copyright © 1968, 1962 by W. W. Norton & Company, Inc. Reprinted by permission of W. W. Norton & Company, Inc. Footnotes supplied.*

Then he[1] commanded each of his men to leave his horse, drive it far away, and walk forward, trusting in his hands and in his good

[1] *I.e.,* Birhtnoth (which means "Bright reputation"), son of Birhthelm ("Bright helmet"). His title of "earl" indicates neither political office nor a seat among a fixed peerage (as it does today); it was applied to all the males of the second highest class recognized in Anglo-Saxon law. Above the *earls* were the *aethelings*, princes of royal blood; beneath them were the *churls,* ordinary freemen.

courage. When Offa's kinsman[2] understood that the earl would not put up with cowardice, he let his beloved hawk fly from his hand toward the woods and advanced to the battle: by this men might know that the youth[3] would not weaken in the fight once he had taken up his weapons. Eadric wished also to serve his lord the earl in the battle; he carried his spear forward to the conflict. He was of good heart as long as he might hold shield and broadsword in his hands; he carried out the vow that he had made, now that he was to fight in the company of his lord.

Then Birhtnoth began to place his men at their stations; he rode about and advised them, taught the troops how they should stand and hold their places, bade them grasp their shields aright, firm in their hands, and have no fear. When he had arranged his folk properly, he alighted among them where it seemed best to him, where he knew his retainers to be most loyal.

Then the Viking's herald stood on the river bank, cried out loudly, spoke words, boastfully proclaimed the seafarers' message to the earl where he stood on the shore: "Bold seaman have sent me to thee. They have commanded me to say to thee that thou must quickly send treasure in order to protect thyself; and it is better for you to buy off this spear-assault with tribute than to have us give you harsh war. There is no need for us to destroy one another, if you are rich enough to pay. With the gold we will confirm truce. If thou that art highest here decide upon this, that thou wilt ransom thy people, and in return for peace give the seaman money in the amount they request, and receive peace from us, we will go to ship with the tribute, set sail on the sea, and keep peace with you."

Birhtnoth spoke, raised his shield, brandished his slender ash-spear, uttered words, angry and resolute gave answer: "Dost thou hear, seafarer, what this folk says? They will give you spears for tribute, poisoned point and old sword, heriot[4] that avails you not in battle. Sea-wanderers' herald, take back our answer, speak to thy people a message far more hateful, that here stands with his host an undaunted

[2] This young man, fond of the aristocratic sport of hunting with birds of prey, is identified only as a kinsman of Offa, who appears later as one of Birhtnoth's chief companions.

[3] In the original, *cniht,* from which derives the form *knight;* in one and a half centuries this would become the generic English term for a well-born mounted warrior, and almost automatically imply vassal status.

[4] The weapons a tenant received from his lord; they were returned by the tenant's heirs upon his death. For a later, lower-class development of this term, see II, 9(b).

earl who will defend this country, my lord Æthelred's homeland, folk and land. Heathen shall fall in the battle. It seems to me too shameful that you should go to ship with our tribute unfought, now that you have come thus far into our land. Not so easily shall you get treasure: point and edge shall first reconcile us, grim battle-play, before we give tribute."

Then he ordered the men to bear their shields forward so that they all stood on the river bank. Because of the water neither band could come to the other: after the ebb, the floodtide came flowing in; currents met and crossed. It seemed to them too long a time before they might bear their spears together. On the river Pant they stood in proud array, the battle-line of the East Saxons and the men from the ash-ships. Nor might any of them injure another, unless one should receive death from the flight of an arrow.

The tide went out. The seamen stood ready, many Vikings eager for war. The earl, protector of men, bade a war-hard warrior—he was named Wulfstan, of bold lineage—to hold the bridge:[5] he was Ceola's son, who with his spear pierced the first man bold enough to step upon the bridge. There stood with Wulfstan fearless fighters, Ælfere and Maccus, bold men both who would not take flight from the ford, but defended themselves stoutly against the enemy as long as they might wield weapons.

When the loathed strangers saw that, and understood clearly that they would face bitter bridge-defenders there, they began to prefer words to deeds, prayed that they might have access to the bank, pass over the ford and lead their forces across. Then in his overconfidence the earl began to yield ground—too much ground—to the hateful people: Birhthelm's son began to call over the cold water while warriors listened: "Now the way is laid open for you. Come straightway to us, as men to battle. God alone knows which of us may be master of the field."

The slaughter-wolves advanced, minded not the water, a host of Vikings. Westward over the Pant, over the bright water they bore their shields: sailors to land brought shields of linden. Opposite stood Birhtnoth with his warriors, ready for the fierce invaders. He ordered his men to form a war-hedge with their shields and to hold the formation fast against the enemy. Now was combat near, glory in battle. The time had come when doomed men should fall. Shouts were raised; ravens circled, the eagle eager for food. On earth there was uproar.

---

[5] Not a bridge in the modern sense, but probably a stone causeway, under water even at low tide; immediately below, it is called a ford.

They let the file-hard spears fly from their hands, grim-ground javelins. Bows were busy, shield felt point. Bitter was the battle-rush. On either side warriors fell, young men lay dead. Wulfmær was wounded, chose the slaughter-bed: kinsmen of Birhtnoth—his sister's son[6]—he was cruelly hewn down with swords. Then requital was made to the Vikings: I have heard that Eadweard struck one fiercely with his sword, withheld not the stroke, so that the warrior fell doomed at his feet; for this his lord gave the chamberlain[7] thanks when he had opportunity. Thus men stood firm in the battle, stern of purpose. Eagerly all these armed fighters contended with one another to see who could be the first with his weapon's point to take life from doomed man. The slain fell, carrion, to the earth. The defenders stood fast; Birhtnoth urged them on, bade each man who would win glory from the Danes to give his whole heart to the battle.

A war-hard Viking advanced, raised up his weapon, his shield to defend himself, moved against Birhtnoth. As resolute as the churl,[8] the earl advanced toward him. Each of them meant harm to the other. Then the seaman threw his southern-made[9] spear so that the fighters' chief was wounded. But he thrust the spear with his shield so that the shaft split and the spearhead broke off and sprang away. The war-chief was maddened; with his spear he stabbed the proud Viking that had given him the wound. Wise in war was the host's leader: he let his spear go through the man's neck, guided his hand so that he mortally wounded the raider. Then he quickly stabbed another, breaking through the mail-shirt: in the breast, quite through the corselet, was this one wounded; at his heart stood the poisoned point. The earl was the blither; the bold man laughed, gave thanks to God that the Lord had given him this day's work.

One of the Vikings loosed a javelin from his hand, let it fly from his fist, and it sped its way through Æthelred's noble thane. By the earl's side stood a lad not yet grown, a boy in the battle, son of Wulfstan, Wulfmær the young, who plucked full boldly the bloody spear from the warrior. He sent the hard spear flying back again: its point went in, and on the earth lay the man who had sorely wounded his lord.

[6] An especially close relationship in the traditions of early Germanic peoples, as well as in the later feudal period.

[7] *I.e.*, Eadweard. The chamberlain (*bur-thegn*—Bower-thane—in the original) was one of the most important officers of a lordly household, being responsible for the safety of his lord's bedroom, in which he slept and kept his richest garments and other treasure.

[8] Here "churl" means something like "villain."

[9] *I.e.*, English or French. The Vikings got even the basic tools of their trade from the lands they raided.

Then an armed Viking stepped toward the earl. He wished to seize the earl's war-gear, make booty of rings and ornamental sword. Then Birhtnoth took his sword from its sheath, broad and bright-edged, and struck at his assailant's coat of mail. Too soon one of the seafarers hindered him, wounded the earl in his arm. Then the gold-hilted sword fell to the earth: he might not hold the hard blade, wield his weapon. Yet he spoke words, the hoar battle-leader,[10] encouraged his men, bade them go forward stoutly together. He might no longer stand firm on his feet. He looked toward Heaven and spoke: "I thank thee, Ruler of Nations, for all the joys that I have had in the world. Now, gentle Lord, I have most need that thou grant my spirit grace, that my soul may travel to thee—under thy protection, Prince of Angels, depart in peace. I beseech thee that fiends of hell harm it not." Then the heathen warriors slew him and both the men who stood by him; Ælfnoth and Wulfmær both were laid low; close by their lord they gave up their lives.

Then there retired from the battle those who did not wish to be there. The sons of Odda were the first to flee: Godric went from the fight and left the good man that had given him many a steed. He leaped upon the horse that his lord had owned, upon trappings that he had no right to, and both his brothers galloped with him: Godwin and Godwig cared not for battle, but went from the war and sought the wood, fled to its fastness and saved their lives—and more men than was in any way right, if they remembered all the favors he had done for their benefit. So Offa had said to him that day at the meeting he had held in the place, that many there spoke boldly who would not remain firm at need.

The folk's leader had fallen, Æthelred's earl: all his hearth-companions saw that their lord lay dead. Then the proud thanes advanced; men without fear pressed eagerly on. They all desired either of two things, to leave life or avenge the man they loved. Thus Ælfric's son urged them on; the warrior young of winters spoke words; Ælfwine it was who spoke, and spoke boldly: "Remember the speeches we have spoken so often over our mead, when we raised boast on the bench, heroes in the hall, about hard fighting. Now may the man who is bold prove that he is. I will make my noble birth known to all, that I was of great kin in Mercia.[11] My grandfather was named Ealhelm, a wise

---

[10] To be a rich leader of men while in the prime of life was impressive enough; to maintain that position even in old age was evidence of even greater distinction.

[11] A large district in west-central England. In the eighth century it had been the most powerful of the several Anglo-Saxon kingdoms.

earl, worldly-prosperous. Thanes among that people shall not have reason to reproach me that I would go from this band of defenders, seek my home, now that my lord lies hewn down in battle. To me that is greatest of griefs: he was both my kinsman and my lord." Then he went forward, bent on revenge, and with the point of his spear pierced one of the pirate band, so that he lay on the earth, destroyed by the weapon. Then Ælfwine began to encourage his comrades, friends and companions, to go forward.

Offa spoke, shook his ash-spear: "Lo, thou, Ælfwine, hast encouraged us all, thanes in need. Now that our lord the earl lies on the earth, there is need for us all that each one of us encourage the other, warriors to battle, as long as he may have and hold weapon, hard sword, spear and good blade. The coward son of Odda, Godric, has betrayed us all; when he rode off on that horse, on that proud steed, many a man thought that he was our lord. Therefore here on the field folk were dispersed, the shield-wall broken. Curses on his action, by which he caused so many men here to flee."

Leofsunu spoke, raised the linden buckler, his shield to defend himself; he answered the warrior: "I promise that I will not flee a footstep hence, but I will go forward, avenge my dear lord in the fight. Steadfast warriors about Sturmer[12] need not reproach me with their words that now that my patron is dead I would go lordless home, abandon the battle. But weapon, point and iron, shall take me." Full wrathful he went forward, fought fiercely; flight he despised.

Then Dunnere spoke, shook his spear; humble churl,[13] he cried over all, bade each warrior avenge Birhtnoth: "He who intends to avenge his lord on the folk may not hesitate nor care for life." Then they advanced: they cared not for life. The retainers began to fight hardily, fierce spear-bearers, and prayed God that they might avenge their patron and bring destruction to their enemies.

The hostage[14] began to help them eagerly. He was of bold kin among the Northumbrians, the son of Ecglaf: his name was Æscferth. He did not flinch at the war-play, but threw spears without pause. Now he hit shield, now he pierced man: each moment he caused some wound, as long as he might wield weapons.

Eadweard the Long still stood in the line, ready and eager, spoke boasting words, how he would not flee a footstep nor turn back, now

---

[12] The Essex village where the speaker lived.
[13] See notes 1 and 8.
[14] Among Germanic peoples, hostages of high rank generally fought on the side of the warriors who held them hostage.

that his chief lay dead. He broke the shield-wall and fought against the foe until he had worthily avenged his treasure-giver on the seamen—before he himself lay on the slaughter-bed.

2. FEUDAL GUARANTEES OF SECURITY

The organization of local security remained a pressing problem even when Vikings ceased to challenge central governments. One solution was the development of feudalism, a complex set of arrangements affecting military service, landholding, personal relationships, and political authority. The homeland of classic European feudalism lay in those regions between the Rhine and the Loire which had been the core area of the Carolingian Empire; its classic period of development stretched from the late ninth to the early twelfth century.

Selection (a) illustrates some of the dangers inherent in the life of the ruling classes against which the creation of well-defined feudal bonds usually afforded protection. Richeldis, whom the chronicler Gilbert calls "a most prudent and powerful woman," was the widow of two counts. Her first husband, Herman I of Hainaut (1039–51), came from a great family which had treated the populous county of Hainaut as a hereditary possession since the 920's. They had extended its boundaries, established a regular seat of government in the castle they built at Mons, and successfully resisted the efforts of several German Emperors to reassert imperial authority. Her second husband, Baldwin I of Hainaut (1051–70) and VI of Flanders (1067–70), was a scion of the neighboring feudal dynasty founded in the last quarter of the ninth century, which had transformed a desolate stretch of coastal plain into an exceptionally rich county efficiently run from the fortress of Bruges. Richeldis' eldest son by Baldwin, Arnulf, was to inherit his father's ancestral Flanders; however, within seven months after his father's death, despite the full apparatus of feudal guarantees and the armed support of his liege lord and first cousin, King Philip I of France, the fifteen-year-old Arnulf had lost his patrimony to his paternal uncle Robert the Frisian and his life to a treacherous liege vassal named Gerobodo. In order to save Hainaut for her younger son, Baldwin II (who ruled it successfully until his death in 1098), Richeldis made it a fief of its second most powerful neighbor, the territorial principality which had grown up around the episcopal city of Liége. By getting several other neighboring lords to witness and approve this act, she achieved the effect of a non-aggression pact with the feudal "states" bordering Hainaut to the east and south, and so could concentrate on the threat of Flemish attack from the west and north. Fortunately for Richeldis and young Baldwin, the rapacious Robert was kept busy on *his* western frontiers by a plot to deprive his mighty brother-in-law, William the Conqueror, of the newly-acquired kingdom of England. The concluding section shows the sort of internal difficulties which feudal lords of such rank had constantly to face. No county could be defended without a network of strong castles, but many a count must have worried more about the nearly hereditary castellans commanding those castles than about his avowed enemies.

A native of Mons, Gilbert rose high in the service of Count Baldwin V of Hainaut (1168–95), acting as his notary, chaplain, chancellor, occasional ambassador, and as provost of Mons, Namur, and several churches and abbeys. After his patron's death, he combined documentary evidence with oral traditions in the compilation of an official chronicle of Hainaut from the mid-eleventh century to 1195. Although Baldwin VI fulfilled an old family ambition by ruling both Hainaut and Flanders (which he inherited from his mother), he did not return the chronicler of his dynasty's glory to high secular office. Too loyal to express any disappointment which he may have felt, Gilbert lived in honorable semi-retirement as provost and canon of St. Waudru and several other churches until his death in 1224.

Gilbert of Mons: *Chronicle of Hainaut*

From La Chronique de Gislebert de Mons, *ed. Léon Vanderkindere (Brussels: Riessling et Cie., 1904)* , *pp. 10–14, 35–36. Footnotes supplied.*

8. Let us return now to the Countess Richeldis, who built the castle of Beaumont[1] with its tower and other defenses, and established there a chapel in honor of St. Venantius, for which she provided quite a handsome endowment. This same countess, in concert with her son Baldwin, made hereditary the offices of the seneschals, butlers, bakers, cooks, chamberlains, and gatekeepers in her court, and conferred them on men of Hainaut and also on some Flemings who had left their goods in Flanders to follow their lady and her son into exile in Hainaut. Many others, both nobles and of servile condition, left Flanders in grief at their lord's spoliation of the countess and settled in Hainaut

[1] Twenty-five miles southeast of Mons, near the borders of Liége and Namur.

with her and her son, who bestowed respectable fiefs and holdings on them.

Mourning bitterly the death of her son Arnulf, and taking very ill the disinheriting of her surviving son, the Countess Richeldis offered all her allods[2] located in Hainaut to Theoduin,[3] Bishop of Liége, a powerful and neighboring prince, so as to get help from him in her vengeance against the aforesaid Robert, especially by getting money to hire mercenary soldiers. After holding a council of the church of Liége and of his vassals, both nobles and *ministeriales,*[4] Bishop Theoduin gratefully accepted those splendid allods, further distinguished by such a complimentary offer, and conferred them as liege[5] fiefs on Richeldis and her son Baldwin, adding a large sum of money besides. This purchase seriously drained the gold and silver in the treasuries of the conventual churches of the whole diocese of Liége. This transaction was passed and ratified at Fosse;[6] Godfrey, Duke of Bouillon,[7] Count Albert of Namur,[8] the Count of Louvain,[9] the Count of Cluny, the Count of Montaigu in the Ardenne, and many others, vassals of the church of Liége, both noble and of servile condition, served as witnesses. Bishop Theoduin, an adroit and powerful man, at that time enjoyed much favor and influence at the court of the Holy Roman Empire; through gifts and services rendered he arranged for the Emperor to confer on the Church of Liége all the fiefs which the Count of Hainaut held from the Emperor, such as the lay abbacy of Mons and the advocacy of its church, and the administration of justice in the county. Richeldis and her son Baldwin gave their consent and approval, and so came to hold all their former allods, dependents, and fiefs from the Bishop of Liége as their

[2] Land owned outright, without any subjection to a higher lord.

[3] Bishop 1048–75. The bishops of Liége had been counts of all their church's possessions since Bishop Notger (972–1008); their state would last until 1794.

[4] Serfs given positions (sometimes hereditary) of administrative or military importance, but without the free status usually accompanying them.

[5] Most vassals owed fealty to several lords. In case of conflict among his feudal superiors, the vassal was supposed to follow his *liege* lord rather than any other. The *liege fief* was the standard guarantee of such precedence.

[6] A castle in the bishop's territory.

[7] Titular Duke of Lower Lorraine (1069–76), the province of the Holy Roman Empire which contained all the feudal states involved in this agreement. Richeldis (but not Baldwin II) was a personal vassal of Godfrey, who acted as an intermediary between her (but not Baldwin II) and the Bishop of Liége. His nephews Godfrey and Baldwin were leaders of the First Crusade and the first Latin Kings of Jerusalem.

[8] Count 1064–1102; his domain lay between Hainaut and the greater part of Liége. His great-granddaughter Alix would marry Baldwin IV of Hainaut (1120–71); his great-great-grandson Rudolph would become bishop of Liége (1167–91).

[9] Henry II (1062–79), whose daughter Ida would soon marry Baldwin II. Louvain shared boundaries with Flanders, Hainaut, Namur, and Liége.

sole liege lord. Their successors did likewise. Excepted from this general homage, however, were the allods belonging to the church of Saint Waudru[10] in the castle of the town of Mons and in the villages of Quaregnon and Jemappes, Frameries and Quévy, Braine-la-Wilhote and Braine-le-Château, Hal, Castres, Hérinnes: Saint Waudru had kept them for herself during her lifetime, and left them in perpetuity to the church which she built at Mons, then known as Castrilocus. Also excepted were Cuesmes, Nimy, Ville-sur-Haine[11] and other property which had been given to that church afterwards.

9. In arranging the transfer of so many important allods and fiefs to the church of Liége, along with the liege homage of a person as great as the Count of Hainaut, the following stipulations were agreed upon. The Count of Hainaut owes his lord the Bishop of Liége aid and service in all things and against all men, with the full force of his men, both knights and foot soldiers; but once the Count leaves the County of Hainaut on such a mission, his expenses will be paid by the Bishop. If the lord Count comes to the lord Bishop to be invested with his lands, the lord Bishop owes him his expenses once he leaves the County of Hainaut. When the lord Bishop calls the Count of Hainaut to his court or to any conference, he owes him expenses similarly. If the lord Emperor of the Romans calls the Count of Hainaut to his court for any reason, the Bishop of Liége ought to bring him safely to court and back again, and support and answer for him at the court. If anyone should advance against the land of Hainaut to do evil, the Bishop of Liége should at his own cost match the army raised by the Count of Hainaut. If the Count of Hainaut should besiege any castle belonging to his fief, or be besieged himself in any such castle, the Bishop should assist him with five hundred men at his own cost, and the Count should provide him with a market for provisions at a fair price: if there is grass standing in the fields, or other fodder necessary for horses, the Bishop and his men may take it as they wish. The Bishop of Liége owes the Count of Hainaut this aid three times a year, for forty days on each occasion. Three castellans of Hainaut, to wit, those of Mons, Beaumont, and Valenciennes,[12] render homage to the Bishop of Liége along with the Count of Hainaut. At Christmas the Bishop of Liége owes the Count of Hainaut three suits of clothes, each garment being worth six

[10] A great Frankish lady who died about 688. Wife of St. Vincent Madelgarus and mother of four more saints, Waudru (or Waldetrudis) retired to a convent when her husband became a monk. Mons grew up around the two nuclei of her convent and the fortress of the later Counts of Hainaut.

[11] All these villages lay within a twenty-five mile radius of Mons.

[12] Twenty miles southwest of Mons; added to the county by Herman I.

marks of silver, Liége weight, and he also owes garments, each worth six marks, to each of the aforementioned castellans. Should any allod in the county of Hainaut be given the Count, and then given back by him as a fief, or should he acquire within the boundaries of his county any allod, or any serfs or servingwomen, he shall from the moment of acquisition hold them as part of his fief from the Bishop of Liége. And although very many men of high rank, such as dukes and barons and counts, along with other nobles and the men of their peace,[13] have to answer and give satisfaction to the judicial authority of Liége, the counts of Hainaut and the men of their peace are in no way answerable to that justice. . . .

*　　*　　*

21. While Baldwin[14] was ruling in Hainaut, a certain nobleman named Goswin, a native of Oisy in the region of Cambrai and a peer of the castle of Mons, was given by him a great deal of property in the territory of Avesnes[15] and in many other places in Hainaut; wherefore he did liege homage to the Count, owing him uninterrupted garrison duty at the castle of Mons for all he had received. But violating the fealty which he had sworn, he began to build a tower in Avesnes in defiance of the rights of his liege lord the Count of Hainaut and despite his explicit prohibitions. His lord warned him that he had better appear in his court to account for his actions, but he declined to do so, and so the Count took up arms against him. Goswin had the temerity to face him at the river Sambre[16] with all the force he could gather. There was bitter fighting there for two days; on the third day the Count vindicated his rights by winning the victory, and led Goswin back to Mons with him in captivity. But yielding to the petitions of the noblemen who were his vassals, the Count let Goswin return home after shaving off his beard.[17] Later, having won his lord's favor again, Goswin completed his tower in Avesnes, the strength of which was more than once thereafter to be a nuisance to the Counts of Hainaut.

[13] The law codes promulgated by many Lowland counties were called *peaces;* that of Liége was established in 1082.

[14] Actually Baldwin III (1098–1120).

[15] Goswin (died 1127) inherited the barony of Avesnes (25 miles due south of Mons) and with it a place among the twelve Peers of Mons from his maternal uncle in 1105.

[16] About halfway between Mons and Avesnes.

[17] At that time a striking symbol of humiliation. Clerics shaved their faces and tonsured their heads to symbolize their renunciation of secular values.

Internal Subdivisions

3. THE PROBLEMS OF AN EXTENDED FAMILY

Medieval men used terms like "noble" or "gentle" to describe a wide range of persons and families, from dynasts of the blood royal to obscure country gentlemen barely holding out on the frontiers of starvation. The nobility was anything but a homogeneous class. Modern students often find it difficult to understand how people of such diverse fortune could have been assigned by their contemporaries to the same general social category. The explanation probably lies in the medieval notion of a family unit, which extended much farther both lineally and laterally than does ours. The earlier centuries of the Middle Ages provided an ideal environment for the functioning of clanlike groups which came to include practically everyone of importance in a given region, linking them by ties of blood, marriage, and roughly comparable modes of life. This traditional pattern was subjected to severe strains by the economic evolution and increased pace of social and political mobility which in the eleventh century began to alter many aspects of European life. The social conscience of the nobility was intensely conservative, however, and even the most inconvenient of the old ways died hard. The following selection shows both the pressures produced by the new order, with its increasingly individual definition of private property, and the stubbornness of the ancient habits. Particularly striking is the legal topic in the discussion of which this passage occurs. *Compaignie* was a type of association with heavy legal consequences, which could be established by birth, marriage, the formation of a chartered society, economic partnership, and the act of sale, as well as by the ratification of kinship by common sustenance, which is the issue here. For this rich and diffuse term the word *company* is obviously a poor translation, but no genuine equivalent is still current in our vocabulary.

The source of the passage is a treatise on the customary law of the Beauvais district, composed by Philippe de Remi, Lord of Beaumanoir (1250?–96), a knight from the Ile-de-France who was a competent poet and high royal official as well as one of the greatest legal commentators of the Middle Ages. His family ranked among the notables of the region between Campiègne and

Noyon at least since the middle of the twelfth century, and a close relative had fought with distinction at the battle of Bouvines (1214), in which King Philip Augustus led an army of faithful vassals to a dramatic and decisive victory against the combined forces of the German Emperor, the King of England, and the Count of Flanders. Philippe's father became a *bailli* (royal agent of the first rank) in the service of St. Louis; in 1256, he was given the noble fief of Beaumanoir, named for a hamlet near the small market town of Remi, from which his family had derived its name. Philippe spent several boyhood years in England as a page, was knighted probably soon after his return to France, and spent the years of his youth and early manhood composing several courtly romances and lighter types of verse, as well as acquiring wide knowledge of Roman and of several varieties of customary law. From 1279 until his death he served Kings Philip III (1270–85) and IV (1285–1314) as *bailli* of six prosperous districts, and on one occasion as ambassador to the pope. For all the sophistication of his experience, he was distinctly a product of his ancestral *pays*. The neighboring county of Clermont-en-Beauvaisis was his first administrative post and the occasion for his famous treatise, and the nobility of his homeland provided him with the central themes of his literary efforts as well as with a wife, Mabile de Boves (see I, 2[b]).

Philippe de Beaumanoir: *Customs of the Beauvais District, Chapter 21*

From Philippe de Beaumanoir, Coûtumes du Beauvaisis, *ed. Beugnot (Paris: Jules Renouard et Cie., 1842), I, 305–9.*

5. The fourth way in which company is established is the most perilous and the one in which I have seen most men deceived. For company can be established, according to our customs, simply by dwelling together, from one bread and one pot, for a year and a day, after which the movable property of both parties involved is considered as one. Because of this we have seen many rich and powerful men take in their nephews and their nieces or some other of their poor kinsmen out of kindness, and if the latter chance to have any movable property they brought it to the former to take care of and as a guarantee to the one who admitted them to company in good faith; nevertheless, they contributed so few goods to those who took them into their household,

that no company was established after they had been there a year and a day.

We have also seen a case in which a man who did not bring to the company the value of 40 pence and was not there more than two years and did not contribute to anything, who was there simply because of a kind uncle's offer of support, demanded a partition of property on the basis of company, and was awarded in a judgment more than the value of 200 pounds. From that judgment you can see what peril there is in receiving such company. In order to protect oneself from being deceived in like manner, and so as not to have to abandon, because of this sort of suspicion, the good deed of calling one's poor kinsmen around one, we will tell how one can do it without peril.

6. Whoever wishes out of kindness to have his poor kinsman reside with him, in such a way that company will not be established, should take in only his person, without combining anything that he may possess with his own property. And if the kinsman is under age, he should make a public appearance with him before the lord under whose authority he resides, in the presence of two or three of the minor's closest relatives, and say: "Sir, I have invited this child to stay with me for God's sake, and I wish you to know that I do not wish for him to be able to demand anything from me by reason of company, because I have taken him in. I do not wish to combine what little he has with my property, unless it be in such a way that his property may be in your wardship or that of his friends, to the value of a certain sum of money; and that sum of money I shall be held accountable either to hand over to him or to invest to his profit." Whoever does it in this manner is safe from any danger in company.

7. [Agreement to pay a fixed sum—however nominal—for one's expenses has the same effect.]

8. The fifth way in which company can be established, as long as the parties are commoners, is this: when a man or a woman marries two or three times, and there are children of each marriage, and the children of the first marriage reside with their step-parent without making a partition and without a firm agreement concerning possessions. In such a case they can gain and lose along with their father and their stepmother, or with their mother and stepfather. And when the children wish to make partition, they take all the inheritance which comes to them from their dead father or mother, as well as a third of the acquisitions and the movable property gained while the company lasted.

9. This company of which we have spoken above, which can be estab-

lished according to custom among commoners, has no effect among gentlemen. In their case when the children of the first or second marriage reside with their father or mother and their stepfather or stepmother, their association is called not company, but *wardship;* and according to custom this wardship ceases when the child reaches his majority and wishes to take away with him the inheritance of his dead father or mother. . . . And if there was movable property at the time that their father or mother died, they should take half of it; and if there were more debts than movable property, and the father or mother has paid them during the period of wardship, the children are not held to any compensation therefor: for it is licit and fitting for the father or mother during wardship to disencumber their children's succession from the other parent, but not to charge it with debt.

10. When gentlemen or gentlewomen hold their children in wardship after the death of the other parent, and their inheritance includes manorial holdings from the succession of the dead parent, all the profit and all the income from the manor should be kept for the children so that they can have the profit therefrom when they come of age. No one may by reason of wardship or of bail make his own the produce of the manors which belong to the children for whom he is responsible: that is, this applies to gentlemen, for among commoners the income from manorial holdings can belong to any established company as long as it lasts.

4. THE JUVENILE PROBLEM

One consequence of feudal tenure was to make a large family inconvenient. Even great lords hesitated to disperse their collection of fiefs by leaving shares of even roughly equal size to several of their children; noble families of modest estate were reduced to near penury by such a practice, standard in ancient as well as modern law. Most lords tried to prevent vassals from diminishing their fiefs in this fashion, since a fief too poor to support a well-equipped warrior on extended campaigns was no use to any of its lords. On the other hand, intentional limitation of legitimate progeny was an invitation to disaster in that age of constant military risk—especially for the class whose normal profession was warfare. Most noblemen seem to have felt that too many heirs were better than none.

One compromise adjustment was primogeniture, selection of the eldest son (or daughter, if no sons survived) as the privileged recipient of the greater part of his parents' landed property; younger children could be compensated by bequests consisting primarily of movable wealth. Primogeniture was no panacea, however; in some ways it created new inheritance problems. The foremost of these was impatience on the part of the designated prime heir. The average nobleman married fairly young, and so had a full-grown eldest son to provide for and get along with while still in his own vigorous maturity, with many years of potential ruling ahead of him. The nature and conventions of feudal tenure made it much more difficult for a noble to associate his son with his fief's management than for a bourgeois father to take his son—or indeed, sons and sons-in-law—"into the company." The son might claim his mother's dowry if she had died (childbearing then was probably as hazardous as bearing arms), but even that transfer could cause tensions. The eldest son had to have the wherewithal to maintain his contacts in the world of noble affairs, if only so as to be a well-connected and respected successor to his father when the right time came. Besides, some provision still had to be made for younger sons.

In order to satisfy these divergent requirements, the European nobility developed in the twelfth century a special pattern of behavior for its post-adolescent males. For the noble of sufficient means, "youth" extended from knighthood to marriage, from his late teens or early twenties possibly into his forties, by which age he would be ready and able (if not desperate) to settle down. If he were an eldest surviving son, his inheritance awaited him; if younger, he would presumably have had ample opportunity to win his own support, whether from a well-endowed wife, a generous lord, or a conquered fief. In the meantime he had to be kept busy and amused, preferably away from home.

This was the environment in which tournaments arose and flourished, along with the romantic literature which idealized the knight-errant in search of adventure, a lady, and his own identity. It is hardly necessary to add that these roving *juvenes,* or "bachelors" (only later did the latter word come to designate any unmarried adult), made a major contribution to crusade recruitment and domestic war, the cult of manners fostered in many lordly courts, the support of professional entertainers of both sexes and several talents, and the sermons of elder moralists whose interest in the relative stability of their social order kept encouraging the behavior they deplored. Some youths did their jousting in Latin, and won their accreditation as bachelors or better in the cathedral schools and universities that multiplied contentiously across the face of Europe, typically visiting several of them before entering the service of a prince or subsiding into the medieval equivalent of academic tenure. Certain features of this mode of life should not appear excessively unfamiliar to twentieth-century youth.

The following account of one typical pack of noble youths comes from the *History of the Counts of Guines* composed between 1194 and 1205 by a hereditary priest of Ardres named Lambert. The County of Guines, subject to the princely County of Flanders to its north, was a wedge of territory stretching about thirty miles inland from the Strait of Dover, between Calais and Boulogne. From the 980's to 1282 it was ruled by one vigorous family, with which Lambert was connected by marriage. He was on intimate though not always friendly terms with the eighth and ninth Counts, Baldwin II (1140?–1205) and Arnold II (1160?–1220). Lambert's Latin style is a strange blend of erudition and crudity, pomposity and directness, and his interests were unabashedly provincial, but the delight with which he narrated and commented upon the deeds and misdeeds of his patrons and their kinsmen more than compensates for those historiographic defects.

Lambert of Ardres: *History of the Counts of Guines*

From Chronique de Lambert d'Ardre, *ed. Godefroy Menilglaise (Paris: Jules Renouard & Cie., 1855), 198–207, 214–19, 362–65; also ed. I. Heller, in MGH, Scriptores, XXIV (Hannover: Hahn, 1879), 603–5, 607, 637. Footnotes supplied.*

90. Now I direct my tale and turn my pen to Arnold, the eldest son of Count Baldwin.[1] Arnold spent the years of his boyhood in his homeland with his father. When he began to grow to manly strength and to frequent jousts and tournaments here and there, his father sent him to that venerable and memorable prince, Count Philip of Flanders,[2] to learn manners and get introduced to the exercise of the military pro-

[1] Lambert calls Arnold Baldwin's *primogenitus*, which can mean either "first-born" or "eldest surviving." Arnold had at least 2 brothers and 3 sisters from Baldwin's sole marriage to Christiane of Ardres (see note 8), besides some two dozen illegitimate half-brothers and -sisters. Lambert insists that Baldwin made some sort of decent provision for all of his illegitimate children. Another chronicler reports that 33 of Baldwin's children attended his funeral in 1205.

[2] Philip of Alsace, who ruled Flanders 1168–91. He maintained a lavish and literate court, famed throughout Europe. He was Baldwin of Guines' immediate feudal lord: the County of Guines had been created by a Count of Flanders in the late tenth century, and Baldwin had done homage for it to Philip's father Thierry. Arnold's ancestry included several Counts of Flanders and many nobles who had served them as Counts of Boulogne and St. Pol and castellans of Ghent, St. Omer, and other key locations.

fession. At his court Arnold came to be reputed first among the foremost youths of the nobility of Flanders. Although he had not yet received the accolade[3] of knighthood, he showed himself to be agile in arms, outstanding for feats of prowess, brilliant in courtly repartee, swift in obedient service, in generosity I might almost say prodigal; he always wore a happy expression, but at the same time he bore himself more decorously than any of his contemporaries, and was so modest and affable toward everyone, that all men said he was gracious in every way, as indeed he was. After a few years had passed in this fashion, his age and his promise of future prowess called for his enrollment with due ritual as a knight. Although the most revered lord Philip, Flanders' predominant glory, wished to make him a knight and to do him that honor at his own expense and with his own arms,[4] Arnold wished to please his father in all things and in every way, reserving for him the first honors of his knighthood, so he prudently took leave of the Count on the best of terms, and hastened away to his father and his own homeland of Guines, accompanied by his good friend Eustace of Salperwick.

91. Count Baldwin his father showed by the most evident signs how much joy he felt at his son's return. He assembled his sons and his friends and acquaintances in his court at Guines on the holy day of Pentecost, in the year 1181 of the Incarnation of the Lord, and gave his son the knightly accolade[5] and initiated him to full manhood with the appropriate ritual. He also conferred the honor of knighthood, with all its instruments, expenses, and ceremonies, on Eustace of Salperwick, Simon of Nielles, Eustace of Ausque, and Wallon of Preures.[6]

---

[3] A ritual blow on the cheek, administered by the conferring knight as a sign of the new knight's need to withstand real blows. This seems to be a conscious imitation of the blow given by the bishop to the mature Christian in the sacrament of Confirmation, which admitted the candidate to full Christian citizenship as a "soldier of Christ."

[4] The conferrer of knighthood often gave the aspirant to that order a sword, a horse, armor, or other appropriate equipment, all of which was very expensive. Besides those basic costs one had to figure the cost of the feasting which ideally accompanied knighting.

[5] Pentecost (May 24 in 1181) was the traditional date for formal knightings, as well as other courtly business. Readers of Arthurian romances will remember how many memorable quests either begin or end at one of King Arthur's Pentecost courts; see also III, 10. Baldwin himself had been knighted by Thomas à Becket, then Chancellor of England, in 1155; his family had held fiefs in England since the days of William the Conqueror.

[6] All of these young gentlemen knighted with Arnold came from fiefs within 20 miles of Ardres, which was only 7 miles east of Guines. Salperwick, 12 miles east of Ardres, lay within the castellany of St. Omer, and Preures (20 miles south) lay in the County of Boulogne; Nielles and Ausque were 2½ and 5 miles southeast of Ardres, safely within its territory.

That solemn festive day, a day of timeless joy, they spent amidst the most lavish and delicious food and drink and every form of delight to which expression could be given. Arnold had barely been attired in his knightly garments when he leapt into the midst of the crowd, and to minstrels and mimes and good-for-nothings and valets and jesters and jongleurs and indeed to anyone who called his name, he distributed his bounty so satisfactorily that he won their swift praise and gratitude in return. For he gave whatever he had or was able to acquire with a liberality bordering on dissipation, as though he were standing among naked and pure intellects from the first pages of Porphyry;[7] bestowing great gifts and little, his own property as well as what he was provided with by his own people and what he could purchase from others, he barely left himself his own person. On the following day he was received in the church at Ardres in a procession, to the ringing of bells, the voices of monks and clerics singing *"Summae Trinitati honor et virtus"* joyously to God in his honor, and the vociferous exultation of the common people as well.

For nearly two years from that day, Arnold frequented tournaments throughout many provinces and regions, not without the fostering aid of his father; and Eustace of Salperwick was his inseparable companion.

92. Much against his father's will, Arnold began to listen to the advice of Philip of Mongardin, who persistently urged him to demand from his father the town of Ardres and all that came to him from his mother. Finally, after many speeches, days, and conferences, it was accomplished. After Arnold had received Ardres and Colvède with some (though not all) of their appurtenances,[8] he was reconciled with his father through the latter's continuing affection; at his advice and that of Count Philip of Flanders, Arnold took as his counselor in tournament and in expenditure—in effect, his tutor and mentor—Arnold of

---

[7] Lambert parades his erudition by this reference to the treatise *On Abstinence* of the third-century Greek philosopher Porphyry, of which he might have read in the works of Boethius (among others).

[8] Arnold's mother Christiane was the daughter of Arnold IV of Ardres, who was Viscount of Merck (the chief territorial fief to the north of Guines, containing the port of Calais) and vassal for some of his estates to Baldwin of Guines. Baldwin considered this marriage to his vassal's daughter no step downward, since she brought as her dowry the fortified town of Ardres and the castle of Colvède (or Colewide), equidistant from Ardres and Guines, the construction of which had been a favorite project of Arnold of Ardres. Christiane had died in 1177. Philip of Mongardin belonged to a family which had a castle 11 miles southwest of Ardres (5 miles southwest of Colvède) in the Forest of Licques; one of his close relatives, Christiane of Mongardin, married Arnold of Guines' brother Giles, who became a knight after pursuing a formal education.

Caieu,[9] a nobleman skilled in arms and prudent and discreet in counsel. But since Arnold of Caieu was unable to be at his side uninterruptedly, he recommended to him as instructor in arms a nephew of exceptional military achievement, who had previously been a companion-in-arms to Henry, the Young King of England.[10] After a few days, without consulting his father and brothers, Arnold conferred Herbinghem near Licques on his counselor's nephew as a fief in perpetuity.[11] Eustace of Salperwick and Hugh of Malnis remained his inseparable friends and companions-in-arms, but then they were joined by Henry the son of Henry of Campagne,[12] and all the tourneying knights of the land of Guines flowed to Arnold as to their lord and head. He extended the hand of liberality to all of them as far as he could and beyond, and led them back and forth from one tournament to another. But when he was at home Philip of Mongardin kept in close touch with him, and by wit and pleasantries prompted him to moral enterprise.

93. When, as we have related, Arnold of Guines had been commended by his father to the guardianship and care of Arnold of Caieu, and had as household companions Eustace Rasoir, Eustace of Salperwick, and Hugh of Malnis, and also Henry of Campagne and many other noble and illustrious knights, he preferred to go adventuring in foreign parts out of eagerness for the glory to be gained in tournaments: rather than remain at ease in his homeland, he chose to live so as to gain worldly honor.

Arnold of Guines' reputation for heroic prowess spread so widely

[9] He came from a knightly family long important in the County of Boulogne, and married Adelis of Balinghem, a third cousin of Arnold's who was related to him through an illegitimate daughter of Manasses, 5th Count of Guines. Balinghem was a castle 5 miles west of Ardres.

[10] Henry Curtmantle, 1155–83, son of Henry II of England and Eleanor of Aquitaine. His father wanted him designated king quite early, to obviate the succession disputes which had beset the English monarchy for several generations. The young Henry was crowned twice, in 1170 and 1172 (the second time along with his wife Margaret, daughter of Louis VII of France). Despite his father's generous allowance and continuing affection, contrary to the wise counsel of William Marshal, an older bachelor of proud but modest Norman family, the Young King kept trying to seize direct rule of his immense inheritance on the Continent. He died 6 years before his father, leaving Richard the Lion-Heart as next in line, to the elder Henry's intense grief.

[11] The nephew's name was Eustace Rasoir; Herbinghem is 20 miles south of Ardres, on the other side of the Forest of Licques.

[12] Hugh may have come from Moulle, 10 miles southeast of Ardres, quite close to St. Omer. The elder Henry of Campagne was lord of a sizeable fief to the northwest of Colvède; his brother (the younger Henry's uncle) was a valiant but evil-tempered knight in the following of Philip of Flanders.

that it came to the attentive notice of Ida, Countess of Boulogne. She was the daughter of Count Matthew of Boulogne, and at his death took up the title and dignity of Countess. She had been betrothed previously, on the advice of her uncle the venerable Count Philip of Flanders, to Count Gerard of Gelders and then to Duke Berthold of Zähringen; but for a variety of reasons she had been deprived of both in a troubled time,[13] and so left without a man, she indulged herself in worldly delights and the pleasures of the body. She fell passionately in love with Arnold of Guines, and tried as hard as she could to seduce him; or rather, with typical feminine fickleness and deception she feigned that emotion. Emissaries and secret tokens passed back and forth between them as indications of certain love. Arnold either loved her or with masculine foresight and prudence pretended to; for he aspired to the land and dignity of the County of Boulogne once he could gain the Countess' favor through love feigned or true.

[Arnold was cheated of his prize by Renault of Dammartin, who abducted Ida to Lorraine. When Ida sent Arnold rather ambiguous— and, as it turned out, completely misleading—messages of enduring love, Arnold rode to her rescue, only to be imprisoned by Renault's allies in Verdun. After a short confinement he was released through the intervention of Archbishop William of Reims. Renault became Count of Boulogne in due order. This embroilment all seems to have occurred in 1190.]

96. After Arnold of Guines had come to himself and come to understand the depths of feminine weakness and inconstancy, he left the confines of Verdun and returned to his fatherland. He was reconciled to his father and his father's wishes in all things, except that he was said to have more companions-in-arms than his father had, incurred more lavish expenses than his resources permitted, and persisted in greater generosity than his father's counsel urged and requested. He still frequented tournaments wherever he could, in the company of his fellows whom he honored with admirable affection. When he returned home from these tournaments he would reside sometimes at Colvède,

[13] Ida was the daughter of Matthew of Alsace, brother of Count Philip of Flanders, and of Marie, heiress of Boulogne. Matthew died in 1173. Ida married Gerard III of Gelders (whose county lay to the north of Flanders) in 1181; shortly after his death in 1183, she married Berthold IV of Zähringen (whose lands lay east of the Rhine, near Alsace)—he died in 1186. Lambert's vagueness about these two marriages (not mere betrothals) is hard to explain. The County of Boulogne was the southern neighbor of that of Guines, and more than twice its size: its acquisition would have been a terrific coup for Arnold, and his failure began a quarter-century of border incidents and insults.

but more frequently at Ardres. There he indulged in jests and games with his knights and household companions, as his youthfulness demanded. He loved to hold conversations with his young contemporaries, but he also respected and kept around him old and decrepit gentlemen who could recount the adventures and fables and histories of olden times, and weave a thread of moral lessons through their tales. Therefore he kept in his household and willingly listened to Robert of Coutances,[14] a veteran knight who stroked his ears with instructive stories of the Roman emperors and Charlemagne and Roland and Oliver, and Arthur King of Britain. Philip of Mongardin contributed to his ears' delight the story of deeds done in the land of Jerusalem and at the siege of Antioch, among the Arabs and the Babylonians in the regions overseas. Arnold's kinsman Walter of l'Ecluse[15] taught him the fables of the English, about Gormond and Ysembard, Tristan and Isolde, Merlin and Merculf, and also the history of the lords of Ardres and of the town's beginnings, since it was the account of their common origin.

On one occasion, about the time that he was betrothed to Eustacia, daughter of Hugh Campdavaine, Count of St. Pol,[16] Arnold was kept indoors at Ardres with his knights and household campanions for two days and a night. The winter rains swole incessantly, the winds let loose in the heavens struggled against the clouds, blew everywhere on high and wandered over the earth in whistling gusts. Arnold had been hearing a great deal about the Roman emperors and Arthur from Robert of Coutances, and more about Jerusalem and Antioch from Philip of Mongardin, when at last Walter of l'Ecluse responded to our request to recite and explain the deeds of the men of Ardres. The rain did not cease, but the fury of the winds abated as though gentled for our hearing's sake. Walter sat before us all; putting his right hand to his beard and combing and twisting it back and forth with his fingers as old men often do, he began to speak:

[Here follows a long narrative, beginning with the earliest recollections of Arnold's mother's family in the late tenth century.]

---

[14] A native of western Normandy, a region famed for hardy younger sons who sought their fortunes elsewhere.

[15] Walter's mother Adele was the daughter of a canon named Ralph, who was an illegitimate son of Arnold's great-great-grandfather, Arnold I of Ardres. His repertory included some of the most fashionable stories of the time; the great poet Chrétien de Troyes dedicated his *Tristan and Isolde* to Philip of Flanders.

[16] She was the second daughter of Hugh IV of St. Pol. Her elder sister Elizabeth married Gaucher of Châtillon, who inherited the County through her. St. Pol is about 40 miles south of Ardres, beyond the County of Boulogne and the castellany of St. Omer.

149. About four years later [1194], the noble youth Henry, only son and heir of the deceased Walter, most noble castellan of Bourbourg,[17] died around the feast of St. Michael without any heir of his own—he had barely attained youthful age—and was buried with full solemnity in the church of St. Mary at Bourbourg. Arnold of Guines abandoned his betrothal to Eustacia the daughter of Hugh Campdavaine, Count of St. Pol, and left her behind. At the advice of his father Count Baldwin of Guines (who was still alive and in good health), and with the assistance of the noble Advocate William of Béthune and his brothers Conon, Count Baldwin of Aumale, John, later the venerable bishop of Cambrai,[18] and last but not least, Henry of Bailleul who was then in command of the castellany of Bourbourg, Arnold married and joined to himself in lawful wedlock the sister of the most noble youth Henry, castellan of Bourbourg, who had just died and been buried. She was a young lady of the most vigorous nobility, a maiden of the most noble stock and lineage, very learned in the liberal arts, renowned for her behavior and style of life beyond the requirements of her tender years, envied for the exceptional beauty of her figure which was more outstanding than that of Cassandra or of Helen, comparable to Minerva in every variety of wisdom, equal to Juno in resources, and the sole legitimate heiress to the castellany and title of Bourbourg. Consent was obtained from those venerable rulers of Holy Mother the Church, Archbishop William of Reims and Bishop Lambert of Thérouanne; Arnold granted her as dowry Ardres and Colvède with all their appurtenances.[19]

[17] The castellany of Bourbourg, almost as large as the County of Guines, touched the northeastern borders of Ardres, and included the prosperous port of Gravelines on the North Sea. The castle of Bourbourg itself (like that of Guines) lay about 8 miles in from the coast, and about 14 miles northeast of Ardres. Walter was the seventh son of Henry I of Bourbourg, but outlasted his brothers. He married Mathilda of Béthune, whose father was Advocate of that ecclesiastical fief forty miles to the southeast.

[18] These gentlemen are all maternal uncles of Henry and his sister Beatrice. William the Red became Advocate of Béthune in that very year. Conon of Béthune was one of the most famous poets connected with the brilliant court of Champagne, went on the Fourth Crusade in 1204, and became a dominant figure in the Latin Empire of Constantinople, ruled largely by noblemen from Flanders and Champagne. Baldwin married the widowed Countess of Aumale. John, after having been named dean of the cathedral of York, became Bishop of Cambrai in 1200. Henry of Bailleul was related to Henry and Beatrice on their father's side; his family ruled a town about 15 miles north of Béthune.

[19] Dowries were given as security by both partners to a marriage, not simply by (or for) the wife. Beatrice, who for all her superlative achievements is not named in this paragraph, was educated by the nuns at Bourbourg.

5. MARRIAGE: REPUDIATION OF THE CID'S DAUGHTERS

The institution of marriage helped define differences of rank within the nobility in two ways: a successful marriage marked with unique vividness the advance of a man or family on the rise; on the other hand, the difficulties attending such an achievement emphasized disparity of status more forcefully than anything else. Rodrigo Díaz (1043?–99), Lord of Vivar, belonged to the middle gentry of Old Castile. He won his heroic epithets, *El Cid* (from the Arabic for *lord*) and *Campeador* (Spanish for *champion warrior*), in the course of a career which brought him several positions of near-royal authority and the greatest fame of any man in Christian Spain. With his conquest of the Moorish kingdom of Valencia in 1089, wealth joined his other assets. Impressed by his new opulence as well as by his stubborn and punctilious loyalty despite mistreatment, King Alfonso VI of Castile and León (1065–1109) removed the sentence of banishment which he had imposed upon Rodrigo, and restored him to all the privileges of royal vassalage. As a sign of his renewed favor, Alfonso arranged a marriage between Rodrigo's two beloved daughters and two scions of the Beni-Gómez clan, which had dominated the valley of the river Carrión in the kingdom of León for at least seven generations. The relationship was tense, since several members of that arrogant family had resented the Cid's rise to prominence and had used their great influence with Alfonso to effect his exile.

The following selection from the *Poem of My Cid,* an anonymous Castilian epic composed about 1140, recounts the collapse of this marriage-sealed reconciliation. The poet tells at length how the Cid's two spendthrift sons-in-law, while in Valencia for their wedding, showed their cowardice by avoiding combat with the Moors and fleeing in terror when a lion which the Cid could control broke loose from its cage. Unable to bear their shame and plotting ignoble revenge, they set out on the long journey to Carrión with their wives, who were accompanied by much movable wealth but only one kinsman. After the fortunate miscarriage of the Heirs' vengeance, the Cid exacted his by getting a judgment from their mutual lord, Alfonso: the Heirs returned all the dowry, paid heavy fines for which they could barely raise the money, and were defeated in public combat by Rodrigo's champions, one of whom was the girls' first cousin, Pedro Bermúdez.

The daughters' second marriages were far grander than their first: one became the wife of Ramón Berenguer the Great, Count of Barcelona (1096–1131); the other married Ramiro of Monzón, nephew of the king of Navarre—through their son, García Ramírez the Restorer (King of Navarre 1134–50), the blood of the Cid gradually flowed into the veins of all the major royal dynasties of Europe.

The poet's account of these events is naturally heightened for literary effect. Nevertheless, almost all the characters and major events of his narrative are historically verifiable, and his social sentiments seem to be entirely in accord with the conventional reactions of his audience.

Poem of the Cid, Cantar Three

From Poem of the Cid, trans. W. S. Merwin, in Medieval Epics (New York: Random House, Inc., 1963), pp. 559–67. Copyright © 1959 by W. S. Merwin. Reprinted by permission of Harold Ober Associates Inc. Footnotes supplied.

128. The Heirs have entered   the oak wood of Corpes;
the mountains are high,   the branches touch the clouds
and there are savage beasts   which walk about there.
They found a glade   with a clear spring.
The Heirs of Carrión   bade their men set up the tent;
there they spend the night   with as many as are with them,
with their wives in their arms,   showing them love;
yet they meant to do them evil   when the sun rose!
They had the beasts of burden   loaded with their riches,
and they have taken down the tent   where they spent the night,
and those who waited on them   have all ridden ahead
as they were ordered to do   by the Heirs of Carrión,
so that none remained behind,   neither man nor woman,
except both their wives,   Doña Elvira and Doña Sol.
They wished to amuse themselves with these   to the height of their pleasure.
All had gone ahead,   only these four remained;
the Heirs of Carrión   had conceived great villainy:
"Know this for a certainty,   Doña Elvira and Doña Sol,
you will be tormented here   in these savage mountains.
Today we shall desert you   and go on from this place;
You will have no share   in the lands of Carrión.
The news of this will go   to the Cid Campeador,
and we shall be avenged   for the story of the lion."
Then they stripped them   of their cloaks and furs;

they left nothing on their bodies   but their shirts and silk undergarments.
The wicked traitors   have spurs on their boots;
they take in their hands   the strong hard saddle girths.
When the ladies saw this,   Doña Sol said:
"You have two swords,   strong and keen edged,
one that is called Colada   and the other Tizón.[1]
For God's sake, we beg you,   Don Diego and Don Fernando,
cut off our heads   and we shall be martyrs.
Moors and Christians   will speak harshly of this,
for such treatment   we have not deserved.
Do not visit upon us   so vile an ensample;
if you whip us   the shame will be yours;
you will be called to account   at assemblies or courts."
The ladies' pleadings   availed them nothing.
Then the Heirs of Carrión   began to lash them;
they beat them without mercy   with the flying cinches,
gored them with the sharp spurs,   dealing them great pain.
They tore their shirts   and the flesh of both of them,
and over the silken cloth   the clean blood ran,
and they felt the pain   in their very hearts.
Oh, it would be such good fortune   if it should please the Creator
that the Cid Campeador   might appear now!
They beat them so cruelly,   they left them senseless;
the shirts and the silk skirts   were covered with blood.
They beat them   until their arms were tired,
each of them trying   to strike harder than the other.
Doña Elvira and Doña Sol   could no longer speak;
they left them for dead   in the oak grove of Corpes.

*   *   *

130. The Heirs of Carrión   left them there for dead,
so that neither   might give aid to the other.
Through the mountains where they went   they praised themselves:
"Now we have avenged ourselves   for our marriage.
We would not have them for concubines   even if they begged us.
As legitimate wives   they were unworthy of us;
the dishonor of the lion   thus will be avenged."
131. The Heirs of Carrión   rode on, praising themselves.
But I shall tell you   of that same Félix Muñoz—

[1] Perhaps the most prestigious items in the dowry; according to the poet, each was worth "more than a thousand marks." The Cid had won Colada in personal combat from Count Ramón Berenguer II of Barcelona, who was attacking Valencia, in 1090. He won Tizón in 1094 from Abu Bekr, commander of the army sent against Valencia by the Almoravid Sultan Yusuf ibn-Tashfin. See I, 10(b).

he was a nephew   of the Cid Campeador—
they had bidden him ride forward   but this was not to his liking.
On the road as he went   his heart was heavy;
he slipped to one side   apart from the others;
he hid himself   in a thick wood,
waiting for his cousins   to come by
or to see what they had done,   those Heirs of Carrión.
He saw them come   and heard something of their talk;
they did not see him there   nor suspect that he heard them;
he knew well that if they saw him   they would not leave him alive.
　The Heirs set spur   and ride on.
Félix Muñoz   turned back the way they had come;
he found his cousins   both lying senseless.
He called, "Cousins, cousins!" Then he dismounted,
tied his horse   and went up to them.
"Cousins, my cousins,   Doña Elvira and Doña Sol,
they have vilely proved themselves,   the Heirs of Carrión!
May it please God   that their punishment find them!"
He stayed there   endeavoring to revive them.
Their senses had gone far from them;   they could not speak at all.
The fabrics of his heart   tear as he calls:
"Cousins, my cousins,   Doña Elvira and Doña Sol,
come awake, cousins,   for the love of the Creator!
Wake now while the day lasts   before the night comes
and the wild beasts   devour us on this mountain!"
Doña Elvira and Doña Sol   come back to themselves;
they opened their eyes   and saw Félix Muñoz.
"Quickly, cousins,   for the love of the Creator!
the Heirs of Carrión   when they miss me
will come looking for me   at full speed;
if God does not aid us   we shall die here."
Then with great pain   Doña Sol spoke:
"If our father the Campeador   deserves it of you, my cousin,
give us a little water,   for the love of the Creator."
Then with his hat,   which was new, with its sheen still on it,
which he had brought from Valencia,   Féliz Muñoz
took up water   and gave it to his cousins;
they were gravely hurt   and both had need of it.
　He urged them a long while   till they sat upright.
He gave them comfort   and made them take heart again
till they recovered somewhat,   and he took them both up
and with all haste   put them on his horse;
he covered them both   with his own mantle,
took his horse by the reins   and went off with them both.
They three alone   through the forest of Corpes

between night and day   went out from among the mountains;
they have arrived   at the waters of the Duero;
at the tower of Doña Urraca   he left those two.
Félix Muñoz came   to San Esteban
and found Diego Téllez,   who was Alvar Fáñez's[2] vassal;
he was grieved in his heart   when he heard the story,
and he took beasts   and fine garments
and went to receive   Doña Elvira and Doña Sol;
he brought them   into San Esteban;
he did them honor   as well as he could.
Those of San Esteban   are always sensible folk;[3]
when they knew of this deed   it grieved their hearts;
they brought tribute from their farms   to the Cid's daughters.
There the girls remained   until they were healed.
   And the Heirs of Carrión   continued to praise themselves.
Through all those lands   the tidings are made known;
the good King Alfonso   was grieved deeply.
word of it goes   to Valencia, the great city;
when they tell it   to My Cid the Campeador,
for more than an hour   he thought and pondered;
he raised his hand   and grasped his beard:
"I give thanks to Christ   Who is lord of the world;
this is the honor they have done me,   these Heirs of Carrión;
I swear by this beard,   which no one ever has torn,[4]
these Heirs of Carrión   shall not go free with this;
as for my daughters   I shall yet marry them well!"
My Cid was grieved   with all his heart and soul,
as were Alvar Fáñez   and all the court.
   Minaya mounted   with Pedro Bermúdez
and Martín Antolínez,   the worthy man of Burgos,[5]
with two hundred knights   whom My Cid sent;
he commanded them strictly   to ride day and night
and bring his daughters   to Valencia, the great city.
They do not delay   to fulfill their lord's command;
they ride with all speed,   they travel day and night;
they came to Gormaz,   a strong castle,
and there in truth   they paused for one night.
The news has arrived   at San Esteban
that Minaya is coming   for his two cousins.
The men of San Esteban,   like the worthy folk that they are,

[2] Alvar Fáñez Minaya, whom the Cid called his right arm, was also his first cousin.
[3] The poet may have been a native of San Esteban de Gormaz.
[4] See III, 2, note 17.
[5] A "hardy lance" who had joined the Cid at the lowest point of the latter's fortunes.

receive Minaya   and all his men;
that night they presented   Minaya with great tribute;
he did not wish to take it   but thanked them deeply:
"Thanks, people of San Esteban,   you conduct yourselves well.
For this honor you do us   in this misfortune
My Cid the Campeador   thanks you from where he is,
and here where I am   I do the same.
By God Who is in heaven   you will be well rewarded!"
All thank him for what he said   and are content;
they go each to his place   for the night's rest.
Minaya goes to see   his cousins where they are.
Doña Elvira and Doña Sol,   fix their eyes upon him:
"We are as glad to behold you   as though you were the Creator,
and give thanks to Him   that we are still alive.
When there is more leisure   in Valencia, the great city,
we shall be able to recount   all our grievance."
   132. Alvar Fáñez and the ladies   could not keep back the tears,
and Pedro Bermúdez   spoke to them thus:
"Doña Elvira and Doña Sol,   forget your cares now,
since now you are healed   and alive, and without other harm.
You have lost a good marriage,   you may yet have a better.
And we shall yet see the day   when you will be avenged!"
They spent that night there   amid great rejoicings.
   The next day in the morning   they mounted their horses.
The people of San Esteban   went with them on their way
as far as the River Amor,   keeping them company;
there they said good-by   and turned back again,
and Minaya and the ladies   rode on ahead.
They crossed over Alcoceba,   on their right they left Gormaz;
where it is called Vadorrey   they came and went by;
in the village of Berlanga   they paused to rest.
Next day in the morning   they rode on again
as far as the place called Medinaceli   where they took shelter,
and from Medinaceli to Molina   they came in one day.
The Moor Abengalbón[6]   was pleased in his heart;
he rode out to receive them   with good will;
he gave them a rich dinner   for the love of My Cid.
Then straightway they rode on   toward Valencia.
   The message came   to him who in good hour was born;
he mounts in haste   and rides out to receive them;
he went brandishing his weapons   and showing great joy.
My Cid rode up   to embrace his daughters;
he kissed them both   and began to smile:

   [6] Lord of Molina, and good friend of the Cid; the Heirs of Carrión had planned
to murder him for his wealth.

"You are here, my daughters! God heal you from harm!
I permitted your marriage   for I could not refuse it.
May it please the Creator   Who is in heaven
that I shall see you   better married hereafter.
God give me vengeance   on my sons-in-law of Carrión!"
Then the daughters   kissed their father's hands.
All rode into the city   brandishing their weapons;
Doña Jimena, their mother,[7]   rejoiced at the sight of them.
  He who was born in good hour   wished no delay;
he spoke in secret   with his own men.
He prepared to send a message   to King Alfonso in Castile.
  133. "Oh, stand before me, Muño Gustioz,   my loyal vassal.
In a good hour I brought you up[8]   and placed you in my court!
Carry my message   to Castile, to King Alfonso;
kiss his hand for me   with all my heart and soul,
since I am his vassal   and he is my lord;
this dishonor they have done me,   these Heirs of Carrión,
I would have it grieve the King   in his heart and soul.
He married my daughters;   it was not I who gave them.
Since they have been deserted   and gravely dishonored,
whatever in this   may redound to our dishonor,
in small things or in great,   redounds to my lord's.
They have taken away wealth   beyond measure;
this should be reckoned in   with the other dishonor.
Let them be called to a meeting,   to a court or assembly,
and give me my due,   these Heirs of Carrión,
for I bear much rancor   within my heart."
Muño Gustioz   mounted quickly,
and two knights with him   to wait upon his will,
and with him squires   of the Cid's household.
  They rode out of Valencia   and with all speed go forward;
they take no rest   by day or night.
In Sahagún   they found King Alfonso.
He is King of Castile   and King of León
and of Asturias   and the city of Oviedo;
as far as Santiago   he is the lord,
and the Counts of Galicia   serve him as their lord.
There Muño Gustioz,   as soon as he dismounts,

---

[7] Jimena Díaz, whose father's family were Counts of Asturias and of Oviedo. On her mother's side she was a great-granddaughter of King Alfonso V of León (999–1028) and first cousin once removed of Alfonso VI, who had bestowed her on Rodrigo in 1074, seven years before banishing him.

[8] The verb *criar* used here is used in medieval Spanish to refer to God's creation of the world, the education of one's children, the training and maintenance of a vassal, and even (though not in this poem) the support of the most menial domestic servants.

knelt to the saints   and prayed to the Creator;
he went up to the palace   where the court was,
and two knights with him   who serve him as their lord.
   When they entered   into the midst of the court
the King saw them   and knew Muño Gustioz;
the King rose   and received them well.
Before King Alfonso   Muño Gustioz
went down on his knees   and kissed the King's feet.
"Grace, King of great kingdoms   that call you lord!
The Campeador   kisses your hands and feet;
he is your vassal   and you are his lord.
You married his daughters   with the Heirs of Carrión;
the match was exalted   because you wished it so.
You know already what honor   that marriage has brought us:
how the Heirs of Carrión   have affronted us,
how they beat and abused the daughters   of the Cid Campeador,
stripped them naked, lashed them with whips   and deeply dishonored them
and abandoned them   in the oak forest of Corpes,
left them to the wild beasts   and the birds of the mountain.
Behold, now his daughters   are once more in Valencia.
For this the Cid kisses your hands   as a vassal to his lord;
he asks you to call these Heirs   to a court or assembly;
the Cid has been dishonored   but you still more deeply;
he asks you to share his grief, King,   as you are wise,
and to help My Cid to receive reparation   from these Heirs of Carrión."
For more than an hour the King   thought, and said nothing.
"I tell you, in truth   this grieves my heart,
and in this I speak truth   to you, Muño Gustioz.
I married the daughters   to the Heirs of Carrión;
I did it for the best,   for his advantage.
Oh, that such marriage   never had been made!
As for myself and the Cid,   our hearts are heavy.
I must see he receives justice,   so may the Creator keep me!
I never expected   such a thing as this.
My heralds shall go   through all my kingdom
and call my court   to assemble in Toledo;
let all gather there,   counts and nobles;
and the Heirs of Carrión,   I shall bid them come there
and give just reparation   to My Cid the Campeador;
he shall not be left with a grievance   if I can prevent it.
   134. "Say to the Campeador,   he who was born in good hour,
to be ready with his vassals   seven weeks from now
and come to Toledo;   that is the term I set for him.
Out of love for My Cid   I call this court together.

Give my greetings to all   and bid them take comfort;
this which has befallen them   shall yet redound to their honor."
Muño Gustioz took his leave   and returned to My Cid.
Alfonso the Castilian,   as he had promised,
took it upon himself.   He brooks no delays,
he sends his letters   to León and Santiago,
to the Portuguese[9]   and the Galicians
and to those of Carrión   and the nobles of Castile,
proclaiming that their honored King   called court in Toledo,
that they should gather there   at the end of seven weeks;
and whoever should not come to the court,   he would hold no longer his
    vassal.
Through all his lands   thus the message ran,
and none thought of refusing   what the King had commanded.

6. AN IDYLLIC PRINCELY MARRIAGE

When a noble marriage was based on a realistic parity of interests, it could transcend them as happily and romantically as
any union founded on that form of personal compatibility which
we fondly call love. One touching example, all the more beautifully unblemished for its brevity, was the marriage of Prince
Ferrando of Mallorca (a great-great-great-great-grandson of the
Cid) to the young heiress of a century-old French principality in
Greece. A younger son of King Jaime I of Mallorca (1278–1311),
Ferrando had to make his fortune elsewhere; like so many Spaniards of his time, he turned eastward to the Mediterranean frontiers of Latin Christendom. He went first to Sicily, ruled by his
cousin Frederick (king 1296–1336), son of Pedro III of Aragon
and of the Hohenstaufen Emperor Frederick II's granddaughter
Constance, heiress of one of the two dynasties which claimed the
Sicilian crown. Frederick sent Ferrando to take command of a
company of Catalan adventurers who had seized Gallipoli, thus
dominating the strategic straits dividing Europe and Asia, and
cutting Constantinople off from the Mediterranean (part of an
old ambition of Sicilian rulers; see I, 8). The Venetians joined
with the Byzantines to thwart their designs and managed to capture Ferrando. After his release and return to Sicily, Frederick
arranged a marriage between Ferrando and Isabel of Aková (or
Matagrifon), heiress of several French families whose forebears had

---

[9] Whom Alfonso had recently placed under the rule of Henry of Burgundy, a land-
less French knight with good connections who had married one of Alfonso's illegitimate daughters; their son would become the first King of Portugal.

conquered the greater part of the Peloponnesus after the Fourth Crusade.

The story of their wedding and its consequences is told by Ramon Muntaner (1264–1336), a faithful gentleman retainer of the royal family of Aragon, Sicily, and Mallorca. Born in Catalonia, burned out of his small ancestral property during a war with the French, he sailed to Greece with the Catalan Grand Company in 1302. He was governor of Gallipoli for the Company until Ferrando's arrival. Entering the service of the young prince, he shared his captivity, and went with him to Sicily after being released. There King Frederick (Fadrique in Catalan) entrusted to him the reconquest and governorship of Jerba and Kerkenna, islands off the east coast of Muslim Tunisia. When he heard that Ferrando was preparing to reclaim his wife's and son's inheritance in Greece, Muntaner was swift to rejoin him. Foreseeing an uncertain period of campaigning, Ferrando gave him the dangerous and highly honorable assignment of bringing the infant prince safely home to the Dowager Queen Esclaramunda of Mallorca (a daughter of the powerful Count of Foix, and great-great-granddaughter of Raymond Trencavel of Béziers—see I, 11(c) and (d)— as well as a descendant of the Cid). Ferrando died in battle in the Peloponnesus before Ramon had a chance to return to his side with reinforcements. In 1325 the little boy whom he had escorted across nearly a thousand miles of sea infested by ransom-hungry freebooters became Jaime III of Mallorca (he would reign until his death in 1349). By then a prosperous husband, father of three children, and master of property in Valencia and the Balearic Islands, Muntaner was full of memories as well as honors. Taking up the pen, he began a vernacular chronicle of the family he had served so well; in its lively pages he shows himself as solicitous of their proper emotions as of their deserved reputation for gallantry and courage.

Ramon Muntaner: *Chronicle*

From The Chronicle of Muntaner, *trans. Lady Goodenough (London: The Hakluyt Society, no. 50, 1921), pp. 631–37. Reprinted by permission of Cambridge University Press. Footnotes supplied.*

Chapter 263. When the son of the count of Aria had celebrated his wedding[1] he entered into possession of the barony of Matagrifon and,

[1] To Margaret, daughter of Prince Louis of Morea, who claimed kinship with the kings of France. Morea was the name given by Westerners to the Peloponnesus.

if ever a lord proved himself worthy, he did; he was very wise and accomplished in all things. And he had, by his wife, a daughter called my Lady Isabel. And when his daughter was born, soon after, he died, whereat all his barons and vassals of the Morea were greatly displeased. And this count of Aria is of the lineage of the counts of Baux, which is the oldest and most honourable house of Provence and they are kinsmen of the Lord King of Aragon. And when the lady lost her husband she was much grieved and did not wish to take another husband. And when the Princess, her sister,[2] died, she claimed the Principality; but those who held it gave her curt answer. She heard that the Lord Infante En Ferrando, son of the Lord King of Mallorca, was in Sicily and had neither wife nor territory. And she thought that there was no man in the world with whom her daughter would be so well situated, provided that he received, freely or by force, all her right to the Principality. And so she sent her messengers to the Lord King of Sicily and to the Lord Infante En Ferrando. In the end it was agreed that the lady and her daughter should come to Messina, and then, if the damsel was what she was said to be, the marriage would please them. The lady, with her daughter and full ten damsels and as many ladies, and twenty knights and twenty sons of knights, and other retinue came to Messina, where much honour was shown her. And when she was at Messina, the Lord King and the Lord Infante saw the damsel and, if they had given him the whole world, the Lord Infante would not have exchanged her for anything, but was so pleased with her that a day was a year to him until the matter was concluded. Indeed, he told the Lord King positively that he wanted this damsel to be his wife, and no other in the world. And it was no wonder if he was enamoured of her, for she was the most beautiful creature of fourteen one could see, the whitest and rosiest and the best. And she was the most learned damsel, for her age, of any in the world. What shall I tell you? The Lady of Matagrifon endowed her daughter during her lifetime and after her death, with all the barony of Matagrifon and all the rights she had with the barony, to do and say according to her will, without any condition.

And when this was done and the documents made of the wedding gifts, by the grace of Our Lord the Lord Infante took my Lady Isabel to wife, with great ceremonies and a great feast made by the Lord

[2] Isabel of Morea, whose last husband, Philip of Savoy, laid claim to Morea despite Prince Louis' provision that it should go to Margaret after Isabel's death. Philip was holding Morea against his sister-in-law Margaret and against the family of the kings of Naples, who coveted it.

King and my Lady the Queen[3] and all the barons of Sicily and the Catalan and Aragonese and Latin knights and all the others of Messina; and the archbishop of Messina said the mass, and the feast lasted full fifteen days, so that everyone marvelled how pleased all were.

And when the feast was over, the Lord Infante took her to Catania with her mother, with all the retinue that had come with her, and gave her Catalan ladies and Catalan damsels, and wives and daughters of knights. And when they were at Catania the Lord Infante made great gifts to all who had come with her; and so they stayed full four months at Catania. And then the lady, mother-in-law of the Lord Infante, returned to the Morea with her retinue, cheerful and content, and the Lord Infante, cheerful and content, stayed with my Lady the Infanta. And it pleased God that she became pregnant, whereat great rejoicing was made when it was known. And when the lady was pregnant, the Lord Infante prepared to go to the Morea with full five hundred horsemen and many afoot.

Chapter 264. And whilst he was getting ready I heard of it at Jerba; and, however much had been given me, I would not have refrained from going to him, and, with him, wherever he wished to go. I sent a message to the Lord King, asking him to be pleased to allow me to come to Sicily. And the Lord King was content and I came to Sicily with all the elder men of the island, who came with me in a galley and a leny, and I left the castle of Jerba and the island under a good chief. And the first place at which I landed in Sicily was Catania. And there I found the Lord Infante well and cheerful and my Lady the Infanta pregnant; before eight days had gone by, she gave birth to a child and had a beautiful son, for which a great feast was made. And when I had descended from the galleys, I had two bales of carpets brought on shore, which came from Tripoli, and anibles and ardiens and almaxies and aquinals and mactans and jucies[4] and jewels. And I had all these displayed before my Lady the Infanta and the Lord Infante and presented them with all, whereat the Lord Infante was very content. And then I departed from them and went to Messina; the Lord Infante told me he would be there before fifteen days had gone by and that he wished to speak to me at length.

And, when I was at Messina, fifteen days had not gone by before a message came that my Lady the Infanta had had a beautiful son,

[3] Eleanor, daughter of Charles II of Naples, whose family also laid claim to the crown of Sicily.

[4] Various articles of apparel, made according to Arabic fashion.

born on the first Saturday in April of the year 1315. May God grant everyone as much joy as I had. And do not ask me if the Lord Infante was joyful and all they of Catania. The feast made in Catania lasted over eight days. And the Lord Infante had him baptised in the cathedral of the blessed Lady Saint Agatha and had the name of Jaime given to him. And if ever an infant was born endowed with all beauty, this Infante En Jaime was. What shall I tell you? When the Lord Infante En Jaime had been baptised and the lady was out of danger, the Lord Infante came to Messina. And when he was at Messina I offered myself to him, in person and property, to follow him wherever he pleased. He was very grateful to me for it and said to me:—"You have to go to the Lord King who is at Piazza, where you will find him, and give up to him the castle and island of Jerba and the Kerkennas, and then you will return to Us and then we shall settle all We have to do."

And so I took leave of him. And whilst I was taking leave of him, a message came to him to hasten to Catania, for my Lady the Infanta was ill, she had been seized with fever and dysentery. And so he rode and, that night, entered Catania. And when my Lady the Infanta saw him, she was better; but she made her will before she got worse, and then confirmed it; and she left the barony of Matagrifon and also all the rights she had in the Principality to her son, the Infante En Jaime, and, if the Infante, her son, should die, she left it to the Infante En Ferrando, her husband. Now it is the truth that it was full two months since her mother had died of illness at Matagrifon, but she knew nothing of it, nor did the Lord Infante wish anyone to tell her whilst she was pregnant, nor likewise after she had been delivered, until she had gone to mass. And therefore the Lord Infante had prepared everything for his journey, and only waited until the Infanta should have been delivered and had gone to mass; after which he and she were to embark at once. All things were ready for embarcation.

Chapter 265. What shall I tell you about it? The Infanta, as it pleased God, passed from this life thirty-two days after the Infante En Jaime, her son, was born; and she died in the arms of the Lord Infante En Ferrando. And he and all the city made the greatest mourning ever seen. And, with great ceremonies, as for one who was pure and had confessed and received Holy Communion and Extreme Unction, she was put into a beautiful tomb, near the body of the Holy Virgin, Saint Agatha, in the church consecrated to her in Catania.

And after this misfortune had happened, the Lord Infante came to Messina to embark and to go to the Morea. And I went to the Lord King whom I found at Piazza, and I went to Palermo and, in the presence of the noble En Berenguer de Sarriá and many other richs homens[5] of Sicily and knights and citizens, I surrendered to him the castles and islands of Jerba and Kerkenna. . . .

And, as soon as I had surrendered the islands and had the letter of discharge, I took leave of the Lord King and returned to the Lord Infante whom I found in Messina, preparing to embark. And I told him that I had come to serve him and to go on board the galleys and also to lend him all I had. And on the day I told him this, he said to me he would answer me on the following day. And next day, when he had heard mass, he summoned a great number of knights and of men of good birth and before all he said to me:—"En Ramon Muntaner, it is the truth that you are the man to whom We are more beholden than to any other." And here he gave many good reasons and acknowledged how I had lost, in his service, all I had brought from Romania;[6] and, again, that I was put into prison with him, and how King Robert[7] had done me much hurt because of him; and how I had lent him of my fortune in Romania and given up all I had; and, again, how I had left all the charges I had in the Company for him, and many other services which I do not remember, which he heard I had done him; especially that, for love of him, I had given up the command of Jerba, which I had had for seven years; again, that I had lent him, at that juncture, all the money I had. "And so," said he, "so many are the services you have rendered me that I could not reward them at all. But now We have arrived at a case in which the service We beg of you will surpass all the other services you have rendered Us; and We beg you, in the presence of these knights, to grant Us this service." And I rose and went to kiss his hand and gave him many thanks for the praise he had given me and for holding himself well served by me. . . .

7. MILITARY MANNERS AND OPPORTUNITIES DURING THE HUNDRED YEARS' WAR

Jean Froissart was probably the most representative contemporary interpreter of the Hundred Years' War, which did as much

---

[5] Literally, *"ruling"* rather than *"rich"* men; a general term for the most important nobles, as distinct from mere knights or bourgeois.

[6] The territory of the Byzantine Empire, which still considered itself Roman.

[7] The previous King of Naples.

as the Black Death to undermine the civilization of the High Middle Ages. Waged sporadically from 1337 to 1461 between adherents of the French and English kings, its main battlefield was the unhappy land of France, but subsidiary campaigns occurred also in Spain, Scotland, Italy, and the western provinces of the Holy Roman Empire. One consequence of eventual French victory was a series of civil upheavals in England known as the Wars of the Roses, which dragged on until 1485. In origin dynastic rivalries, these protracted conflicts ended by producing a new type of national monarchy, increasingly hostile to any power exercised by the nobility. The Hundred Years' War itself was managed by the nobles, however, and provided them with endless opportunities to display both the chivalric manners which their class had developed and their persistent attachment to the warfare endemic in medieval society.

Froissart was born in Hainaut about 1333 and died there about 1410. His exact origins are unknown, and his last employment was as a canon in a minor collegiate church, but his middle life was full of movement and of courtly contacts. He met most of the famous men of his age, including Chaucer and Petrarch, and knew personally a great number of the great and lesser nobles who crowd the pages of his immense *Chronicle* of "Events in England, France, Spain, and the Adjoining Countries" from 1325 to 1400. He went to England about 1357, serving as a secretary to Queen Philippa, daughter of Count William III of Hainaut: the early parts of his *Chronicle* reflect his admiration for the warlike subjects of King Edward III (1327–77). He traveled all over western Europe in the next thirty-five years, during which he gradually became conscious of the ghastly consequences of their gallantry, and his book ends on a different note.

The incidents related here took place in 1370. The French had been humbled by overwhelming defeats at the battles of Crécy (1346) and Poitiers (1356), the capture of their king, John II (1350–64), and the severe terms of the Treaty of Brétigny, which practically awarded the western half of the kingdom to Edward and his allies. Under the leadership of King Charles V (1364–80), the French began a series of scattered attacks against Edward's territories. Edward's and Philippa's eldest son, known to later ages as the Black Prince (of Wales), took up the challenge.

The two leaders of the French effort presented in the following passages came from very different strata of the nobility. Louis II, Duke of Bourbon (1356–1410) was, like Edward III and John II, a great-great-grandson of St. Louis. His mother, Isabelle of Valois, was a sister of King Philip VI of France (1328–50), and his sister Jeanne married Charles V. Two other sisters married King Peter the Cruel of Castile and Count Amedeus VI of Savoy; his father, Duke Peter I (son of Duke Louis I and Marie of Hainaut), was killed at the battle of Poitiers. A vigorous defender and developer of his princely fiefs, Louis II became thereby a staunch supporter of his French royal kinsmen. Bertrand Du Guesclin (1320?–80) belonged to the minor gentry of northeastern Brittany. In the course of a dramatic and bloody life he achieved a long list of triumphs, the last of which was burial with royal honors in St. Denis (see II, 8 [a]). His chief assets were brute strength and superb fighter's instincts, which he could put to use in formal duels, guerilla raids, or long-range campaigns employing both kinds of tactics.

Bertrand's talents were first recognized at a tournament in 1337, after which he entered the service of Charles de Blois and his wife, Jeanne the Lame, Countess of Penthièvre, who claimed to be the rightful Duchess of Brittany and was conducting a feud with Jean de Montfort, actual possessor of the ducal crown (and of a marriage alliance with the daughter of Edward III). After the Peace of Brétigny, the Dukes of Anjou and Orléans and the Count of Alençon (brothers of the future King Charles V) put Du Guesclin in charge of their lands, which he defended with outstanding success against the "free companies" of unemployed soldiers then roaming through defeated France. Charles V rewarded him with the title of royal chamberlain, the post of royal lieutenant for Normandy, the county of Longueville, and permission to marry Tiphaine Raguenel, a Breton heiress. In 1364 Du Guesclin abandoned all but the last of these prizes in order to answer the appeal of his first lord, Charles de Blois, who needed him back in Brittany. In 1367 the king and his brothers swallowed what displeasure they may still have felt, and made Du Guesclin commander of a French army which went to Spain to aid Henry of Trastamara in his fight for the crown of Castile against Peter the Cruel (backed by the Black Prince). Despite a period of English captivity, Bertrand did so well there that the Castilians made him Constable (commander-in-chief of the army) and Duke of Molina. It was from Castile that Charles V summoned him in 1370 to become Constable of France, a post which he held with mounting distinction for the last ten years of his life.

The following passages contain, in fact, portraits of a cross-section of the nobility engaged on both sides of the general conflict. At the top are Charles V and Edward III, fighting at times for the crown as well as the territory of France. Immediately beneath their dispute is that over the large, traditionally autonomous duchy of Brittany. At roughly the same level of the social scale we can discern the involvement of princely figures like Louis of Bourbon or Louis of Anjou, whose English counterparts were Edward the Black Prince, John of Gaunt (Duke of Lancaster), Edmund Earl of Cambridge—three sons of Edward III— and their brother-in-law the Earl of Pembroke. Old families of the "middle" nobility are represented by Moreau de Fiennes or Louis de Sancerre, Marshal and later Constable of France; on the other side we find Jean de Grailly, captal of Buch, who would become Constable of Aquitaine in 1371, and those three Knights of the Garter who were his frequent companions-in-arms: Lord Thomas Percy, Sir John Devereux, and Sir Thomas Felton. Balancing Du Guesclin both socially and militarily (although never really his equal in either category) is Sir Robert Knolles, whose enduring loyalty to Jean de Montfort won him a Breton fief and the confidence of two English kings. Knolles and Du Guesclin fought and respected one another very well through nearly a quarter-century of swiftly rising fortunes; it is hard to say whether posterity has been more just in forgetting Knolles or in transforming the tough Du Guesclin into a paragon of all the chivalric qualities he never tried to cultivate. Beneath all these gentlemen in original status and in final fame are the simple knights, esquires, and lesser officers of the "free companies," whose contributions to the wars were as inevitable and as marginal as the privileges that made them nobles.

Jean Froissart: *Chronicles*

From Sir John Froissart's Chronicles, *trans. Thomas Johnes, Esq. (London: William Smith, 1839), I, 440–42, 452–56. Footnotes supplied.*

Chapter 280. Duke Louis de Bourbon was much enraged that the English and free companies should keep possession of his country, the Bourbonnois, and that Ortigo, Bernard de Wist and Bernard de la Salle, should hold his castle of Belleperche, and detain his mother prisoner in it: he resolved, therefore, to set on foot an expedition of men at arms, and lay siege to the castle of Belleperche, which, he declared he would not quit until he had re-taken it. He spoke of it to the king of France, who instantly promised to assist him in the siege with men and money. He left Paris, having ordered his rendezvous at Moulins in the Bourbonnois, and at St. Poursaint, whither there came a numerous body of men at arms and able combatants.

The lord de Beaujeu came to serve him, with three hundred lances: the lords de Villars and de Roucillon, with one hundred; and numbers of barons and knights from Auvergne and Forêts, of which he was lord paramount, through the lady his wife, the daughter of that gallant lord Beroald count dauphin.[1] The duke arrived and fixed his quarters before the castle of Belleperche, where he built a large and strong redoubt, in which his men might be sheltered every night, and skirmish with the garrison during the day. He had also brought and pointed against the castle four large machines, which kept continually throwing, night and day, stones and logs of wood, so that they broke through the roofs of all the houses, and beat down the greater part of the towers. The mother of the duke of Bourbon, who was a prisoner within the castle, was much alarmed, and sent frequently to entreat her son to abstain from this mode of attack, for these machines annoyed her exceedingly; but the duke, who knew for certain that these requests came from his enemies, replied that he would not desist happen what would.

When the garrison found themselves so much harassed, and that the French force was daily increasing; for sir Louis de Sancerre, marshal of France,[2] had just arrived with a large body of men at arms; they resolved to send and acquaint sir John Devereux, séneschal of Limousin,[3] who resided at La Souteraine, two short days' journey

---

[1] Louis of Bourbon's wife was Anne, daughter of Beroald the Great, Count of Clermont, Dauphin of Auvergne, etc., and of Jeanne, Countess of Forez. Beroald, who fought at the battle of Poitiers, defeated Knolles' raiders in 1359, and fought the English off and on until his death in 1401, was the son of Beroald I and of Marie de Villemur. His third wife was Marguerite de Sancerre. The title of *dauphin* had been borne by the lords of southeastern Auvergne since 1155, as well as by the Counts of Vienne, who bequeathed it to the eldest son of the French king in 1349.

Antoine de Beaujeu (1343–74) fought alongside Du Guesclin in Spain and then against the free companies in central France. His family had ranked high in the region around Lyons since the tenth century. His father, Edouard I de Beaujeu (who bestowed the barony of Beaujolais in Burgundy on Louis of Bourbon), was a Marshal of France and a veteran of Crécy, and was killed by the English in 1352.

[2] Louis de Sancerre (1341–1402), second son of Count Louis I of Sancerre, who died at Crécy. This Louis' elder brother, Count Jean III, destroyed one of the free companies besieging Sancerre (on the upper Loire, the direct route between Paris and the Bourbonnais) in 1364. Louis became Marshal in 1368. He retook Limoges in 1372. The dying Du Guesclin entrusted the Constable's sword to him, and in 1397 he became Constable himself (earning 2000 pounds per month for that post). He was buried near Du Guesclin in St. Denis.

[3] Second Lord Devereux, he came from a Norman family powerful in England since 1140. Having fought first with Du Guesclin in Spain and then against him, he was made high steward of Aquitaine, seneschal of Poitou, and governor of the Limousin by the Black Prince. Captured by Du Guesclin in 1373, he later served Richard II as ambassador and royal steward and went often to Parliament.

from them, of their distress, and who knew that, when these lords of Poitou and Gascony[4] had made an excursion from Quercy, it was upon the faith, that if they should take any castles in France, and were besieged in them, they would be assisted. They wrote their letters, and sent them off in the night by one of their servants to the castle of sir John Devereux. Sir John recognized the messenger by the tokens he mentioned, and, having read the letters, said, "that he would most willingly acquit himself of his engagement, and that the more effectually to do so, he would immediately wait on the prince and the lords who were with him, at Angoulême, and exert himself so that the garrison of Belleperche should be reinforced."

Sir John Devereux set out, after having given proper directions respecting his castle and garrison to his officers, and, being arrived at Angoulême, found there the prince,[5] the earl of Cambridge,[6] the earl of Pembroke,[7] sir John Montague, sir Robert Knolles,[8] lord Thomas Percy,[9] sir Thomas Felton,[10] sir Guiscard d'Angle, the captal de Buch,[11]

---

[4] *I.e.*, vassals of Edward III from those continental territories, who accounted for the bulk of this army.

[5] Edward of Woodstock, the Black Prince (1330–76). Father of Richard II (1377–99) by Joan, daughter of Edmund, Earl of Kent; legend asserts that Edward III founded the Order of the Garter in her honor. The Black Prince acted for his father in Aquitaine from 1356 to 1371, when "fever" contracted in Spain and local resistance to his severe policies convinced Edward III to call him home.

[6] Edmund of Langley (1341–1402). Fifth son of Edward III and Philippa, he fought alongside his father in France (1359–60), became Knight of the Garter in 1362, returned to France in 1369 with 400 men-at-arms and 400 archers. He married Isabella, daughter of Peter the Cruel of Castile, in 1372. Twice regent for his nephew Richard II, he stayed out of dynastic politics; but his great-grandson would become Edward IV (1461–83), first English king of the House of York.

[7] John Hastings (1347–75), second Earl of Pembroke in his family; son of Laurence Hastings and Agnes Mortimer, daughter of the Earl of March. In 1369 he was made a Knight of the Garter and went to France with the Earl of Cambridge, whose sister Margaret he had married. Captured by Du Guesclin in 1372, he was released for a ransom of 120,000 francs.

[8] Robert Knolles (1317?–1407) was born in Cheshire of an inglorious and impoverished family. He began fighting in France in 1346 and was knighted by 1351, when he entered the service of Jean de Montfort, who gave him the castle of Derval in 1365. In the interim he had captured Du Guesclin (1359), led the "Great Company" on an epic sack of Normandy and the Loire valley (1357–60; he declared that he fought "for himself alone" and promised a fortune to any man who would join him), put the 40 castles he had captured at the disposal of Edward III, sacked the Bourbonnais (1364), etc. He fought in Spain in 1366–67, but preferred to stick close to Derval, which never fell to the French during his lifetime. In later years he served with Lord Thomas Percy and led the London citizens' militia against the Peasants' Revolt (1381). He was on good terms with Sir John Hawkewood, who led a free company through northern Italy. His wife Constantia was English, and likewise "of mean birth."

[9] Earl of Worcester (1344?–1403); second son of Henry, baron Percy of Alnwick,

and many others. He explained to them, how these free companies in the castle of Belleperche were besieged and much straitened by the French under the duke de Bourbon. . . . The lords, on hearing this statement, replied with great cheerfulness, that they must be relieved, according to the promises which had been made to them. This business was entrusted to the earls of Cambridge and Pembroke; and the prince issued a summons to all his vassals, who, in sight of it, were to assemble in the town of Limoges. Upon which, knights, squires, free companies, and men at arms, marched to that place, according to their orders; and, when they were mustered, they amounted to upwards of fifteen hundred lances and about three thousand others. They marched to Belleperche, where they encamped themselves opposite to the French. The French kept themselves close in their redoubt, which was as strong and as well fortified as a good town might be. The English foragers were at a loss where to seek for provisions, so that, whenever it was possible, some were brought to them from Poitiers.

Sir Louis de Sancerre, marshal of France, gave exact information of the number and condition of the English to the king of France, and to those knights who had remained at Paris: he sent also a proclamation, which he had affixed to the gates of the palace. It ran in these

---

and of Mary, daughter of Earl Henry of Lancaster. His elder brother Henry was Earl of Northumberland, and his nephew was the Hotspur immortalized by Shakespeare. His service in France began in 1369; at first seneschal of the strategic port of La Rochelle, he was made seneschal of Poitou by late 1370. Captured in 1372, he was ransomed for a strategic castle, and returned to England for seven years. Froissart admired his fidelity to his pledged word.

[10] Thomas Felton (died 1381) came from a highly respectable Northumbrian family. Present at Crécy, Poitiers, and Brétigny, he became one of Edward III's most trusted advisers on continental matters. Seneschal of Aquitaine before 1362, he was left in charge of Bordeaux after both the Black Prince and the Duke of Lancaster had failed to protect the rest of Aquitaine from French reconquest.

[11] Jean III de Grailly (died 1377) came from a distinguished Gascon family: the title of *captal*, meaning *lord*, was used in only three lordships of the area (Buch lay along the Atlantic coast some 60 miles southwest of Bordeaux). His grandfather, Jean I, often represented Edward I (1272–1307) at Paris as a sort of ambassador for Aquitaine. Jean III's mother was Blanche de Foix, and his brother Archambault inherited the county of Foix through marriage as well as kinship. Jean went on a crusade against the pagans in Prussia (1356); he rescued the Dowager Queen Jeanne of France from a violent peasant uprising known as the Jacquerie (1358), and may subsequently have been a suitor for her hand. In 1364 he was captured by Du Guesclin while ravaging the Seine valley between Paris and Rouen; in 1367 he was Du Guesclin's captor in Spain. A year after becoming Constable of Aquitaine, he was captured with Thomas Percy, but refused either to surrender important castles for his ransom or to come over to the side of Charles V, and so died in very polite confinement.

words: "Ye knights and squires who are anxious of renown, and seek for deeds of arms, I inform you for a truth, that the earl of Cambridge and the earl of Pembroke are arrived with their troops at Belleperche, with the intention of raising the siege which we have so long made: we have so much straitened the garrison of the castle that it must immediately surrender, or our enemies beat us in a pitched battle. Come therefore hither, directly, for you will have opportunities of exhibiting your prowess in arms; and know that the English are encamped so much apart, and in such positions, that they may be wonderfully annoyed."

Upon this exhortation and request of the marshal, several good knights and squires of France advanced to those parts; and I know myself that the governor of Blois, named Alart de Toustanne, went thither with fifty lances; as did also the count de Porcien, and his brother sir Hugh de Porcien.

Chapter 281. When the earls of Cambridge and Pembroke had remained before the French army at Belleperche fifteen days, and did not see any signs of the French quitting their redoubt to fight with them, they called a council, in which they resolved to send to them a herald, to know what they meant to do. Chandos the herald [12] was ordered on this business, and it was repeated to him what he was to say: he therefore went to them, and said; "My masters and lords send me to you, and inform you by my mouth, that they are quite astonished you have allowed them to remain fifteen days here, and you have not sallied out of your fort to give them battle. They therefore tell you, that if you will come forth to meet them, they will permit you to choose any plot of ground for the field of battle; and let God give the event of it to whomsoever he pleases." The duke of Bourbon made to this the following reply: "Chandos, you will tell your masters, that I shall not combat as they may wish or desire. I know well enough where they are: but for all that, I will not quit my fort nor raise the siege, until I shall have re-conquered the castle of Belleperche." "My lord," answered the herald, "I will not fail to report what you have said."

The herald set out, and on his return gave the duke's answer, which was not very agreeable. They called another council, and when it was over, gave to Chandos a proposal, for him to carry to the French. He did so, and said: "Gentlemen, my lords and masters let you know,

---

[12] An English herald-at-arms who later wrote a long narrative poem in French about the Black Prince. Such articulate envoys enjoyed a type of diplomatic immunity.

that since you are not willing to accept the offer they have made you, three days hence, between nine and twelve o'clock in the morning, you my lord duke of Bourbon, will see your lady-mother placed on horseback, and carried away. Consider this, and rescue her if you can." The duke answered: "Chandos, Chandos, tell your masters, they carry on a most disgraceful war, when they seize an ancient lady from among her domestics, and carry her away like a prisoner. It was never seen formerly, that in the warfare between gentlemen, ladies or damsels were treated as prisoners. It will certainly be very unpleasant to me to see my lady-mother thus carried off: we must recover her as soon as we can: but the castle they cannot take with them: that, therefore, we will have. Since you have twice come hither with propositions, you will bear this from me to your masters, that if they will draw out fifty men, we will draw out the same number, and let the victory fall where it may." "My lord," replied the herald, "I will relate to them everything you have told me."

At these words, Chandos left them, and returned to the earls of Cambridge and Pembroke and the other lords, and told them the offer the duke of Bourbon had sent them. They were advised not to accept it. Preparations were therefore made for the departure of the army, and to carry off with them the lady and the garrison, which had been exceedingly harassed by the machines of the enemy. When the appointed day arrived, they ordered their trumpets to sound at early morning: upon which every one armed himself and drew up, both horse and foot, in order of battle, as if they expected a combat, with their banners and pennons flying before them. In this manner were they arrayed; and on this day sir John Montacute,[13] nephew to the earl of Salisbury, displayed his banner. They had ordered their trumpets and minstrels to sound very loud; and at nine o'clock the garrison and madame de Bourbon came out of the castle of Belleperche. They mounted her on a palfrey handsomely equipped for her. She was accompanied by her ladies and damsels. The English army marched away at mid-day. Sir Eustace d'Ambreticourt and sir John Devereux attended upon madame de Bourbon; and in this manner they returned to the principality, where the lady remained a considerable time a prisoner to the free companions at La Roche Vaucloix in Limousin.

This capture never pleased the prince, who, whenever it was mentioned, said, that if any others than the free companies had taken the duchess, she should instantly have had her liberty: and when the

---

[13] Knighted by the Earl of Cambridge, John Montacute, or Montague (1350?–1400), became third Earl of Salisbury after his uncle's death in 1390.

captains of these free companies spoke to him on the subject, he told them to make some sort of an exchange, for him to get back his knight, sir Simon Burley,[14] whom the French had taken. You may suppose the duke of Bourbon was greatly incensed when he saw his lady mother carried away from the castle of Belleperche in the Bourbonnois. Soon after her departure, he marched from the redoubt, and sent his men to take possession of his own castle of Belleperche, which the English had left quite empty. Thus ended this grand expedition, and each withdrew to his usual place of residence. The French who were under the duke of Bourbon, retired to the garrisons from whence they had come. The duke returned with his knights and squires to the king of France, who received him with great joy, and entertained him handsomely. The earl of Cambridge went to his brother at Angoulême; and the earl of Pembroke and his troops to Mortagne in Poitou. Those free companies and men at arms who had been in Belleperche went into Poitou and Saintonge, seeking for provisions, and committing many disgraceful acts, from which they had not the inclination to refrain themselves, nor power to restrain others.

Sir Robert Knolles, shortly after this, left the prince, and returned to his castle of Derval in Brittany, where he had not been a month, before the king of England sent him positive orders to set out, without delay, and cross the sea to him in England, as he would find his profit in it. Sir Robert very willingly obeyed this summons: having made his preparations, he embarked and landed in Cornwall, at St. Michael's Mount, and thence continued his road until he arrived at Windsor, where he found the king, who was right glad to see him, as were all the English barons; for they thought they should have much need of him, as he was so great a captain and leader of men at arms.[15]

*   *   *

Chapter 289. Sir Robert Knolles, as has been before related, had entered France with a large body of men, and was marching by short

---

[14] A knight from Herefordshire (1336–88) who served in France 1350–70. A favorite of the Black Prince, he fought alongside him until his capture in 1369. After being exchanged for the Duchess of Bourbon, he returned to England to supervise the education of the future Richard II, of whose marriage with Anne of Bohemia he was one of the chief arrangers. A lover of chivalric literature, he was close to Froissart.

[15] Edward countered a French plan to invade restive Wales by sending Knolles to ravage the north of France.

stages through that kingdom with a magnificence for which the people and the rich provinces paid dearly. The English, as they advanced and retreated, did infinite mischief, at the same time showing as if they only wished for a battle. Having passed through the countries of Artois, Vermandois, the bishopric of Laon, the archbishopric of Rheims in Champagne, they returned into Brie, and from thence came near to Paris, and quartered themselves for a day and two nights in the villages around it.

[The events at Belleperche occurred in January and February. On August 22 the French persuaded the Bishop of Limoges to yield that key city after a token siege and for a considerable sum of money. Shocked and enraged, the Black Prince hastened to besiege Limoges anew.]

Chapter 290. During the time sir Robert Knolles was employed in his expedition, and the prince of Wales with his two brothers were at the siege of Limoges, sir Bertrand du Guesclin with his company, amounting to about two hundred lances, marched through a part of Limousin, but did not encamp in the open plain for fear of the English. He retreated every night into some of the strong places which had lately turned to the French: in that number were the castles of sir Louis de Maleval and sir Raymond de Marneil, and several others: from thence he made daily excursions to conquer other towns and castles. The prince knew well all this; for he received every day information of what was passing, as well as complaints on the subject; but he would not break up his siege, for he had too much at heart the loss of Limoges. Sir Bertrand entered the viscounty of Limoges, a territory which was dependent on lord John de Montfort, duke of Brittany, in the name of the widow of lord Charles de Blois, to whom it had formerly belonged. He made war upon it without any opposition; for the duke of Brittany did not imagine sir Bertrand would carry the war into any part of his property. He came before St. Yrier, where there were not any gentlemen that knew how to defend it; and the inhabitants were so frightened, they surrendered themselves under the obedience of the duchess dowager of Brittany, in whose name the war was made. The Bretons formed St. Yrier into a considerable garrison; by which means they took many other towns in Limousin. But let us return to the prince.

The prince of Wales remained about a month, and not more, before the city of Limoges: he would not allow of any assaults or skirmishing, but kept his miners steadily at work. The knights in the town perceived what they were about, and made countermines to destroy them; but they failed in their attempt. When the miners of the prince (who, as they found themselves countermined, kept changing the line of direction of their own mine) had finished their business, they came to the prince, and said: "My lord, we are ready, and will throw down, whenever you please, a very large part of the wall into the ditch, through the breach of which you may enter the town at your ease and without danger." This news was very agreeable to the prince, who replied, "I wish then that you would prove your words to-morrow morning at six o'clock." The miners set fire to the combustibles in the mine; and on the morrow morning, as they had foretold the prince, they flung down a great piece of wall, which filled the ditches. The English saw this with pleasure, for they were all armed and prepared to enter the town. Those on foot did so, and ran to the gate, which they destroyed as well as the barriers, for there were no other defences; and all this was done so suddenly that the inhabitants had not time to prevent it.

The prince, the duke of Lancaster,[16] the earls of Cambridge and of Pembroke, sir Guiscard d'Angle and the others, with their men, rushed into the town. You would then have seen pillagers, active to do mischief, running through the town, slaying men, women and children, according to their orders. It was a most melancholy business; for all ranks, ages and sexes cast themselves on their knees before the prince, begging for mercy; but he was so inflamed with passion and revenge that he listened to none, but all were put to the sword, wherever they could be found, even those who were not guilty: for I know not why the poor were not spared, who could not have had any part in this treason; but they suffered for it, and indeed more than those who had been the leaders of the treachery. There was not that day in the city of Limoges any heart so hardened, or that had any sense of religion, who did not deeply bewail the unfortunate events passing before their eyes; for upwards of three thousand men,

[16] John of Gaunt (1340-99), fourth son of Edward III and Philippa. He became Duke of Lancaster in 1362 thanks to his marriage to Blanche of Lancaster (daughter of Duke Henry); in 1372 he styled himself King of Castile on account of his marriage to Constance, daughter of Peter the Cruel, who had been defeated and killed by the Trastamara party. He was also Earl of Richmond (an earldom traded by Jean de Montfort for English support in Brittany), Derby, Lincoln, and Leicester. A jealous and ambitious man, better at intrigue than at warfare, he proved to be a disastrous replacement for the Black Prince in Aquitaine. Twenty-five years later he designed the coup which succeeded in deposing his brother's son Richard II, and brought his own son to the throne as Henry IV (1399-1413), first English king of the House of Lancaster.

women and children were put to death that day. God have mercy on their souls! for they were veritable martyrs.

A company of English, in entering the town, hastened to the palace of the bishop, whom they there found and took prisoner, carrying him, without any regard to his dignity, to the prince of Wales, who, eyeing him indignantly, told him that his head should be cut off, and ordered him out of his presence.

We will now speak of those knights who were in the town, sir John de Villemur, sir Hugh de la Roche, and Roger de Beaufort, son to the count de Beaufort, governors of the city. When they perceived the tribulation which was overpowering them, they said: "We shall all be slain for a certainty, if we do not gallantly defend ourselves: let us therefore sell our lives dearly as good knights ought to do." Upon this, sir John de Villemur said to Roger de Beaufort, "You must be knighted." Roger replied, "Sir, I have not as yet signalised myself sufficiently for that honour, but I thank you much for your good opinion in suggesting it to me." No more was said, for they had not time to hold further conversation. They collected in a body and, placing themselves before an old wall, sir John de Villemur and sir Hugh de la Roche displayed their banners, and drew up in good order. They might be, in the whole, about fourscore. The duke of Lancaster and the earl of Cambridge, with their men, advanced upon them, and dismounted, to be on an equality with the enemy. They attacked them with hearty good will. You may easily imagine that this handful of men could not resist the English, but were all slain or made prisoners.

The duke of Lancaster was engaged for a long time with sir John de Villemur, who was a hardy knight, strong and well made. The earl of Cambridge singled out sir Hugh de la Roche, and the earl of Pembroke Roger de Beaufort, who was but a simple esquire. These three Frenchmen did many valorous deeds of arms, as all allowed, and ill did it betide those who approached too near. The prince, coming that way in his carriage, looked on the combat with great pleasure, and enjoyed it so much that his heart was softened and his anger appeased. After the combat had lasted a considerable time, the Frenchmen, with one accord, viewing their swords, said, "My lords, we are yours: you have vanquished us: therefore act according to the law of arms." "By God," replied the duke of Lancaster, "sir John, we do not intend otherwise, and we accept you for our prisoners." Thus, as I have been informed, were these three knights taken. But the business was not here ended, for the whole town was pillaged, burnt, and totally destroyed. The English then departed, carrying with them their booty and prisoners. They marched to Cognac, where the princess had remained, and there the prince disbanded his forces, not intending to do anything more that season; for he did not feel himself at his ease, as every exertion aggravated his disorder, which was increasing, to the great dismay of his brothers and all those about him.

I must inform you how the bishop of Limoges escaped with imprisonment, who had been in imminent danger of his life. The duke of Lancaster asked him of the prince, who consented, and ordered him to be given up to the duke, for him to do with him according as he willed. The bishop having good friends, they sent information of his situation to the pope,[17] who had lately arrived at Avignon; and fortunate was it for the bishop they did so, otherwise he would have been a dead man. The pope wrote such pressing and kind letters to the duke of Lancaster, to request he would give him the bishop, that he was unwilling to refuse, and sent him to the pope, who felt himself exceedingly obliged for it.

We will now say what was going forward in France.

Chapter 291. The king of France was informed of the conquest and destruction of Limoges, and how the prince and his army had left it empty and deserted, which vexed him much on account of the distress and loss of the late inhabitants. It was therefore thought advisable in a council of nobles and prelates, as well as by the common assent of the whole kingdom, to elect a chief or commander, called a constable (for sir Moreau de Fiennes[18] wished to resign the office) who was a valiant and enterprising man, and one to whom all knights and squires would pay proper deference. After all things had been well considered, they unanimously elected sir Bertrand du Guesclin (provided he would undertake the office), as the most valiant, the best informed, the most virtuous and fortunate in conducting affairs for the crown of France of all those who were bearing arms in its defence. The king wrote to him by messengers, for him to come to Paris. Those

---

[17] Urban V (October, 1362–December, 1370). Born Guillaume de Grimoard in southern France, a student of law at Paris and Avignon, professor at Avignon and Montpellier, and abbot at Auxerre and Marseilles, he moved the Papacy from Avignon to Rome in 1367 despite the opposition of his fellow Frenchmen in the College of Cardinals. In September, 1370 he returned to Avignon on account of the disorders afoot in Italy and a desire to end the Anglo-French war. Jean le Cros, Bishop of Limoges 1348–71, rose to become Cardinal-Bishop of Preneste (1377–83).

[18] Constable 1356–70, he died in 1385. His niece inherited the castellany of Fiennes in Picardy, which had been a fief of his family since the eleventh century. He seems to have been a 4-times-great-grandson of Arnold of Guines and Beatrice of Bourbourg: see III, 4.

sent found him in the viscounty of Limoges, taking castles and forts, which he put under the obedience of madame de Bretagne, widow of the late lord Charles de Blois. He had lately taken a town called Brantome, whose inhabitants had surrendered themselves to him, and was then on an expedition against another.

When the king's messengers came to him, he received them handsomely, as he knew well how to do. They gave him their letter, and delivered their message word for word. When sir Bertrand thus saw himself specially ordered, he was unwilling to make any more excuses for not waiting on the king of France to know his will: he set out as soon as possible, having ordered all his men into the garrisons which he had conquered, and appointed his nephew, sir Oliver de Mauny, commander over them. He rode on to Paris, where he found the king surrounded by a number of the lords of his council. He was received by all with great pleasure; and the king told him of his being chosen constable of France. On hearing which, sir Bertrand modestly and sagely excused himself, saying, "he was not worthy of it: that he was but a poor knight and simple bachelor, in comparison with the great lords and valorous men of France, however fortune might have been favourable to him." The king replied, "that his excuses would be of no avail; that he must consent to accept this dignity, for it had been so determined by the decision of the whole of the council of France, and that he would not break through such a resolution." Sir Bertrand used other arguments to excuse himself; adding "Dear lord and noble king, I cannot, I dare not, whatever I may wish, oppose what may be your good pleasure: but in truth I am too poor a man, and of low extraction, for the office of constable, which is so grand and noble that it is proper for those (who wish to exercise it justly and honourably) to command and keep a strict eye more upon the great than the poor. Now Sir, here are my lords your brothers, your nephews and your cousins, who will have different commands in your armies, and in various expeditions; and how shall I dare to order them? Certainly, my dear lord, envy and jealousy are so much abroad, I ought to be on my guard against them; I therefore entreat you will not insist on my taking this office, but give it to some other who will readily accept it, and, who knows better than I do how to execute it." The king made answer: "Sir Bertrand, that excuse will not serve you; for I have neither brother, nephew, cousin, count or baron in my realm but who will obey your orders; and should any one act otherwise, he would so anger me that he should soon feel the effects of it: I therefore beg of you to accept this office with a good will."

Sir Bertrand, finding that no excuse nor any thing he could say would be listened to, accepted the king's offer, but it was much against his inclination. He was invested with the office of constable; and the king, to show him greater affection, made him be seated at his table, and gave him, besides this office, many rich gifts and large domains in land, for him and his heirs. The duke of Anjou[19] was very active in forwarding this promotion.

8. ROYAL REWARDS FOR NOBLE SERVICE

Henry Plantagenet, fourth Earl of Lancaster (1299?–1361), was one nobleman who profited greatly from the Hundred Years' War. A great-great-grandson of King Henry III (1216–72), he supported his second cousin Edward III's attack on France with men, money, and his own person, but reaped the rewards of his loyalty back home in northern England rather than in the conquered territories across the Channel. The following document announces a double recompense. First comes the ritual act of formal admission to a defined rank of nobility topped only by the title of prince—which in England was held exclusively by the heir to the throne. Men of the fourteenth century had come to delight in public ceremonies like formal investitures, the foundation of Orders of chivalry, etc., and evidently found the content of such symbols eminently satisfying. Then come the grants of real power, in the form of profitable judicial rights normally exercised in Norman England by the Crown alone. Finally, in the provision for efficient summoning to Parliament, we note a third consequence of the king's dependence on the military gentlemen of his realm. Edward III knew how to exploit representative assemblies for funds and propaganda, and called them frequently. In the reign of his less adroit grandson, Richard II (1377–99), Parliament began to demand more than it gave, and finally presumed even to depose a king.

Edward apparently saw little danger in his generosity. Eight years after the charter in question, he married his son John of Gaunt to Henry's daughter Blanche, seeing to it that Henry's other earldoms of Derby and Lincoln entered the dowry. Three years later Henry's other daughter, Matilda of Leicester (wife

---

[19] Louis I, Duke of Anjou (1339–84). In 1360 he married Marie, daughter of Charles de Blois and Jeanne de Penthièvre. He got Du Guesclin to command his forces in Provence before the Spanish expedition, and joined him in a clean-up of English forces in most of Aquitaine before the Treaty of 1377, which largely reversed that of Brétigny.

of William of Bavaria, Zealand, etc.) died childless; when John and Blanche produced a son four years afterwards, few of their contemporaries could have failed to notice that they had given the future Richard II a most formidable first cousin. In 1399 that son, Henry of Bolingbroke, parlayed one grandfather's county palatinate and court of chancery into possession of the other grandfather's crown. Carefully avoiding an unequivocal statement of his debt to Parliament, he ruled as Henry IV for fourteen years. Every reader of Shakespeare knows how his son, the fiery Henry V, renewed the war with France that had first brought the house of Lancaster within grasp of sovereignty.

Charter of Edward III, March 6, 1351

From The Charters of the Duchy of Lancaster, *trans. and ed. William Hardy (London: Chancellor and Council of the Duchy of Lancaster, 1845), pp. 9–11. Footnotes supplied.*

For Henry Duke of Lancaster. Edward, by the grace of God, King of England and France and Lord of Ireland, to all to whom the present letters shall come, greeting. Know ye, that if we, weighing with due consideration the noble bearings of all those who laudably and strenuously have served us in our wars, be desirous of raising them to honors, and rewarding them for their valour according to their merits, how much more doth it become us to advance with greater honors and favors our cousins, whom we see excelling others as well in wisdom as in noble bearing, and who have stood and may stand us in better stead. Considering, therefore, the strenuous goodness and excellent wisdom of our most dear cousin Henry Earl of Lancaster, who, yielding to no labor and charges, hath ever shewn himself ready to serve us, and many times in our need intrepidly exposing himself for us to the dangers of war, hath nobly triumphed over our enemies, we do not see how we shall be able to make him a suitable retribution that may honorably record the remembrances of the whole English nation; but, because it is meet such great and valiant deeds should attain the excellence of a more famous name, with the assent of the prelates and nobles assembled in our present parliament convoked at Westminster, we do impose upon the aforesaid Henry the name of Duke of Lancaster, and presently do invest him with the name of Duke of the said place by girding of the sword. And since it is becoming that addition of honor and advantage should accompany excellency of name, we have granted with cheerful heart, for us and our heirs, unto the aforesaid Duke, that he for the whole of his life may have within the same county his chancery, and his writs to be sealed under his seal to be deputed for the office of the chancellor, his justices to hold as well pleas of the crown[1] as all other pleas whatsoever touching the common law, and the cognisance thereof, and all manner of execution to be made by his writs and his ministers there, and all other liberties and *jura regalia* pertaining to a Count Palatine, as freely and entirely as the Earl of Chester is well known to obtain within the same county of Chester:[2] (saving always the tenths and fifteenths, and other contributions and subsidies granted and hereafter to be granted to us and our heirs by the commonalty of our realm, and the tenths and other contributions granted and hereafter to be granted to us by the clergy of the same our realm, or imposed and to be imposed upon the same clergy by the apostolic see;—and the pardon of life and limbs in case that any person of the same county, or other person in the same county, ought for any delict to lose his life or limb;—and also the superiority and power of correcting those things which shall have been erroneously done there in the courts of the same Duke, or if the same Duke or his ministers shall have failed in doing justice there also in the courts of the same Duke). And it is our intention that the same Duke, at the mandates of us and our heirs, be held to send to our parliaments and councils two knights for the commonalty[3] of the shire aforesaid, and two burgesses from every borough of the same shire, to treat with the others of the commonalty of our said realm coming to the same parliaments and councils concerning the affairs of our said realm in the same parliaments and councils to be declared. And that the same Duke shall assign certain trusty and sufficient men for the like tenths and fifteenths, subsidies and other contributions, so often as they shall happen to be granted to us or our heirs in parliament or council; so that we and our heirs may by them be answered in respect of such

[1] This special privilege of having his own chancellor (chief administrative officer) and system of chancery courts was retained by the duke of Lancaster (usually also king of England after the fifteenth century) until 1873, and still survives in an attenuated form.

[2] A count palatine exercised rights usually reserved to the king. Three lay lords on the western and northern frontiers—the Earls of Chester, Pembroke, and Lancaster—and the Bishops of Ely and Durham, held this lucrative and powerful position in medieval England, which was otherwise a model of centralized feudal monarchy.

[3] The knights as well as the burgesses belonged to the "commonalty" because Norman England had a small, privileged class of freemen and no legally distinct nobility within that class. Things were quite different on the continent.

grants. In witness whereof we have caused these our letters to be made patent. Witness ourself at Westminster on the sixth day of March, in the twenty-fifth year of our reign of England, and the twelfth of our reign of France.

A Legally Closed Class

9. THE PROBLEM OF SERVILE BLOOD

In the yeasty eleventh century it was possible for peasant laymen of exceptional determination, strength, or cleverness to rise into the ranks of the actual ruling class. In the twelfth century such feats of self-improvement became progressively rarer, and in the thirteenth they were declared technically illegal. This change in noble status from descriptive title to prescriptive right is well illustrated in the following anecdote from the life of Garnier de Mailly, who was abbot of the monastery of St. Stephen in Dijon and also its provost (administrative representative of its secular lord) in the middle of the eleventh century. The anonymous author, probably a monk of St. Stephen, wrote his admiring biography about 1164. Despite the lapse of a century he seems quite well informed on the genealogical lore of his part of Burgundy, and his social values are anything but radical. He is entirely typical in his respect for Garnier's distinguished parentage and in his assumption that the ultimate proof of unfree status was the payment of a tax levied on the serfs as though they were so many "head" of inferior creatures. Elsewhere in Europe, particularly in the Holy Roman Empire (see III, 2), a special class of serf-knights was recognized in law; in Norman England, the rigid line between villeins and freemen permitted little crossing, but great mobility above that barrier. Whatever the regional variations, the European ruling class became very conscious of its lower limits in the course of the twelfth century.

Life of the Lord Garnier, Provost of St. Stephen of Dijon

From Histoire des institutions et des faits sociaux, *ed. J. Imbert, G. Sautel, and M. Boulet-Sautel (Paris: Presses Universitaires, 1961), pp. 53–54.*

On the day after Christmas, when the venerable feast of St. Stephen is celebrated, it is the custom for those who are subject to the *census* [head tax] to present themselves before the altar, and there pay their dues in the presence of the abbey's ministers. For that reason a certain provost of the viscount of Dijon, whose name we do not mention so as not to give offense to his heirs who today shine with all the honors of knighthood, placed the *census* of the head tax on the altar in the absence of any witness, before the abbey's officers had assembled. When it was time for the procession, the illustrious Provost Garnier asked the ministers as they gathered around him if the *census* had been paid in its entirety. When they answered that all had paid the *census* except the aforesaid person, the lord Garnier forced him before them all, despite his urgent protests, to carry his *census* once more to the altar in that very assembly, in the presence of the congregation, before the procession could begin.

10. SOCIAL-CLIMBING THROUGH THE CLERGY

Jean de Joinville (1224–1319), seneschal of Champagne and personal vassal of St. Louis (king 1226–70), epitomizes the French nobility at the thirteenth-century apex of its confidence. His biography of the saintly king (Louis was canonized in 1297) is one of the chief monuments of medieval vernacular prose, although to modern eyes it often seems to reveal more about the author than the subject. Joinville wrote his masterpiece in the years immediately preceding 1309, by which time he had become disgruntled with the slippery policies of Louis' grandson, Philip IV (1285–1314). The following selection describes an encounter which probably took place in the comfortable days before the young king departed for the Sixth Crusade in 1248. In interpreting this passage, it is important to realize that Master Robert of Sorbon was an old crony of Joinville's, for whom the octogenarian author felt unmistakable nostalgia.

Joinville was born at the castle of the same name in Champagne, son of the boisterous Simon of Joinville and Beatrix of Auxonne, daughter of Count Stephen of Auxonne and Beatrix, Countess of Châlons-sur-Saône. Close kin to most of the higher nobility of the area, the young Jean received a standard aristocratic education, compounded of the Bible, devotional works in French and Latin, legal and poetic literature in French, and steady repetition of the deeds and connections of his ancestors. Foremost among them was his great-grandfather Geoffrey III de Joinville, who had been made hereditary seneschal of the rich county of Champagne on account of his bravery during the ill-fated crusade led by King Louis VII in 1147–49 (see I, 8). When Jean was 16 he married Alix of Grandpré, sister of Count Henry VI of Grandpré. In the same year he acted as seneschal for the gallant Count Thibaut IV of Champagne during a ceremonious visit to the court of the young king, who was nine years his senior. In 1243 Jean took over full management of his father's estates from the firm hands of his mother, whom he always regarded with some awe (not only because of her distant kinship to Emperor Frederick II). He was dubbed a knight about the same time. Five years later he followed Louis on crusade with three knights and 200 men-at-arms, and returned from the Holy Land with his royal lord at the bitter end of that expedition in 1254. The remaining six decades of his life were spent in managing his estates, dabbling with outspoken opinions but discreet actions in the politics of Champagne and France, and finally in reminiscence. His only child by his first marriage wed a daughter of the Villehardouin family, who had established thriving branches in Ireland and the Morea (see III, 5) as well as producing another famous crusading chronicler. By his second marriage, to Alix of Reynel (another noblewoman of Champagne), he had one son and three daughters, one of whom contracted a childless marriage with Earl Henry of Lancaster (1281–1345), the father of the Duke Henry of III, 7.

Robert of Sorbon (1201–74) was born of an ambitious peasant or bourgeois family in the county of Rethel, a northern neighbor of Champagne. His distinguished clerical achievements brought him from the cathedral chapter of Cambrai to that of Paris in 1258; in the decade before that date he had become an adviser, friend, and perhaps confessor of St. Louis. In 1257 he founded a residential college for serious students of theology at the university of Paris, which survives in a much-altered state today as the Sorbonne. Blessed though he was with managerial skill and, thanks to that, with wealth, Robert's prime talent seems to have been a contagious sense of moral propriety. His Latin treatises on confession, matrimony, and conscience won the king's respect, and probably Joinville's as well. The reader may be excused if he concludes that Louis had a keener perception of character than either his low-born chaplain or his aristocratic vassal.

Jean de Joinville: *Life of St. Louis*

From *Jean de Joinville*, Histoire de St. Louis, ed. *Natalis de Wailly (Paris: Société de l'histoire de France, 1868), pp. 12–13. Footnotes supplied.*

One Pentecost the saintly King was at Corbeil,[1] and he had eighty knights there with him. After dinner the King went down to the courtyard below the chapel, and was talking in the doorway to the Count of Brittany,[2] the father of the present Duke,[3] whom God protect! Master Robert of Sorbon came to seek me there, and took me by the cloth of my cloak and brought me to the King, and all the other knights came after us. Then I asked Master Robert, "Master Robert, what do you want of me?" And he said to me, "I want to ask you this: if the King sat down in this courtyard, and you went to take a seat higher than he on the bench, would you not be very much to blame?" And I said yes, that I would. And he said to me, "Then you are doing something very deserving of blame when you dress more nobly than the King; for you dress yourself in parti-colored fur and green cloth, which the King doesn't do." And I said to him, "Master Robert, saving your grace, I do nothing blameworthy if I dress myself in green cloth and fur, for my father and my mother left me this habit. But you do something worthy of blame, for you are the son of a peasant and a peasant woman and have left the habit of your father and your mother, and are dressed in richer camel's hair than the King's." And then I took the flap of his surcoat and of the King's surcoat, and said to him, "See if I'm not telling the truth." And then the King took it upon himself to defend Master Robert in argument with all his might.

After all this, my lord the King called to my Lord Philip his son,[4] the father of the present King, and to King Thibaut,[5] and sat down at the door of his oratory and put his hand to the ground, and said, "Sit here close to me, so no one will hear us." "Ha, Sire!" they said,

[1] A town and royal palace about 30 miles up the Seine from Paris, close to Champagne.

[2] Jean I (1237–86). He married Blanche, daughter of Count Thibaut IV, in 1235, so he was the brother-in-law of Joinville's liege lord Thibaut V.

[3] Jean II, First Duke (1286–1305). In 1260 he married Beatrix, daughter of Henry III of England.

[4] Philip III (1270–85).

[5] Thibaut V of Champagne and II of Navarre (king 1253–70), Louis' son-in-law and Joinville's liege lord.

"we would not dare sit so close to you." And he said to me, "Seneschal, sit here." And I did so, so close to him that my clothes touched his; and he made them sit after me and said to them, "You have done an ill thing in full view, being my sons and yet not doing right away what I commanded you; take care that it does not happen again." And they said that it would not. Then he said to me that he had called us over to confess that he had wrongfully defended Master Robert against me. "But," as he put it, "I saw that he was so discomfited that he really needed me to come to his aid. So don't pay any attention to what I said in defending Master Robert, for just as the Seneschal said, you should dress well and trimly so your ladies will love you better and your men will esteem you more. For, as the wise man says, 'One should array himself with clothes and with weapons in such a way that the respectable men of this world will not say that he does too much, nor the worldly youth say that he does too little.' "

11. LETTERS OF NOBILITY

The rulers of the later Middle Ages devised a formal technique for admitting new talent to the hereditary nobility. The practice of ennobling by legal charter appeared in southern France at the end of the thirteenth century, but was quickly claimed as a royal prerogative throughout Europe. The first of the following letters of nobility concentrates on the accomplishments of a single recipient, while the second seems more concerned with his family and hereditary rights; it also permits the reader to discern the discreet influence of wealth on such transactions.

Charles IV was King of Bohemia and Holy Roman Emperor from 1346 to 1378. A man of cosmopolitan culture strongly influenced by things French (his family rose to greatness as Counts of Luxemburg and his father, King John of Bohemia, was killed by the English at Crécy), Charles enjoyed ingenious political arrangements. In 1356 he issued the famous Golden Bull, which finally settled the constitution of the Empire, and in 1355 and 1358 he participated in a series of revolutions in Siena, of which he was only nominally the overlord. Perhaps his favorite project was the University of Prague, which he founded in 1348 and supported lavishly throughout his reign. The University had the first endowments in Europe for a library, faculty residences, etc.; its charter contained several provisions concerned with the harmonious organization of the different "nations" of students; and its faculty recruitment and curriculum policies sought to combine the best features of the two earlier models of university organization, Paris and Bologna. The jurist Wycker, who held a double doctorate in civil and in canon law—Bologna's most prestigious degree—was just the sort of man Charles wanted to attract to his university and his imperial service.

Charles VIII of France (1483–98) was a monarch whose ambitions gravitated toward foreign conquest and the gallantries of an earlier, more chivalric age. Robinet le Mercier's achievements are less easy to discern than those of Wycker. His family name suggests mercantile origins, but the part of Charles' entourage dominated by La Trémouille was even more warlike than the king and in 1492 was hard at work recruiting support for the forthcoming invasion of Italy (1494–97). In any case, Robinet's descendants quickly intermarried with the older feudal families of central Normandy and showed relatively little interest in urban life or activities until the seventeenth century.

Charter of Charles IV for Wycker, J.U.D.

From O. J. Thatcher and E. H. McNeal, A Source Book for Mediaeval History *(New York: Charles Scribner's Sons, 1905), pp. 550–51.*

Charles IV, by divine clemency emperor of the Romans, Augustus, and king of Bohemia, sends his favor and wishes all good to the honorable Wycker, *scholasticus*[1] of the church of St. Stephen of Mainz, his chaplain, intimate table companion, and devoted and beloved member of his household.

Beloved and devoted: Although, according to your birth and to the standards of the world, you were not born of a noble family and are not reckoned as a knight, nevertheless, because you are adorned with so great and remarkable knowledge of both the civil and canon law, that it supplies what you lack by birth, in imitation of our predecessors, the emperors of great and renowned memory, we regard your knowledge and ability as the equivalent of nobility, and out of the fulness of our imperial power we decree that you are noble and knightly, and of the same rank, honor, and condition as any other noble and knight. Therefore we strictly command all princes, ecclesiastical and secular, counts, chiefs, nobles, and all our other faithful subjects, to whom this letter may come, under threat of the loss of imperial favor, to regard, hold, and treat you as such [that is, as a knight], in all places;

[1] That is, he was a professor in the school connected with that church.

and out of reverence for the holy empire to admit you to all the rights, privileges, etc., which noblemen are accustomed to enjoy. . . .

Charter of Charles VIII for Robinet le Mercier

From an *unpublished charter registered in the* Régistre Mémorial de la Cour des Aides de Rouen (*Archives de la Préfecture du Département de la Seine-Inférieure, Rouen, 1594*), *X, 144–46 v°. Footnotes supplied.*

CHARLES by the grace of God King of the French:

The upright merit, the noble and praiseworthy deeds, and the signs of courage by which some persons are deservedly distinguished and adorned, induce Us to reward them according to their accomplishments in conformity with the example of the Creator Himself, and to elevate them and their posterity with commensurate favors and the marks of honor due to nobles, so that the name may correspond to the fact. Let them enjoy this order of prerogative and let others aspire all the more ardently to the performance of good deeds, hastening eagerly to achieve honors arising from meritorious virtues and good works.

Therefore we declare to all men present and to come that, observing the praiseworthy life, honorable behavior, fidelity, and numerous other meritorious virtues which We have come, through the trustworthy witness of many, to recognize in Our beloved Robinet le Mercier, and on account of which he has rendered himself ever more welcome and acceptable to Us, We wish to honor his person and his descendants in a manner that will redound to the perpetual honor of his person and his descendants. Therefore, from the fullness of Our royal power and authority and as a special grace, We do by these presents ennoble and have ennobled Robinet le Mercier with all his posterity and descendants of either sex procreated and to be procreated in lawful marriage, and We make them nobles and render them capable of all and every thing which the other nobles of Our kingdom enjoy and are able and accustomed to enjoy.

Therefore Robinet himself and his male descendants and posterity procreated and to be procreated in wedlock may receive the belt of knighthood from whichever knight they wish. We concede to the same Robinet and to his descendants and posterity procreated and to be procreated in lawful marriage that each of them shall be accorded full noble standing by everyone in judgments and in all cases. They shall have the benefit of whatever privileges, prerogatives, franchises, honors, liberties, and rights of nobility the other nobles of Our aforesaid kingdom may enjoy and use in peace, freedom, and tranquillity. We concede furthermore that the aforesaid Robinet and his descendants and posterity procreated and to be procreated in lawful marriage may acquire noble fiefs and rear-fiefs[1] and other noble properties of whatever sort and whatever authority may attach to them . . .[2]

Wherefore, by the tenor of these presents, We instruct Our beloved and faithful agents of the Chambre des Comptes[3] and of Our treasury in the *Baillage*[4] of Rouen, and Our other justiciars and officials or those who serve in their place, both present and to come, whomever of them it may concern, to assist the aforesaid Robinet le Mercier and his descendants and posterity of either sex procreated or to be procreated in lawful marriage, in the enjoyment and use of Our grant of nobility, gift, remission, and favor, and [We instruct them] to leave them in peace and quiet; let no one in contradiction of the tenor of these presents disturb or molest them in any way either now or at any time in the future.

In order that Our decree remain firm and stable forever, We have ordered Our seal to be attached to these presents: saving Our right in other matters and that of any other party in all. Given at St. Denis in France in the month of March in the fourteen-hundred-and-ninety-second Year of Our Lord, the tenth of Our reign.

(Signed on the reverse fold:)
For the King:
  the Count de Bucy,
  the Seigneur de la Trémoille,[5]

---

[1] A rear-fief was a fief held by vassal *C* of lord *A*, through an intermediate bond with *B* (lord of *C*, vassal of *A*). Some fiefs were designated as *noble* in order to distinguish them from those which could legally be bought by bourgeois. Robinet's heirs tended for several generations to be direct vassals ("tenants-in-chief") of the King in his capacity as Count of Montfort.

[2] In the later medieval and nearly modern periods, the French Crown made a regular policy of selling certain administrative or judicial posts to anyone belonging to certain qualified groups. The office concerned and the public authority connected with it then became a piece of property, dear to the officeholder's family for reasons either of financial profit or of prestige. "Property-in-office" was finally abolished in France by the Revolution of 1789.

[3] The royal financial bureau, which had "branches" in several of the more important provincial capitals.

[4] The district administered by a *Bailli*, who was the top royal official in any given area. The *Baillage* de Rouen extended some 15 miles north, east, and south of Normandy's capital city, and some 45 miles west into the district involved in this document. The law courts and financial agencies sitting at Rouen exercised jurisdiction over all or most of Normandy, however.

[5] Probably Louis II de La Trémouille, Viscount of Thouars, Prince of Talmont, etc. Called the "Chevalier sans reproche" in his lifetime, Louis was one of the great

the Seigneur de Myolans,
the Seigneur d'Aubigny,[6]
and others present.

(Bound with red and green silk, with a seal in green wax. Further down on the reverse appears this endorsement:)

The Treasurer of Our Lord the King has received and transmitted to the same Lord from Robinet le Mercier, feudal Seigneur of Les Vieux in the viscounty of Pont-Audemer, in the parish of Écaquelon,[7] *the sum of fifty gold écues which he owed the agents of the Chambre des Comptes for the costs of the ennobling of his person and his descendants and posterity [etc.] by virtue of the letters of the aforesaid Lord King in the form of a charter given at St. Denis in France in the month of March, 1492; assessed by the aforesaid Treasurer for the burden and execution of entering the aforesaid document in the same Treasury, 17 March 1493.*

---

nobles of France. Lord of one of the realm's largest collection of estates, he supported the young and uncertain Charles VIII against all his foreign and domestic enemies, and received many high commands (like the lieutenant-generalcy of Poitou) in return. His family, well-known since the eleventh century, had produced numerous French military heroes, all of whom Louis II surpassed by his feats in the Italian wars. Born in 1460, he died at the battle of Pavia in 1525.

[6] Probably Robert Stewart, seigneur d'Aubigny (died 1544). The fief of Aubigny (near Sancerre) was given to his ancestor John Stewart, Lord Darnley, in 1423 by King Charles VII, and stayed in the family until 1672. Robert's greatest military feat was bringing the remnants of Charles VIII's army out of Italy with relative safety; returning to later Franco-Italian wars, he served Francis I as Governor of Milan and Viceroy of Naples.

[7] The town of Pont-Audemer is about 40 miles west of Rouen, on the river Risle. Écaquelon is about 12 miles up the Risle from there, on the edge of the forest of Montfort.

THE PEASANTS   IV

The peasants were the most essential members of medieval European society, but the least favored and, of course, the least articulate. The relative silence of normal sources of historical evidence on their thoughts, attitudes, and values presents the modern student with a serious dilemma. We are forced to rely almost entirely on the judgments of those who exploited the peasantry or had left it behind them; even when we have a "strictly factual" record to deal with, we have no guarantee that the categories used in it, or even the facts reported, would have seemed right to the peasants in question. One is tempted, for the sake of strict accuracy, to say rather little about this faceless multitude. On the other hand, how can one really justify ignoring that vast majority of medieval Europeans, without whose strenuous labor the history-makers would have found it difficult if not impossible to eat, drink, clothe themselves, or undertake the ambitious enterprises we are inclined to remember?

This chapter's selections attempt to show several approaches to discovering the character of peasant life across a span of four centuries marked by a fair amount of social change. It begins with three literary evocations of the peasant image, each deriving from a different social context. Then come extracts from three solemnly authoritative legal texts, one an early estate register, the next a model code for judicial reform, the last a classic treatise on customary law. These are followed by several documents which reveal the dramatic twelfth- and thirteenth-century improvement in formal status and in economic leverage that permanently elevated the position of the peasantry in France, but was to undergo a frustrating reversal east of the Rhine. The final selection, a series of excerpts from the regular proceedings of a minor rural court, has been included in order to suggest (among other things) both the invariable monotony and the intense particularism which characterized most peasant communities in medieval Europe as well as in other regions and periods of history.

The Peasant Image

1. A CLERICAL VIEW

The following selection presents a stilted and somewhat idealized picture, which is hardly surprising since it comes from an interlinear Latin and Old English textbook composed by an idealistic Benedictine monk, Aelfric of Eynsham (955?–1020?). Nevertheless, it shows us how the basic activities of the peasant world looked in the eyes of a well-educated cleric, and it contains one of the earliest echoes of the unfree peasant's fundamental discontent. Aelfric was the sort of man who would be sympathetic to the plight of the poor folk, at least to the extent that he could understand it. Although he was intent on the reform of literary education and monastic discipline and deeply involved with archbishops of Canterbury and wealthy lay patrons in the realization of those goals, most of the books he wrote were designed to be instruments for improving the state of average religious practice among the laity. His numerous works in Old English indicate his sensitivity to the nuances of popular speech; it may be that he had a good ear for popular sentiments, too.

Aelfric of Eynsham: *Colloquy*

From *Aelfric of Eynsham,* Dialogue of the Teacher, *trans. W. R. Parish, in Allen R. Benham,* English Literature from Widsith to the Death of Chaucer *(New Haven: Yale University Press, 1916), pp. 26–33. Reprinted by permission of the publisher.*

Pupil. We children beg you, teacher, to teach us how to speak Latin correctly, for we are very ignorant and make mistakes in our speech.

Teacher. What do you want to talk about?

Pupil. What do we care what the subject is, provided the language be correct, and the discourse be useful, not idle and base? . . .

Teacher. I ask an answer to this: What is your work at present?

Pupil. I am a monk by profession and I sing every day at seven services of the hours with my brethren and am occupied with reading and singing, but nevertheless I should like, between times, to learn Latin.

Teacher. What do these your comrades know?

Pupil. Some are plowmen, some shepherds, some oxherds; and some are hunters, some fishermen, some fowlers, some merchants, some shoemakers, some salters, and some bakers.

Teacher. Plowman, what can you say for yourself? How do you do your work?

Plowman. O, dear master, I work very hard; I go out at daybreak, drive the oxen to the field and yoke them to the plow. Never is winter weather so severe that I dare to remain at home; for I fear my master. But when the oxen are yoked to the plow and the share and coulter fastened on, every day I must plow a full acre or more.

Teacher. Have you any one to help you?

Plowman. I have a boy who urges on the oxen with a goad. He is now hoarse from cold and shouting.

Teacher. Do you do anything else in the course of a day?

Plowman. I do a great deal more. I have to fill the bins of the oxen with hay and water them and clean their stalls.

Teacher. Oh! Oh! that is hard work!

Plowman. The labor is indeed great, because I am not free.

Teacher. What is your work, shepherd, have you anything to do?

Shepherd. Yes indeed, master, I have. In the early morning I drive my sheep to their pasture and stand over them in heat or cold with dogs lest wolves devour them. I lead them back to their folds and milk them twice a day. In addition I move their folds, make cheese and butter and am faithful to my master.

Teacher. Well, oxherd, what is your work?

Oxherd. O my master, my work is very hard. When the plowman unyokes the oxen, I lead them to pasture and all night I stand over them and watch for thieves. Then in the early morning I turn them over to the plowman after I have fed and watered them.

Teacher. Is this one of your friends?

Oxherd. Yes, he is.

Teacher. Can you do anything?

Hunter. I know one craft.

Teacher. What is it?

Hunter. I am a hunter.

Teacher. Whose?

Hunter. The king's.

Teacher. How do you carry on your work?

Hunter. I weave my nets and put them in a suitable place, and train my dogs to follow the wild beasts until they come unexpectedly to the nets and are entrapped. Then I kill them in the nets.

Teacher. Can't you hunt without nets?

Hunter. Yes, I can hunt without them.

Teacher. How?

Hunter. I chase wild beasts with swift dogs.

Teacher. What wild beasts do you catch?

Hunter. Harts, boars, does, goats and sometimes hares.

Teacher. Did you go out to-day?

Hunter. No, because it is Sunday; but I was out yesterday.

Teacher. What luck did you have?

Hunter. I got two harts and a boar.

Teacher. How did you catch them?

Hunter. The harts I took in a net and the boar I slew.

Teacher. How did you dare to kill a boar?

Hunter. The dogs drove him to me, and I, standing opposite to him, slew him suddenly.

Teacher. You were very brave.

Hunter. A hunter should not be afraid; for many kinds of wild beasts live in the woods.

Teacher. What do you do with your game?

Hunter. I give the king what I take because I am his hunter.

Teacher. What does he give you?

Hunter. He clothes me well and feeds me. Occasionally he gives me a horse or a ring that I may pursue my craft more willingly.

Teacher. What craft do you follow?

Fisherman. I am a fisherman.

Teacher. What do you gain by your craft?

Fisherman. Food and clothes and money.

Teacher. How do you catch your fish?

Fisherman. I go out in my boat, throw my net in the river, cast in my hook baited and take in my creel whatever comes to me.

Teacher. What if they are unclean fish?

Fisherman. I throw the unclean ones back and keep the clean for meat.

Teacher. Where do you sell your fish?

Fisherman. In the city.

Teacher. Who buys them?

Fisherman. The citizens; I do not catch as many as I could sell.

Teacher. What sorts of fish do you catch?

Fisherman. Eels and pike, minnows and turbots, trout and lampreys; in short, whatever swims in running water.

Teacher. Why don't you fish in the sea?

Fisherman. Sometimes I do, but seldom; because a large boat is needed for sea-fishing.

Teacher. What do you catch in the sea?

Fisherman. Herring and salmon, dolphins and sturgeons, oysters and crabs, mussels, periwinkles, cockles, flounders, sole, lobsters and many others.

Teacher. Wouldn't you like to catch a whale?

Fisherman. No.

Teacher. Why not?

Fisherman. Because it is a dangerous thing to catch a whale. It is safer for me to go to the river with my boat than to go with many ships to hunt whales.

Teacher. Why so?

Fisherman. Because I prefer to take a fish that I can kill than one that with a single blow can swallow not only me but my companions also.

Teacher. Yet, many catch whales without danger and get a good price for them.

Fisherman. I know it, but I do not dare; for I am very timid.

Teacher. What have you to say, fowler? How do you catch the birds?

Fowler. I entice them in many ways, sometimes with nets, sometimes with nooses, sometimes with lime, sometimes by whistling, sometimes with a hawk and sometimes with traps.

Teacher. Have you a hawk?

Fowler. Yes.

Teacher. Can you tame it?

Fowler. Yes; what good would it be to me, if I could not tame it?

Hunter. Give me a hawk.

Fowler. I will gladly, if you will give me a swift dog. Which hawk do you prefer, the larger or the smaller?

Hunter. Give me the larger one.

Teacher. How do you feed your hawks?

Fowler. They feed themselves and me in the winter, and in the spring I let them fly in the woods. In the autumn I take the young birds and tame them.

Teacher. And why do you let the tame ones go?

Fowler. Because I don't want to feed them in the summer, since they eat a good deal.

Teacher. Many people feed those that they have tamed, even through the summer, that they may have them ready again.

Fowler. Yes, so they do; but I do not take so much trouble for them, because I can get others, not one only, but many more.

[Conversations with the merchant, shoemaker, and salter follow.]

Teacher. Salter, how is your craft useful to us?

Salter. Who of you would relish his food without the savor of salt? Who could fill either his cellar or his storeroom without the aid of my craft? behold, all butter and cheese would you lose, nor would you enjoy even your vegetables, without me.

Teacher. And what do you say, baker? Does any one need your craft, or could we live without you?

Baker. Life might be sustained for a while without my craft, but not long nor well. Truly, without my skill, every table would be empty. Without bread all food would cause sickness. I strengthen the heart of man. I am the strength of men and few would like to do without me.

Teacher. What shall we say of the cook? Do we need his skill for anything?

Cook. If you should send me away from your midst, you would be compelled to eat your vegetables green and your meat uncooked, and you could have no nourishing broth without my skill.

Teacher. We do not need your skill, nor is it necessary to us; for we ourselves could cook the things which should be cooked and roast the things that should be roasted.

Cook. If you send me away, that is what you will have to do. Nevertheless, without my skill, you cannot eat.

Teacher. Monk, you who are talking with me, I have persuaded myself that you have good comrades and that they are very necessary. Now, who are these?

Pupil. I have smiths—a blacksmith, a goldsmith, a silversmith, a coppersmith, a carpenter and many other workers at various trades.

Teacher. Have you any wise counselor?

Pupil. I certainly have. How could our community be ruled without a counselor?

Teacher. What would you say, wise man? Among these crafts which seems to you the greatest?

Counselor. I tell you that among all these occupations the service of God seems to me to hold the first place; for thus it is written in the Gospels: "Seek ye first the kingdom of God and his righteousness and all these things shall be added to you."

Teacher. And among the worldly crafts which seems to you to be first?

Counselor. Agriculture, because the farmer feeds us all.

Blacksmith. Where would the farmer get his plowshare, or mend his coulter when it has lost its point, without my craft? Where would the fisherman get his hook, or the shoemaker his awl, or the tailor his needle, if it were not for my work?

Counselor. Verily, you speak the truth; but we prefer to live with the farmer rather than with you; for the farmer gives us food and drink. What you give us in your shop is sparks, noise of hammers and blowing of bellows.

Carpenter. How could you spare my skill in building houses, in the use of various tools, in building ships and in all the things I make?

Counselor. O comrades and good workmen, let us quickly settle these disputes, and let there be peace and harmony among us. Let each one benefit the others with his craft and agree always with the farmer who feeds us and from whom we get fodder for our horses. And this advice I give to all workers, that each one shall follow his own craft diligently, for he who forsakes his craft shall be himself forsaken by his craft. Whoever you are, priest or monk or layman or soldier, exercise yourself in this. Be satisfied with your office; for it is a great disgrace for a man to be unwilling to be what he is, and what it is his duty to be.

Teacher. Well, children, how have you enjoyed this conversation?

Pupil. Pretty well, but you speak profoundly and beyond our age. Speak to us according to our intelligence that we may understand what you say.

2. A NOBLE PARODY

Here is a parody of peasant types composed for the delectation of the thirteenth-century French nobility. The anonymous vernacular romance from which it is taken has an excellent time making friendly fun of fathers, lovers, clerics, Saracens, and several other major elements of medieval society. The chief appeal of this elegant tale partly in prose and partly in verse (for which we fortunately have the musical score), has always been to the young at heart or in wish; its chief serious message seems to be that being serious is usually absurd. Aucassin, its entirely fictional hero, is the son of Count Garin of Beaucaire (a real city on the river Rhone between Arles and Avignon), who is disgusted at the romantic nonsense going on between his son and the beautiful but sensible and quite virtuous Nicolette, a Saracen captive of mysterious but evidently high birth. Garin banishes Nicolette, whereupon Aucassin sulks and then follows her; everything turns out wonderfully of course, with a revelation of Nicolette's royal birth, the lovers' marriage, etc. The peasants' reactions to all this alternate between gruesome boorishness and bucolic lyricism—both caricatures were destined for a long life in European literature, but are not therefore necessarily unworthy of the serious student's consideration.

Aucassin et Nicolette

From Aucassin et Nicolette, *ed. and trans. Francis W. Bourdillon (London: Macmillan & Co., Ltd., 1897), pp. 63–67, 75–77, 83–89.*

Now they say and tell and relate.

Nicolette made great lamentation, as you have heard. She commended herself to God, and went on till she came into the forest. She durst not go deep into it, for the wild beasts and for the serpent kind; and she crept into a thick bush, and sleep took her; and she slept till the morrow at high Prime, that the herdboys came out of the town, and drove their beasts between the wood and the river; and they draw aside to a very beautiful spring which was at the edge of the forest, and spread out a cloak and put their bread on it. While they were eating, Nicolette awoke at the cry of the birds and of the herdboys, and she sprang towards them.

"Fair children!" said she, "may the Lord help you!"

"May God bless you!" said the one who was more ready of speech than the others.

"Fair children," said she, "know you Aucassin, the son of the Count Garin of Beaucaire?"

"Yes, we know him well."

"So God help you, fair children," said she, "tell him that there is a beast in this forest, and that he come to hunt it. And if he can catch it he would not give one limb of it for a hundred marks of gold,—no, not for five hundred, nor for any wealth."

And they regard her, and saw her so beautiful that they were all bewildered.

"I tell him?" said he who was more ready of speech than the others; "sorrow be his who shall ever speak of it or who shall ever tell him! 'Tis fantasy that you say, since there is not so dear a beast in this forest, neither stag nor lion nor wild boar, whereof one of the limbs were worth more than two pence, or three at the most; and you speak of so great wealth! Ill sorrow be his who believes you, or who shall ever tell him! You are a fay, and we have no care for your company, but keep on your way!"

"Ah, fair children!" said she, "this will you do! The beast has such a medicine that Aucassin will be cured of his hurt. And I have here five sous in my purse; take them and tell him! And within three days must he hunt; and, if in three days he find it not, never more will he be cured of his hurt!"

"I' faith!" said he, "the pence will we take; and if he comes here we will tell him, but we will never go to seek him."

"I' God's name!" said she.

Then she takes leave of the herdboys, and goes her way.

Here they sing.

> Nicolette, that bright-faced may,
> From the herdboys went her way,
> And set forth upon her road
> Right amid the bosky wood,
> Down an ancient path foregone,
> Till a highway she came on, . . .

[After various adventures, Aucassin comes upon the herdboys singing:]

Quoth the one: "Fair comrades mine,
Pray God help young Aucassin!
Aye, i' faith! the pretty lad!
And the girl in bodice clad,
Who of yellow had her hair,
Bright her face, her eyes of vair.
Her that did the pence bestow
Which to buy us cakes shall go,
Eke a sheath, and eke a knife,
Eke a flute, and eke a fife,
Crooks and whistlepipes moreover.
    God him recover!"

Now they say and tell and relate.

When Aucassin heard the shepherd boys, he minded him of Nicolette his most sweet friend whom he loved so much; and he bethought him that she had been there. And he pricks his horse with the spurs, and came to the shepherd boys.

"Fair children, may God help you!"

"May God bless you!" said he who was more ready of speech than the others.

"Fair children," said he, "say again the song that you were saying just now!"

"We will not say it," said he who was more ready of speech than the others. "Now sorrow be his who shall sing it for you, fair sir!"

"Fair children," said Aucassin, "do you not know me?"

"Yes, we knew well that you are Aucassin, our young lord; but we do not belong to you, but we belong to the Count."

"Fair children! you will do so, I pray you!"

"Hear, by Gog's heart!" said he. "Why should I sing for you, an it suited me not? Since there is not so rich a man in this country,—saving Count Garin's self—if he found my oxen or my cows or my sheep in his meadows or in his wheat, that he would be so venturesome for to have his eyes put out as to dare to chase them from it. And why should I sing for you, an it suited me not?"

"So God help you, fair children, you will do so! And take ten sous which I have here in a purse!"

"Sir, the pence will we take, but I will not sing to you, for I have sworn it. But I will tell it to you, if you will."

*   *   *

Now they say and tell and relate.

Aucassin went through the forest from way to way, and his good steed bore him on a great pace. Think not that the briars and thorns spared him! Not a whit! But they tore his clothes, so that one could hardly have knotted over at the soundest, and so that the blood flowed from his arms and from his sides and from his legs in forty places or thirty; so that, after the boy, one could have followed the track of the blood that fell upon the grass. But he thought so much on Nicolette, his sweet friend, that he felt neither hurt nor pain; and he went all day through the forest, in such wise that never heard he news of her. And, when he saw that the evening was drawing on, he began to weep because he found her not.

Along an old grassy way he was riding, and he looked before him amid the way, and saw a boy such as I will tell you. Tall was he and wonderful and ugly and hideous. He had a great shock head blacker than a coal, and had more than a full palm-breadth between his two eyes; and he had great cheeks, and an immense flat nose, and great wide nostrils, and thick lips redder than a broiled steak, and great teeth yellow and ugly; and he was shod in leggings and shoes of ox-hide, laced with bast as far as above the knee; and he was wrapped in a cloak with two wrong sides, and was leaning on a great club. Aucassin sprang towards him, and had great fear when he considered him.

"Fair brother, may God help thee!"

"May God bless you!" said he.

"So God help thee, what doest thou there?"

"What matters it to you?" said he.

"Nothing," said Aucassin; "I ask you not save for good."

"But for what are you weeping," said he, "and making such sorrow? Certès, if I were as rich a man as you are, all the world would not make me weep!"

"Bah! Do you know me?" said Aucassin.

"Yes. I know well that you are Aucassin the son of the Count; and if you tell me for what you are weeping I will tell you what I am doing here."

"Certès," said Aucassin, "I will tell you right willingly. I came this morning to hunt in this forest; and I had a white greyhound, the most beautiful in the world, and I have lost it; for this am I weeping."

"Hear!" said he, "by the heart the Lord had in His body! That you wept for a stinking dog! Foul sorrow be his who ever again shall esteem you! Since there is no such rich man in this land, if your father demanded of him ten, or fifteen, or twenty, he would not have given them too willingly, and be too glad. But I should weep and make sorrow."

"And thou for what, brother?"

"Sir, I will tell you. I was hired to a rich villein, and drove his plough —four oxen there were. It is now three days since there befell me a great misadventure, that I lost the best of my oxen, Roget, the best of my team; and I am going in search of it. And I have neither eaten nor drunk these three days past; and I dare not go to the town, as they would put me in prison, since I have not wherewith to pay for it. Of all the wealth in the world have I nothing more worth than you see on the body of me. A wretched mother had I, and she had nothing more worth than a mattress, and they have dragged it from under her back, and she lies on the pure straw; and this troubles me a deal more than for myself. For wealth comes and goes; if I have lost now I shall gain another time, and I shall pay for my ox when I can; nor ever for this will I weep. And you wept for a dog of the dunghill! Foul sorrow be his who ever again shall esteem you!"

"Certès, thou art of good comfort, fair brother! Blessed be thou! And what was worth thine ox?"

"Sir, twenty sous do they ask me for it; I cannot abate a single farthing."

"Now take," said Aucassin, "twenty which I have here in my purse, and pay for thine ox!"

"Sir," said he, "Gramercy! And may God grant you to find that which you seek!"

He takes his leave of him; and Aucassin rides on. The night was fine and still; and he went on till he came to the place where the seven roads fork, and he looked before him, and saw the lodge which Nicolette had made; . . .

3. A PEASANT DAYDREAM

The following selection is a nearly complete *fabliau*, a modest example of a kind of short tale in jingly verse immensely popular in thirteenth- and fourteenth-century France. Crude compositions of wandering minstrels who usually belonged to the lower bourgeoisie or to those elements of the peasantry that had managed to get a little schooling, the *fabliaux* were favorite entertainments at rural or urban fairs. Generally full of ribaldry and frank social satire, occasionally flashing an acute insight, these crude poems were excellent vehicles for the expression of the poor peoples' self-image. This translation has sacrificed any sense of the original rhythmic pattern in order to preserve the original metaphors and phrasing as exactly as possible. The basic structure of this *fabliau* is an extended pun on the word *buffet,* which in Old French, as in modern English, meant both a blow with the fist and a table or cabinet for eating. The reader should note that the central criticism is directed not at the authentic nobleman, but at his pushy manager, whose behavior was probably supposed to suggest humble origins. Those of us who have been conditioned by modern assumptions about self-conscious class struggle may find this medieval priority of hostilities surprising; it is well attested by a wide range of less imaginative sources, however, and appears to be quite normal.

The Peasant and the Buffet

From Le vilain au buffet, *in* Recueil général et complet des fabliaux des XIIIe et XIVe siècles, *ed. Anatole de Montaiglon and Gaston Raynaud (Paris: Librairie des Bibliophiles, 1878), III, 199–208. Footnotes supplied.*

Once upon a time, as the story goes, a count had in his household a seneschal who was treacherous, greedy, and spiteful, and full of every evil trait; you may be sure that nobody who got bad treatment when he came there would ever lodge a complaint against him!

If his lord did anyone a favor, he would be filled with rage; over even a little thing he would be ready to burst with resentment, irritation, and envy. The count, who led a good life and had a great reputation, was not amused at his seneschal's maliciousness, for he saw perfectly well that he disliked everyone who received hospitality at the count's residence. Everybody knew about his malice and the control he exercised, and everybody detested him. And the villainous[1] creature grew fat as a pig, and filled his guts with the wine he had stolen; many a fat capon and many a spring chicken he ate all alone in his office, without even thinking of letting anyone else in on it!

The count, who was both honorable and wise, sent messages everywhere, announcing that he wished to hold court. Rumor, which runs

---

[1] In the original, *vilain,* a term which technically meant "unfree peasant," but popularly (as well as in upper-class language) also meant "ugly," whether physically or morally. Both the hero and the villain (note that derivative word!) of this punning *fabliau* are called *vilains.*

about everywhere, spread through the countryside. Squires, knights, and ladies who don't do as much for their souls as they are well used to doing for their bodies, came to court without delay. . . . What abundance was spread out there! Whoever wished could enter the court: there came many of the sort who, believe me, had never had their fill either in winter or in summer; but everyone had enough to eat, both meat and wine without stint, for so the count had ordered.

"Well, we're falling in debt to disaster now," said the seneschal. "They don't contribute anything of their own to all this. Each one that comes asks for whatever pops into his head and suits him, as if it didn't cost the price of an egg. I can see thirty-nine right now who haven't had a full belly in a long time."

At that moment a peasant named Raoul entered. He was a cowherd who had just left the plow. The seneschal turned his eyes right on the peasant, who suddenly realized that he was in an embarrassing situation, since he was unwashed and his head was shaggy—it had been about fifty years since he'd had a cap on his head. Malice, which puts it in the head of many a man to offend and do villainous and cruel deeds, got hold of the seneschal so strongly that he was almost in pain. As soon as the peasant entered, he went to block his way, furious and swollen with anger.

"Look at this guzzler of peas! By the Holy Spirit, it's in spite of me that you've come in here! He must have rolled in the straw to get so frizzy. Look how he makes like an empty pot: it'll take many a bowl of leek soup to stuff that belly!" . . . And so the seneschal raved on, dying with pain and irritation: "Whoever showed you the way here should be drowned in a latrine!"

At the sound of all this, the peasant made the sign of the Cross with his hight hand. "Sir," he said, "by St. Germain,[2] I have just come to eat, for I've heard say that nobody gets refused here; but I don't know where to sit."

"I'll show you where to sit," the seneschal said mockingly; he raised his fist, knocked him down with a great buffet, and then said with a sneering laugh, "Sit down there! It's here, at this buffet, that you should be seated!"

The seneschal went away whistling, so as to taunt the peasant. He had a napkin brought him, and food and wine aplenty; he thought

---

[2] Perhaps St. Germain of Auxerre (in southern Champagne), a great converting bishop of the fifth century. More probably St. Germain of Paris (496–561), who was known as "Father of the Poor" on account of his charities, and continued to work miracles from his tomb in the abbey of St. Germain-des-Prés.

the peasant would not fail to get himself drunk, and that then he would beat him so thoroughly that he would lose any desire to show up again in a lord's court.

Why stretch this story out any longer? The count had the minstrels come in, and announced that he would give his brand-new robe of scarlet to whoever would tell or perform the best joke. At once the minstrels began encouraging one another to show their talents. One played a drunkard, another an idiot; one sang and another accompanied him; one started a debate, another answered him back; and those who knew how to juggle performed in front of the count. There was one who recited a *fabliau* full of mockery, while another one told the story of the *Herberie*,[3] which was greeted with a lot of laughter.

The peasant, who was thinking how to avenge himself for the bad treatment the seneschal had given him, waited until everyone had finished. Then the seneschal, I don't know why, went to tell the count something. While the seneschal was talking, the peasant picked up his napkin; very smoothly, without any rush, he made his way up to the count and right next to the seneschal, who was so intent on his lord that he didn't notice him. Then he raised his hand, which was hard and full of calluses—as hard as you could want, since there wasn't a stronger man this side of Wales—and struck him a great blow, and said: "Here's your buffet and your napkin: I don't want to take them away. It's a bad deal when a man doesn't give back what's been lent him."

The count's men ran up in a flash to assault the peasant, for they were furious at the sight of the seneschal wiped out at the count's feet. But the count said he wanted to hear the story, and the reason why he had struck him, so they fell still since their lord commanded it.

Then the count asked the peasant why he had wounded his seneschal: "Your spirits were too high when you struck him in front of me! You've fallen into a bad situation, and committed a real outrage; I will have you put in my prison."

"Sire," said he, "please listen to me, and hear me out for just a moment. When I came in here I ran into your seneschal, who is cruel, filthy, and a miser. His vile and stingy manners told me off and made fun of me; he gave me a great buffet and then told me for a joke that that's what I should sit at, and what he'd provide me with. Then he brought me some food, and now that I've eaten and drunk, sire Count,

[3] Another, better-known *fabliau* of the time.

what should I do with his buffet besides give it back to him? I know very well that if I'd lost it, he would have been quick to take offense; so here I've returned it to him before witnesses, as you have seen yourself. Sire Count, before you go to wash your hands, judge if I have committed any crime for which I should be held here. It's only right for the seneschal to let me pass, since I've well returned what he provided me. Here I am, ready to give him another buffet, if the one he's gotten isn't enough!"

The count, whose name was Lord Henry,[4] let out a laugh, and a general roar of laughter started that took a long time to stop. The seneschal didn't know what to do; he held his hand in front of his face, which was frying with shame. He was furious at those he saw laughing, and would have done many disgraceful things to the peasant, but did not dare for fear of the count, who sternly forbade it.

Then the count said to the seneschal, "He has given you back your buffet, and all that he had of yours." And then he said to the peasant, "Take my robe which is brand-new, for you have come up with a better joke than all the minstrels."

The minstrels all agreed with the count and said: "Indeed, Sire, you say the truth: he deserves a very fine prize! I have never seen such a good peasant; he served your seneschal very well in paying back his mockery. The man who provokes evil and goes to a lot of trouble for its sake is a fool: the gifts of a lord and the griefs of a serf aren't worth crying over.[5] They are a lost and useless race of men who guard what they have in their care so tightly that they do no good with it! Nothing that's in their hands gives anyone either profit or comfort. Wealth which does not honor the lord is evil indeed. Let's all say 'God be praised!' for this seneschal who got knocked down; to the flames with those who turn good to ill!"

The peasant left the court, carrying the lord's robe away with him. When he had gotten outside the gate, he said to himself, " 'He who

[4] Possibly a reference to Count Henry the Liberal of Champagne and Brie (1152–81), who fought with distinction on the Second Crusade (as did Jean de Joinville's great-grandfather, his vassal, whom he made hereditary seneschal after their return; see III, 10). He died shortly after his return from another Crusade. His wife was Marie, daughter of Louis VII of France and Eleanor of Aquitaine. Their son Henry II ruled Champagne 1181–97, and claimed the crown of Jerusalem in his wife's right after 1190. A third Henry ruled Champagne and also the kingdom of Navarre 1270–74; he was the son of Thibaut IV, and brother of Thibaut V (see III, 10). But the court presented in this *fabliau* is a far cruder and more rustic affair than that of the opulent Counts of Champagne and Kings of Navarre!

[5] Compare the remarks of the ploughman in the forest to Aucassin in the previous selection.

sits gets thirsty' "; and then, " 'He who gets moving, gets a lick.' If I'd stayed home in my hut, it would have been a long time before I got a brand-new scarlet suit: 'He who hunts well, gets a good bag!' "

The Legal Order

4. A CAROLINGIAN MONASTERY'S MANOR ROLL

In the early Middle Ages, the vast majority of western Europeans lived in rather tightly organized agricultural communities which it is most convenient to call villages, although some historians prefer the term *manor*. The pattern of village life was already very old, deriving largely from the "Agricultural Revolution" of the Late Stone Age, and responding slowly to technological or social change. By the time of Charlemagne, most of these communities had become subject to some sort of lord, who exacted a portion of the produce and controlled the normal operation of the law. He did not exactly "own" the land, however; the peasants retained considerable control over their village and maintained its unity when more than one lord had rights to revenue or the exercise of power.

The demands of local farming conditions and the powerful insistence of custom made for a certain amount of variation within the generally stable order of village life. In some regions the peasants' houses were scattered throughout the area belonging to the village, in others all the buildings clustered around a nucleus. Some village areas were broken up into many fields by hedges or fences, while the plowed land of others made one great open field; in most cases arable land was supplemented by forest, meadows, watercourses, etc. The lords and peasants of certain favored regions devoted much time and territory to such specialized crops as grapes, apples, olives, or other fruit, but the staple crop was usually some form of grain. Cattle and poultry of various kinds also contributed to the diet and the economy. In most villages of whatever type, the lord possessed a *demesne,* a portion of usable land from which all the produce went directly to him. The rest of the village was divided into *mansi,* units of exploitation (often scattered widely), each adequate for the support of a peasant household after the required dues were paid to the lord.

The legal status of the individual peasants could vary within a single community, as could physical layout from one region to another. In the following ninth-century document from the heartland of the Frankish empire, we can discern the existence of two basic classes, freemen and serfs. The village *mansi* were divided according to the same classification, and differed somewhat in the nature of their dues, but a man's (or woman's) personal status did not necessarily correspond to that of the land he held. Also present is a third group with many names (*forenses, forastici, accolae, aubains,* etc.), those who for one reason or another were outside the jurisdiction of the court of the village in question, but who lived and worked in close association with the village. According to the traditions of Germanic law, such aliens were not without rights if some full legal member of the community would stand as a pledge for them or take them under his patronage—in this case, that person was the village's lord, the abbot of the monastery of St. Remi at Reims.

Named for and original burial place of the legend-encrusted archbishop (459?–533?) who baptized the Frankish king Clovis after his conversion to Catholic Christianity, the monastery grew up outside the old city walls, and became in turn the nucleus of a suburb, as well as the possessor of rich lands scattered throughout Champagne (King Dagobert—see II, 8(a)—seems to have been an outstanding benefactor). After a period of decline and royal spoliation, the monastery was taken under the protection of the archbishop, who was its abbot from the 780's to 945. Perhaps the most vigorous of its rulers during this period was Hincmar (806–82), a member of the Frankish aristocracy who entered the great monastery of St. Denis near Paris as a boy and came to Reims as archbishop and abbot in 845. Author of several strongly assertive books on dogmatic theology, canon law, political theory, history, and biography (including *Lives* of Dagobert and St. Remigius), Hincmar was an indefatigable builder; among his projects were a new city wall, a hostel for pilgrims and paupers, and a new abbey church (consecrated in 852). His consequent need for construction material is clearly reflected in the following excerpts from the general survey of the abbey's rural property which he initiated very soon after his arrival.

Aguilcourt was and is a nucleated village about 10 miles north of Reims, less than a mile south of the river Aisne which had constituted the chief natural boundary of the *pays Rémois*. The abbey was lord of the entire village. Its population at the time of the selection which follows appears to have numbered about 325 (100 more than its population in 1962); perhaps an equal number of "outsiders" appear in the abbey's tally of Aguilcourt and its associated resources. Cernay-en-Dormois is about 75 miles up the curving valley of the Aisne from Aguilcourt, and about 30 miles due east of Reims on the Roman road that then begins to cut through the wooded uplands of the Argonne on its way to the Rhineland. Now numbering only 305 souls (less than half its nineteenth-century population), Cernay was a relatively important center of local administration in the Middle Ages, being the seat of a deanery of the archdiocese and later of a sizable lay barony. Situated at a crossroads commanding its sector of the Aisne valley, Cernay knew ruin as well as prosperity. Destroyed by Magyar horsemen on their way to Reims in 933, it was burned to the ground in 1359 by an English force under Duke Henry of Lancaster (see III, 8), retreating from an unsuccessful siege of Reims. The city's ranking abbey was fortunate to have in that large village a defensive buffer as well as four productive *mansi*. For a comparison with the relationship of similar communities to their ecclesiastical lord in another part of Europe four and a half centuries later, see II, 9(b).

Polyptych of the Abbey of St. Remi of Reims

From Polyptyque de l'Abbaye de St. Rémi de Reims, *ed. B. Guéranger (Paris: Imprimerie Impériale, 1853), pp. 42, 44–46, 49, 54–58, 64–65. Footnotes supplied.*

XVII: Curtis Agutior [Aguilcourt]. 1. In Aguilcourt there is demesne land with buildings, a garden and resting area, and subsidiary buildings conveniently situated. There are two fenced fields in which 24 *modii*[1] of rye can be sown; 9 fields which yield 2848 *modii* of spelt;[2] 2 pastures, one measuring 4 *mappae*[3] and the other, ½. There are also 3 mills: the first grinds 20 *modii* of wheat, and 40 of mixed grains; the second grinds 20 *modii* of wheat, but 50 of mixed grains; and the third grinds 10 *modii* of wheat and 30 of mixed grains. And when the lord or the provost comes there, they meet him with offerings of the best they can manage or the property provide. There is 1 brewery there.

[1] A *modius* was roughly equal to a bushel, which in the case of grain would amount to about 50 pounds.

[2] A type of bearded wheat with small, triangular grains. Traditionally the first food of the ancient Romans, it is rarely cultivated anywhere today.

[3] Units of surveying measure, difficult to determine with precision in this case.

2. These are the names of the men who have free *mansi* there:

Godoard and Ragnoard, freemen, hold 1 free *mansus*. For the winter sowing they plow [an area] 100 perches[4] long and 4 wide, and they do the same for the summer plowing. They also owe 4 *corvées*[5] and they collect the produce due from all this. They pay a field tax in winter wheat or barley or both. For their head tax[6] they give one *modius*. Every other year they give a tithe[7] in sheep. Each year they give for army service[8] 8 pennies. They also owe 3 hens and 15 eggs; 1 wagonload of wood to be brought to the monastery . . . , 100 shingles, and 50 planks of wood; otherwise, they cut wood in the forest for 15 days, and bring it in. They also do plaiting-work[9] in the manor house yard, stable duty, and work on the garden enclosure. They owe carting duty for wine or grain, wherever it needs to be brought. They owe 15 days at grape-gathering time, and they do manual work at the wine-press, whether that of the monastery or of some other place. To pay for the oxen who carry the wine to Aachen,[10] they owe 1 penny every year.

3. Heribert, Ragentulf, and Stacher, freemen, hold 1 free *mansus*. They owe and do all things as above.

Herigaud, freeman, likewise.

Hrotm, freeman, likewise.

Hairoin, freeman, likewise.

Ursin and Alecramn, freemen, likewise.

* * *

[4] A *perch* was a unit of plowland measurement, varying greatly from region to region; perhaps 10–12 feet long in this case.

[5] Periods of work on some task designated by the lord. "Four *corvées*" means 4 days of such labor.

[6] The field tax, a portion of the produce of a given field, was not so much "rent" in our sense of the word as a recognition of the lord's dominant relationship to the village: he did not "own" the plowland in any simple sense. In Aguilcourt the head tax indicated the same relative status, and was not, as elsewhere, a sign that the payer was a serf (see III, 9).

[7] A portion of the produce, ideally one-tenth, collected by the lord for the support of the church.

[8] A survival of the primitive obligation of all Germanic freemen to render military service, commuted to a money payment as the military profession became increasingly expensive and specialized. Serfs usually did not owe this payment.

[9] Presumably with reeds or with strips of wood or bark, to make thatch work, partitions, or coverings as well as baskets.

[10] Capital of the Frankish empire, some 140 miles to the northeast of Reims (as the crow flies). The royal palace may have been using this monastery as a regular source of Champagne's most popular export, and was clearly requiring the exporter to pay the transportation costs.

14. Blithelm and Teutbert, serfs, likewise.
    Salaco and Sigbert, freemen, likewise.
    Alecrimm and Hairoald, freemen, likewise.
    Aint and Divisom, freemen, likewise.
    Aittramn and Elts and Sicmand, freemen, likewise.

*　　*　　*

18. Waremfrid, freeman, likewise.
    Rimar and Lanfrid and Baldwin, freemen, likewise.
    Hairoard, freeman, and Adelmann and Dominic, *forastici*,[11]
likewise.
    Flotgis, freeman, likewise.
    Gisentrude, freewoman, likewise.

*　　*　　*

21. The *mansi* recorded above give each year 10 shillings of silver
altogether.
    22. The following hold servile *mansi*.
        Ripuin, a freeman, holds 1 servile *mansus*. For the winter sowing
he plows [an area] 100 perches long and 4 wide; likewise for the summer
sowing. He owes 4 *corvées*. Gathering all the produce due from these
services, he transports it to the monastery. Each year he gives 1 *modius*
of barley, 8 pennies for army service, 3 hens, and 15 eggs. He pays a
field rent. He cuts wood in the forest for 15 days, but does not bring it
in. He does winepress work in the monastery or in another place, like
the free *mansi*. Each year he gives 1 wagonload of thornbushes for
enclosures. He does grape gathering for 15 days, and plaiting-work in
the manor house yard, stable work and garden work. He also stands
watch, and harvests the lord's grain. He does Aachen service, too, giving
1 penny for the Aachen ox.

*　　*　　*

25. Cristemia, a serf, likewise.
    Wandreher and Amalhad and Gosmund, freemen, likewise.
    Trutbold, freeman, and Haimeric, serf, likewise.
    Vuandrehard and Heirbold, serfs, likewise.
    Fermenold and Inguis, serfs, likewise.

*　　*　　*

[11] See note 14, below.

28. Amalhad and Godwin, Anglebold and Hairoin, freemen; Ursold and Adroin and Ursiaud, freemen; hold one *accola*.[12] They give on that account 1 sheep each year.

Hrodra, Madelvinn, Fainulf, freemen, likewise.

Godefrid holds 1 *accola*. He pays 12 pennies.

Teutbert and Hrodoer, freemen, hold 1 *accola*. They plow the measures and do the *corvées* of free *mansi*, and each one gives for his head tax 1 *modius* of barley.

There is one *accola* belonging to Aguilcourt in the manor of Conciacum (Coucy-lez-Eppes),[13] held by Hairoald, Buroald, and Hrotfrid, blood brothers and freemen. That *accola* has 2 fields, amounting to 6 *mappae*, which get 9 *modii* of rye at sowing. They also have 3 *mappae* of common woodland, for making the enclosure. From this they pay each year 1 shilling.

29. These are the names of the women and of certain men holding *mansi* in the aforesaid manor:

Anglehild, freewoman, with 3 children.

Brannoaid, freewoman.

Ermentrude, freewoman, with 4 children.

Angletrude, freewoman, with 4 children.

Euresia, freewoman, with 2 children.

* * *

60. These are the names of the aforesaid men and women who are strangers[14] to the aforesaid manor: each of them owes yearly 4 silver pennies, on the Vigil of St. Remigius.[15]

Hilprad, freeman.

Erlind, freewoman. Adelulf her son, Odelind her daughter.

Hrotgerd, freewoman. Elari her son.

Blithari, freeman.

Blitga, freewoman. Ailhari her son.

* * *

[12] A piece of land in a neighboring community. *Accola* can also mean the person cultivating such a holding.

[13] A village across the Aisne, about 5 miles north of Aguilcourt and, like it, lying somewhat off the Roman road connecting the two episcopal cities of Reims and Laon.

[14] *Forenses* in the original. People in so vulnerable a legal position were in danger of being equated with serfs, or at least their children were. Most of the men and women in this list are free, however, and a few of the women had even acquired freedom by charter.

[15] September 30. Compare the practice reported in III, 9.

114. Here follow the names of all the serfs, male and female, inside or outside, of the same village, each one owing (that is, if he is of mature age) 12 pennies—the women 12 pennies, too. Unless they have some part of a *mansus,* the serf women owe three unbaked loaves and 15 eggs.

Warher, serf. Waifer, his son, serf. Waldemia, his daughter, serf. Baldor, serf. Himlind, his daughter, serf. Plictrude, his daughter, serf. Teudolina, his daughter, serf.

Merulf, serf. Aldo, his son, serf; his wife Salia, serf. Gotselind, his daughter, serf. Hugbold, his son, serf, of two years.[16]

Hildegrimm, serf.

*   *   *

122. The mayor[17] of the same village, if he does not have more than one free *mansus,* owes according to ancient custom the following dues: at Christmas and Easter he must do reverence to his lords in the monastery, with these offerings: 2 bottles of honey and 2 of wine—or then 1 of honey and a second of wine; 4 hearth cakes, 6 hens, 1 goose. The priest, likewise; the dean,[18] likewise. The cellarer,[19] if he has one servile *mansus,* owes 4 hearth cakes, 4 hens, and bottles full of wine.

123. There is in the above village a church dedicated to St. Martin,[20] which possesses: 2 altar curtains; 1 pallium, 2 corporals of shiny cloth; 1 silver pyx, 1 silver chalice with a silver paten, weighing together 10 shillings; 1 chasuble of green silk, 1 stole with pearls, 1 maniple, 1 tin crown above the altar, 1 lamp of tin; a Gregorian missal with Gospels and readings, and breviary with antiphons, all in 1 volume; a Gelasian missal in 1 volume; 1 volume of the books of the Gospels, 1 volume of Epistles, 1 volume of Gospels and Epistles, 4 booklets of glosses, 1 psalter, 2 volumes of canons; 3 bells, 1 of bronze, 2 of iron.[21]

This church has one *mansus* in demesne.

---

[16] Reduced to servile status two years previously? if so, why? or two years old? if so, the only child so listed. A good example of the enigmatic entries which complicate the interpretation of documents of this type.

[17] Probably an overseer appointed by the abbey rather than a manager elected by the peasants themselves (although this type of mayor existed even this early).

[18] Perhaps the deacon assisting the priest—possibly a cleric stationed there more or less permanently by the monastery/archdiocese.

[19] The man in charge of the wine and beer supply, distinctly a responsible figure!

[20] Bishop of Tours (died 397; see II, 2), a miracle-working saint very popular among the rustic inhabitants of Gaul. By the ninth century, hundreds of villages had been named after churches dedicated to him.

[21] Compare this inventory with the standards proposed in the beginning of the next century by Regino of Prüm, in II, 4.

124. Baldigisus, a freeman, holds 1 free *mansus,* owing and doing like the others of the same village. There is 1½ a servile *mansus* there, taxed like the others of the same village. There are 2 *accolae.* One pays 2 shillings, 2 hens, and 10 eggs; the other pays 12 shillings. From this the priest pays every year 1 silver pound.[22]

125. Witnesses to the matter: Adroin the mayor, Hagroin the dean, Geimfrid the juryman,[23] Ursold, Frederic, Ursiaud, Hrodera, Erleher, Betto.

126. Summary of Aguilcourt. Excepting the demesne land, there are 92½ free *mansi,* 35 servile *mansi,* 6 *accolae;* 20 female serfs, 6 male serfs, 1 church. It yields 7 silver pounds, 8 shillings; 207 *modii* of barley, 4 sheep, 382½ hens, 39 unbaked loaves, 2107½ eggs, 92½ wagons of wood, 9250 shingles, 4625 planks, 35 wagons of material for enclosures. All the *mansi* pay a field tax and a tithe in sheep; altogether they pay 10 shillings and 7½ pennies for oxen to transport the wine to Aachen; and from month to month they owe 30 day laborers on 30 days.

The strangers each owing 4 pennies are 306 in number. From this source should be received, on the vigil of St. Remigius, 5 pounds, 1 ounce, and 4 pennies.

127. At the command of Archbishop Hincmar, Aguilcourt was visited by his envoys, to wit: Sigloard, priest and head of the school of the holy Church of Reims, and the noble man Dodilo, vassal of the same bishop. Presiding over the public court and investigating the justice of St. Remigius and of the aforesaid lord, they heard a rumor that the bondsmen whose names are listed below should by right be serfs because of their genealogy, since Berta and Avila, their grandmothers, had been purchased with the lord's money. When the aforesaid envoys heard this, they inquired diligently into the matter. These are the names of those who, being present, were interrogated: Grimold, Warmher, Leuthad, Ostrold, Adelard, Ivoia, Hildiard her daughter. But they answered and said, "It is not so, for we ought to be free by birth." The aforesaid envoys asked if anyone were there who knew the truth of this matter, and would give proof. Then the oldest witnesses advanced, whose names are Hardier, Tedic, Odelmar, Sorulf, Gisinbrand, Gifard, and Teuderic; and they testified that the others' origins had been purchased by the lord's money, and that by justice and law they ought to be serfs rather than free men and women. Then the

---

[22] This paragraph explains how the "demesne" land of the parish church is allotted for exploitation.

[23] In the original, *scabinus,* a member of the community designated by a royal official of some sort to sit on all or most of the cases that came before the local court.

envoys asked if the witnesses said the truth against them. But they, seeing and recognizing the truth of the matter and how capable of proof it was, immediately resubmitted themselves, and gave pledges once more for the service which had been for many days unjustly held back and neglected. This was done according to the judgment of the jurymen, whose names are Geimfrid, Ursold, Frederic, Ursiaud, Hrodera, Herleher, Ratbert, and Gislehard.

Done at Aguilcourt on the third day before the Ides of May,[24] in public court, in the sixth year of the glorious reign of King Charles, and the third year of Archbishop Hincmar's reign over the holy see of Reims.

* * *

XIX, 9: In Colonia Cirsinniaca [Cernay]. Hrotveus, a serf, his wife Odelindis a freewoman, with their 4 children, and Rothard a serf, have 1 servile *mansus*. For the winter sowing he plows 2 *mappae* 40 perches long and 7 wide; for the summer sowing, 1 *mappa*. He does 9 *corvées* in a year. Each year he gives 4 *modii* of wine for the head tax; 2 *modii* of acorns to feed the pigs; 3 hens, 15 eggs, 150 shingles, 1 *modius* of hops. They do 2 bans,[25] one for wood, the other for the stable, half a cart for each. They do carting and hand labor, and as their service for the Aachen ox [they pay], 1 penny.

10. Ermenold a freeman, his wife Ransoid, with 1 child; and Madelveus a freeman, his wife Uniard a freewoman, hold 1 *mansus* likewise.

11. Randoin a serf, his wife Adeltrude a freewoman, with 4 children and Odoin their son, hold 1 servile *mansus*. They pay 3 *modii* of wine; all else as above.

12. Dominica, a freewoman, has 1 servile *mansus*. For the winter sowing she plows 1 *mappa* 40 perches long and 5 wide; likewise for the summer sowing. She does 9 *corvées* in a year, and everything else as above.

5. A RHINELAND BISHOP'S REFORM PROGRAM

The previous excerpts presented a static ideal of peasant order —ideal in the lord's eyes, anyway. The following selection gives us some idea of how smoothly such arrangements actually worked out, and also shows how an ecclesiastical lord concerned with legal tranquillity rather than regular revenue would set about

[24] May 9.
[25] Very similar to a *corvée*.

imposing order on the lives of his dependent peasantry. Burchard of Worms (965–1025) was the son of a powerful noble family of western Franconia, the province of the German Empire of which he became an important clerical magnate. Educated at the monastery of Lobbes in the southern Lowlands, he served the archbishop of Mainz as judge of the cathedral city, which, like many administrative districts of the Empire, was subject to its bishop in secular as well as in spiritual matters. Burchard's performance in that office brought him to the attention of the imaginative and reform-minded Emperor Otto III, who in the year 1000 had him made Bishop of Worms, a diocese in the Franconian Rhineland directly south of Mainz. During the quarter-century of his episcopate Burchard was a leader of reform movements throughout Germany; in the century after his death the influence of his legal codifications and his example would spread throughout Latin Christendom (see II, 4). His last and in a sense his most ambitious effort at reform concentrated on his own lay dependents. Although some of the *Laws and Statutes* promulgated in the last two years of his life affected the noble vassals and urban subjects of the Bishop of Worms, Burchard was chiefly concerned with the rural serfs and lesser freemen under his lordship.

The paternalist quality of Burchard's interest is evident in his choice of the extended family as the organizing metaphor for the group for whose behavior he was trying to propose systematic norms and sanctions. It is worth noting that the father figure in this metaphor is less the bishop than St. Peter, patron saint of the diocese: the bishop serves as his representative (steward, judge, vicar in general—almost a local pope). Notice also how much the terminology of status in eleventh-century Franconia differed from that of ninth-century Champagne, even though both areas lived under closely related varieties of Frankish customary law.

Burchard of Worms: *Laws and Statutes of the Family of St. Peter of Worms*

From O. J. Thatcher and E. H. McNeal, A Source Book for Medieval History (New York: Charles Scribner's Sons, 1905), pp. 553–62. Footnotes supplied.

Because of the frequent lamentations of my unfortunate subjects and the great injustice done them by many who have habitually wronged the family of St. Peter, imposing different laws upon them and oppressing all the weaker ones by their unjust judgments and decisions, I,

Burchard, bishop of Worms, with the advice of my clergy, knights, and of all my family, have ordered these laws to be written, in order that hereafter no advocate,[1] nor vidame, nor official, nor any other malicious person may be able to add any new law to the detriment of the aforementioned family, but that the whole family, rich and poor alike, may have the same law.

1. If anyone of the family of St. Peter legally marries a woman who is also a member of the family, and gives her a dower and she has peaceable possession of it for a year and a day, then if the man dies, the wife shall hold the whole of the dower until she dies. When the woman dies, if they had no children, the dower goes to the nearest heirs of the man. If the woman dies first, the same disposition shall be made of it. If after marriage they acquire property, when one of them dies, the other shall have it and do what he will with it. If the wife brought any property to her husband at the time of marriage, at the death of both, their children, if they have any, shall inherit it. If they have no children, it shall return to her relatives unless she gives it away before her death. If the children die after inheriting it, it shall return to the nearest relatives of their mother.

2. If anyone has inherited a piece of land with serfs, and becomes poor and is forced to sell it, he must first, in the presence of witnesses, offer to sell it to his nearest heirs. If they will not buy it, he may sell it to any member of the family of St. Peter. If a piece of land has, by judicial process, been declared forfeited to the bishop [because the holder has not paid the proper dues or rendered the due services], and any one of the heirs of the one who held it wishes to pay the back dues, he may do so and receive the land. But if no heir wishes to pay the back dues, the local official may let the land to any member of the family he may wish, and the one thus receiving it shall hold it. If after a few years someone comes and says: "I am the heir. I was poor, I was an orphan, I had no means of support, so I left home and have been supporting myself in another place by work," and if he tries by his own testimony alone to dispossess him who, with the consent of the bishop, received the land, and who has cultivated it well and improved it, he shall not be able to do so. For since there was no heir at the time who was willing to pay the back dues, let him to whom the local official gave it keep it. For [it may be said to the new claimant]: "If you were the

---

[1] A layman who performed military and coercive functions for the bishop, and might also preside over the three annual sessions of the full local court, collect fines arising therefrom, etc. He was assisted by one or more vidames.

heir, why did you go away? Why did you not stay at home and look after your inheritance?" No hearing shall be granted him unless he has a good and reasonable excuse.[2] If anyone who has a piece of land by hereditary right dies leaving a child as heir, and this child is not able to render the service due, and there is a near relative who is willing to render the due service for this land until the heir becomes of age, he may do so. But let the heir not be disinherited because of his youth. We beg that he may be treated mercifully in this matter [that is, that he may receive his inheritance when he comes of age].

3. If anyone on our domain land dies leaving an inheritance, his heir shall receive it without being bound to give us a present,[3] and thereafter he shall render the due service for it.

4. If any member of the family dies leaving free property,[4] unless he has given it away, his nearest heirs shall inherit it.

5. If anyone in the presence of witnesses and with the consent of his wife parts with any piece of property, no matter what it is, the bargain shall stand unless there is some other good reason for breaking it.

6. If anyone sells his land or his inheritance to another member of the family in the presence of one of his heirs, and that heir does not object at the time, he shall never afterwards have the right to object. If an heir were not present, but, after learning of the sale, did not object within that year, he shall afterwards not have the right to object to it.

7. If anyone is, by the judgment of his fellows, put "into the bishop's hand," he and all his possessions are in the bishop's power.

8. If anyone takes some of his fellows and does some injustice to a member of the family, he shall pay a fine for himself and for his accomplices and each one of them shall pay his own fine.

9. Five pounds of the *wergeld* of a *fisgilinus* go to the bishop's treasury and two and one-half pounds go to his friends [kin].

10. If a man and his wife die leaving a son and a daughter, the son shall receive the inheritance of the servile land [*i.e.*, the land which the father held], and the daughter shall receive the clothing of her mother and all the cash on hand. Whatever other property there is shall be divided equally between them.

[2] *E.g.*, absence due to military service, imprisonment by an enemy of the bishop's, etc.

[3] A convenient and customary legal fiction for a type of inheritance tax, often consisting of the best animal, piece of furniture or clothing, etc.

[4] *I.e.*, property on which no dues are or were owed to any lord, such as items bought with surplus produce.

11. If anyone has received a piece of land and serfs by inheritance, and takes his bed because of illness so that he cannot ride on horseback or walk alone, he shall not alienate the land and serfs to the disadvantage of his heirs, unless he wishes to give something for the salvation of his soul. All his other property he may give to whomever he wishes.

12. In order that there may not be so many perjuries, if any member of the family has done some wrong to a fellow-member in the matter of land, or vineyards, or any other less important thing, and the case has been brought before the local official, we desire that the local official shall, with the aid of his fellows, decide the case without having anyone take an oath.

13. If any *fisgilinus* does an injustice, either great or small, he shall, like the *dagewardus,* pledge five solidi to the treasury of the bishop and pay five solidi as composition to him to whom he did the wrong, if he is of the same society. If he is outside his society he shall pledge one ounce and no oath shall be taken.

14. If anyone from the bishop's domain lands marries someone who belongs to a fief which is held from the bishop, he shall continue to be under the bishop's jurisdiction. If anyone from such a fief marries someone from the bishop's domain land, he shall continue under the jurisdiction of the lord of the fief on which he lives.

15. If anyone marries a foreign woman [that is, one who does not live on the bishop's territory], when he dies two-thirds of their possessions shall go to the bishop.

16. If a *fisgilinus* marries a *dagewarda,* their children shall be of the lower rank; and likewise if a *dagewardus* marries a *fisgilina.*

17. If anyone makes an unjust outcry in court, or becomes angry and leaves the court, or does not come in time to the court, and those sitting in the court with him do not convict him of this, he shall not take an oath about it, but the *Schoeffen*[5] shall decide it.

18. If anyone has a suit against his fellow, he alone shall take an oath about it. But if it concerns a feud, or is against the bishop, he shall have six men to take an oath with him.

19. It has frequently happened that if one lent his money to another, the borrower would repay as much as he wished and then swear that he owed no more. In order to prevent perjury we have decreed that the lender need not accept the oath of the borrower but may, if he wishes, challenge him to a duel, and so [by defeating him] prove his indebted-

---

[5] In the original, *scabinus.* See IV, 4, note 23.

ness. If the lender is so important a person that he does not wish to fight the borrower on such an account, he may appoint someone to fight for him.

20. If anyone in the city of Worms is convicted by losing a duel, he shall pledge sixty solidi. If he is defeated by a member of the family who lives outside of the city, he shall pay the victor three times the amount of the fine, because he challenged him unjustly, and he shall pay the bishop's ban,[6] and twenty solidi to the advocate, or he shall lose his skin and hair [that is, he shall be beaten and his head shaved].

21. If anyone of the family of St. Peter buys a piece of land and serfs from a free man [that is, one who is not a member of the family], or has acquired it in any other way, he shall not dispose of it to anyone outside of the family, unless he exchanges it [for other land and serfs].

22. If anyone attempts to reduce a *fisgilinus* to the rank of a *dagewardus* and subject him to an unjust poll tax, the *fisgilinus* shall prove his rank by the testimony of seven of his nearest relatives, but he shall not hire them for this purpose. If the charge is made that his father was not a *fisgilinus,* two female witnesses shall be taken from his father's family and one from his mother's. If it is said that his mother was not of that rank, two shall be taken from her family and one from his father's family, unless he can prove his rank by the testimony of the *Schoeffen* or of his relatives.

23. If any member of the family enters the house of another with an armed force and violates his daughter, he shall pay to her father, or to her guardian, three times the value of every piece of clothing which she had on when she was seized, and to the bishop his ban for each piece of clothing. And he shall also pay to her father a triple fine and the bishop's ban. And because the law of the church does not permit him to marry her, he shall appease her family by giving to twelve members of it twelve shields and as many lances and one pound of money.

* * *

29. If the bishop wishes to take a *fisgilinus* into his service, he may put him to work under the chamberlain, or the cup-bearer, or the steward [dish-bearer], or the master of the horse, or under the official who has charge of the bishop's lands and collects the dues from them [*i.e.,* the advocate]. But if he does not wish to serve the bishop in any

---

[6] A fixed sum, in this case 60 *solidi,* serving as the basic unit for the assessment of fines in one jurisdiction.

of these departments of the bishop's household, he may pay four denars every time the bishop is summoned by the king to call out his men for the purpose of fighting, and six when the bishop is summoned to accompany the emperor to Rome, and he must attend the three regular sessions of court which are held every year, and then he may serve whomsoever he wishes.[7]

30. Homicides take place almost daily among the family of St. Peter, as if they were wild beasts. The members of the family rage against each other as if they were insane and kill each other for nothing. Sometimes drunkenness, sometimes wanton malice is the cause of a murder. In the course of one year thirty-five serfs of St. Peter belonging to the church of Worms have been murdered without provocation. And the murderers, instead of showing penitence, rather boast and are proud of it. Because of the great loss thus inflicted on our church, with the advice of our faithful subjects, we have made the following laws in order to put an end to such murders. If any member of the family of St. Peter kills a fellow member except in self-defence, that is, while defending either himself of his property, . . . we decree that he shall be beaten and his head shaved, and he shall be branded on both jaws with a red-hot iron, made for this purpose, and he shall pay the *wergeld* and make peace in the customary way with the relatives of the man whom he killed. And those relatives shall be compelled to accept this. If the relatives of the slain man refuse to accept it and make war on the relatives of the murderer, anyone of the latter may secure himself against their violence by taking an oath that he knew nothing of the murder and had nothing to do with it. If the relatives of the slain man disregard such an oath and try to injure the one who took it, even though they do not succeed in doing so, they shall be beaten and have their heads shaved, but they shall not be branded on the jaws. But if they kill him or wound him, they shall be beaten and their heads shaved, and they shall be branded on the jaws. If a murderer escapes, all his property shall be confiscated, but his relatives, if they are innocent, shall not be punished for him. If the murderer does not flee, but, in order to prove his innocence [that is, that he acted in self-defence], wishes to fight a duel with some relative of the slain man, and if he wins, . . . he shall pay the *wergeld* and satisfy the relatives of the slain man. If no relative of the slain man wishes to fight a duel with the mur-

---

[7] Such an elite group of serfs, generally called *ministeriales,* often proved more useful and faithful to a lord than his less tractable noble vassals. By the end of the century many major lords of the Empire (see III, 2) were appointing *ministeriales* to posts of honor and high responsibility; their descendants became a hereditary class with the right to knighthood and several other prerogatives of the free nobility.

derer, the murderer shall clear himself before the bishop with the ordeal of boiling water, and pay the *wergeld,* and make peace with the relatives of the slain man, and they shall be compelled to accept it. If through fear of this law the relatives of the slain man go to another family [that is, to people who do not belong to the family of St. Peter], and incite them to violence against the relatives of the murderer, if they will not clear themselves by a duel [that is, prove that they did not incite them, etc.], they shall clear themselves before the bishop by the ordeal of boiling water, and whoever is proven guilty by the ordeal shall be beaten, his head shaved, and he shall be branded on the jaws. If any member of the family who lives in the city kills a fellow member except in self-defence, he shall be punished in the same way, and besides he shall pay the bishop's ban, and the *wergeld,* and make peace with the relatives of the slain man, and they shall be compelled to accept it. If any foreigner . . . who cultivates a piece of St. Peter's land, . . . kills a member of the family of St. Peter except in self-defence, he shall either be punished in the same way, . . . or he shall lose his fief and he shall be at the mercy of the advocate and the family of St. Peter [that is, they may carry on a feud against him, and slay him]. If anyone who is serving us . . . or one of our officials commits such a crime, . . . it shall be left to us to punish him as we, with the advice of our subjects, may see fit.

31. If one member of the family has a dispute with another about anything, such as fields, vineyards, serfs, or money, if possible, let it be decided by witnesses without oaths. If it cannot be decided in that way, let both parties to the case produce their witnesses in court. After the witnesses have testified, each for his side, . . . two men shall be chosen, one from each side, to decide the suit by a duel. He whose champion is defeated in the duel shall lose his suit, and his witnesses shall be punished for bearing false witness, just as if they had taken an oath to it.

32. If any member of the family commits a theft not because of hunger, but from avarice and covetousness, or habit, and the stolen object is worth five solidi or more, and it can be proved that the thief, either in a public market or in a meeting of his fellow members, has restored the stolen object, or given a pledge to do so, we decree for the prevention of such crimes that as a punishment of his theft the thief shall lose his legal status—that is, if anyone accuses him of a crime, he cannot clear himself by an oath, but must prove his innocence by a duel or by the ordeal of boiling water or red-hot iron. The same punishment shall be inflicted on one who is guilty of perjury, or of bearing false

witness, and also on one who is convicted by duel of theft, and of those who plot with the bishop's enemies against the honor and safety of his lord, the bishop.

6. THE ESTATE OF SERFDOM

Back to northern France, two and a half centuries later. The following passage comes from Philippe de Beaumanoir's classic treatise on the law of the county of Clermont-en-Beauvaisis, forty miles northwest of Paris (see III, 3). Note this royal lawyer's articulated sense of the relationship of serfdom to the other states and orders of society, his strong anticlerical sentiments, and his tendency to derive general principles of equity—just a step short of social theory—from the precedents of local customary law. Most of his specific precedents and general maxims are in line with the central tradition of medieval ruling-class attitudes toward the serf: one good example is Beaumanoir's use of the term "man of the body," a classic phrase implying either that the serf is an extension of his lord's person (not entirely unlike Burchard of Worms' use of the family metaphor in the previous selection), or simply that the serf's body is his lord's rather than his own to dispose of (a logical but rather crude corollary of the former interpretation). On the other hand, in the intriguing discussion of title sixteen, we can also note the growing sense that serfdom is a distinct social estate, not merely a catchall description of the lowest, most exploited position in society. We can hardly miss throughout this passage the implication that serfs were constantly eluding their former subjection, in an upward movement going faster than lords' and lawyers' attempts to freeze the former state of affairs.

Philippe de Beaumanoir: *Customs of the Beauvais District,* Chapter 45

From *Philippe de Beaumanoir, Coûtumes du Beauvaisis, ed. Beugnot (Paris: J. Renouard & Cie., 1842), II, 221–27.*

12. The serf who disavows his servile status should be pursued by his rightful lord on the basis of his origin, at the court of the person under whose authority he resides, if he makes himself out to be a freeman, or in the court of the lord whose man of the body he recognizes himself

to be. Against the argument of origin he has no reply, if it is based on proofs of his actual descent. But if the lord who wishes to reclaim him attempts to prove his origin by evidence other than that of his descent, he can counter that evidence so long as he has grounds for rebutting it, and after giving some surety.

13. He who is pursued on the charge of servile status can defend himself on the following grounds. The first ground is this: that he and his mother were in the state of freedom all their lives, without paying any of the fees exacted from serfs, in the full sight and knowledge of the lord who wishes to pursue him, or of his predecessors. However, they may have been enjoying the state of freedom in vain, if the lord who is pursuing him on the basis of origin can prove that the mother of the defendant's mother was his serf; this applies even if he had resided for a long time outside the jurisdiction of the lord who pursues him, for it would appear then that he had gone away in order to escape serfdom.

But if the lord can not prove his case, the defendant remains in the state of freedom; nor can the lord's charge then be based on any other grounds than origin. For it is not lawful for anyone to say to someone who has always been in the state of freedom, "You are my serf, and I intend to prove it." So if he does not make his case on the basis of origin, or on the ground that the defendant has at some time paid a fee due from serfs, he should not be heard, and the defendant should remain in the state of freedom.

14. The second ground on which one pursued on the charge of servile status can defend himself, is this: that he knows that his mother (or grandmother or great-grandmother) was a serf, but that she was freed by someone who had the power to grant freedom. He may prove this by that lord's letters or by eyewitnesses, and this proof is sufficient to maintain him in the state of freedom.

15. Thus we can see that servile status comes through the mother, for all the children that a serf bears are serfs, even if the father was a free man. Even if a knight marries a serf, all the children that he has from her would be serfs, and would be debarred from noble status to the extent that they could not be knights. For it is not lawful for serfs to become knights even though nobility, through which one is capable of knighthood, should come through the father. It is customary in the kingdom of France that men who are of noble blood on their father's side can become knights even if their mother is a commoner, so long as she is not a serf: in that case it cannot be, as is stated above. When the mother is a noblewoman and the father is not, the children cannot become knights. However, the children do not lose all the effects of

the noble state, and so are maintained in that condition in regard to their persons, and can certainly hold fiefs, which is something no free commoner can do.

And from these cases one can see that full nobility comes through the father only, and serfdom comes through mothers who are serfs. And also it is clear that when a man is a serf and takes a free woman, all the children are free. And from this one can understand what was said above.

16. The third way in which one pursued on the charge of servile status can defend himself, is by means of an argument which is not very polite, but which we have often seen employed nonetheless: that is, when he claims and can prove that he is a bastard. Once he proves it, he is free of serfdom. And the way in which one can prove bastardy is by showing that one was born before his mother married a husband, or if she had, by proving that at the time he was born and ten months before, the husband was overseas or in distant foreign regions, without having returned: from this evidence it becomes clear that he cannot be the son of the aforesaid husband. But if he wishes to present as evidence the fact that the husband had been gone for the ten months mentioned above (or longer) on account of a quarrel or debts or banishment, that will do him no good, for it often happens that men who have gone away for such reasons come and go from time to time, finding their wives secretly and resting there. And on such trips children can be begotten, which is better to believe than the alternative explanation. The third way in which one can prove bastardy is by proving that he was born ten months or more after the death of his mother's husband and during the time of her widowhood; and when he proves this, he is released from serfdom.

And if some people think that none should benefit from being a bastard, the reason for the above customs is that the bastard succeeds to the condition neither of his father nor of his mother, neither in lineage nor in inheritance nor in any other matter; and since he has no share in their goods nor in the advantages of their conditions, he should not have a share in the disadvantages of their conditions nor in the duties which they owe their lords.

17. The fourth ground on which one who is pursued for serfdom can defend himself is this: when he is a cleric, and has been in the estate of the clergy for ten years, in the full sight and knowledge of his lord who now pursues him and has taken no previous action against him. It is entirely lawful for a lord whose man of the body has become a cleric, to take him before the bishop and demand that the bishop not give

him tonsure, and if he has given it to take it away: and the bishop is required to comply. But this must occur before he has been admitted to higher orders, for if he has risen so far as to achieve higher orders, he remains in a state of freedom. And if the bishop makes any serf a cleric against my will, I can take action against him [the ex-serf] to demand damages to the extent of his own worth, both personal and in movable property: for there is no doubt that a cleric can possess and dispose of his inheritance.

18. It is a good thing for those who wish to purchase freedom from serfdom, to have their enfranchisement confirmed by their lord's suzerain. For if I have some serfs whom I hold from another lord and I free them, I lose them: by rights I have control over their freedom to the extent of its worth to me, but then my lord will get control over them, and they will become serfs again. And if I have taken any price from them, I will be bound to return it, since I am unable to guarantee their franchise. And I will also be held liable for damages to my lord, for having diminished his fief, and the damages will amount to 60 pounds.

19. Serfdom arose in many ways. The first of these was that it became so difficult to sow the fields in olden times because of the armies in the field and the battles against the Crown, that those who were unable to obtain justice became and remained serfs, both themselves and their heirs. The second is that in past times many gave themselves, their heirs, and their property to the saints out of great devotion, and paid dues which they had thought up in their own hearts. The agents of the churches wrote down what they paid and whatever else they could get from their connection, and so the agents exploited them and have always done so more and more, out of the malice which has grown in them beyond measure: so what was done at first in good faith has been turned to the disadvantage and degradation of the heirs. The third way was by sale: for example, if someone succumbed to poverty and said to some lord, "You give me so much, and I will become your man of the body." And sometimes they became so by outright gift of themselves, so as to be protected from other lords or from some enmity afoot against them. Serfdom arose through all these causes in the past, for according to the natural law everyone is free, but this natural freedom has been corrupted by the acquisitions stated above. And there are still some lands where a free person who is not of noble lineage, whether man or woman, becomes after a year and a day of residence a serf of the lord under whose authority he wishes to reside; but that custom has no force whatever in the county of Clermont. If a free man

wishes to live there, he does not lose his free status on that account, whether he takes up residence among serfs or elsewhere. And if a serf comes to dwell there from another *pays,* and his lord pursues him, he must be surrendered to him; and if he disavows his servile status, it is appropriate for the lord to take him to court and prove his case on the basis of origin, as has been explained above.

* * *

21. It is entirely lawful, according the custom which holds currently, for each male or female serf to buy freedom for himself and his children, if he can obtain it from his lord and by his suzerain's authority. But if he has achieved his and his children's freedom, and then returns to servile status, he does not thereby return his children to it; for it is lawful to enfranchise one's children, but not to subject them.

Upward Mobility

7. GERMAN FRONTIER SETTLEMENT INDUCEMENTS, 1106

The external and internal frontiers of an expanding Europe, added to the advances in farming technique mastered by the peasants from the eleventh century onward, gave skilled agricultural workers a strong bargaining position in the twelfth and thirteenth centuries. This improved leverage showed large-scale results quite early on the Slavic borderlands of Latin Christendom. Frederick, nineteenth bishop of Bremen and sixteenth of Hamburg (1104–23), was forced to concentrate his eminently political energies on the internal development of his half-missionary double archdiocese since his administration of it began with Rome's rejection of its claims to a kind of patriarchal authority over the Church in Scandinavia (see I, 9). One of the most striking features of the following document is its failure, despite careful precision in other matters, to make the slightest reference to the legal status of the Lowland peasants in question. This may be due to the fact that serfdom was comparatively rare in the northern Netherlands or to the startling degree of autonomy in internal matters which Frederick was conceding, but it is at least possible that ignoring such issues was a special inducement to peasant settlers. This last possibility is particularly interesting in view of Frederick's attempt to embarrass a troublesome lay magnate by claiming in open court (in a procedure similar to that outlined by Beaumanoir) that his enemy was in fact his serf, because of his grandmother's and great-grandmother's status after they suffered shipwreck on the coasts of the archdiocese of Bremen.

Charter of Frederick, Bishop of Hamburg

From O. J. Thatcher and E. H. McNeal, A Source Book for Mediaeval History (New York: Charles Scribner's Sons, 1905), pp. 572–73. Footnote supplied.

1. In the name of the holy and undivided Trinity. Frederick, by the grace of God bishop of Hamburg, to all the faithful in Christ, gives a perpetual benediction. We wish to make known to all the agreement which certain people living this side of the Rhine, who are called Hollanders, have made with us.

2. These men came to us and earnestly begged us to grant them certain lands in our bishopric, which are uncultivated, swampy, and useless to our people. We have consulted our subjects about this and, considering that this would be profitable to us and to our successors, have granted their request.

3. The agreement was made that they should pay us every year one denarius for every hide of land. We have thought it necessary to determine the dimensions of the hide, in order that no quarrel may hereafter arise about it. The hide shall be 720 royal rods long and thirty royal rods wide. We also grant them the streams which flow through this land.

4. They agreed to give the tithe according to our decree, that is, every eleventh sheaf of grain, every tenth lamb, every tenth pig, every tenth goat, every tenth goose, and a tenth of the honey and of the flax. For every colt they shall pay a denarius on St. Martin's day [Nov. 11], and for every calf an obol [penny].

5. They promised to obey me in all ecclesiastical matters according to the decrees of the holy fathers, the canonical law, and the practice in the diocese of Utrecht.[1]

6. They agreed to pay every year two marks for every 100 hides for the privilege of holding their own courts for the settlement of all their

---

[1] The settlers' home diocese, about 175 miles southwest of Bremen; Utrecht was subject to the archdiocese of Cologne, Bremen-Hamburg's western neighbor.

differences about secular matters. They did this because they feared they would suffer from the injustice of foreign judges. If they cannot settle the more important cases they shall refer them to the bishop. And if they take the bishop with them [that is, from Hamburg to the colony] for the purpose of deciding one of their trials, they shall provide for his support as long as he remains there by granting him one-third of all the fees arising from the trial; and they shall keep the other two-thirds.

7. We have given them permission to found churches wherever they may wish on these lands. For the support of the priests who shall serve God in these churches we grant a tithe of our tithes from these parish churches. They promised that the congregation of each of these churches should endow their church with a hide for the support of their priest. The names of the men who made this agreement with us are: Henry, the priest, to whom we have granted the aforesaid churches for life; and the others are laymen, Helikin, Arnold, Hiko, Fordolt, and Referic. To them and to their heirs after them we have granted the aforesaid land according to the secular laws and to the terms of this agreement.

8. EMANCIPATION OF THE SERFS OF ORLY, THIRTEENTH CENTURY

The four documents following record one dramatic incident and several gradual developments in the movement of enfranchisement which freed most of the serfs around Paris in the second half of the thirteenth century. Orly today is a bustling suburb of Paris (population over 18,000 in 1962), some ten miles southeast of the cathedral of Notre Dame, whose chapter the village recognized as lord in some form or degree through most of the Middle Ages. Across Orly's flat and once-fertile fields stretch the runways of France's greatest airport, and under the government of Charles de Gaulle the town became the new wholesale-produce center for metropolitan Paris, direct successor to the Halles established by King Philip Augustus on the north-west edge of his capital city over seven centuries ago. Orly has only recently achieved such distinction, however. In 1901 it had only 832 residents, probably not many more than its medieval population, and in other respects as well it appeared to be a typical village of the area. Consequently, its experience can be taken as a valid indicator of the ebb and flow of peasant fortunes and formal status in the middle valley of the Seine.

Orly is an old village whose original name of Aureliacum suggests the presence or influence of a significant Gallo-Roman estate. If we may extrapolate from the evidence of comparable villages, its inhabitants lost their relatively free status sometime between Charlemagne and the First Crusade: its neighbor Thiais (originally Theodosiacum), two and one-half miles down the road to Paris, counted 160 heads of families in the early ninth century, of whom 130 enjoyed the status of *coloni,* 11 were slaves, and 19 were "outsiders" paying a yearly head tax; in the mid-thirteenth century, almost everyone in Thiais was a serf. As time passed, Orly came increasingly under the dominance of the cathedral chapter, which finally consolidated its ownership of the village in the early thirteenth century.

Other forces, which would reverse the tide of seignorial control, were also at work in the twelfth century. The exploitation of previously uncultivated lands and the improvement of agricultural techniques gave the serfs both surpluses and alternatives close at hand. One typical manifestation of this new situation was Villeneuve-le-Roi, founded in the twelfth century on the originally marshy bottomlands of the Seine one mile east of Orly. In the century following that and similar foundations, the older villages of the area began agitating for more autonomy in their management and a more honorable status for their inhabitants. About 1250 the peasants of Orly seem to have begun a campaign for enfranchisement. Since their lord had jurisdiction over all legal suits ("high and low justice"), the peasants turned to a tactic of combined slowdown (to which agricultural "employers" are peculiarly vulnerable, especially if they cannot—or may not —bring in substitute labor) and selective public demonstrations. Selection (a) tells briefly how successful these tactics were; its sympathy is particularly striking since it comes from an "authorized" history of the French monarchy composed in the vernacular at the monastery of St. Denis (see I, 8 and II, 8) for the edification of visiting lay noblemen. Blanche of Castile, daughter of the embattled Castilian king Alfonso VIII (1158–1214), had been Regent of France for eight years (1226–34) during the minority of her son, St. Louis, and served in that capacity again while he was away on a protracted Crusade (1248–54). During the first regency she had depended heavily on episcopal support in her conflicts with power-hungry lay magnates, who had treated her with little gallantry. It was typical of her stern piety that even the memory of such past favors did not incline her to overlook the disedifying behavior of the Paris canons during her second regency.

Selections (b), (c), and (d) come from the massive *Cartulary* (collection of public records) of the chapter of Notre Dame, and show us how the skillful clerics of that privileged corporation tried to cope with a serious and mounting threat to their valuable interests. Beneath all its turgid and slippery legal formulae, selection (b) is an attempt to fix the *fait accompli* of 1252 in terms as official and favorable as possible. Despite the assiduous ingenuity of the chapter's lawyers, however, the peasant community of Orly gained nearly complete control of its own activity: in 1337, for example, the village bought its mill from the chapter for the relatively cheap rent of 17 pounds a year. In 1360 Orly was sacked and burned by English soldiers after a heroic resistance, thereby contributing, like Cernay-en-Dormois the year before (see IV, 4) to the defense of its local metropolis; but the freedom and long-range solvency of the community survived even a disaster of that magnitude.

Selection (c) shows us, among other things, how some of the chapter's swiftly-rising serfs hastened to take advantage of the situation of the 1250's. This charter does not mention a charter of emancipation which Robert Meunier got from the chapter in May of 1255 for himself, his wife, their son Guillaume, and four other children, presumably on conditions similar to those spelled out in (a). The later charter reproduced below was probably designed to protect the career prospects of an ambitious eldest son from the consequences of any possible default, as well as from a delay of perhaps six years. The price and the risks of either alternative were high, but these new bourgeois from a thriving artisans' suburb had the money and the drive to take them on. Selection (d) demonstrates that the security of serfdom still had some appeal for the less dynamic and less mobile peasants of the area: very few social movements proceed on a course unruffled by contrary currents.

Why were the peasants so successful in thirteenth-century France, especially since the same century saw a decline in peasant freedoms east of the Rhine? These selections should suggest some of the answers. Unlike their east-European counterparts, these French serfs relied primarily on passive resistance rather than armed uprisng; in this atmosphere free of physical threat, their complaints could elicit optimum response from those members of the political establishment who had guilty social consciences— and in the brisk mental climate of a city like Paris, such consciences were not rare (*cf.* Beaumanoir's theoretical epilogue to IV, 6). Secondly, assistance was forthcoming from one group within the establishment whose interests were served by the embarrassment of the peasants' immediate lords. Finally, the peasants themselves had the money and the morale to follow up their initial legal victories. Unfortunately for most medieval tillers of the soil, circumstances were not always or everywhere so favorable, nor their leadership so canny.

The Great Chronicles of France: St. Louis, Chapter 64

From Les Grandes Chroniques de France, ed. *Jules Viard (Paris: Société de l'histoire de France, 1932), VII, Chapter 64. Footnotes supplied.*

In the year of Grace 1252, it happened that Queen Blanche was at Melun[1] on the Seine. There her heart began to hurt very badly, and she came to feel weighted down with illness. So she had her train decamp and her coffers packed up and went with haste to Paris. There she was so hard pressed by her disease that she had to give up her spirit. When she was dead, the nobles of the country carried her around Paris in a gilded chair, all attired like a queen, the golden crown on her head. The crosses and the marchers of the procession brought her thus to an abbey of nuns close by Pontoise,[2] which she had built during the time she was alive.

The little people were troubled by her death, for all that she had done had relieved them from oppression by the rich and had upheld good justice. An example of this had occurred when the canons of Paris arrested all the men of the village of Orly and of Châtenay[3] and of other neighboring villages who were tenants of their church, and imprisoned them closely in a house belonging to the chapter, and left them there without sustenance. They made them suffer so much from discomfort that they were like to die. When the queen knew of it, she requested very humbly that they be released on pledge and that a voluntary inquest be held to handle the matter. The canons answered that it was none of her affair to take cognizance of their serfs or their villeins, whom they could arrest or kill or subject to such justice as they wished. On account of the fact that a complaint had been made

[1] For over a century a favorite occasional residence of Capetian rulers, Melun was a royal town about 30 miles up the Seine valley from Paris, and 20 miles southeast of Orly.

[2] A royal town and palace about 25 miles northwest of Paris (beyond St. Denis), near the confluence of the rivers Seine and Oise. It was at Pontoise that Louis, after recovering from a dangerous illness, had sworn to go on Crusade.

[3] A village 7 miles west of Orly, and 4 miles southwest of L'Hay. See selection (d).

before the queen, the canons imprisoned their women and children; and they were in such discomfort from the heat caused by such crowding that several of them died.

When the queen knew of it, she had great pity for the people who were so tormented by those who should protect them and show them good example and doctrine. So she called up her knights and bourgeois and armed them and set out on the road, and came to the house of the chapter where the people were imprisoned. She ordered her men to tear down and break up the gate, and struck the first blow herself with a baton she held in her hand. As soon as she had struck the first blow, her men knocked the gate to the ground and released the men and women; and the queen put them under her protection and held the canons in such great contempt that she took all their temporal possessions in her hand until they should amend everything according to her will. [The canons] were not so rash as to judge [the peasants], and so they were freed [*franchis*] for a sum of money which they owe every year to the chapter of Paris. This and much other good justice the queen did while her son was in the Holy Land.

General Emancipation of Orly

General Emancipation of Orly, Charter of the Chapter of Paris to Robert Meunier and Avelina His Wife, Natives of Orly, and Their Son Guillaume, *and* Charter of the Chapter of Paris Concerning Pierre Le Roy of L'Hay, Residing at Chevilly *from* Cartulaire de l'Eglise Notre-Dame de Paris, *ed.* M. Guérard (Paris, Crapelet, 1850), II, 3–7, 19–21, 41. Footnotes supplied.

To all who shall examine these letters, greetings in the Lord from the officers of Jean and Raoul, archdeacons of the church of Paris, and from the officers of the chancellor of Paris. We declare that Aveline Lathoma and Guillot her son, acting for themselves and for Tyonot, Maciot, Gibeline, and Marie her children, assembled in our presence together with others of the village and native to the village of Orly. They recognized of their own free will and from certain knowledge declared that they, as well as their ancestors, were and had been men of the body[1] of the church of Saint Mary of Paris, and were attached to those venerable men the dean and the chapter of that church by the yoke of the servile condition since time immemorial.

They recognized and declared further, spontaneously, not under

----
[1] See IV, 6.

duress, and from certain knowledge, that the dean and the chapter had emancipated from the yoke of serfdom and of mortmain[2] by which they had been attached to the same church of Paris, both themselves and their children, both those that they have and those that they will procreate legitimately of their own flesh; this was done in response to their supplication and their various petitions, at the prompting of piety, according to the conditions and in the manner recorded beneath, which have been added to and inserted in this charter of emancipation not in order to encumber their liberty, but with the willing and express assent of each and every one of the aforesaid persons expressly consenting thereto, after thorough deliberation and discussion on the part of the same persons, both for themselves and for their posterity of whatever degree of descent.

They recognized and declared what in that act of emancipation the dean and chapter had retained (according to the voluntary and express assent of the same men) over their own persons, children, and heirs begotten of their flesh unto posterity, and over their property, wherever it was or had been situated in the territory and jurisdiction of the church of Saint Mary of Paris, or to whatever place the aforesaid emancipated persons and their children might transfer it: to wit, honor, due reverence, and those things which freedmen ought to and customarily do show their patrons,[3] as well as other rights recorded below.

Among those rights they recognize especially, under the name of tallage, [the right to] sixty pounds of Paris to be paid each year to the aforesaid dean and chapter on the feast of St. Andrew the Apostle[4] by themselves or their successors or the possessors of the houses,

[2] Property to which the lord had an inalienable right, and which always reverted to him upon the death of tenants using it, was said to be within his *mortmain—i.e.*, under his hand at (his tenants') death. A person living and working predominantly on such property—the classic situation of the serf—was by extension said to be under his lord's mortmain.

[3] This stipulation resembles Roman legislation of the fourth and fifth centuries (*Theodosian Code* IV, 10, 1–2, for example) which provided for the return to servitude of an emancipated slave who acted in an injurious manner toward his former master or went to court against him or his heirs. Whatever thirteenth-century French serfs understood by this stipulation, whatever practical advantage the chapter's lawyers hoped to get from it, it does suggest the revived study of Roman law which did much to alter the relationship between ecclesiastical lords and their serfs. In earlier, harsher centuries churches were usually the most lenient lords, but the relative permanence of clerical records and the introduction of learned distortions like equating medieval serfdom with classical slavery soon made ecclesiastical lords less convenient than their less-literate lay counterparts.

[4] From an Old French word meaning (literally) a "cut." The payment date was November 30.

homesteads, rental tenancies, and possessions of the village and territory of Orly, whoever they may be, or by anyone to whom such property and possessions shall fall by any title or means, since before that manumission the dean and chapter had the right to levy tallage at will and to their pleasure on those persons and goods or possessions. However, the tallage will be levied and assessed by those appointed thereto by the chapter of Paris.

Further, a rightful and lawful tithe,[5] upon the lands, vines, and any other possessions whatsoever. It shall be assessed as follows: they themselves and their heirs or successors shall pay on their lands and vines and other possessions, both acquired and to be acquired, . . . as shall those to whom such lands and vines and other possessions may fall in whatever manner or by whatever title, whoever they may be and to whichever order[6] they may belong, a sixteenth part or a *cuppa*[7] of wine from the first pressing, and a third part of the second pressing; of the winter wheat, spring wheat, beans, peas, vetch, woad, pulse,[8] and any other kind whatsoever of grain, legume, woad, or other seed, an eleventh part or every eleventh sheaf.

The tithe shall be counted and taken or levied by the agents of the chapter in the following manner: the wine tithe, before anything is removed or taken away from the *cuppa* measure or the wine press; and the tithe of winter wheat, spring wheat, beans, peas, woad, and any other kind of grain, legume, or seed, before anything is removed from the fields, plots, or gardens. Whoever by himself or through another shall remove, take away, abscond with, or arrange for the like before (as has been said) the counting and collection, shall be held responsible for making it up to the aforesaid dean and chapter or their local representative, as though he had committed a theft. However, the agent or agents appointed to count and levy the tithe shall take an oath each year in the chapter house that they shall attend to it faithfully and carefully, both on behalf of the chapter and on behalf of the aforesaid men [of Orly].

They also recognized and declared that the same dean and chapter

---

[5] See IV, 4, note 5.

[6] *I.e.*, order or rank of society; more specifically, whether serf, free, cleric, etc.

[7] A liquid measure, hard to define exactly in this case; not a large amount, though surely more than a modern American *cup*.

[8] Pulse: beans, peas, and other related leguminous foods. Vetch, like clover, makes good cattle fodder; woad is an herb providing a blue dye. This list gives some sense of the varied uses the chapter found for the produce of its dependent villages. Little if any wine is produced near Orly today; like Aguilcourt (IV, 4), it lies near the northern limit of practical viticulture.

had in that emancipation retained the following rights over themselves and their successors and over whatever goods and possessions they have or will have within the territory, tributary land, or jurisdiction of the church of Paris, to wit: all field taxes which they owed previously, revenues, *corvées*,[9] levies, dues, and all other customary obligations; and all manner of justice, as much in small or in minor as in major cases, as much high as low or lesser, and the fines, damages, right to determine possession, and all other legal rights formerly belonging to the dean and chapter, except for the royal tallage collected through the chapter, whenever it shall happen to be levied. To all these they shall be held, both themselves and their heirs or successors, as well as those to whom such goods or possessions shall fall by whatever title or manner, with this added condition: that they and their heirs [etc.], even if they be citizens of Paris[10] or of any other city whatever, shall be held responsible to the dean and chapter in regard to damages, jurisdiction, and liabilities, should it happen that they default in payment of the field taxes and other revenues within the appointed time limits. To the payment of each and every one of these dues the aforesaid men have committed and obligated themselves and their heirs or successors as well as anyone having a suit on their account concerning the aforesaid goods and possessions by whatever title, as well as those goods and possessions; they have fully and expressly willed that such property be encumbered and obligated in favor of the church of Paris.

They also recognized that they had been emancipated in such a way that neither they nor their heirs or successors shall be able to seek, have, or hold any further goods or possessions by right of parental affinity or consanguinity, nor to inherit them whether by will or through an intestate succession, so long as the other parties involved are in the condition of serfdom and mortmain to the dean and chapter of Paris. Nor will they be able to have or to acquire or gain possession by purchase or any other manner of title, any goods or possessions of other men of the church of Paris who are or will in future be in the condition of serfdom or mortmain to it. They also add that neither they nor their heirs [etc.] will bring any men or foreigners[11] subject

[9] See IV, 4, note 5.

[10] *I.e.*, if they possess the rights enjoyed by the bourgeoisie of Paris through grant or by inheritance.

[11] See IV, 4, especially note 4. The "rental tenancies" referred to in this chapter would presumably be rented to such *hospites*. The men of Orly might encounter such *hospites* in a number of other places and situations, of course, and this contingency is foreseen here as well.

to the jurisdiction of the dean and chapter of the church of Paris, before any court or to any jurisdiction other than the jurisdiction or court of the chapter of Paris, so long as the aforesaid chapter or some delegate thereof shall be ready to do full justice in their case.

The aforesaid persons also willed and conceded, in their name and in that of their heirs or successors and in the name of those on whose behalf they may obligate themselves (as herein contained), and on the part of all who may have a suit on their account affecting the homesteads, rental property, lands, and other possessions aforesaid, that those to whom their lands, vines, and rental property (insofar as they are held from the aforesaid dean and chapter) shall fall, . . . shall be held responsible for paying the aforesaid sixty pounds of Paris under the name of tallage, just as they were held to it, and also to the tithe and to each and every one of the rights aforesaid.

They have also asserted and recognized that it was not the intention of the chapter nor did they in any way intend to emancipate anyone originally from the aforesaid village besides those who at the time of the present emancipation were residing in the village of Orly, and those who would be hereafter procreated by them or designated [as heirs?]. An exception is made for Jean of Cossigny, Avelina of Dumus, and Garnier of Larchant[12] and their sons and daughters, on this added condition: they shall not in any way rejoice in such liberty until they shall have paid the dean and chapter the full sum of four thousand pounds of Paris, which they have promised to pay for such emancipation within the span of eight successive years, at the rate of five hundred pounds of Paris each year, before the feast of St. Andrew. But they shall be free of this condition in regard to marriage, and can henceforth marry wherever they will. And when that sum of money is paid in entirety, then shall they first rejoice in the liberty that has been conceded them, as set forth above. But if, before the

[12] Cossigny (population approximately 225 in 1962) is a nucleated village on the uplands of the *pays de Brie,* on the western edge of the Forest of Armainvilliers, about 20 miles by road due east of Orly across the Seine. Its parish, whose tithes seem to have been collected by the bishop rather than the chapter of Paris, was founded in the twelfth century; by that time the Counts of Brie (and Champagne, etc.) had been at work converting the woodlands of the region into the grainfields and pastures for which it is still outstanding. Larchant (population 508 in 1962) is 40 miles southeast of Orly up the valley of the Seine, on the southwest edge of the Forest of Fontainebleau. In the thirteenth century Larchant boasted strong walls and a large Gothic church dedicated to St. Mathurin, an eloquent converter of local pagans in the fourth century (he died in 388) whose relics continued to draw pilgrims until the sixteenth-century Wars of Religion. I have been unable to locate Dumus, though it must have been very close to the villages of Chevilly and L'Hay, 4 and 5 miles northwest of Orly. See selection (d).

aforesaid sum has been paid in full, there shall occur any escheat under mortmain[13] of any of the aforesaid emancipated persons whose goods should revert to the chapter of Paris, . . . the dean and chapter of Paris shall freely and without hindrance take possession of the goods escheated or under mortmain of those deceased in such a state, just as though they had not been emancipated; with this further condition, that nothing will be subtracted or withdrawn from the aforesaid price of emancipation on account of such escheat or mortmain. Neither shall the dean and chapter be held responsible for anything which the deceased shall owe in any way; rather, the emancipated survivors shall be held responsible for such debts of the deceased and for freeing the chapter of Paris in such a case.

Finally, concerning the payment of the sum stated above and the inviolable observance of each and every one of the above conditions, the aforesaid persons have obligated and committed themselves and all their heirs for all time to come and any other successors whatever and those who shall have a suit concerning them, and also whatever possessions of theirs may lie within the aforesaid territory, jurisdiction, and control of the church of Paris; swearing an oath, they have touched the most holy Gospels. Furthermore, presenting sureties and taking an oath in person, they have promised and obligated themselves to do each and every thing stated above and to see that they are inviolably observed, notwithstanding any legal prescription however ancient in date or any privilege granted or to be granted by anyone. As a testimonial, memorial, and confirmation of the matter, and so that the agreement stated above may gain the force of perpetual durability, we have, at the petition of the same persons, considered it fitting to attach our seals to the present document. Done in the year of Our Lord 1263, in the month of May.

[13] Escheat: reversion of property to the lord after a tenant's death, either because of a lack of heirs or (in this case) since the natural heirs would no longer be under the lord's mortmain.

Charter of the Chapter of Paris to Robert Meunier and Avelina His Wife, Natives of Orly, and Their Son Guillaume

To all who shall examine these present letters, greetings in the Lord from an officer of the court[1] of Paris. We declare that before

[1] *I.e.*, the diocesan court, a distinct rival of the royal court structure (as all these documents indicate).

us in our official capacity appeared Robert Meunier, Avelina his wife, natives of Orly as they asserted, now residing at Paris in the neighborhood called Beaubourg,[2] and Guillaume, their son. They declared that they were men of the body of the church of Paris, and that they had humbly besought the venerable dean and chapter of Paris to grant clerical tonsure to the aforesaid Guillaume. The dean and chapter granted the aforesaid tonsure to the same Guillaume, as the aforesaid Robert, Avelina his wife, and Guillaume their son asserted, on the conditions stated below.

The same Guillaume shall be held to display honor and due reverence forever to the dean and chapter of Paris, and all that freedmen customarily owe their patrons.[3] He shall be a cleric and remain in the clergy, and if it shall happen that hereafter he should rush into marriage or abandon clerical tonsure, he shall revert to the state of his original serfdom and be a man of the body of the aforesaid chapter, just as he was before the emancipation in question, notwithstanding that emancipation.

The same Guillaume renounced before us in our official capacity, of his own free will and from certain knowledge, all inheritance and paternal and maternal succession and recognized that he would not be capable of acquiring any possessions by right of consanguinity, purchase, or any other title or way, from any kinsmen so long as they shall be in the condition [of serfdom] and mortmain to the aforesaid chapter, except by license obtained from the chapter. And if anything shall come to the same Guillaume from the succession of any kinsman of his who was in the aforesaid chapter's mortmain, he shall be held to selling it within a year, putting it beyond his hand,[4] to someone within the chapter's mortmain. Otherwise, after a year, the dean and chapter may take the aforesaid effects into their hand as their own.

---

[2] Beaubourg was a suburb which grew up, largely in the twelfth century, along the chief Roman street (now the *rue St. Martin*) heading north from the original island-city of Paris. About halfway between the Abbey of St. Martin-in-the-Fields and the merchant settlement which in Carolingian times constituted Paris' only suburb on the Right Bank, Beaubourg was left outside the walls built by Louis VII (1137–80), but enclosed by those built under Philip Augustus (1180–1223). The *IIIe Arrondissement* of today's Paris covers most of medieval Beaubourg.

[3] See note 3 in the previous selection, and notice paragraph five of this charter.

[4] Notice the affinity of hand metaphors to medieval attempts to express freedom of action. One vivid application of this symbol occurred in the ceremony of homage, in which the vassal placed his hands between those of his future lord; sometimes peasants went through a similar ritual with their manorial lords.

The aforesaid Guillaume, in the presence of his aforenamed father and mother, willed and accepted each and every one of the foregoing conditions, and before us in our official capacity consented of his own free will, giving his promise with sureties and swearing an oath, having touched the most holy Gospels, to the following stipulation: that he would not hereafter contest the foreging conditions in a suit, either in his own person or through another. Rather, he will hold, fulfill, and observe inviolably each and every one of them as set forth above.

The aforesaid Guillaume also swore and promised, having offered sureties and taken an oath, that he would not summon or bring any man of the body of the aforesaid dean and chapter, or any other person within their jurisdiction, before any other judge ecclesiastical or secular, unless he has previously sought and obtained license to do so from the chapter, or unless the aforesaid chapter should be negligent in giving him justice in the matter.

As testimony and confirmation of all these matters, at the request of the aforesaid Guillaume and his aforenamed father and mother, we have caused the present charter to be fortified with the seal of the court of Paris. Given in the year of Our Lord 1256, on the vigil of the Assumption of the Blessed Virgin Mary.[5]

[5] *I.e.,* August 14.

Charter of the Chapter of Paris Concerning Pierre Le Roy of L'Hay, Residing at Chevilly

To all who shall examine these letters, greetings in the Lord from an officer of the court of Paris. We declare that there appeared before us Pierre called Le Roy, a native of L'Hay, residing in Chevilly,[1] who asserted and recognized before us in our official capacity, of his own free will, not under duress, and from certain knowledge, that he had for a long time been married to Gila, formerly wife of the

[1] L'Hay-les-Roses lies about 7 miles southeast of the cathedral of Notre Dame of Paris, and about 4 to 5 miles northwest of Orly. Its parish church (dedicated to St. Leonard) was established by the cathedral chapter in the thirteenth century, although the village was probably of earlier foundation than that. Its population in 1901 was about 900; now, a suburb of metropolitan Paris, it has over 18,000 people. Chevilly-la-Rue is about 1 mile to the southeast, on the way to Thiais and Orly; numbering a little over 800 scattered people in 1901, its population today is over 12,000. Most of Chevilly's serfs were emancipated in 1259.

deceased Pierre of Origny,[2] now herself deceased, a woman of the body of the church of Paris. The aforesaid Pierre also asserted and recognized before us in our official capacity that on that account, according to the general custom of the country[3] he himself became a man of the body of the church of Paris; and the aforesaid Pierre promised, swearing an oath in person before us and having touched the most holy Gospels, that he would have the dean and chapter of Paris for his lords in other respects as well, and would obey them as his lords, and would in no way call on any other lord beside them. Furthermore, on Monday in the church at Chevilly,[4] at the hour of the parish mass, immediately after the Gospel of that mass, he will publicly and before everyone profess himself a man of the body of the church of Paris in every respect, and will swear in that very place that he will consider himself a man of the body as regards the dean and chapter, and will in no wise call on any other lord beside them. And the aforesaid Pierre swore before us that the foregoing were true. In testimony whereof, at the request of the aforesaid Pierre, we have had the seal of the court of Paris attached to the present letters. Given in the year of Our Lord 1267, in the month of January.

9. THE SPECIAL PEASANT PERSPECTIVE: NORTH WALES, 1294–96

To give a more balanced picture of peasant concerns in their encounter with the techniques and structures of the law, we move now to northern Wales, a region which, unlike the Ile-de-France, was marked by little social change but by a great deal of political upheaval in the second half of the thirteenth century. The following selection consists of excerpts from the registers of two local courts in the Clwyd valley, which had been part of the Welsh principality of Gwynedd until the last quarter of the century. In 1277 Llewellyn ap Gruffydd, lord of Gwynedd and Prince of Wales, revolted against his overlord, the English king Edward I (1272–1307); in 1282 his brother David did the same. By 1283 Edward had defeated all their forces, detached the Clwyd

---

[2] About 30 miles due east on the uplands of the Brie, on the eastern side of the Forest of Armainvilliers (see selection [b], note 12). Origny has now been absorbed into the commune of Tournan.

[3] In the original, *patria*, perhaps a translation of the French *pays* (does it refer to Chevilly, or the whole *pays Parisis?*). Compare the different custom of Clermont-en-Beauvaisis, 45–50 miles northwest, as shown in IV, 6.

[4] Ste. Colombe, built in the tenth century by the chapter; a Gothic tower was added in the thirteenth.

valley and neighboring districts from Gwynedd, and handed that territory out to faithful vassals of Anglo-Norman stock. The upper Clwyd valley, with its commanding fortress of Ruthin, was given to Reginald Grey, the founder of a long line of Greys de Ruthin ruling the Lordship of Dyffryn-Clwyd (which simply means Valley of the Clwyd—which means "strong"—in Welsh); the lower valley with its town of Denbigh went to Henry de Lacy, Earl of Lincoln, and the upper valley of the Dee across the ridges to the south was given as a fief (called the Lordship of Bromfield and Yale) to John de Warenne, Earl of Surrey.

A more profound change came in 1284 with the Statute of Wales, which imposed English criminal law and reorganized the whole judicial hierarchy. This act did away with Welsh laws and practices codified three and a half centuries before, finally converted the courts of the local *commotes* (from the Welsh word for neighborhood) into territorial jurisdictions beyond the reach of tribal initiative, and put the responsibility for law enforcement firmly in the hands of the new lords and justiciars.

This drastic revision was followed immediately by revolts which flared up in several parts of Wales for a variety of reasons, and were not quieted until 1292. Two years later, in September of 1294, Madoc ap Llewellyn, son of a poor but ancient family of Merioneth, led a general uprising of the northern Welsh against all these impositions. Considerable numbers flocked to his standard in the mountains, and the fact that it took Edward only seven months to defeat and disperse them is no small tribute to his military talents. The king cemented his victory with the construction of several great royal castles, most of which survive today in good condition. The policy of repressive occupation of which they are massive monuments seems a familiar phenomenon to modern observers, as do the risings of the native Welsh, which we naturally liken to those nationalistic resistance movements, loaded with ethnic self-consciousness and resentment, for which the nineteenth and twentieth centuries have been famous.

This last impression is distinctly not borne out, however, by the records of ordinary business left by the commote courts of the Lordship of Ruthin (as castle-dominated Dyffryn-Clwyd soon came to be known). Some care is taken to make the juries half-Welsh and half-English, one prophetic boast is recorded (enigmatically at that), and we notice that some of the men named are imprisoned or fugitive; but by and large the great rebellion of Madoc figures as an occasion for stealing cattle and brewery equipment, encroaching on the lord's forest rights, and so on. When one of these peasants felt like insulting another (apparently a favorite pastime), he looked for an excuse in the spheres of sex or honesty or daily competence, rather than in the realms of ethnic or political identification. We should be hesitant to decide that these rolls present only a peripheral or repressed aspect of daily life in the valley of the Clwyd (as may be true of most police-court records today): notice how constantly and enthusiastically the sparse population of these commotes went to law, and how well attended the sessions seem to have been.

Court of Llannerch[1] Held on Thursday in Whitsun-week, in the Twenty-second Year of the Reign of Edward I (June 10, 1294)

Court of Llannerch *and* Court of Ruthin *from* The Court Rolls of the Lordship of Ruthin, or Dyffryn-Clwydd, of the Reign of King Edward the First, *ed. and trans.* Richard A. Roberts *(London: Honorable Society of the Cymmrodorion, 1893)*, Cymmrodorion Record Series, 2, *pp. 2–10, 13, 15–17, 19–21, 23.*

Itth. Vacchan complains of Houa Madoc for that he beat him with a stick. The parties appearing, the said Houa was accused. He did not deny. Therefore [he is] in mercy. He gives 12*d*.[2] [*12d.*]

Cad. ap Blethin ap Howel complains of Henry de Riggebi, of the county of Lancaster, that he stole his iron-grey horse, against the lord's peace. The parties appearing, the said Henry was accused of the said theft. He appeared and put himself upon the country:[3] six English-

---

[1] Perhaps Llanfair-Dyffryn, a small community about 2 miles southeast of Ruthin. No attempt is made in these notes to indicate the distances of most of the places named in these rolls from one another, first because most are clearly within a 10-mile radius of Ruthin, and second because many of them are most uncertain at this distance in time. Unlike the Ile-de-France, the Vale of Clwyd was an area of scattered homesteads in which social bonds had been expressed more through tribal association than through the physically close activities of a nucleated village or joint cultivation of open fields. The sessions of commote court would be held at some churchyard, marketplace, or fortress, as is made strikingly clear by the names of the two commotes here cited: Ruthin comes from the Welsh Rhudd-din, meaning Red Fortress, and whether the other court belonged to Llannerch or Llanfair, the prefix *Llan-* indicates an enclosure, quite often that around a parish church and its immediately dependent buildings.

[2] *I.e.*, he had to pay a fine, the amount of which, in the original record, is usually indicated in the left-hand margin. The lord got the fine; damages paid the injured party are not usually noted in this record. If theft was involved, restitution of the stolen goods or their value was of course required.

[3] *I.e.*, appealed to a trial by jury composed of men from the neighborhood. This entry shows clearly the variety of ethnic origins of this commote's residents. Cad

men and six Welshmen: who were sworn and say that the said Henry took the horse without his leave and not thievishly. Therefore the said Henry is in mercy. And the said Cad. in mercy for a false complaint. [*Quit. 6s. 8d.*]

William le Crothor of Llannerch declared that Iorwerth ap Kenwric ap Ririt on Whitsunday demanded from Thomas ap Gilth Crist his homage [and] his rent, and says that this demand was made by the Constable's order; and then he [Iorwerth] of his evil will cursed the Constable's beard and afterwards his head if he would not give orders to go again into France, and he swore by the body of Christ that before the middle of the month the Constable and other English will hear such rumours[4] that they will not wish to come again into Wales. The said Iorwerth was called and comes not. Therefore, etc. [*i.e.*, he is in mercy.]

Wilin ap Howel was attached because he received a cow of a black colour, which belonged to William, the lord's shepherd. Being called, he was accused. He vouches Wyn his brother to warranty.[5] The said Wyn appeared and vouched a certain woman named Alice to warranty. The said Alice appeared and was interrogated. She answers and says that the aforesaid cow is her own, of her own calving and pasture. And Leuke, wife of the said William, asked, Who warrants this day the aforesaid cow? The said Win warranted it, and took the cow by the ear; and forasmuch as William was not present, therefore he is commanded to come at the next Court: and said Win finds pledges for bringing up the said cow. Pledges: Wilin ap Howel and Howel ap Cadugan.

Ieuan Boolbleyt was attached because he depastured land which was in the lord's hands, by Robert de Haggele. He appeared and gives 6d. [*Quit. 6d.*]

Willin ap Howel attached because he has not brought up a cow

---

ap Blethin ap Howel is a Welshman, the son of Blethin who is the son of Howel. Henry de Riggebi is an Englishman whose Norman name-form suggests a fair degree of family pride; he is apparently an immigrant from England proper. Anglo-Norman family names like *le Walker* also occur, as do a few Welsh family names (Vacchan or Vaghan). Individuals of both races also carry names showing function, such as John the Forester or Martin the Baker. Do not expect too much consistency in the spelling of even one person's name in these records.

[4] This enigmatic but vivid report shows that political opinions were not necessarily alien to this type of record. Iorwerth was obviously privy to some plans for the great uprising which actually began on the following September thirtieth, after the King's agents had distributed arms to many Welshmen who agreed to accompany him on expeditions to Flanders and to Gascony, against the French king.

[5] *I.e.*, as a witness with "certain knowledge."

of a dun colour to this Court, according as he found pledges for bringing it up. He appeared and brought it not. Therefore he is in default. Pledge: the Ringildre,[6] and he is to bring it up at the next Court. [*Quit. 2s.*]

Iorwerth ap Iago attached because he depastured the lord's land without leave. Pledge: the Ringildre. [*Quit. 6d.*]

Map Goue for the same. [*Quit. 6d.*]

David ap Howel for the same. [*Quit. 6d.*]

Jokin the tailor, for the same. [*Quit. 6d.*]

Kenwric Vaghan for the same. [*Quit. 6d.*]

Maddoc ap Keheylin attached because he lost the lord's hay going towards Merioneth.[7] [*Quit. 6d.*]

Court of Llannerch Held on Friday next before the Feast of Saint Barnabas, in the Twenty-third Year of the Reign of King Edward I (June 10, 1295)

Maddoc ap Edeneuet was made bailiff in the office of the forest in Llannerch with John the Forester, and finds pledges for his faithful service, Griffith ap Maddoc *Ddu*, Wilin ap Griffith, Llewelyn Vaghan, Caruet ap Iorwerth, and Blethin ap Howel.

Wilin ap Howel was attached because he concealed a cow of a dun colour with a white head, which belonged to a certain woman whose husband was with Maddoc ap Llewelyn, the lord the King's felon, and stood against the peace. He appeared and acknowledged the truth of it. Therefore the aforesaid Wilin is at the will of the lord, and the cow by judgment remains to the lord, price 5s. Pledge for doing the will of the lord. He made fine as below. [*Quit. one cow.*]

Wyn ap Howel brought up a black cow which was replevied[8] at the last preceding Court, and when in full Court he came with the aforesaid cow, there appeared Leuke, late the wife of William the Shepherd, and accused Win concerning the said cow, that it was her own on the same day when the said William was alive and dead, on Saturday after the departure of the lord from Dyffryn-Clwyd, at Cilken, and the said Win [charges] that he bought the said cow

---

[6] Welsh for *bailiff*. See the first entry of the next session.

[7] A shire or *cantred* (an administrative unit composed of several commotes) about 30 miles to the southwest of Ruthin, up the valley of the Dee.

[8] Handed over to the keeping of one of the parties in the dispute, on the understanding that it must be returned if the judgment ultimately goes against that party.

from English Alice and vouched [her] to warranty, and she warranted it, and immediately he releases the cow and puts himself in the lord's mercy. Pledge: [*name not filled in.*] The same Leuke by 12 men sworn to credit proved the cow to be her own, and had it after oath made. Afterwards she made fine with Wilin ap Howel. [*Mercy.*]

Wilin ap Howel attached for receiving a cow of a black colour which Lewke, widow of William the Shepherd, claimed to be her own proper chattel, which was her husband's on Saturday, the Feast of St. Michael in Monte Tumba, at Cilken, when he was killed there. Afterwards he made satisfaction with 5*l.* Pledges: Caruet ap Iorwerth, Blethin ap Howel, Grathcornu, Iorwerth ap Mereduth, Blethin Ddu, Gronou ap Maddoc Palnen, Cad. ap Maddoc, Houa ap Cadugan, Blethin Voil, and Cad. ap Blethin; to pay on Sunday after the Feast of St. John the Baptist, 20*s.*; on Sunday after the Feast of St. Peter ad Vincula, 20*s.*; on the Feast of the Assumption of the Virgin Mary, 20*s.*; on the Feast of St. Matthew, 20*s.*; on the Feast of All Souls, 20*s.* He has paid 20*s.* Likewise 13*s.* 4*d.* Likewise 6*s.* 8*d.* on the Feast of the Assumption of the Blessed Virgin [August. 15]. Likewise 6*s.* 8*d.* at the Feast of St. Matthew [Sept. 21].[9] [*5l.*]

Iorwerth Vaghan ap Iorwerth ap Ithel gives to the lord 40*d.* for having the lord the King's peace for the benefit of Lloyden his son. It is written in the Constable's Roll.[10]

Kenwric ap Iorwerth ap Adaff gives to the lord for having peace concerning two oxen taken from the chattels of the said lord, 16*s.* 8*d.* He has paid 8*s.* 4*d.* Likewise he has paid 6*s.* 8*d.* Quit. [*16s. 8d.*]

*   *   *

Hugh the Chaplain was attached against John the Forester for opposing him. Both consented to a verdict of four arbitrators, to wit, the Constable, Richard the Chaplain, William Passevaunt, Massy. Pledges for abiding by their award: Almari le Mareys and Massy; and the said Sir Howel is in mercy, and is to make amends to the said John. [*Condoned.*]

Matthew of Ludlow complains of Sir Ririth the Chaplain for that

---

[9] William the Shepherd had been killed on October 16, 1294, presumably by rebels against his lord Reginald Grey. All these dates for payment lie between June 21 (St. John the Baptist) and November 1 (All Souls).

[10] A man of importance (as the form of his name suggests) buys official forgetfulness for some deed of his son's; may we surmise some role in the rebellion? The last sentence of this entry is written in a different hand, probably somewhat later on.

on Friday before the Feast of St. Luke[11] he came to his house and there took feloniously and thievishly one red cow, to his damage of 13s. 4d. He appeared and led the cow into court, and says that if the said Matthew make oath that the said cow was his, that he would restore it; and he swore and had the cow. Therefore it is decided by judgment of the adjudicators that the said Ririth remain in mercy for the theft in [the sum of] 7l. Pledges: Maddoc ap Howel, Llewelyn ap Ririth, Maddoc his brother, Llewelyn Voyl, Carewet Waghan, Maddoc ap Griffith. He paid 13s. 4d. Also 40d. Also 40d. By the hands of Jokin, 6s. 8d. Also 13s. 4d. [4l.]

Court of Llannerch Held on Friday next after the Feast of St. Bartholomew, in the Twenty-third Year of the Reign of King Edward I (August 26, 1295)

John the Forester complains of Iorwerth Goch for that he carried away his toll from the mill of Carthtanan on Friday before the Feast of St. Luke the Evangelist,[12] to the value of 20s. and more. Besides, before the coming of the lord, he despoiled the said mill of the mill-iron belonging to it, to the value of 40d., through which the same John bought the aforesaid mill-iron for 19d. in the presence of Richard the receiver. He appeared and puts himself upon the country, who say that the aforesaid Iorwerth is guilty concerning the mill-iron and concerning three baskets of the toll of the mill. Therefore, etc. He finds pledges: Amari de Mareys and Howel the Chaplain, of Llanfair. [*Mercy. 6d. Quit.*]

Matthew of Ludlow complains of Kenwrick ap Ievan of Lanbennogh for that at Michaelmas he hired his grange in order to put his corn into it. The said Kenwrick, after the Feast of St. Luke,[13] did his will with the said corn, to the value of 20l., and against the peace. He appeared and was accused. He stood in peace, and neither said any-

---

[11] October 15, 1294: compare the date of William the Shepherd's death. Considering also the previous entry, it would seem that the Welsh clergy were active in the uprising. The notations of payment at the end of this entry were probably added after each payment.

[12] The same date as that of the theft dealt with in the previous entry. The "toll of the mill" was that portion of the grain ground exacted from each user as a payment to the lord; John the Forester seems to have collected it.

[13] Michaelmas is September 29, the day before the rebellion broke out. The Feast of St. Luke the Evangelist is October 18, by which time things were clearly hopping around Ruthin.

thing nor denied anything. Wherefore it was decided by judgment of the adjudicators that the said Kenwrick should be in mercy towards the lord and [make] amends to the said Matthew, [and] because in no manner did he deny, nor wished to deny, it seemed to the adjudicators that the said Kenwrick as it were consented to and confessed all things charged against him. Pledges of the amercement: Maddoc Goch, Maddoc ap Howel. He paid 40*d.* Also 40*d.* Also 40*d.* Also half a mark. [*Mercy. 20s.*]

William Howel complains of Madin Kyte for that he came to his house in Llannerch and there brewed in the time of Maddoc ap Llewelyn, and afterwards the said William came into those parts with the army of the lord the King,[14] and discovered his utensils to the value of 20*s.* He appeared and put himself upon the country, who say that he is guilty. Therefore he is in mercy. [*Mercy. Quit. 6d.*]

* * *

Jokin Brich complains of David ap Adaf of Mod . . . of shedding of blood. The said David puts himself in mercy and to make amends to the hurt person. [*Quit. 1 mark.*]

Ievan Thloynoch was attached in the forest of Thlunbrand. He appeared and does not deny. Therefore he is in mercy. [*Mercy. Quit. 6d.*]

Maddoc ap Anian of Thoth . . . . attached because he cut green wood in the forest. Convicted. [*Mercy. Quit. 6d.*]

Maddoc ap David attached with his cattle feeding in the forest . . . . He does not deny. Therefore, etc. [*Mercy. Quit. 6d.*]

Iorwerth Vaghan attached because during the time when Maddoc ap Llewelyn made himself lord, with the leave of the said Maddoc he cut one tree.[15] Therefore, etc. [*Mercy. Quit. 6d.*]

Kenwrick ap Thomas attached for carrying away old wood from Nantclwyd.[16] Convicted. Therefore, etc. [*Mercy. Quit. 6d.*]

Anian Cryyth attached for that he cut down boughs of oak for his oxen without licence. Therefore, etc. [*Mercy. Quit. 12d.*]

Kenwrick ap Maddoc Kethen attached with eleven beasts in the lord's forest. Therefore, etc. [*Mercy. Quit. 5½d.*]

[14] Edward marched through the Vale of Clwyd in December, 1294 and July, 1295 (two months after imposing quiet).

[15] Note his purchase of the King's peace for his son during the previous session.

[16] A forest and estate 4 miles upriver (south) from Ruthin; it means "dale of the Clwyd."

Helin ap Griffin attached because he cut rods in the forest without licence. Therefore, etc. [*Mercy. Quit. 2d.*]

Iorwerth Goch attached because he cut and carried away green wood out of Nantclwyd. Convicted. Therefore, etc. [*Mercy. 2s.*]

Total, 14s. 5½d.

Court of Ruthin Held on Tuesday next after Michaelmas Day, in the Twenty-third Year of the Reign of King Edward I (October 4, 1295)

Robert le Walker complains of Henry de Brencreden for that when he was pledge of the said Henry against Richard Russel of Chester of 11s. 6d., for which money the said Robert was imprisoned in Chester,[17] and so being compelled, he made satisfaction to the said Richard, as appears by the tally which he has concerning the said money. The said Henry appeared, and denies, and says that he never was his pledge, nor ever paid for him one penny; and concerning these he puts himself upon the country. Who say that the said Henry is debtor of the said money, and that the said Robert, compelled by force, paid the said money. Therefore the said Henry is in mercy 6d., and let him render to the said Robert the said money. [*Mercy. 6d.*]

Maddoc ap Wian complains of Henry de Brecredin for that he unjustly detains one quarter of oats which he sold to the said Maddoc. He finds pledges to prosecute. The parties appeared, and the said Henry was accused. He denied: therefore to the law.

Court of Ruthin Held on the Eve of St. Andrew in the Twenty-fourth Year of the Reign of King Edward I (November 29, 1295)

Anian ap Candelow complains of Mabbe, the maid of Sandre of Southwell, that she upbraided him with disgraceful words, and that she defamed him. She appeared and denies. Therefore to the law;

---

[17] Chester was the well-fortified capital of the County Palatine (see III, 7) to the east of Gwynedd. Commanding the lower valley of the Dee, it had been an important Roman fort (*castrum,* whence its Saxon name), and after the coming of the Normans became the seat of one of the semi-autonomous "Marcher" lordships created to contain and exert pressure on the upland Welsh. Reginald Grey, grandson of a Norman Earl of Pembroke (see II, 9), was Justiciar of Cheshire before Edward I made him lord of Ruthin, 20 miles to the west.

and she has made law. Therefore the said Anian in mercy for a false complaint. [*6d.*]

* * *

Walter of Ludlow, in full Court, claimed one brazen pan, price 5*d.*, of Angharet, daughter of Gronon of Roos, to be his own chattel. They have a day for settling the ownership of the chattel, until the next Court, by consent of the parties. He proved, and had it. Therefore the said Angharet in mercy. Pledge, Ithel ap Bracerooh.

Hugh Picot, demanding one coat from Wladusa the laundress, on Tuesday before the feast of the Exaltation of the Holy Cross, in the 23rd year.[18] The said Hugh was called, and comes not. Therefore it is adjudged by the Court that he should remain in default, and the said Wladusa should depart quit with the said coat, and the other in mercy for default. [*6d.*]

Edith, wife of the said Hugh Picot, Complains of Wladusa the laundress concerning one coat unjustly retained from whose possession it slipped she knows not how. She finds pledges to prosecute, [viz.] Richard Picot and Adam son of Maddoc, and the said Wladusa finds pledges for having the coat, with the hood, and doing what justice shall require. The pledges, Gronon Waghan of Lannanneys[19] and Llewelyn ap Maddoc. The said Wladusa made law that ever [she had] the coat with the hood; and because she has made law, therefore [she is] quit, and the said Edith in mercy for false complaint; and because she was poor, it was condoned. [*They are quit.*]

* * *

Leuke, wife of Henry le Porter, complains of Roger of Wenlock for that she delivered to him three shillings to carry to her husband in prison at Chester, of which money he paid 22*d.* and retained 14*d.* The parties appeared, and the said Roger said that he expended 11*d.* at Chester awaiting the presence of the Constable of Ruthin, and this by command of the husband of the said Leuke, and called him to warranty. He finds pledges for having his warranty at the next Court. Pledges, Howel Goch and Philip the baker. [*He is fugitive.*]

* * *

[18] September 13, 1295.
[19] Three miles down the Clwyd (north) from Ruthin.

*Court of Ruthin Held on Tuesday the Eve of St. Thomas the Apostle,
in the Twenty-fourth Year of the Reign of King Edward I
(December 20, 1295)*

Wladusa the laundress essoins[20] [herself] against Edith the wife of
Picot, by Gronon ap Leward, because she is sick: attested by oath of
the Ringildre.

* * *

Jowkin of Montgomery complains of Martin the baker, of one mare
sold to him, and he detains the debt. They have a day of concord,
[to wit] this Thursday next following. Pledges, Mascii and Peter the
cobbler. [*Terminated.*]

John the bailiff complains of John the tailor concerning one horse
detained. [*Terminated.*]

Neste, wife of John de Moles, appeared against William of Rue the
tiler. He was called and came not. Therefore he is in mercy.

*Court of Ruthin Held on Tuesday within the Octave of the
Epiphany of the Lord, in the Twenty-fourth Year
of the Reign of King Edward I (January 10, 1296)*

On the same day is given a love-day,[21] at the request of the parties,
between Adam of Aston, petitioner, and Ralph of Hassal, defendant,
concerning pledgery.

Thomas essoins against Adam of Aston concerning a plea whereof
(they are) at law, by Richard Palfrey: second time.

John the tailor essoins himself against John Balle in a plea of debt,
by Walter of Ludlow: second time.

Roger of Wenlock essoins against Leuke, wife of Henry le porter,
in a plea, by William the baker; second time.

David the ditcher, of Lanworrock, [essoins] against Richard de
Thabeleg in a plea of trespass, by Roger the barber: first time.

Martin the baker essoins against Ralph del Peeck in wager of law,
by Richard Picot: first time.

Richard Belamy essoins against John Lewerich in a plea of debt,
by Richard the cobbler: first time.

---

[20] *I.e.,* she sends a valid excuse for non-attendance, which Gronon brings to court.
Wladusa and the Picots clearly had a long-standing feud.

[21] A day appointed for the settlement of differences by arbitration, without fine.

Court of Ruthin Held on Tuesday before the Feast of St. Luke the Evangelist, in the Twenty-fourth Year of the Reign of King Edward I (October 16, 1296)

It is commanded to attach David Clostok and the wife of Cerwin for two hoppers of wheat and rye to be made good to the carter, according to their conviction by inquest. [*In the Court of Dogveylin.*]

It is commanded to attach Philip Ddu of Llanelidan[22] for that he carried fire to the house of Thomas the cobbler to burn it. [*In the Court of Llannerch.*]

Mariot', the wife of Walter of Ludlow, complains of Christian Schot for that he defamed her with opprobrious words and called her whore, to her loss and shame in 20s. and more. He appears and denies: therefore to the law; and, because he cannot find pledges, therefore, by judgment of the Court, let him go to the punishment which is called Thewe.[23] Afterwards they agreed in such form that the said Christian Schot remains in mercy, and is to make amends to the said Mariot'. [*6d.*]

* * *

It is commanded to attach Iorwerth Goch, Saer, to answer Walter of Ludlow of one sword, two sacks, and 5s. of silver taken from him by violence, feloniously, and against the peace, as before. They have a love-day.

It is commanded to attach Philip Troynok for the goods of Robert le Walker, carried away against the peace, as before. The said Troynok is not found. [*In the Court of Llannerch.*]

It is commanded to attach Grono ap Houa for the utensils of Robert le Walker, taken away against the peace, as before. He is not found.

It is commanded to attach William his brother.

---

[22] Five and one-half miles south of Ruthin, 4 miles southwest of Llanfair; but there is no indication where the near-victim lived. The lord's representative at this session is issuing judgments applicable throughout the several commotes of the region.

[23] Sitting on the cucking stool at the marketplace, to general comment and merriment.

THE BOURGEOISIE V

This chapter's readings will probably seem more immediate and less in need of explanation than any other part of this book. With them, we are tracing the emergence and rise of that class of medieval European society which outlasted or unseated its parents and rivals, and has become in our age the dominant and almost the only style-setting class of the modern Western world. It came to full self-consciousness relatively late in medieval history, although its remote origins can be discerned in the tracks left by merchants who led a distinct way of life in even the most stagnantly rural centuries of the Dark Ages.

As in the previous two chapters, the first few selections to follow will present several views of the merchant (the original and continuously the quintessential bourgeois) through the eyes of older and prouder orders of medieval society. After that we will turn our attention to four documents revealing characteristic techniques or concerns of the expanding bourgeoisie of the High Middle Ages. Finally, we shall take a brief look at four urban environments which proved supremely sympathetic to the self-expression of this new, variable, and marvelously inventive class.

The Merchant's Rise to Recognition

1. THE SNOW CHILD (LATE TENTH CENTURY)

Here is a poem, a parody of current liturgical verse forms, written in Latin in tenth-century Germany. Its anonymous author must have gotten a good clerical education in order to dress this fable in the symmetrical meters and Vergilian vocabulary which it wears so incongruously; his portrayal of the merchant as a heartless slave trader whose crudity is relieved only by his cleverness is surely consistent with the clergy's generally dubious view of the normal activities of a merchant's calling. On the other hand, the author seems to take a certain pleasure in the way this abused man employs his dangerous craft to turn the tables on his wife. Even in Swabia many a man who went to clerks' schools to learn Latin led the rest of his life as a lawyer, notary, or trader in the towns that were just beginning to thrive in the tenth century. Besides, it seems very likely that this versifier was simply trying out his scholastic talents on a tale currently circulating among the tough and wily merchants of the region.

The Snow Child

Translated from the Latin text in The Oxford Book of Medieval Latin Verse, *ed. F. J. E. Raby (Oxford: The Clarendon Press, 1959), pp. 167–70. Footnotes supplied.*

Pay attention to a laughable tale, all you people, and hear how a woman defrauded a Swabian and he defrauded her.

A minor Swabian, a citizen of Constance,[1] transporting treasure across the deep in ships, left too lusty a wife at home.

Barely had he cut the surly sea with his oars when, all of a sudden, a tempest arose. The sea raged, the blasts struggled with one another, the waves surged high about him—and after a lot of this the south wind [2] threw him as a vagrant exile on a distant shore.

But in the meantime his wife wasn't leaving their house empty! Strolling actors were there, youths followed them, and she, quite forgetting her castaway husband, was delighted to take them all in. The next night she was pregnant, and on the right day she let out an unrightful son.

After two years had rolled 'round, the aforesaid wanderer returned. His faithless wife rushed up to him, dragging the little boy after her. When they had exchanged kisses the husband said to her, "From whom do you have that boy? Tell, or suffer the ultimate penalty!"

But she, in fear of her husband, cast about in all directions for a ruse, and finally said, "My dear husband, one time when I was thirsty

[1] A city in southern Germany on Lake Constance, through which the Rhine flows. The poet is obviously not concerned about the geographical difficulties involved in having his merchant go on what sounds like a trip across the Mediterranean.

[2] In the original text, *nothus*, which is strictly a misspelling of *notus* (the south wind), and means illegitimate: hence, a learned pun ("that bastard of a south wind") is intended. This bizarre and consciously gruesome mixture of vulgarity and elevated vocabulary is the poet's hallmark.

up in the Alps I quenched my thirst with some snow. Impregnated then and there by it, I conceived—alas!—that boy whose birth has been so ruinous to me."

After all of this five years or more passed by. The roving merchant repaired his oars, fixed up his shattered ship, and then set his sails and took the snow child with him.

When he had traversed the sea he brought the boy forth, handed him over to another merchant to bind a transaction worth a hundred pounds,[3] and rich from his sale of the child, returned.

Coming in to his house, he says to his wife, "Be consoled, wife; be consoled, my dear one: I have lost your son, whom even you could certainly not have loved more than I.[4]

"A tempest arose, windy fury drove us onto shallow sandbanks. The sun burned down fiercely on all of us, and that son of snow just melted!"

And so did the Swabian cheat his faithless wife; thus did fraud overcome fraud. For the sun rightly dissolved what the snow begot!

2. THE WAGON OF NÎMES (TWELFTH CENTURY)

Here is an aristocratic view of the merchant, taken from the robustly feudal epic *Le Charroi de Nîmes*. It was written down in the middle of the twelfth century, and reflects many of the basic social attitudes of the audiences to which it was sung or recited in many castles and less-elevated residences of the rural nobility throughout northern France. Its title derives from a ruse related to the Trojan horse, which William Fierebrace was said to have employed in his capture of the city of Nîmes from the Saracens. Fierebrace, also called William Short-Nose and William of Orange, was the hero of several epic stories belonging to the cycle of Charlemagne and Roland. His numerous feats seem to represent a distant and almost totally distorted memory of a

[3] In medieval commercial law, the most effective way to bind a transaction was for the buyer to hand over to the seller an object of value over and above the amount of the sale. It is not clear whether the poet means that the Swabian used the snow child for this purpose, and got a kickback of 100 pounds, or whether the child was his only merchandise (of a sort eagerly sought after by slave traders, not only in Islam), and that he got 100 pounds for him in outright sale, with no further pledges required (except perhaps as a legal cover-up). In either case, the poet demonstrates that he knows some fancy classical vocabulary and a fair amount of contemporary commercial practice.

[4] Or, "whom surely you did not love more than [you love] me"—a Latin wordplay of which English is incapable.

saintly Count William of Gothia (a Frankish administrative district between the river Rhône and the Pyrenees; see I, 10), who died in Spain in 812. Nîmes, a beautiful city full of Roman remains undoubtedy even more impressive then than now, and a center of considerable trade in Roman and early medieval times despite its location on a tiny river 25 miles inland from the Mediterranean, was actually recovered for Christendom by Charles Martel a few years after being sacked by the Saracens in 725.

We should not try to make the historic Carolingian count fit the image of the fictional twelfth-century hero, who appealed to his own age primarily as an embodiment of the vigorous and narrow feudal virtues which made such a spectacular success of the First Crusade. We should also notice that, beneath his stressing of the differences between the wiles of a French baron and those of outlandish merchant types, the poet betrays in his caricature no little knowledge of the trade routes, export commodities, and mercantile habits of his time.

Le Charroi de Nîmes

From Le Charroi de Nîmes, *trans. Henri J. Godin (Oxford: Basil Blackwell, 1936), pp. 22–25, 28–31. Reprinted by permission of Henri J. Godin and Basil Blackwell & Mott Ltd.*

32. They put on their hauberks, and lace on their bejewelled helmets, they gird on their swords with the golden hilts inlaid with black enamel, they mount into the saddles of their spirited steeds; from their necks hang strong shields, in their hands they hold their lances inlaid with black enamel. They come out of the town in close and well-ordered ranks, they have their oriflame displayed before them; they make straight for Nîmes. That is where so many glittering helmets were to be seen! In the vanguard was Bertrand the illustrious, Gautier de Termes and the Scotchman Gilemer, and Guielin, the brave and wise. In the rear was William the valiant with ten thousand Frenchmen well armed and ready for the fray. They had not covered a distance of four leagues when they met a serf in the middle of the road. He comes from St Giles where he has spent some time. He has four oxen which he had bought, and three of his own children. The serf, who was no fool, reflected that salt is expensive in the kingdom where he was born; he raised a cask on his cart and filled it with

salt to the brim. His three children play and laugh and hold in their hands large pieces of bread; they play marbles on the salt.

The French are amused; how could they help it! Count Bertrand addressed him in these words: "Tell us, serf, by your law, where were you born?" And he replied: "You will hear the truth: by Mahomet,[1] Sir, I come from Laval on Cler. I am returning from St Giles,[2] where I have done business. I am going home to garner my corn. If Mahomet would save it for me, I should be well provided for I have sown so much." The French say: "You have spoken like a fool, since you believe that Mahomet is God, and that it is thanks to him that you have riches and plenty, cold in winter and heat in summer. We ought to cut your limbs off (to teach you a lesson)." And William said: "Barons, calm yourselves. I shall talk to him about something else."

33. Count William began to say to him: "Look, now, serf, according to the law by which you live, have you been to Nîmes, the strong and powerful city?" "Yes, indeed, Sir, they wanted me to pay toll, but I am too poor, and I could not give it to them; they let me in for the sake of my children whom they saw."

"Tell me, serf, about the mode of life in the city." And he replies: "That I can well tell you. There we have seen large loaves costing but a farthing; the same food costs two in another town; it is a very good city, unless it has grown worse (since I was there)."

"Fool," said William, "that is not what I am asking you at all. But I wish to know about the Pagan knights in the town, King Otrant and his company." The serf said: "I know nothing about these, and I shall never tell lies on that subject."

There was Garnier, a noble knight; he was a vassal expert in wiles and a master in deceit. He looked at the oxen who were turning about (i.e. moving in such a way as to make the cart turn in a circle). "Sir," said he, "so help me God, if we had now a thousand casks similar to the one standing on this cart, and if we filled them with knights, and led them all the way to Nîmes, we would capture that city in fine style." And William said: "By my head, you speak truly. I shall do it if my barons consent."

34. According to William's orders the serf is brought before them,

[1] The writers of epic poems like this thought that the Muslims worshiped three gods: Mahomet, Tervagam, Apollin.

[2] An important shrine 10 miles southeast of Nîmes, in the eleventh century a favorite possession of the Counts of Toulouse; the rest of the geography in this passage is pretty fanciful.

they bring him plenty to eat: bread, wine, mead, and spiced-wine. And the serf and his children ate for they were very hungry. And when he (the serf) had eaten his fill, Count William convened his barons who come there without delay. When he sees them he addresses them in these terms: "Barons," said he, "listen to me. If we had now a thousand hooped casks similar to the one you see in this cart, and if they were full of armed knights, and if we led them along the highway straight to Nîmes, that good city, we could thus enter it in fine style. Not a lance would be thrust nor a bow drawn." And they reply: "You speak the truth. Sir William, true knight, please think about it. In this land there is a great deal of carting, there are plenty of carts and chariots. Send your men back by way of Ricordane through which we passed, and have the oxen seized by force." And William said: "That is a good plan."

35. Following the advice given by the barons, Count William sent his men back fourteen long leagues to Ricordane. They take the carts, the oxen and the casks. The good serfs who make them and join them strengthen the casks and turn over the ploughs (yoke the teams?). It matters little to Bertrand whether the serfs grumble: some, for having uttered a word, were afterwards greatly sorry; they lost their eyes and were hanged by the neck.

36. If you could but have seen the hard serfs walking about, carrying adzes and hatchets, hooping casks and renewing everything, strengthening the carts and chariots by means of pegs and bars, the knights entering the casks, you would have been reminded of great deeds. To each (knight) is brought a big mallet, for, when they reach the city of Nîmes and hear the sound of the great horn, our Frenchmen will be able to look after themselves.

37. In the other casks are placed the lances, and on each cask they have two signs engraved, so that when the soldiers of France mix with the monstrous race, they may not encounter difficulties.

38. In another cask they placed the shields, making two marks on the bottom of each cask, so that when our Frenchmen come among the Saracens they may not be endangered.

39. The count hastens to make ready the carts. If then you could but have seen the serfs of the kingdom hooping, rebuilding and fixing new bottoms on the casks, turning over and upside down the big chariots, the knights entering the casks, you would have been reminded of great deeds. Now we must sing of Lord Bertrand and of the way in which he had rigged himself out. He wore a smock of smoke coloured serge; his feet were shod with wonderful shoes; they

are big and made of ox-hide and the tops are gaping. "O God," said Bertrand, "beauteous king of majesty, "here are shoes which will soon cripple my feet." On hearing these words, William burst out laughing. "Nephew," said the Count, "listen to me. Drive these oxen forthwith down that valley." And Bertrand said: "You speak in vain. I know neither how to goad nor to strike sufficiently to make them move a step." At these words, William burst out laughing. But it was an unfortunate thing for Bertrand that he had not learnt that trade. He never knew a word of it, and so he drove into the mud; the cart went in as far as the hub; Bertrand sees this and very nearly loses his senses. If you had seen him step in the mud and lift the wheel with his shoulders, you would have looked upon him with great admiration. His mouth and nose were bruised. William sees him and begins to make fun of him. "Good nephew," said he, "listen to me. You have taken on an occupation of which obviously you know very little." Bertrand hears him and very nearly goes out of his mind.

* * *

43. . . . Fierebrace dismounted. He took his purse and loosened the money; he draws out the good coins in handfuls; he tells the official in charge of the toll that for all the world he does not want anyone to harm them (him and his followers). The Pagans say: "Have no fear; there is no one, however high in rank, whom we would not hang by the neck from a tree if he uttered impertinent or rude words in your presence."

44. While they are speaking thus and talking to Count William, behold Harpin and Otrant who are asking for the famous merchant. The Pagans who were looking at him say: "There he is, the goodly looking man; see his hat and his long beard; he gives orders to all the others."

King Otrant called William before him: "Whence do you come, merchant, good friend?"

"Sire, we come from the great country of England and from Canterbury, the valiant city."

"Have you a wife, merchant, good friend?"

"Yes, she is very beautiful, and I have eighteen children. They are all small; two only are grown-up; one is called Begues and the other Sorant. Here they are, if you don't believe me." And he shows them Guielin and Bertrand: they were his nephews, sons of Bernard of Brabant. The Pagans look at them and say: "It is wonderful, what beautiful children you have. If only they knew how to dress becomingly."

King Otrant called him at once: "What is your name, merchant, good friend?" "Good sweet Sire, Tiacre, indeed." The Pagans say: "It is the name of a low class. Brother Tiacre, what are the wares you are carting?"

"Silks, Sire, taffeta and buckram, scarlet, green and blue cloths of great value, white hauberks and strong glittering helmets, sharp spears and good heavy shields, shining swords with hilts of gleaming gold." Otrant replies: "You are well stocked, merchant." And William said: "Barons, wait a while; behind come the most costly goods." "What are they, then?"

"Right in front are inks and sulphur, incense and quicksilver, alum, grain, pepper and saffron, furs, sheepskins, Cordovan leather, sable-skins which are useful in winter."

At these words, Otrant laughs heartily, and the Saracens make great mirth.

45. King Otrant called out to him: "Brother Tiacre, in the name of your religion, if you please, tell me the truth. To my knowledge you have great possessions which you are transporting this way on your carts; for mercy's sake, let us have a share of them. Give some to me and to the others; we are all knight-bachelors. You will derive great profit if you remain in this country."

And William replied: "Good Sire, have patience; I shall never leave this city: this is a good town, and I shall remain here. To-morrow noon shall not pass nor vespers toll nor the sun set but that I give you so much of my possessions that the strongest among you will hardly bear his load." The Pagans say: "Merchant, you are too noble, but your generosity resides only in your words. If you are really an honest man, we shall soon know it." "Indeed, that I am," said he, "and more than you think, I have never been a traitor nor a miser; all my possessions are freely given to my intimate friends." The Count called one of his men. "Prithee, have all my carts entered now?" "Yes, truly, Sir, thanks be to God." He begins to lead his carts through the streets, here they are unloading on the large squares, for he does not wish to be hemmed in, so that in case of emergency he may have freedom of movement. They have blocked the entrance to the palace in such a way that the Saracens will experience difficulty in entering.

46. King Otrant began to speak to him: "Brother Tiacre, by the law under which you live, in what country have you conquered such rich

possessions, and in what country and in what fief do you live?" And William said: "That I can well tell you: 'tis in sweet France indeed that I got all this. And now, in truth, I am going into Lombardy, in Calabria, in Apulia and in Sicily, in Germany and hence into Rumania, in Tuscany and hence into Hungary; then I am returning from there by way of Galicia through the rich land of Spain, and through Poitou and hence into Normandy; it is in England and in Scotland that I live. I shall not stop until I reach Wales. I shall lead my vassals straight to Cracow to a fair famous throughout the ages. As for my exchange office, I have fixed it in the kingdom of Venice." The Pagans say: "You have visited many lands, it is no wonder, serf, that you are rich."

47. Hearken, Lords, in the name of God of majesty, how on that day William acted with great cunning. Otrant, the King, began to look at William when he heard him speaking so well. Then he saw the scar on his nose. He then remembered William with the short nose, son of Aymeri of Narbonne-on-Sea.[3] This vision well nigh drove him out of his senses. All at once the blood surged in his veins, his heart fails him, and he almost faints. He addresses William in courteous terms; and speaks to him in the way you are going to hear: "Brother Tiacre, by the law which you obey, who caused you to have that great scar on your nose? Take care not to hide it from me, for you remind me of William with the short nose, son of Aymeri, who is so greatly feared, and who has killed my noble kinsmen. Would to God, who is my protector, and to Tervagam and his sacred bounty, that I might hold him prisoner here, just as I am holding you whom I see standing before me. By Mahomet, he would already have been lynched, hanged on the gallows and swinging in the wind, or burnt in the fire or held up to shame."

On hearing these words, William burst out laughing: "Sire," said he, "listen to me. As to the question you are asking me, I shall reply to you willingly and with pleasure. When I was young, as a youthful nobleman and a knight-bachelor, I became an extraordinary thief and besides a master cheat: I never saw anyone like myself. I used to cut purses and well-fastened belts. And so the master-bachelors blamed me for it and so did the merchants whom I had robbed. They cut my nose with their knives, then they allowed me to go without any further harm. Then I began the trade which you see me ply. Thanks to God, I have acquired as many possessions as you can see here before your

---

[3] An old, archiepiscopal city very like Nîmes, 80 miles to the southwest on the Mediterranean coastal plain, and a famous site of Christian-Saracen encounters.

eyes." The Pagans say: "You have acted valiantly. Never shall you hang from the gallows."

3. GODRIC OF FINCHALE, THE MERCHANT SAINT (1170)

Godric of Finchale died as a hermit in 1170 and was venerated as a saint shortly thereafter in his native England. The selection below comes from the biography written by an admiring disciple before the holy man's death. It bears clear testimony to Godric's outstanding practice of both mercantile subtlety and ascetic devotion, two sets of human virtues not usually considered compatible at the time. We should not fail to notice that Reginald can approve of Godric's earlier life as much as he does because Godric eventually left it for a recognized form of Christian achievement. On the other hand, that retired piety should not blind us to Godric's skill at parlaying a little chance capital into the means for making large investments, or to the really impressive (and perilous) distances covered in his voyages. Who can be sure that on all those pilgrimages he did not mix some sales with saintliness, or that he might have seen less wrong in that than the proper Reginald would have?

Reginald of Durham: *The Life of St. Godric*

From G. G. Coulton, Social Life in Britain from the Norman Conquest to the Reformation *(Cambridge: Cambridge University Press, 1918), pp. 415–20. Reprinted by permission of the publisher. Footnotes 2–4 supplied.*

This holy man's father was named Ailward, and his mother Edwenna; both of slender rank and wealth, but abundant in righteousness and virtue. They were born in Norfolk, and had long lived in the township called Walpole. . . . When the boy had passed his childish years quietly at home; then, as he began to grow to manhood, he began to follow more prudent ways of life, and to learn carefully and persistently the teachings of worldly forethought. Wherefore he chose not to follow the life of a husbandman, but rather to study, learn and exercise the rudiments of more subtle conceptions. For this reason, aspiring to the merchant's trade, he began to follow the chapman's way of life, first learning how to gain in small bargains and things of insignificant price; and thence, while yet a youth, his mind advanced little by little to buy and sell and gain from things of greater expense. For, in his beginnings, he was wont to wander with small wares around the villages and farmsteads of his own neighborhood; but, in process of time, he gradually associated himself by compact with city merchants. Hence, within a brief space of time, the youth who had trudged for many weary hours from village to village, from farm to farm, did so profit by his increase of age and wisdom as to travel with associates of his own age through towns and boroughs, fortresses and cities, to fairs and to all the various booths of the market-place, in pursuit of his public chaffer. He went along the high-way, neither puffed up by the good testimony of his conscience nor downcast in the nobler part of his soul by the reproach of poverty. . . .

Seeing that he then dwelt by the sea-shore, he went down one day to the strand to seek for some means of livelihood. . . . The place is called Wellstream, hard by the town of Spalding; there, when the tide was out, the country-folk were wont to scour and explore the stretches of sand, discovering and converting to their own use whatever wreckage or drift the sea might have brought to shore; for hence they sometimes get wealth, since they are free to seize there upon whatsoever goods or commodities they may find by the shore. The saint, then, inspired by such hopes, roamed one day over these stretches of foreshore; and, finding nothing at first, he followed on and on to a distance of three miles, where he found three porpoises lying high and dry, either cast upon the sands by the waves or left there by the ebb-tide. Two were still alive and struggling: the third, in the midst, was dead or dying. Moved with pity, he left the living untouched, cut a portion from the dead fish, and began carrying this away upon his back.[1] But the tide soon began to flow; and Godric, halting under his burden, was overtaken by the waves; first they wet his feet, then his legs; then his upper body was compassed about by the deep; at length the waters went even over his head; yet Godric, strong in faith, bare his burden onwards even under the waves, until, by God's help, he struggled out upon the very shore from which he had gone forth. Then, bringing the fish to his parents, he told them the whole tale, and exhorted them to declare the glory of God.

Yet in all things he walked with simplicity; and, in so far as he yet knew how, it was ever his pleasure to follow in the footsteps of the truth. For, having learned the Lord's Prayer and the Creed from his

[1] Fats were rare and costly in the Middle Ages; therefore porpoise was highly esteemed and always fetched a considerable price.

very cradle, he oftentimes turned them over in his mind, even as he went alone on his longer journeys; and, in so far as the truth was revealed to his mind, he clung thereunto most devoutly in all his thoughts concerning God. At first, he lived as a chapman for four years in Lincolnshire, going on foot and carrying the smallest wares; then he travelled abroad, first to St Andrews in Scotland and then for the first time to Rome. On his return, having formed a familiar friendship with certain other young men who were eager for merchandise, he began to launch upon bolder courses, and to coast frequently by sea to the foreign lands that lay around him. Thus, sailing often to and fro between Scotland and Britain, he traded in many divers wares and, amid these occupations, learned much worldly wisdom. . . . Thus aspiring ever higher and higher, and yearning upward with his whole heart, at length his great labours and cares bore much fruit of worldly gain. For he laboured not only as a merchant but also as a shipman . . . to Denmark and Flanders and Scotland; in all which lands he found certain rare, and therefore more precious, wares, which he carried to other parts wherein he knew them to be least familiar, and coveted by the inhabitants beyond the price of gold itself; wherefore he exchanged these wares for others coveted by men of other lands; and thus he chaffered most freely and assiduously. Hence he made great profit in all his bargains, and gathered much wealth in the sweat of his brow; for he sold dear in one place the wares which he had bought elsewhere at a small price.

Then he purchased the half of a merchant-ship with certain of his partners in the trade; and again by his prudence he bought the fourth part of another ship. At length, by his skill in navigation, wherein he excelled all his fellows, he earned promotion to the post of steersman. . . .

. . . In labour he was strenuous, assiduous above all men; and, when by chance his bodily strength proved insufficient, he compassed his ends with great ease by the skill which his daily labours had given, and by a prudence born of long experience. . . . He knew, from the aspect of sea and stars, how to foretell fair or foul weather. In his various voyages he visited many saints' shrines, to whose protection he was wont most devoutly to commend himself; more especially the church of St Andrew in Scotland, where he most frequently made and paid his vows. On the way thither, he oftentimes touched at the island of Lindisfarne, wherein St Cuthbert had been bishop, and at the isle of Farne, where that Saint had lived as an anchoret, and where St

Godric (as he himself would tell afterwards) would meditate on the Saint's life with abundant tears. Thence he began to yearn for solitude, and to hold his merchandise in less esteem than heretofore. . . .

And now he had lived sixteen years as a merchant, and began to think of spending on charity, to God's honour and service, the goods which he had so laboriously acquired. He therefore took the cross as a pilgrim to Jerusalem, and, having visited the Holy Sepulchre, came back to England by way of St James [of Compostella].[2] Not long afterwards he became steward to a certain rich man of his own country, with the care of his whole house and household. But certain of the younger household were men of iniquity, who stole their neighbours' cattle and thus held luxurious feasts, whereat Godric, in his ignorance, was sometimes present. Afterwards, discovering the truth, he rebuked and admonished them to cease; but they made no account of his warnings; wherefore he concealed not their iniquity, but disclosed it to the lord of the household, who, however, slighted his advice. Wherefore he begged to be dismissed and went on a pilgrimage, first to St Gilles[3] and thence to Rome the abode of the Apostles, that thus he might knowingly pay the penalty for those misdeeds wherein he had ignorantly partaken. I have often seen him, even in his old age, weeping for this unknowing transgression. . . .

Godric, when he had restored his mother safe to his father's arms, abode but a brief while at home; for he was now already firmly purposed to give himself entirely to God's service. Wherefore, that he might follow Christ the more freely, he sold all his possessions and distributed them among the poor. Then, telling his parents of this purpose and receiving their blessing, he went forth to no certain abode, but whithersoever the Lord should deign to lead him; for above all things he coveted the life of a hermit.[4]

4. WILL OF THE GRISKIN: A HUMBLE SUCCESS
(mid-thirteenth century)

Here is the pious report of another Norfolk farm boy who rose high in the world of business. Unlike Godric, he did not

[2] In northwestern Spain; perhaps the most sought-after place of pilgrimage in Europe, after Rome. Along the land routes leading there, Romanesque churches and less permanent inns, markets, etc. sprang up in the eleventh and twelfth centuries.

[3] See V, 2, note 2.

[4] Which Reginald tells us he led for 40 years before his death. His final hermitage was at Finchale, near Reginald's monastery in Durham.

finally forsake that world, although he kept reserved in his opulent house something like a hermit's cell, and so could qualify for clerical approval. The so-called *Lanercost Chronicle* was compiled by a friar living in the Scottish Lowlands about a century and a quarter after Reginald of Durham. However much or little literal truth we may wish to attribute to the details of this short anecdote, we should not fail to notice that the author was perfectly familiar with the kind of swift upward mobility that brought Will from a very modest piece of initial capital to a rich foreign bride, and then a place among the councils of the great. Success of that sort makes a good story in any age, not only that of Horatio Alger; by the thirteenth century it was evidently entirely possible, even for men whose hearts stayed pure.

The Lanercost Chronicle (1244)

From Life in the Middle Ages, *ed. and trans.* G. G. Coulton *(Cambridge: Cambridge University Press, 1930), III, 21–22. Reprinted by permission of the publisher.*

About this time, as I think, there thus grew up in France, from small beginnings, a man of substance and of worthy memory. There lived in Norfolk a simple countryman who had many children, among whom he specially loved a little boy named William, for whom he set aside a pigling and the profits thereof, in order that, grown to manhood, he might provide for himself without burdening his parents, wheresoever Fortune might favour him. The boy followed his father's bidding; and, leaving his fatherland, he hastened to France with naught else in his purse but the profits of that pig; for at home his playfellows were wont to call him the Boy of the Griskin.[1] Now it came to pass, amidst the miseries and evils of those folk, he so advanced himself as to espouse an honourable matron, the widow of a man of some substance; with whom he had wealth and honour and a household of servants. This he did; and, being a man of diligence in all his works, he profited much, and was oftentimes summoned to business councils by the king and his great men. From henceforward, even as this honest man grew in substance, so did the fickle favour of the people grow with him; and, lest he should find his prosperity as false and perilous as adversity, he caused a most comely chamber to be built and painted within according to his own choice; whereof he committed the key to none

[1] Little pig.

save unto his own care, nor suffered any other, not even his wife, to enter therein. It was his wont, whensoever he returned from the courts of the great, forthwith to neglect all other business and enter into this secret chamber, wherein he would stay as long as he desired, and return in melancholy mood to his family. In process of time, as this custom became inveterate, all were amazed and agape to know what this might mean that they saw; wherefore, having taken counsel, they called all his friends together to solicit this wise man for the reason of his so strange behaviour in this chamber. At last, besieged and importuned by their complaints, he unlocked the door and called them all together to see his secret, the monument of his poverty thus set forth. Amid other ornaments of this chamber, he had caused a pigling to be painted and a little boy holding him by a string; above whose heads was written, in the English tongue—

Willé Gris, Willé Gris,
Thinche cwat you was, and qwat you es!

Which may be confirmed by that saying of St Gregory: "We can then keep our present state well, when we never neglect to consider what we were."

Bourgeois Techniques and Ambitions

5. CHARTER OF A GENOESE TRADING COMPANY

The following document from the notarial archives of Genoa, one of the first genuinely capitalist cities in Europe—perhaps, depending on your definition of capitalism, in the world—is a representative example of one of the many kinds of formal partnership contracts developed by the Italian bourgeoisie during the economic boom of the High Middle Ages. It is not a particularly early example, but it contains several important pieces of evidence. First of all, it shows a general concern for a precise statement of the newly-formed company's investments, liabilities, and shares of potential profit. The day of the solitary adventurer-capitalist was pretty much over by 1308, at least in economically sophisticated circles like these. A second point of interest is the variety of the original assets and of the types of business projected. Finally, we may at least surmise that this venturesome young *societas* is being launched at least partly by young men and against a background of relatively modest circumstances.

Charter of a Genoese Trading Company (1308)

From Medieval Trade in the Mediterranean World, *trans. and ed. Robert S. Lopez and Irwin W. Raymond (New York: Columbia University Press, 1955), pp. 191–92. Reprinted by permission of Columbia University Press. The footnotes originally accompanying this selection have been deleted with the permission of the publisher.*

Genoa, January 19, 1308

In the name of the Lord, amen. Percivalle Grillo, son of Andreolo; Daniele Grillo; Meliano Grillo; Benedetto Contardo and Nicola Contardo, brothers, sons of the late Luchetto Contardo; Manuele Bonifacio; Antonino Grillo, son of Andreolo, acknowledge to each other that they have formed and made a *societas* for the purpose of maintaining a bank in the city of Genoa and of engaging in commerce and business in Genoa and throughout other [and] different parts of the world, according to what shall seem [proper] and shall be the pleasure of the partners themselves, to continue, God willing, for the next two succeeding years. This *societas* they acknowledge to be of £9,450 Genoese, in which sum they acknowledge to each other that each of them has or has deposited as below, viz.: said Percivalle, £3,500; said Daniele, £2,000; said Meliano, £1,000; the aforesaid Benedetto Contardo and Nicola, his brother, £2,000; said Manuele Bonifacio, £450; and said Antonio Grillo, £500. This capital they acknowledge to be in the hands of said Percivalle in money, in credits,[1] in exchange to be received in France, and in a vein of iron in Elba.[2] And the aforesaid partners have waived the exception and legal right by which they could speak against or oppose the aforesaid. And said Percivalle is to use this money in business and commerce in Genoa in said bank which he maintains, in the buying and selling of wares, and in exchange both in France and throughout other [and] different parts of the world, by sea and by land, personally and through his factors

---

[1] In the original, *in debitoribus*, *i.e.,* in debtors—a very concrete way of looking at it, faintly reminiscent of distant times in which men could be sold into slavery for their debts.

[2] An island just off the coast of Tuscany, 130 miles southeast of Genoa by sea, but not politically subject to her.

and messengers, according as God may dispose better for him, up to the time limit mentioned above, at the risk and fortune of the [partners]. And he has promised said partners of his to act in good faith [and] efficiently for the increase and preservation of said *societas*. And the aforesaid partners promised each other to guard and to preserve the goods and wares and money which may come into the hands of any one of them from the aforesaid *societas,* and not to defraud one another in anything. The profit which God may grant in the aforesaid *societas* shall be allocated to each of them pro rata to his capital; and if any accident befall said *societas* or the goods of said *societas*—may God be our help—it shall be allocated similarly to each of them pro rata to his capital. And they have promised each other in good faith to come to the accounting of the capital and profit of said *societas* at the end of the time limit; and each of them is to deduct his capital and to divide among them the profit pro rata to the capital of each one. The aforesaid *societas* and each and all of the above [conditions] the aforesaid partners promised each other, etc. Firm, etc., and for it, etc. And said Benedetto acknowledges that he is more than twenty-four years old, and said Nicola acknowledges that he is more than nineteen years old, and said Antonio acknowledges that he is more than nineteen years old. And they swore by the sacred Gospels of God, putting their hands on the Scriptures, to undertake and to observe [everything] as above stated and not to do anything or to act contrary in any way by reason of their being minors or by any other cause. And they made the aforesaid [agreement] with the counsel of the witnesses written below, whom for this [purpose] they call their relatives, neighbors, and counselors. Done in Genoa in the Church of Santa Maria delle Vigne, in the year of the Nativity of the Lord 1308, fifth indiction, January 19, about nones.[3] Witnesses: Arnaldo of Spigno, dealer in poultry; Manfredo; and Pagano of Moneglia, dealer in poultry.

6. A TRAVELING AGENT'S EMPLOYMENT CONTRACT

The following contract was made between one Ugo Gigone and the venerable and far-flung Sienese firm of the Salimbeni, and so represents a far less equal relationship among active members of the bourgeoisie than the previous agreement. The Salimbeni, originally a younger branch of the rural feudal family of the Forteguerri, became important money changers and bankers in Siena and abroad, especially in France, by the early thirteenth

[3] *I.e.,* about 3 P.M.

century. Twenty-two years before this contract, the Salimbeni had offered the commune of Siena the enormous sum of 118,000 florins to defray the costs of a defensive war against the Florentines (a victorious effort, as it turned out). Their massive stone *palazzo* remained a center of political influence in that upland Tuscan republic for centuries, although their fortunes declined drastically, as did everything Sienese, after the trauma of the Black Death.

This document gives no indication of Ugo Gigone's social position, or even of his citizenship. One suspects that they were irrelevant, once the Salimbeni knew his personal qualifications and were prepared to risk some of their fortune on his performance. The summary of business ethics contained in the conditions designed to protect that risk should not sound too unfamiliar to any modern traveling salesman.

Contract between Ugo Gigone and the Salimbeni (1282)

From Medieval Trade in the Mediterranean World, *trans. and ed. Robert S. Lopez and Irwin W. Raymond (New York: Columbia University Press, 1955), pp. 215–17. Reprinted by permission of Columbia University Press. The footnotes originally accompanying this selection have been deleted with the permission of the publisher.*

Siena, October 13, 1282

In the year of the Lord, 1282, eleventh indiction, the third day before the Ides of October. I, Ugo, [son] of the late Ugolino Gigone, entering into a solemn and legal written stipulation for fee and salary, promise and make agreement with you, Alessandro and Ser Giovanni, [son] of the late Salimbene, receiving [the obligation] for yourselves and for the partners and the *societas* of the Salimbeni . . . to stay and to remain . . . as factor and agent of your business in your behalf from the next feast of All Saints' Day up to [the end of] the four years directly following that date. And [I promise] to go and to remain wherever you wish and order me throughout Tuscany and Lombardy and the kingdoms of France, England, and Sicily and elsewhere, wherever you direct and wish [me] to do business and to gain a profit and to carry on your business well and advantageously and lawfully, acting in good faith, without fraud, to your advantage and to that of your *societas*. Also [I promise] to preserve and to guard your property and goods which come into my hands, and what I receive and have from you or from another in your behalf in the future in gold and silver, [notarial] instruments, books, letters, and other things of whatsoever kind, acting in good faith and without fraud. And [I promise] to return and to consign to you or to any one of you or to whomever you wish, direct, and order me by letter, by word of mouth, or by writing, a correct and legal accounting of each and all that . . . or I have managed, and in regard to all your goods which come into my hands [I promise] both to consign and to return and to give intact these goods to you whenever and as many times as you ask and express the wish; and [I promise] not to do anything fraudulent with them nor to conceal them nor to retain [any money] except the salary granted to me by you.

And I also promise you that whatever may be donated or given to me in money or gold or silver or anything else by any person or locality or community or baron or prelate in any way, so long as I remain your factor, I shall turn over and give all to you and to your *societas* and I shall send it to your *societas*, keeping back nothing.

And I promise you that as long as I remain your factor, as is stated above, I shall not gamble in any game of dice with pledge or money, nor shall I have carnal relations with any married woman, virgin, or religious, nor shall I make any expenditures on them out of your goods.

I also promise you to observe and to have carried out each and all that you order me by word of mouth or by a messenger or by letter, acting in good faith and without fraud, and that I shall keep every confidence which you shall order me [to hold] and that I shall not disclose any to anyone without your permission.

Furthermore I promise you not to make or to form any *societas* with any person or persons without your permission and will. I assert and acknowledge that I do not have and did not invest in your *societas* or in another *societas* any amount of money or any cash, neither in your behalf nor for the common work of your *societas*, except the said salary of mine, promised me by you, as shall be apparent from another instrument by the hand of Orlando, notary undersigned.

And I promise you to undertake and to observe all these aforesaid conditions, article by article, under penalty of 100 marks of silver,[1] which I promise to give you, just as is stated, if I do not observe or if I act contrary to the conditions: and [I promise] to observe what is stated above, whether the penalty is paid or not. And for these conditions I pledge myself and my heirs to you and your heirs, and I pledge as security my goods; these goods you are to be allowed to sell and use as security, and to receive possession of them by your own authority

---

[1] A prohibitively heavy penalty.

without requesting [permission of] the court or the judge; and I designate myself to have and to hold them meanwhile in your name.

And I do and I promise [to do] this for you because you have promised and made agreement to give me £450 Sienese as my fee and salary for the said four years on account of the said service and because of all the aforesaid, as must be apparent by another instrument by the hand of Orlando, notary undersigned; wherefore I waive the exception that the promise and obligation has not been made, [the exception] that the salary has not been established and promised, [the exception] that the affair has not been carried out in this way, the privilege of tribunal, and every legal right and remedy of law. And of my own free will I swear on the holy Gospels of God, having placed my hand on the book, to observe all the aforesaid, article by article, and not to violate it nor to act contrary to it.[2]

And Orlando, notary undersigned, admonished the abovesaid Ugo, willing and acknowledging the abovesaid agreement, that by reason of the oath and of the guarantee he must observe this instrument, article by article, in regard to the aforesaid Ser Alessandro and Ser Giovanni mentioned above. Done in Siena in the presence of Jacopo, [son] of the late Ser Uguccione Lotteringhi, and Ventura, [son] of the late Accursio, and Giannino Benini, Lombard, witnesses invited.

I, Orlando, notary, son of the late Ottaviano mentioned above, was present, and having been invited, I wrote and published these things.

7. A BURGESS OF NEWCASTLE LEASES A MANOR

Northern Europe knew merchants, both traveling and settled, from the beginning of the Middle Ages. In the thirteenth and fourteenth centuries the North Sea made valiant efforts to catch up with the Mediterranean as a zone of active trade. In some of the coastal regions bordering on those cold seas this swift economic expansion led to the emergence of political and social structures as dominated by the bourgeoisie as were the urban republics of Italy (see V, 11). Such developments were exceptional rather than normal, however; in the vigorous and politically integrated feudal kingdoms of England and France the bourgeoisie was generally content to accept a privileged but less than supreme position beneath the Crown's protection. Consequently, final success for a Northern dynasty of merchants or financiers con-

---

[2] Compare the form of this oath with that of the previous contract and with the concluding sentences of IV, 8(b), (c), & (d).

tinued to mean blending with the feudal nobility, whose decline in wealth and power did not noticeably tarnish the glamor of their social leadership. In England neither the nobles nor the kings placed major obstacles in the way of such amalgamation. The following document shows us the process whereby a rich burgess, proprietor of a good deal of real estate in and around the town of Newcastle in Northumbria, worked his way into the feudal order of the surrounding countryside. Whether he leased these two villages, one of them a manor with all that meant in judicial profits (see II, 9(b); IV, 8(b); and IV, 9) for income, prestige, or both, is unclear: the leasing nobleman's worry about losing peasant dependents or ultimate control is unmistakable. In time the likes of the Lord of Warkworth lost their standoffishness, however; the descendants of Thomas of Carlisle rooted themselves firmly among the local gentry, and by the seventeenth century they ranked high in the Northumbrian establishment.

Covenant between Robert of Wirkeword and Thomas de Karliolo (1280)

From Northumberland and Durham Deeds, trans. A. M. Oliver (Newcastle: Newcastle-upon-Tyne Records Committee, 1929), pp. 77–79. Reprinted by permission of Rev. T. M. Oliver. Footnotes supplied.

Tuesday before Philip and James App. (30 April) 1280.[1] Covenant between Robert son of Roger lord of Wirkeword and Thomas son of Thomas de Karliolo[2] burgess of Newcastle, namely that Robert granted

[1] I.e., the Feast of Sts. Philip and James, Apostles. For at least 10 years before this date Thomas had been leasing such properties or buying them outright from various local gentlemen and gentlewomen.

[2] I.e., of Carlisle, a prosperous town on the Irish Sea, 75 miles west of Newcastle. Both Carlisle and Newcastle owed their foundation to the Romans, having been the main garrison stations at respectively the western and eastern ends of Hadrian's Wall. They shrank during the Saxon centuries but never entirely disappeared, and got a new lease on life in the eleventh and twelfth centuries. Godric of Finchale (V, 3) was active around Newcastle, a natural port on the deep estuary of the river Tyne. By the time of this document Newcastle had a significant "colony" of Spanish merchants, with whom our Thomas had many dealings.

Wirkeword is usually spelled Warkworth; in the thirteenth century it was a major castle on the Northumbrian coast, about 27 miles north of Newcastle and 15 miles southeast of Caluley (more usually Callaly) and Yetlington. Both Robert and Roger had been involved in suits with Avice, widow of Gilbert of Callaly (probably a former vassal of theirs), over the legal title to Callaly and Yetlington. Perhaps Thomas the burgess was a convenient person to keep them running while their ownership was still in question.

and demised to Thomas his manor of Caluley and the vill of Yetlington[3] with all its appurtenances without any retention whether in demesnes, services, rents, works, mills, woods, wards, reliefs, escheats, villeins, cottars and all their chattels and broods, merchets, heriots, amercements of court[4] and all other profits and appurtenances as well not named as named, appurtenant to the said manor and vill or which ought to be appurtenant without any retention, saving nevertheless to Robert and his heirs the land which Avice widow of Gilbert de Caluley held by way of dower on the day of the making of this writing in Caluley if she shall die within the term of seven years and saving that the villeins or cottars of the said vills shall not be tallaged within the said term of seven years; to hold and have to Thomas and his heirs or assigns of Robert and his heirs or assigns freely etc. to the end of seven years next following fully complete until he shall receive thereout seven crops and seven yearly farms, for a certain sum of money which Thomas paid in hand to Robert. Warranty in consideration of the said money paid in hand. In witness whereof each has affixed his seal to the chirograph writing of the other. And for further security Robert finds the following sureties namely sir Hugh de Euere, Hugh Gubiune,[5] John de Oggle, Roger Mawdute, Roger de Widerington, of whom each are bound as principal for the observance of the said covenant and for keeping the said Thomas and his heirs and assigns

[8] The manor of Callaly and its dependent hamlet of Yetlington (population of both, 306 in 1842) are about 30 miles northwest of Newcastle, on the eastward slopes of the desolate Cheviot Hills. They first appear in the records in the second half of the twelfth century, although Callaly Castle is the successor of British and Saxon fortifications, and the Romans built a military road right through the site of the present village. Poor as they probably were, they dated at least to Saxon times: Callaly comes from an Anglo-Saxon name meaning either "bare clearing" or "calf pasture" (it was probably both), and Yetlington originally meant "farmstead of the sons of the little Geat." In any case, it is hard to imagine their being a prime investment even in the abnormal prosperity of the late thirteenth century. It is too bad that we do not know how much Thomas paid Robert for the privilege of this lease.

[4] *Villeins:* residents of vills (villages), a general term for the semi-dependent peasantry in France as well as England (see IV, 3). *Cottars:* poor peasants literally on the fringes of such vills, owing the lord a day or two of work per week in return for a cottage and a small plot of land, to do with what they willed. Cottars were particularly widespread among the hills and moorlands of Northern England, Wales, and Scotland; town-dwelling entrepreneurs often put them to work spinning wool. The much sought-after Cheviot tweeds were produced at least partly in that fashion until relatively recent times.

Merchet or *marchet* was a fee paid by a tenant to his lord for the privilege of marrying his children to spouses not of the same jurisdiction. The other dues listed here are defined elsewhere. See especially II, 9(b); IV, 8(b), (c), and (d); IV, 9.

[5] Sheriff of Northumberland.

indemnified in all things concerning the said covenant to the end of the said term and who have for themselves and their heirs affixed their seals to this present writing remaining with the said Thomas. And be it known that neither sir Robert nor his heirs nor Thomas nor his heirs or assigns shall remove villeins or cottars of the said vills from their villein or cottar holdings nor in any manner subtract or alienate their chattels during the said term, saving nevertheless to Thomas his heirs or assigns amercements of court as is aforesaid. And moreover Robert granted for himself and his heirs that Thomas and his heirs or assigns shall have timber for repair and amendment of the mills of Caluley and Yetlington, as often as shall be necessary, within the forest of Rothbury[6] during the said term. At the end of the said term the manor of Caluley and the vill of Yetlington with their appurtenances without any retention shall peaceably revert to Robert and his heirs without hindrance of Thomas and his heirs or assigns.

> Seals, of grantor; of Eure; of Widdrington;
> of Gubion (round, armorial, barry, a label:
> S. Hvgonis Gvbioune).

8. THE GOODMAN OF PARIS' IDEAL WIFE

About 1393 an aging pillar of the high bourgeoisie of Paris completed a thick book of instructions for his teen-age bride, whose unimpeachably noble birth had prompted him to marry her despite the fact that she was an impoverished orphan and the strong probability that before too long she would be spending his considerable fortune on a younger, and undoubtedly more exciting, husband. Manuals of female perfection written by men usually make entertaining reading; thanks to the fact that its anonymous author was as prolix and as free of self-criticism as he was rich, this book is a mine of information for social historians of the later Middle Ages. Even the casual reader will discern the chief notes of the new style which the high bourgeoisie was then creating for itself (despite great pains taken to act very much like country gentlemen), and which would undergo little substantial change before its triumphant takeover of European manners and morals in the Victorian era. The student of English literature may enjoy reading further in the Goodman's book and then comparing his version of the perfect bourgeois wife with that put into the

---

[6] A forest along a ridge of the Cheviot Hills stretching perhaps 15 or 20 miles southwest of Callaly at that time.

mouth of the Wife of Bath by Geoffrey Chaucer: the elderly Parisian entertained his adolescent bride with several tales which appeared within that very decade in more effective and amusing form along that not-so-fictional road to Canterbury.

The Book of the Goodman of Paris

From The Goodman of Paris, *trans. Eileen Power (London: George Routledge & Sons, Ltd., 1928), pp. 52–53, 188–90, 217–19. Reprinted by permission of Routledge & Kegan Paul Ltd. Footnote supplied.*

The First Section. The second article saith that when you go to town or to church you should be suitably accompanied, according to your estate, and especially by worthy women, and flee suspicious company and never go near any suspected woman, or suffer one to be in your company. And as you go, bear your head straight, keep your eyelids lowered and still and look straight before you about four rods ahead and upon the ground, without looking nor turning your gaze upon any man or woman to right or to left, nor looking up, nor glancing from place to place, nor laughing, nor stopping to speak to anyone in the road. And when you have come to church, choose a secret and solitary place before a fair altar or image, and there remain and stay without moving hither and thither, nor going to and fro, and hold your head upright and keep your lips ever moving saying orisons and prayers. Moreover keep your glance continually on your book or on the face of the image, without looking at man or woman, picture or else, and without hypocrisy or feint, keep your thoughts always on heaven and pray with your whole heart; and so doing go to mass each day and often to confession; and if you do this and fail not therein, honour will befall you and all good will come unto you. And what is said above should be sufficient for a beginning, for the good wise dames whom you frequent, and the good examples you take from their ways and teaching, the good wise honest old priests to whom you confess and the sound mother-wit God has given you will increase this and provide the rest of the second article.

* * *

The ninth article showeth how that you shall be wise when your husband beareth him foolishly, as young and simple folk often do, and that you should gently and wisely draw him away from his follies. First, if he is in mind to be wroth and deal ill with you, take heed that by good patience and gentle words you slay his proud cruelty, and if thus you can do, you will so have vanquished him that he will rather be dead than do you ill, and he will remember him so often hereafter of your goodness, howbeit he saith no word thereof to you, that you shall have him wholly drawn unto you. And if you cannot move him that he turn his wrath from you, take heed that you make not plaint thereof to your friends or to others, so that he may perceive it, for he will think the less of you and will remember it another time; but go you into your chamber and weep gently and softly in a low voice, and make your plaint to God; and thus do all wise ladies. And if perchance he be prone to wrath against another person less near unto him, do you wisely restrain him. . . .

Wherefore I say unto you that it behoveth good ladies, subtly, cautiously and gently, to counsel and restrain their husbands from the follies and silly dealings whereunto they see them drawn and tempted, and in no wise to think to turn them aside by lording over them, nor by loud talk, by crying to their neighbours or in the street, by blaming them, by making plaint to their friends and parents, nor by other masterful means. For all this bringeth nought but irritation and the making of bad worse, for the heart of man findeth it hard to be corrected by the domination and lordship of a woman, and know that there is no man so poor nor of so small value that would not be lord and master when he is wed.

Again will I not be silent concerning an ensample of how to reclaim a husband by kindness, the which ensample I once heard my late father —God rest his soul—tell; who said that there was a citizen's wife, dwelling at Paris, hight dame Jehanne la Quentine, that was wife to Thomas Quentin. She knew that the aforesaid Thomas her husband foolishly and lightly desported himself, and went with and sometimes lay with a poor girl that was a spinner of wool at the wheel, and for a long time, without seeming to be aware of it or saying a single word, the said dame Jehanne bore with it and suffered it very patiently; and at last she sought to find where this poor girl lived and sought so that she found out. And she came to the house and found the poor girl, who had no provisions of any kind, neither wood, nor tallow, nor candle, nor oil, nor coal, nor anything, save only a bed and a coverlet, her spinning wheel and full little furniture beside. Then she spoke to her saying: "My dear, I am bound to keep my husband from blame, and because I know that he takes pleasure in you and loves you and that he comes here, I pray you that you speak of him as little as you can in company, to spare him from blame and likewise me and our children, and that for your part you hide it; and I swear to you that you and he shall be well hidden for my part, for since it haps that he loves you, it is my intent to love you and help you and aid you in all that you have to do, and you shall perceive it well; but I pray you with all my heart that his sin be not revealed nor spread abroad. And because I know that he is of good birth and has been tenderly nurtured, well fed, well warmed, well bedded and well covered according to my power, and I see that you have little wherewith to do him ease, rather would I that you and I together should care for him in health, than that I alone should care for him in sickness. So I pray you that you love and keep and serve him so that by you he may be restrained and kept from leading a light life elsewhere in divers dangers; and without his knowledge I will send you a great pail that you may often wash his feet, and store of wood to warm him, a fair bed of down, sheets and coverlets according to his estate, nightcaps, pillows, and clean hose and linen; and when I shall send you clean ones, so shall you send me those that be soiled, and he shall know naught of all that is between you and me, lest he be shamed; for God's sake bear you so wisely and secretly towards him that he learn not our secret." Thus it was promised and sworn and Jehanne la Quentine departed and carefully sent all things as she had promised.

When Thomas came at eventide to the young girl's house, his feet were washed and he was laid in a fair bed of down, with great sheets spread and hanging on each side, very well covered and better than had been his wont, and on the morrow he had white linen, clean hose and fair new slippers. Greatly did he marvel at this new thing . . .

[Needless to say, this astute man of affairs saw immediately that his best interests lay at home, and dropped his proletarian dalliance.]

The Second Section. . . . [Let] me say that your steward ought to know that each week he must examine and taste your wines, verjuice and vinegar and look at the grain, oil, nuts, peas, beans and other stores. And as to wines, know that if they fall sick, their sickness must be cured in the following manner:

First, if the wine should go bad, he must set the barrel in winter in the midst of a courtyard upon two trestles, so that the frost catches it, and it will be cured.

Item, if the wine be too tart, he must take a basket full of black grapes very ripe, and put it into the barrel through the bunghole, and the wine will improve.

Item, if the wine smell ill, he must take an ounce of powdered elder wood and an equal quantity of grain of Paradise [cardamon] powdered and put each of the powders aforesaid in a little bag and pierce it with a stick, and then hang both the bags inside the cask on cords and stop up the bunghole firmly.

Item, if the wine be muddy, take twelve eggs and set them to boil in water till they be hard, and then cast away the yolks and leave the whites and the shells together, and then fry them in an iron frying pan and put them, still hot, into a bag pierced with a stick as above, and hang them in the cask by cords.

Item, take a big new pot and set it above an empty tripod, and when it is well baked, break it into pieces and throw them into the cask and they will cure the muddiness.

Item, to take the redness out of white wine, take a basket full of holly leaves and cast them into the cask through the bunghole.

Item, if the wine be bitter, take a crock of water and pour it in, that it may separate the wine from the dregs, and then take a dish full of corn and set it to soak in water, and then throw away the water and set it in fresh water to boil, and boil it therein until the grain is on the point of bursting and then take it out; and if therein there be burst grains, cast them away, and then pour the hot corn into the cask. And if the wine refuseth to clear for this, take a basket full of sand well washed in Seine water and cast it into the cask through the bunghole and it will clear.

Item, to make a strong wine of the vintage do not fill up the cask with more than about two gallons of wine, and rub all round the bung and then it cannot drip out and it will thereby be stronger.

Item, to tap a cask of wine without letting air into it, bore a little hole with a drill near the bunghole, and then take a little wad of tow of the size of a silver penny and set it thereon, and take two little sticks and put them crosswise over the aforesaid wad, and set another wad upon the sticks. And to clear thick wine, if it be in a cask, empty two quart pots of it, then stir it up with a stick or otherwise, until the dregs and all are well mixed, then take a quarter of a pound of eggs, and beat up the yolks and the whites for a long while until the whole is fine and clear like water, and then cast in a quarter of pounded alum and immediately thereon a quart of clear water and stop it up, otherwise it will run away by the bunghole.

And after this and with this, fair sister, bid master Jehan the Dispenser to order Richart of the kitchen to air, wash and clean and do all things that appertain to the kitchen, and see you that dame Agnes the Béguine[1] for the women and master Jehan the Dispenser for the men, set your folk to work on all sides: the one upstairs, the other downstairs, the one in the fields, the other in the town, the one in the chamber, the other in the solar, or the kitchen, and send one here and the other there, each after his place and his skill, so that these servants all earn their wages, men and women according to what they know and have to do; and if they do so, they will do well, for know you that laziness and idleness be the root of all evil.

Nathless, fair sister, at times fitting cause them to be seated at table, and give them to eat one kind of meat only, but good plenty thereof, and not several varieties, nor dainties and delicacies; and order them one drink nourishing but not intoxicating, be it wine or something else, and not several kinds. And do you bid them to eat well and drink well and deeply, for it is reasonable that they should eat at a stretch, without sitting too long over their food and without lingering over their meat, or staying with their elbows on the table. And so soon as they shall begin to tell tales and to argue and to lean upon their elbows, order the Béguine to make them rise and remove their table, for the common folk have a saying: "When a varlet holds forth at table and a horse grazes in the ditch, it is time to take them away for they have had their fill." Forbid them to get drunk, and never allow a drunken person to serve you nor approach you, for it is perilous; and after they have taken their midday meal, when it is due time, cause your folk to set them to work again. And after their afternoon's work, and upon feast days, let them have another meal, and after that, to wit in the evening, let them be fed abundantly and well as before, and if the weather be cold let them warm themselves and take their ease.

After this, let your house be closed and shut up by master Jehan the Dispenser or by the Béguine, and let one of them keep the keys, so that none may go in or out without leave. And every evening ere you go to bed cause dame Agnes the Béguine or master Jehan the Dispenser to go round with a lighted candle, to inspect your wines, verjuice and vinegar, that none be taken away, and bid your farmer find out from his men whether your beasts have fodder for the night. And when you have made sure by dame Agnes or master Jehan that the fires on the

---

[1] The Béguines (women) and Beghards (men) were devout lay persons who followed a life of service and personal asceticism compatible with activity in the world. They originated in the Lowlands, especially among the bourgeoisie of the towns, who defended them against the occasional charges of heresy leveled against them by the clergy. Sometimes the line between Beghards and Waldensians (see I, 12(b)) seemed pretty thin.

hearths be everywhere covered, give to your folk time and space for the repose of their limbs. And make you certain beforehand that each hath, at a distance from his bed, a candlestick with a large foot wherein to put his candle, and that they have been wisely taught how to extinguish it with mouth or hand before getting into bed, and by no means with their shirts. And do you also have them admonished and told, each separately what he must begin to do on the morrow, and how each must rise up on the morrow morn and set to work on his own task, and let each be informed thereon.

The Cities of the Bourgeoisie

It may seem gratuitous to remark that without *bourgs* there would have been no bourgeoisie. It is clear, nonetheless, that the development of the bourgeoisie as a fully articulated and self-defining class was inseparably attached to the development, gradual at first and then quite swift, of a special sort of urban center. What was needed was a kind of defensible town which could serve as an inspiration and a training-ground for its special type of citizens, besides being merely one of the many locations on which they might ply their characteristic trades.

9. PAVIA, A TENTH-CENTURY IDEAL

Pavia, capital of the Lombard Kingdom of Italy, is a good example of official but essentially alien encouragement of mercantile activity and organization. Situated near the confluence of the rivers Ticino and Po in the middle of the great plain of northern Italy, Pavia had been an important and much-favored crossroads in Roman times, and knew even better days under the rule of its Germanic kings, who succumbed early to Mediterranean luxury and a Mediterranean sense of the advantages of commerce. The following selection comes from an early eleventh-century description of tenth-century regulations, and shows, among other things, how far Italy had advanced beyond the rest of Latin Europe in such matters. It also shows that Pavia's economic life in that period was run according to patterns followed more successfully in the Byzantine Empire and the busy cities of the Islamic world than in the backward West. There is already something nostalgic in the tone of this probably over-schematic description, and rightly so: its ideal was soon to give way to techniques and habits both more dynamic and more distinctively European.

Regulations of the Royal Court at Pavia

From Medieval Trade in the Mediterranean World, *trans. and ed.* Robert S. Lopez *and* Irwin W. Raymond *(New York: Columbia University Press, 1955), pp. 56–60. Reprinted by permission of Columbia University Press. The footnotes originally accompanying this selection have been abridged with the permission of the publisher.*

2. . . . . Merchants entering the kingdom [of Italy] were wont to pay the *decima*[1] on all merchandise at the customs houses and at [the beginning of] the roads appertaining to the king.[2] And the [customs houses] are these: the first is Susa, the second Bard, the third Bellinzona, the fourth Chiavenna, the fifth Bolzano, the sixth Volargne, the seventh Trevile, the eighth San Pietro di Zuglio on the Monte Croce road, the ninth near Aquileia, the tenth Cividale del Friuli.[3] All persons coming from beyond the mountains into Lombardy are obligated to pay the *decima* on horses, male and female slaves, woolen, linen, and hemp cloth, tin, and swords. And here at the gate they are obligated to pay the *decima* on all merchandise to the delegate of the treasurer. But everything that [pilgrims] bound for Rome to Saint Peter's take with them for expenses is to be passed without payment of the *decima*. No one ought to exact the *decima* from the pilgrims themselves bound for Rome or to hinder them in any way.[4] And if anyone does so, let him be anathema.

3. As for the nation of the Angles and Saxons, they have come and were wont to come with their merchandise and wares. And [formerly], when they saw their trunks and sacks being emptied at the gates, they

[1] A ten-percent tax.

[2] Roads subject to the jurisdiction of the king as parts of the royal demesne; public highways under royal administration as opposed to private roads maintained and exploited by vassals.

[3] The list includes both those customs houses which Italy had recently lost—when part of its territory was transferred to the German kingdom—and the new customs houses established along the new borders. Each *clusa* or fortified customs house was situated in the first town inside Italy along a road from one of the Alpine passes. The list mentions the *clusae* in their geographical order from west to east, but it mentions no customs house along some of the most important roads crossing the Alps.

[4] The exemption of pilgrims was both rooted in custom and guaranteed in certain cases by law. The same conditions prevailed in the Muslim countries.

grew angry and started rows with the employees (*ministrales*) of the treasury. The [parties] were wont to hurl abusive words and in addition very often inflicted wounds upon one another. But in order to cut short such great evils and to remove danger [of conflicts], the king of the Angles and Saxons and the king of the Lombards agreed together as follows: The nation of the Angles and Saxons is no longer to be subject to the *decima*. And in return for this the king of the Angles and Saxons and their nation are bound and are obligated to send to the [king's] palace in Pavia and to the king's treasury, every third year, fifty pounds of refined silver, two large, handsome greyhounds, hairy or furred, in chains, with collars covered with gilded plates sealed or enameled with the arms of the king, two excellent embossed shields, two excellent lances, and two excellent swords wrought and tested. And to the master of the treasury they are obligated to give two large coats of miniver and two pounds of refined silver. And they are to receive a safe-conduct from the master of the treasury that they may not suffer any annoyance as they come and go.

4. As for the duke of the Venetians with his Venetians, he is obligated to give every year in the [king's] palace in Pavia fifty pounds of Venetian deniers. These deniers are of one ounce each, equally good as the Pavian deniers in regard to weight and silver [content]. And to the master of the treasury [he is obligated to give] one excellent pall [5] on account of [the rights] that appertain to the king of the Lombards. And that nation does not plow, sow, or gather vintage. This tribute is called *pact* because [by it] the nation of the Venetians is allowed to buy grain and wine in every port[6] and to make their purchases in Pavia, and they are not to suffer any annoyance.

5. Many wealthy Venetian merchants were wont to come to Pavia with their merchandise. And they were wont to pay to the Monastery of Saint Martin, which is called Outgate, the fortieth solidus on all merchandise. When the Venetians [or rather] the *maiores* [among them] come to Pavia, each of them is obligated to give to the master of the treasury every year one pound of pepper, one pound of cinnamon, one pound of galanga, and one pound of ginger. And to the wife of the master of the treasury [they are obligated to give] an ivory comb and

[5] The word *palium* is almost exclusively used for silk cloaks of Byzantine manufacture.

[6] *Portus* in the early Middle Ages does not necessarily mean "port" in the modern sense, but any center to which commodities are carried or any legitimate mart under the control of public authorities.

a mirror and a set of accessories, or else twenty solidi of good Pavian [deniers].

6. Likewise the men of Salerno, Gaeta, and Amalfi were accustomed to come to Pavia with abundant merchandise. And they were wont to give to the treasury in the king's palace the fortieth solidus. And to the wife of the treasurer [they gave] individually spices and accessories just as did the Venetians.

7. As for the great and honorable and very wealthy *ministri*[7] of the merchants of Pavia, they have always received from the emperor's hand credentials with every honor,[8] so that they suffer no harm or annoyance in any way, wherever they may be, whether in the market or [traveling] by water or by land. And whoever acts contrary to this is obliged to pay a thousand gold *mancusi*[9] into the king's treasury.

8. As for the *ministerium* of the mint of Pavia, there are to be nine noble and wealthy masters above all the other moneyers, who are to supervise and to direct all other moneyers jointly with the master of the treasury, so that they never strike deniers inferior to those they always have struck in regard to weight and silver [content], to wit, ten out of twelve.[10] And those nine masters are obligated to pay for the rent of the mint twelve pounds of Pavian deniers into the king's treasury every year and four pounds of the same to the count [palatine] of Pavia. If a mint master discover a forger, [they are to act] in this wise: They, together with the count of Pavia and the master of the treasury, are under obligation to have the right hand of that forger cut off. And [they must see to it] that all the property of the forger is turned over to the king's treasury.

9. As for the moneyers of Milan, they are to have four noble and wealthy masters, and with the advice of the treasurer in Pavia are to strike Milanese deniers, equally good as Pavian deniers in regard to silver [content] and weight. And they are obligated to pay rent to the

---

[7] *Ministri* simply means members of a *ministerium* ("mystery" or "craft"; usually, but not necessarily, a craft gild).

[8] *Preceptum cum omni honore*. This *preceptum* must have been a charter promising imperial protection to the Pavian merchants throughout the territory of the Empire. Similar charters were issued in behalf of the *negociatores* of many other cities. The word *honor* is much more ambiguous. It may mean specific privileges of a fiscal character (exemption from some tribute?) or merely "honor" in its modern meaning of esteem or token of esteem.

[9] All Muslim (nonfigured) gold coins and all imitations of these coins that were struck in Western Europe were most commonly called *mancusi*.

[10] This seems to mean that the moneyers retained two deniers out of twelve as their fee.

master of the treasury in Pavia twelve pounds of good Milanese deniers every year. And if they discover a forger, they are under obligation to cut off his right hand and to turn over his entire property to the king's treasury.[11] . . .

13. There are other *ministeria*. All shipmen and boatmen are obligated to furnish two good men as masters under the authority of the treasurer in Pavia. Whenever the king is in Pavia, they themselves are obligated to go with the ships and these two masters are obligated to outfit two large vessels, one for the king and one for the queen, and to build a house with planks, and to cover it well. As for the pilots, they are to have one vessel, so that [people] may be safe on the water. And they, together with their juniors, are to receive every day their expenses from the king's court. . . .

17. And in regard to all these *ministeria* you should know this: that no man is to perform [his functions] unless he is one of the *ministri*. And if another man does, he is obligated to pay the *bannum*[12] into the king's treasury and to swear that he will no longer do so. Nor ought any merchant to conclude his business in any market before the merchants of Pavia do, unless he is one of the merchants of Pavia. And whoever acts contrary to this, let him pay the *bannum*. . . .

10. FLORENTINE GREATNESS, 1336-38

Florence was a different kind of city from early-blooming royal Pavia. A Roman town of no great significance in Classical times or under the Lombard and Frankish Dukes of Tuscany, Florence grew to economic greatness and then unrivalled aesthetic splendor under her own direction. A commune government headed by elected consuls achieved practical independence for the city by 1138. Two centuries later an intensely patriotic native Florentine wrote the radiantly proud but statistically precise eulogy of his city from which the following selection is taken. Ten years later the Black Death would deal Florence a crushing blow; although she would recover much more successfully than most of her sister cities (Siena, for example) and reach a unique climax of cultural leadership in the two centuries following, Florence would never regain the dominant position in the European economy that her unabashedly bourgeois sons had won for her just before the Plague.

---

[11] We omit here the description of a number of *ministeria* carrying out various crafts—gold washers, fishermen, leathermakers, soapmakers.

[12] *Bannum* was the fine due from one incurring the ban.

Giovanni Villani was born to a modest family of Florentine citizens sometime in the last quarter of the thirteenth century. By 1345 he had become enough of a capitalist to be ruined by the failure of the international but Florence-based banks of the Bardi and Bonaccorsi families. In the meantime, after several years of youthful travel to Rome, France, and Flanders, he had risen high in the politics and service of his city. In 1346 he published a *New Chronicle* in twelve books, tracing Florentine history from fabulous Antiquity to the very year of publication. The *Chronicle* is distinguished for its nearly unprecedented attention to statistics, the substantial accuracy of which has been solidly established, rather than for the ardent patriotic and moral values which might have been expected. After Giovanni's death the *Chronicle* was continued with less originality by his brother Matteo and nephew Filippo.

Giovanni Villani: *New Chronicle, Book XI*

From Medieval Trade in the Mediterranean World, *trans. and ed. Robert S. Lopez and Irwin W. Raymond (New York: Columbia University Press, 1955), pp. 71–74. Reprinted by permission of Columbia University Press. The footnotes originally accompanying this selection have been abridged with the permission of the publisher.*

Chapter 94. Since we have spoken about the income and expenditure of the Commune of Florence in this period, I think it is fitting to mention this and other great features of our city, so that our descendants in days to come may be aware of any rise, stability, and decline in condition and power that our city may undergo, and also so that, through the wise and able citizens who at the time shall be in charge of its government, [our descendants] may endeavor to advance it in condition and power, seeing our record and example in this chronicle. We find after careful investigation that in this period there were in Florence about 25,000 men from the ages of fifteen to seventy fit to bear arms, all citizens. And among them were 1,500 noble and powerful citizens who as magnates[1] gave security to the Commune. There were in Florence also some seventy-five full-dress knights. To be sure, we find that before the second popular government now in power was formed there were more than 250 knights; but from the time that the people

[1] The legislation against the nobility required magnates to put up bail with the Commune.

began to rule,[2] the magnates no longer had the status and authority enjoyed earlier, and hence few persons were knighted. From the amount of bread constantly needed for the city, it was estimated that in Florence there were some 90,000 mouths divided among men, women, and children, as can readily be grasped [from what we shall say] later; and it was reckoned that in the city there were always about 1,500 foreigners, transients, and soldiers, not including in the total the citizens who were clerics and cloistered monks and nuns, of whom we shall speak later. It was reckoned that in this period there were some 80,000 men in the territory and district of Florence. From the rector who baptized the infants—since he deposited a black bean for every male baptized in San Giovanni and a white bean for every female in order to ascertain their number—we find that at this period there were from 5,500 to 6,000 baptisms every year, the males usually outnumbering the females by 300 to 500. We find that the boys and girls learning to read [numbered] from 8,000 to 10,000, the children learning the abacus and algorism from 1,000 to 1,200, and those learning grammar and logic in four large schools from 550 to 600.

We find that the churches then in Florence and in the suburbs, including the abbeys and the churches of friars, were 110, among which were 57 parishes with congregations, 5 abbeys with two priors and some 80 monks each, 24 nunneries with some 500 women, 10 orders of friars, 30 hospitals with more than 1,000 beds to receive the poor and the sick, and from 250 to 300 chaplain priests.

The workshops of the *Arte della Lana*[3] were 200 or more, and they made from 70,000 to 80,000 pieces of cloth, which were worth more than 1,200,000 gold florins. And a good third [of this sum] remained in the land as [the reward] of labor, without counting the profit of the entrepreneurs. And more than 30,000 persons lived by it. [To be sure,] we find that some thirty years earlier there were 300 workshops or thereabouts, and they made more than 100,000 pieces of cloth yearly; but these cloths were coarser and one half less valuable, because at that time English wool was not imported and they did not know, as they did later, how to work it.

The *fondachi* of the *Arte di Calimala*,[4] dealing in French and Transalpine cloth, were some twenty, and they imported yearly more than

---

[2] *Poichè'l popolo fu,* literally, "after the people was." "People," of course, means commoners or bourgeoisie as opposed to magnates or patriciate (*grandi*).

[3] The gild of wool merchants and entrepreneurs in the woolen industry.

[4] The gild of importers, refinishers, and sellers of Transalpine cloth. Their name is derived from Calle Mala, the "bad street," where their shops were located.

10,000 pieces of cloth, worth 300,000 gold florins. And all these were sold in Florence, without counting those which were reexported from Florence.

The banks of money-changers were about eighty. The gold coins which were struck amounted to some 350,000 gold florins and at times 400,000 [yearly]. And as for deniers of four petty each, about 20,000 pounds of them were struck yearly.

The association[5] of judges was composed of some eighty members; the notaries were some six hundred; physicians and surgical doctors, some sixty; shops of dealers in spices, some hundred.

Merchants and mercers were a large number; the shops of shoe-makers, slipper makers, and wooden-shoe makers were so numerous they could not be counted. There were some three hundred persons and more who went to do business out of Florence,[6] and [so did] many other masters in many crafts, and stone and carpentry masters.

There were then in Florence 146 bakeries. And from the [amount of the] tax on grinding and through [information furnished by] the bakers we find that the city within the walls needed 140 *moggia*[7] of grain every day. By this one can estimate how much was needed yearly, not to mention the fact that the larger part of the rich, noble, and well-to-do citizens with their families spent four months a year in the country, and some of them a still longer period.

We also find that in the year 1280, when the city was in a good and happy condition, it needed some 800 *moggia* of grain a week.

Through [the amount of] the tax at the gates we find that some 55,000 *cogna* of wine entered Florence yearly, and in times of plenty about 10,000 *cogna* more.

Every year the city consumed about 4,000 oxen and calves, 60,000 mutton and sheep, 20,000 she-goats and he-goats, 30,000 pigs.

During the month of July 4,000 *some* of melons came through Porta San Friano, and they were all distributed in the city. . . .[8]

[Florence] within the walls was well built, with many beautiful houses, and at that period people kept building with improved techniques to obtain comfort and richness by importing designs of every kind of improvement. [They built] parish churches and churches of

---

[5] *Collegio* was similar to but not quite identical with an *arte* or gild.

[6] These were the factors or agents of the companies of merchant bankers which had branches abroad.

[7] The *moggio* was a dry measure equal to 16.59+ bushels.

[8] We omit here a description of the different magistracies having jurisdiction in the city. Their large number seemed to Villani another proof of the greatness of Florence.

friars of every order, and splendid monasteries. And besides this, there was no citizen, whether commoner or magnate, who had not built or was not building in the country a large and rich estate with a very costly mansion and with fine buildings, much better than those in the city—and in this they all were committing sin, and they were called crazy on account of their wild expenses. And yet, this was such a wonderful sight that when foreigners, not accustomed to [cities like] Florence, came from abroad, they usually believed that all of the costly buildings and beautiful palaces which surrounded the city for three miles were part of the city in the manner of Rome—not to mention the costly palaces with towers, courts, and walled gardens farther distant, which would have been called castles in any other country. To sum up, it was estimated that within a six-mile radius around the city there were more than twice as many rich and noble mansions as in Florence.

11. STATUTES OF THE HANSEATIC LEAGUE, 1230–65

The following brief excerpts from the vast body of documents that make up the constitution of the Hanseatic League may give the reader some sense of the fundamental concerns of those North German merchants who turned their confederate cities into the next thing to a sovereign state after the Holy Roman Empire lost control over the southern coasts of the Baltic and the North Sea. We have met Lübeck and Hamburg, the League's two parent cities, in other, earlier contexts (see I, 9 and IV, 7). The formal pact they concluded in 1241 against the pirates who threatened their interests capped an earlier friendliness evident in the first selection, and reoriented that quite common type of association in a most unusual direction. Nearly a hundred other trading cities from the Gulf of Finland to the English Channel eventually joined this protective and demanding League, extending to one another varying degrees of mutual citizenship and paying heavy dues to the central treasury at Lübeck for the maintenance of a common fleet. Even cities like London, Bruges, and Novgorod, capitals of proud and powerful governments, were pleased to charter Hanseatic colonies with their own walls, police, and extraterritorial liberties. In 1370 the League imposed a humiliating peace treaty on the King of Denmark, nominal lord of the Straits linking the Baltic with the North Sea and the open Ocean.

Despite such triumphs, the Hanseatic League stopped short of genuine political sovereignty, and slid slowly into genteel decline under the tolerant eyes of resurgent post-Renaissance monarchies; its last general assembly met in the late seventeenth century. Perhaps the League's failure to make that final step was due to a more exclusively mercantile and hence more purely bourgeois attitude toward such things than even the Italian republics were able to develop. On the other hand, the reason may have been simply a thoroughly bourgeois realism about wealth: even at the peak of its prosperity in the 1380's, Lübeck's commerce seems to have been worth only one-tenth that of Genoa one and a half centuries before.

Agreement between Hamburg and Lübeck, c.1230

Agreements between Hamburg and Lübeck, *and* Decrees of the Hanseatic League *from O. J. Thatcher and E. H. McNeal,* A Source Book for Mediaeval History *(New York: Charles Scribner's Sons, 1905), pp. 609–12. Footnotes supplied.*

To their honorable and beloved friends, the advocate, aldermen, and other citizens of Lübeck, the advocate, aldermen, and the commune of Hamburg, greeting, etc. . . .

We wish you to know that we desire by all means to preserve the mutual love and friendship which have hitherto existed between you and us. We desire that we shall have the same law, so that whenever your citizens come into our city, bringing goods that are unencumbered [that is, about which there is no dispute or suit pending], they may possess and enjoy them in peace and security, in the same way as our citizens. . . .

Agreement for Mutual Protection between Lübeck and Hamburg, 1241

The advocate, council and commune of Lübeck. . . . We have made the following agreement with our dear friends, the citizens of Hamburg.

1. If robbers or other depredators attack citizens of either city anywhere from the mouth of the Trave river to Hamburg, or anywhere on the Elbe river,[1] the two cities shall bear the expenses equally in destroying and extirpating them.

[1] Lübeck is an island on the river Trave, about 15 miles from the open Baltic. Hamburg is situated where the Elbe opens into a large estuary emptying into the North Sea. The Elbe itself rises in northern Bohemia. In other words, an ambitious policing project is being proposed here.

2. If anyone who lives outside the city, kills, wounds, beats, or mishandles, without cause, a citizen of either city, the two cities shall bear the expenses equally in punishing the offender. We furthermore agree to share the expenses equally in punishing those who injure their citizens in the neighborhood of their city and those who injure our citizens in the neighborhood of our city.

3. If any of their citizens are injured near our city [Lübeck], they shall ask our officials to punish the offender, and if any of our citizens are injured near their city [Hamburg], they shall ask their officials to punish the offender.

Lübeck, Rostock, and Wismar[2] Proscribe Pirates, 1259

To all the faithful subjects of Christ. . . . The communes of Lübeck, Rostock, and Wismar. . . . Since most merchants are not protected on the sea from pirates and robbers, we have, in a common council, decreed, and by this writing declare, that all who rob merchants in churches, in cemeteries, or on the water or on the land, shall be outlawed and proscribed by all cities and merchants. No matter where these robbers go with their booty, whatever city or land receives them shall be held equally guilty with them, and proscribed by all the cities and merchants. . . .

[2] Wismar is about 40 miles by sea east of Lübeck, and Rostock (which had only been founded in 1218) another 40 miles farther east along the Baltic.

Decrees of the Hanseatic League, 1260–64

We wish to inform you of the action taken in support of all merchants who are governed by the law of Lübeck.

(1) Each city shall, to the best of her ability, keep the sea clear of pirates, so that merchants may freely carry on their business by sea. (2) Whoever is expelled from one city because of a crime shall not be received in another. (3) If a citizen is seized [by pirates, robbers, or bandits] he shall not be ransomed, but his sword-belt and knife shall be sent to him [as a threat to his captors]. (4) Any merchant ransoming him shall lose all his possessions in all the cities which have the law of Lübeck. (5) Whoever is proscribed in one city for robbery or theft shall be proscribed in all. (6) If a lord besieges a city, no one shall aid him in any way to the detriment of the besieged city, unless the besieger

is his lord. (7) If there is a war in the country, no city shall on that account injure a citizen from the other cities, either in his person or goods, but shall give him protection. (8) If any man marries a woman in one city, and another woman from some other city comes and proves that he is her lawful husband, he shall be beheaded. (9) If a citizen gives his daughter or niece in marriage to a man [from another city], and another man comes and says that she is his lawful wife, but cannot prove it, he shall be beheaded.

This law shall be binding for a year, and after that the cities shall inform each other by letter of what decisions they make.

Decrees of the Hanseatic League, 1265

We ought to hold a meeting once a year to legislate about the affairs of the cities.

(5) If pirates appear on the sea, all the cities must contribute their share to the work of destroying them.

12. VENICE ELECTS A DOGE, 1268

For the thousand years between Charlemagne's unsuccessful siege and Napoleon's eventual dissolution of her aristocratic Republic in 1806, no one in Western Europe had any serious doubts about the sovereignty of Venice. She half-recognized the Byzantine Empire's claim to ultimate lordship by giving her supreme executive the title of Doge (meaning *Duke;* he was at first an appointed Imperial official), but that fiction disappeared for good in 1204 when a Venetian fleet carrying an army of French Crusaders captured Constantinople for the first time in that imperial city's history. From the thirteenth to the seventeenth century one of the most powerful of Mediterranean states, and for the centuries before that the chief depot for Mediterranean trade with northern Europe, Venice was founded in the 450's by refugees fleeing from the unspeakable but land-bound Hunnish horsemen. The sandy islands on which they settled lay in a lagoon, safe from the Adriatic's famous storms and the occasionally awesome inundations of the Po as well as from the Huns, but they had no other natural advantages, not even drinking water. Consequently, in order to meet the minimum requirements of survival, the Venetians had to trade. Over the centuries they turned their necessity first into a virtue and then into fabulous wealth and a glittering maritime empire.

The following (and concluding) selection comes from the *Venetian Chronicle* of Martino da Canale, a native of the Italian mainland who became an official in the Venetian maritime bureau, and for several years before his death (c.1275) composed a glowing tribute to the unique city of which he had become a naturalized citizen. The first part of his *Chronicle* simply continues an earlier, anonymous history of Venice from its origins to 1229; with the election of the popular Lorenzo Tiepolo as Doge in 1268 (probably the year he began to write), Martino comes into his own. He wrote in elevated French prose so as to reach a wider audience, and it is with a like purpose that his account of the Republic's inaugural celebration dwells lovingly on every possible paraliturgical ritual and chivalric trapping. It is as though this first-generation citizen of the oldest, most coherent, and incomparably freest of Europe's merchant cities can think of no higher compliment for his Republic than to proclaim its parity with the noble order of continental (indeed, Transalpine) Latin Christendom. Fortunately, we cannot help discerning beneath all the slightly fantastic ceremony (which did have a peculiar attraction for the most authentic of Venetians, after all) many of the fundamental institutions and much of the merited self-confidence of the Serene Republic which managed its millennium of precarious freedom without one real revolution.

Martino da Canale: *Venetian Chronicle*

From Martino da Canale, Cronaca Veneta, ed. F. L. Polidori and G. Galvani, in Archivio storico italiano, ser. Ia (1845), VIII, 594, 600–602, 620–26. Footnotes supplied.

Chapter 259. When these forty-five were assembled in the [Ducal] Palace,[1] forty-five little balls of wax were readied for them, and in eleven of those were little pieces of parchment with the word *Elector* written on them. The balls were placed in the chapel, and each one came to the chapel, and the little child gave one to each, just as I have already related to you, until eleven of the forty-five had the balls

[1] The seat of the Republic's executive government, a visible symbol as well as an actual working building. It was located very fittingly between the cathedral of St. Mark and the main harbor into which the Grand Canal opens, at the east side of the public square (Piazzetta San Marco, famous today for the pigeons and the tourists) stretching from the main Piazza to the harbor.

that contained the word *Elector*. Then the Vicar[2] made them take an oath according to the statutes. After they had sworn the oath before all who were present, they betook themselves to a chamber. Now you should understand that these eleven had to choose forty-one men on whom nine of them agreed; and you must understand that I do not want their names to be forgotten. Messer Maffeo Milano was the first, and the second was Messer Michele Moresino, and the third Messer Marino Veniero, and the fourth Messer Giovanni Brasolano, and the fifth Messer Giovanni Albino, and the sixth Messer Simone Giusto, and the seventh Messer Marco Aurio, and the eighth Messer Filippo Mano-lesso, and the ninth Messer Piero Salomone, and the tenth Messer Bartolomeo Dolfino, and the eleventh Messer Marino Gradenigo, the knight.[3] These eleven men, as I have told you, elected forty-one men of those who seemed advisable to them, and these forty-one had to elect a Doge on whom twenty-five of them could agree. When they had chosen him, they let the Vicar and the members of the Council and the Chiefs of the Fifty[4] know; then they made them come to the Palace and swear before the Council to elect him Doge according to the statutes which had been promulgated to the whole people in the Church of My Lord Saint Mark and which the people had acclaimed, and they made them swear also on their souls to recognize as Doge and as lord the one who had been chosen by the forty-one, according to the regu-lations which had been established by the men who had been elected

[2] An interim executive officer chosen by the Grand Council, which was the highest in a hierarchy of councils governing Venice.

[3] Practically a microcosm of the proudest families of the Venetian patriciate. The last elector mentioned, Marino Gradenigo, served as Captain of the Venetian armed forces at one time; his family were generally the leaders of the most conservative wing of this elite group during the thirteenth century. They claimed descent from the original refugees who fled to Venice from Grado (on the mainland) and provided the Republic with numerous Doges, archbishops, admirals, etc. His cousin Pietro Gradenigo would reign as Doge from 1288 to 1311 after a long career of service as a naval commander and governor of Venetian colonies. In 1289 Pietro led a move-ment known as the Closing of the Grand Council, which limited its membership to descendants of a select group of Venetian patricians. Despite bitter popular resent-ment, two attempted uprisings, and papal excommunication (for another reason—his attack on Ferrara), Pietro and his constitutional reform survived, the latter until the Republic's ultimate dissolution. His family and allies considered it only prudent to bury him in the family church of San Cipriano on the glass-making island of Murano, however, rather than in St. Mark's as would have been normal for a Doge. Another relative, Marco Gradenigo, was governor of the colony at Constantinople, defeated the perennially-rival Genoese at the great naval battle of Trapani, etc.

[4] Different bodies checking and balancing one another in the complicated and ingenious Venetian constitution, which tended naturally to ever more oligarchic discipline.

by the Grand Council. I want you to know the names of the forty-one who elected the noble Doge. . . .

* * *

Chapter 261. . . . and at the end of all these speeches they declared that they had elected Messer Lorenzo Tiepolo[5] Doge of Venice. And now Messer Lorenzo was taken up and acclaimed, and all his [outer] garments were stripped from his back, and he was conducted before the altar of My Lord Saint Mark. There he swore the oath, chapter by chapter as it was read to him by the canons of Saint Mark. After that he was handed the banner of Saint Mark, all covered with gold, [by one] among the canons and Messer Nicolao Michele the Vicar, and he took it.

But if you had been there, my lords, you would have seen a throng and a passing great throng, festivity and passing great festivity, joy and passing great joy. And through that throng and festivity and joy My Lord the Doge went up into the Palace. But he stopped on the stairway of the Palace, the banner in his hand, to receive the Ducal acclamations uttered by the canons of My Lord Saint Mark, who were already going up to the Palace from beneath. They were as follows: "Christ, conquer; Christ, reign; Christ, rule! [6] To our lord Lorenzo Tiepolo, by the grace of God glorious Doge of Venice, Dalmatia, and Croatia,[7] and

[5] Leader of the popular element, with an especially firm following among the lesser sailors and small-boat owners, Lorenzo Tiepolo came from a family which rose to prominence in the eleventh century, and by the thirteenth was as firmly ensconced in the patriciate as was the Gradenigo family. Among his achievements before election were victory over the Genoese naval forces at Acre (on the coast of Palestine, in the declining Latin Kingdom), from which triumph he brought columns back to the Piazzetta San Marco, where they still stand; governorships over cities subject to Venice on the Italian mainland (Padua, 1264; Fermo, 1266; Fano, 1268). He reigned as forty-sixth Doge (according to a traditional reckoning) from July 23, 1268 to August 16, 1274. Among his imperial victories in office were a defeat of a league formed at Bologna to reduce Venice by a blockade of her mainland food supply, and the acquisition of some salt-producing territory, to protect the Venetian monopoly. Salt was probably Venice's first export product, and remained one of her most preciously-guarded ones.

[6] These opening acclamations, dating from the first Christian centuries of the Roman Empire, were in Latin; the rest of the text was in the vernacular tongue.

[7] In other words, a sizable portion of modern Yugoslavia, the coastal part of which was obviously vital to control of the Adriatic Sea.

[8] *I.e.*, the Byzantine Empire. This fraction had been agreed on in the negotiations following the fall of Constantinople and the erection of a Latin Empire (see III, 6) in 1204. Venice held on to much of her territory after the Greeks retook Constantinople in 1261.

lord of a fourth part and a half of all the Empire of Romania,[8] salvation, honor, life, and victory! Saint Mark, aid him!"

Then My Lord the Doge went up into the Palace, and was put in possession of his authority, and there he swore an oath in such wise as had been established. He spoke a few words there afterwards, and then came and addressed the people with great wisdom, and was acclaimed lord and Doge by all. And the canons went to Sant' Agostino[9] where My Lady the Dogaressa was waiting, and sang the Ducal acclamations to her also.

At the time that My Lord Lorenzo Tiepolo was made Doge the Venetians were equipped to travel in their ships or in their war galleys to go overseas and to every other place where they were wont. Messer Piero Michele was Captain over them all; Messer Giacomo Tiepolo, nephew of My Lord Lorenzo Tiepolo, the noble Doge of Venice, went as governor to Acre; Messer Filippo Boccaso, a valorous man and wise and well spoken, went as representative-ambassador to Alexandria; and Messer Andrea Dandolo went as governor to Negropont.[10] My Lord the Doge Lorenzo Tiepolo had a governor elected [for the colony in] Constantinople: this was Messer Giovanni Dolfino, a valorous man and wise; but he died a deadly death, and Messer Marino Giustiniano, the brother of Messer Marco, was elected in his place. . . . And My Lord the Doge had galleys armed to accompany the caravan,[11] twenty galleys well staffed by valiant men of Venice. My Lord Lorenzo Tiepolo had them equipped for launching on the second day of August. Then Messer Piero Michele, the noble Captain, got himself ready to go to sea with all the navy, both galleys and [other kinds of] ships, which

[9] A church and *contrada* (combined ward, parish, military district, and just plain neighborhood) two parishes over from St. Mark's, about 350 yards away. Typically enough, this strongly Tiepolo *contrada* seems to have had its church built by a Gradenigo endowment.

[10] Negropont was the Venetian name for the large island of Euboea in the Aegan Sea, northeast of Athens. The Doge Enrico Dandolo and Conrad of Montferrat (a North Italian feudal lord), the two leaders of the Fourth Crusade, fought over its control, but a little later Venetian suzerainty was recognized by the French barons initially loyal to Conrad. Venice gained complete control in the late fourteenth century, and lost Negropont to the Turks in the late fifteenth. Andrea Dandolo was the son of Giovanni Dandolo, who became Doge in 1280 and was succeeded by Pietro Gradenigo 8 years later (although Lorenzo Tiepolo's son Giovanni almost got the Ducal title then). Despite the rivalry between those two wings of the patriciate, Andrea Dandolo was given major commands by both the Tiepolo and the Gradenigo Doges.

[11] *I.e.*, the ships that met the caravans from China at their termini either on the Black Sea or in Syria. In 1269 Marco Polo's father and uncle would return from a journey of many years to China and back.

came to the number of fifty, as strongly outfitted as I have told you. And My Lord the Doge was in a state of great joy and great festivity as I shall tell you below.

* * *

Chapter 263. First I shall tell you of his gracious acts. The day after he was made Doge of Venice, he sent messengers to seek out those who were not on good terms with him, he embraced them and made peace, and bestowed on them his grace and good will, and made them his friends. But I would also have you know of the passing great festivity which the Venetian people celebrated to honor the noble Doge Messer Lorenzo Tiepolo. The men of each craft dressed themselves very richly, each craft assembled together, and went to see their new lord, Messer Lorenzo Tiepolo, the noble Doge of Venice. And when they had seen My Lord the Doge, they turned around and went to see their lady. My Lady Marchesina,[12] the noble Dogaressa, right there where she lived in the *contrada*[13] of Sant' Agostino, . . . each craft at a time, with their trumpets and their banners before them.

* * *

Chapter 279. You have heard in what manner those who sell salted meat and cheese went to see their noble lord; now I shall tell you about those who sell birds from the shore and fish from the sea and rivers. They put their banner in front, and then the trumpets and other instruments, and then rich silver cups and flasks of wine; and they dressed themselves up in rich garments and squirrel fur, and on their heads rich garlands of pearls and gilded strawberries.[14] They lined up behind their banner under the direction of good marshals, and they marched two-by-two, singing about their new lord. In such a fashion as I have told you they went to the Palace and mounted the steps; when they found their new lord there, they greeted him and he as their lord returned their greeting. And you should know, my lords, that when Messer Lorenzo Tiepolo, the noble Doge of Venice, saw the company of those who sell fish, he must have remembered very well indeed how many fine sturgeons and trout and other great fish he had bought from them. What shall I tell you? With great joy and great festivity they

[12] She was the daughter of Bohemond of Brienne, an nobleman of French stock who was King of Serbia at the time of their marriage.

[13] See note 9.

[14] Compare Jean de Joinville's attire in III, 10. A design of pearls and gilded strawberry leaves would become standard for ducal coronets in the heraldry of Northern Europe.

descended from the Palace, and went to see their lady the Dogaressa, there where she was; and they greeted their lady and she returned their greeting. . . .

Chapter 280. You have heard how those who sold fish and the birds of the shore went to see their lord; and I shall tell you in what manner the master barbers went there. They clad [15] their bodies very richly, and garlands of pearls were on their heads. They had with them two horsemen fully armed who called themselves knights-errant; and they had with them four damsels, two on horseback and two on foot, and these four damsels were very strangely apparelled. What shall I tell you? These master barbers put their banner in the fore, the trumpets and other instruments, the silver cups and the flasks full of wine, and they had good marshals. They went two-by-two. . . . They mounted the steps up to the top floor of the Palace, both those on horseback and those afoot, and then they greeted My Lord the Doge, and he as lord returned their greeting. And now one of those who was on horse dismounted, fully armed, and said to the Doge: "Sire, we are two knights-errant, who have ridden abroad to find adventure; and we have suffered such pain and travail that we have conquered these four damsels. So we have come to your court, and if there is any knight hereabouts who will come forth to try his body and conquer these strange damsels from us, we are prepared to prevent him."

Now My Lord the Doge answered, and said they were welcome, and that he hoped the Lord God would give them leave to enjoy their conquest. "I will," he said, "that you be honored in my court, and do not wish anyone of my court to gainsay you; they will acquit you of anything you desire."

Then the knight-errant mounted and they all cried out: "Long live our lord Lorenzo Tiepolo, the noble Doge of Venice." And then they turned around . . . [etc.]

* * *

Chapter 282. So you have heard of the master glassmakers,[16] how they went to see their new lord and their new lady; and I shall tell you how the masters who make combs went to see their lord. They put their banner in front, and put themselves in ranks two-by-two behind the trumpets right skillfully; and they had good marshals, and they went right before My Lord the Doge, expressing great joy. And when they

---

[15] The verb used here, *abouber,* was normally used in France in reference to the investiture of a knight.

[16] One of Venice's most famous and sought-after crafts, then and now.

were before him, a skilled comb master of theirs, named Master
Ughetto, went in front to salute him, and said, "Sire, I pray Jesus Christ
and His sweet Mother and My Lord Saint Mark, that they grant you
health and life and victory, and to govern the honorable Venetian people in victory and honor for all the rest of your life!" And My Lord
the Doge answered him very wisely, and they all cried out together:
"Long live our lord, the valiant Messer Lorenzo Tiepolo, the noble
Doge of Venice!"

Know, my lords, that these masters of comb- and lantern-making had
with them a lantern full of birds of diverse kinds: and to give pleasure
to My Lord the Doge, they opened the door [of the lantern]; the birds
all rushed out and went flying hither and thither as they wished. And
if you had been there, my lords, you would have seen laughter on every
side. . . .

Chapter 283. . . . Know that My Lord the Doge was put in possession of the noble Venetian Duchy on a Monday, and until the following Sunday the Venetian people did nothing besides going to see their
lord and their lady, all in such wise as I have told you. Now I want you
to know in what manner the master goldsmiths went to see their lord.
They clad their bodies with rich vestments and their heads and backs
with pearls and gold and silver and rich precious stones, to wit: sap-
phires, emeralds, diamonds, topazes, jacynths, amethysts, rubies, jas-
pers, carbuncles, and other precious stones; and even their servants
were very richly clad.